Museum, Media, Message

This volume considers in depth the most up-to-date approaches to museum communication – museums as media, museums and audience and the evaluation of museums.

Museum, Media, Message begins by placing museum communication in the context of mass communication and media studies. The book is divided into three sections, the first analysing how museums and galleries construct and transmit complex systems of value and legitimation through processes of collection and exhibition. The second section raises philosophical and management issues and explores examples of work with specific audiences. The third section uses examples and case-studies to introduce methods for studying the audiences' experiences of communication events in museums.

Museum, Media, Message is compiled for people who want to develop a more critical and informed professional practice in relation to museum and gallery audiences. The mix of philosophical discussion and practical examples will enable readers to develop their skills of analysis and reflection on day-to-day activities. The book will also be of value to people in related fields who are interested in current debates and issues in museums.

Eilean Hooper-Greenhill is well known internationally for her work on museum communication. She has been a lecturer in Museum Studies at the University of Leicester since 1980 and is the author of *Museums and the Shaping of Knowledge* (1992, Routledge) and *Museums and their Visitors* (1994, Routledge).

Museums: New Visions/ New Approaches

Series editor Eilean Hooper-Greenhill

Museums: New Visions/New Approaches is a new series within the *Heritage*: *Care–Preservation–Management* programme designed to present innovative views of the roles of museums and art galleries as we move into the twenty-first century.

As museums reinvent themselves, refashioning ideas and institutional processes scarcely changed since the nineteenth century, relevant theories and case-studies are urgently needed. Drawing on a broad range of thinkers in cultural and communication studies, sociology, psychology, linguistics, feminism and educational theory, writers in the series will suggest new ways to imagine and recast museums.

Heritage: Care–Preservation–Management
Editor-in-chief Andrew Wheatcroft

Architecture in Conservation:
Managing development at historic sites
James Strike

The Development of Costume
Naomi Tarrant

Forward Planning: *A handbook of business, corporate and development planning for museums and galleries*
Edited by Timothy Ambrose and Sue Runyard

The Handbook for Museums
Gary Edson and David Dean

Heritage Gardens: *Care, conservation and management*
Sheena Mackellar Goulty

Heritage and Tourism: *in the global village*
Priscilla Boniface and Peter J. Fowler

The Industrial Heritage: *Managing resources and uses*
Judith Alfrey and Tim Putnam

Museum Basics
Timothy Ambrose and Crispin Paine

Museum Exhibition
David Dean

Museum Security and Protection: *A handbook for cultural heritage institutions*
ICOM and ICMS

Museums 2000: *Politics, people, professionals and profit*
Edited by Patrick J. Boylan

Museums and the Shaping of Knowledge
Eilean Hooper-Greenhill

Museums and their Visitors
Eilean Hooper-Greenhill

Museums without Barriers: *A new deal for disabled people*
Fondation de France and ICOM

The Past in Contemporary Society: *Then/Now*
Peter J. Fowler

The Representation of the Past: *Museums and heritage in the post-modern world*
Kevin Walsh

Towards the Museum of the Future: *New European perspectives*
Edited by Roger Miles and Lauro Zavala

Museum, Media, Message

Edited by

Eilean Hooper-Greenhill

London and New York

First published 1995
by Routledge
11 New Fetter Lane, London EC4P 4EE

Simultaneously published in the USA and Canada
by Routledge
29 West 35th Street, New York, NY 10001

Typeset in Sabon by Florencetype Ltd, Stoodleigh, Devon

Printed and bound in Great Britain by T J Press Ltd, Padstow, Cornwall

British Library Cataloguing in Publication Data
A catalogue record for this book is available from the British Library

Library of Congress Cataloging in Publication Data
A catalog record for this book has been requested

ISBN 0-415-11672-4

Contents

Figures

Tables

Notes on contributors

Michel Allard is Professor at the Department of Education of the Université du Québec à Montréal, and teaches the MA in Museology and the MA in education. He has published many articles and books relating to pedagogy in the museum, in particular, *Le musée et l'école* (1991). His researches focus on the elaboration, experimentation and validation of models. He is now director of the Groupe de recherche sur l'éducation et les musées and director of the interest group on education and museums of the Canadian Society for the Study of Education.

Sandra Bicknell is the Visitor Studies Manager, at the Science Museum, London. She is based in the Public Understanding of Science Research Unit, which forms part of the Museum's Science Communication Division.

Since the establishment of a designated evaluation function within the Science Museum (in 1990) Sandra has been responsible for the production of over forty internal evaluation reports, most notable to date being evaluations of Launch Pad – the museum's interactive gallery – and the museum's drama programme.

Sandra Bicknell also teaches evaluation to two groups of postgraduate students: the MSc in Science Communication at Imperial College, and the MA in Museum Studies at the University of Leicester.

Colette Dufresne-Tassé gained a PhD in psychology at Université de Montréal and a Doctorate in sociology at the Sorbonne (Université de Paris).

She taught for several years in the Department of Andragogy at the Université de Montréal and she is now the head of the Maîtrise en muséologie at this university.

She is currently doing research on the psychological functioning of the adult visitor. This research has been funded since 1987 by the Conseil de Recherches en Sciences Humaines du Canada and by the Fonds pour la Formation de Chercheurs et l'Aide à la Recherche of the Quebec Provincial Government.

She is the former president of the Canadian Educational Researchers Association and of the Canadian Association for the Study of Adult Education. In 1992, she received the Jackson Award for an issue of the *Canadian Journal of Education* that she published on Museum and Education.

Anne Fahy trained as an archaeologist and worked in field archaeology in the UK and abroad, before moving into museum work at Southampton City Museums. In 1988, she became Deputy Registrar at the Tate Gallery, London, and then Lecturer in Museum Studies at the Department of Museum Studies, University of Leicester, where she taught courses in collections management and museums documentation. She is now Documentation Officer at the Victoria and Albert Museum where she continues to develop her interests in collections management and documentation. Anne Fahy has been actively involved in the standards work of the Museum Documentation Association and has published on the subject of museums documentation.

Rosemary Flanders is an art historian with special research interests in the development of nineteenth-century museum culture. A graduate of the University of Melbourne and Oxford University she is currently undertaking doctoral research at St John's College, Oxford, on the foundation of the museum and fine art collections of several provincial cities in both the United Kingdom and Australia in the nineteenth century. Her research is particularly concerned with the way the new museum culture reflects the period's civic and educational aspirations. Other educational interests have included convening and editing the proceedings of a symposium 'Higher Education: Towards the 21st Century', which was published as a special issue of the *Oxford Review of Education*.

Janet Hall has an honours degree in Archaeology from the University of Cape Town. She has been employed at the Albany Museum in Grahamstown since 1982 and has been, inter alia, research assistant in the Archaeology Department, librarian, shops manager and for the last eight years Education Officer. In January 1994 she became Public Relations Officer for the museum.

She has published a major paper in the *Journal of Education in Museums*, vol. 12, 1991, 'Museum education adapting to a changing South Africa', and has published numerous popular articles for the museum's magazine, *The Phoenix*, and its newsletter, *The Elephant's Child*.

Her main field of interest is the development of partnerships between museums and their communities. This requires a major shift in focus by museums from being highly specialized and inward-looking to being highly creative and outward-looking. Passionate about the African continent as a whole, Janet Hall professes a great love for the music, jewellery, arts and crafts, clothing, foods, colours, patterns and general richness of the people and their traditions.

Eleanor Hartley is a lecturer in the Department of Adult Education at Leicester University and Director of the Richard Attenborough Centre. She has a background in Social Science and the history of education. She is responsible for special needs provision within the Department and has been jointly responsible for a number of exhibitions which have travelled to museums and galleries throughout the country. The latest of these, 'Finding form: an exhibition of sculpture to touch', completed a widely acclaimed tour in 1992. Her idea of an arts education centre which gives priority to disabled users has been the foundation of the Richard Attenborough appeal for an innovative arts facility at Leicester University.

George E. Hein, Professor in the Division of Liberal Studies and Adult Learning at Lesley College Graduate School, Cambridge, Massachusetts, USA, is also Director of the Program of Evaluation and Research Group, which he founded in 1976. The Group carries out visitor studies in museums as well as large-scale qualitative programme evaluations, primarily in the fields of science and mathematics education. He is the author of *An Open Education Perspective on Evaluation* (1975) and the editor of *A Handbook for Assessment of Hands-On Elementary Science* (1991). With Sabra Price he has recently completed *Active Assessment for Active Science* (forthcoming 1994). During the 1992–5 triennial, Professor Hein serves as chair of ICOM/CECA, the international professional organization for museum educators.

Eilean Hooper-Greenhill trained as a sculptor and taught sculpture at Holland Park Comprehensive School in London until the birth of her two sons. A period of freelance work in museums, galleries and art centres led to the post of Education Officer at the National Portrait Gallery, London. Since 1980 she has been lecturer in Museum Studies at the University of Leicester. Her MA and PhD were awarded by the University of London. Her research interests span museum education and communication, museum histories and ideologies. She is the author of *Museum and Gallery Education* (1991), *Museums and the Shaping of Knowledge* (1992), and *Museums and their Visitors* (1994).

Andrew Jones is Director of the Archaeological Resource Centre, a project of the York Archaeological Trust. After graduating in Zoology in 1971 he worked for four years on a variety of archaeological digs in England and Scotland, as an excavator, photographer and environmental archaeologist. In 1977 he joined the University of York to study animal and plant remains from excavations in York, including the excavations at Coppergate. As a University of York Research Fellow he studied the latrine pits and other faecal deposits and helped with the development of the Jorvik Viking Centre.

He gained a PhD for work on fish remains from Pictish and Viking Age levels in northern Scotland. He has written numerous scholarly articles and reports, has co-authored a book on fish remains in archaeology, *Fishes*, in the Cambridge University Press series Manuals in Archaeology, and is a lively and entertaining broadcaster and speaker.

Flora E. S. Kaplan is Professor of Anthropology, and founder and Director of the Program in Museum Studies, Graduate School of Arts and Science, New York University. She has carried out fieldwork in Nigeria, Mexico, and the United States. From 1983 to 1985 she was Fulbright Professor at the University of Benin, Nigeria, where she taught anthropological theory and art, and did research on royal women. Before coming to New York University in 1976, she taught anthropology from 1970 to 1976 at H.H. Lehman College, the City University of New York. She was formerly Curator of the Department of Africa, Oceania, and New World Art, at The Brooklyn Museum. She has published widely on art and cognitive systems, museums, pottery and graffiti; and she has curated exhibitions of African art, including Benin court art, in the United States and Nigeria.

Her publications include *A Mexican Folk Pottery Tradition: Cognition and Style in Material Culture in the Village of Puebla, Queens, Queen Mothers, Priestesses and Power: Case Studies in African Gender* and , as editor, *Museums and the Making of 'Ourselves': The Role of Objects in National Identity*. She has served on the Executive Committee of ICOFOM, and was twice elected to the United States AAM/ICOM Board.

Gaynor Kavanagh is a Lecturer in the Department of Museum Studies at the University of Leicester. She teaches and writes on issues of museum provision and professionalism and on the theory and practice of history curatorship. She has produced four books since 1990, each with Leicester University Press. *History Curatorship* was published in 1990. Two edited volumes, *Museum Languages: Objects and Texts* and *Museum Profession: Internal and External Relations*, were published in 1991. Her most recent work is *Museums and the First World War: A Social History*, published in 1994.

Ian Kelman spent seventeen years teaching art and design in grammar and comprehensive schools in Northamptonshire. His interest in educational research and evaluation began with a Diploma in Education course at Leicester Polytechnic. The MA course in Museum Studies offered the opportunity to observe the educational role of museums at a time of rapid change. Since moving to Northumberland he continues to teach and work as a freelance museum educator.

Hadwig Kräutler took up the post of Head of Museum Public Services at the Österreichische Galerie im Belvedere in Vienna in 1992. In 1984 Hadwig Kräutler completed her MA degree at the Department of Museum Studies, University of Leicester, with research concerning 'Museum education in Austria – the present state and a proposal for development' (unpublished MA thesis). This led to practical application in the then newly established Museums-pädagogischer Dienst (a central museum educational service for the Austrian Federal Museums) as well as to theoretical work and publications centring on questions of institutional awareness and provisions for museum communication concerns. Since 1991 she has been researching for her doctoral thesis on the museum and exhibition work of Otto Neurath at the Department of Museum Studies, University of Leicester.

Stephen Locke is Director of Hampshire County Council Museums Service and President of the Museums Association with a special interest in professional training and development.

He qualified as a geologist at Leicester University and has worked in a variety of museums since 1966.

He has been a member of Museums and Galleries Commission working parties concerned with professional museum training and curatorial standards and was for many years Secretary of the South Western Federation of Museums and Art Galleries.

He is a firm believer in local management of museums supported by larger-scale networks of specialist support, and has written a number of articles about museum management and organization from this perspective.

Sally MacDonald is Principal Museum Officer for Croydon. Croydon's new museum and exhibition gallery are due to open early in 1995.

Ivo Maroević graduated in Art History at the Faculty of Philosophy, University of Zagreb (1960) and holds a PhD in Art History at the University of Zagreb (1971).

He was museum curator at the Museum Sisak from 1965 to 1969, conservationist and director of the Restoration Institute of Croatia, Zagreb (1969–83), and Professor at the Faculty of Philosophy, University of Zagreb (from 1983) where his teaching subjects are Introduction to Museology, Protection of Museum Collections and Conservation of Cultural Heritage.

He is founder of the graduate study programme and the Chair of Museology within the Department of Information Sciences at the same Faculty (1984). He is also a member of ICOM (ICTOP, ICOFOM), AHF (Arbeitskreis fuer Hausforschung) (since 1975) and ICOMOS (since 1976), a participant at many international meetings. He was the winner of the Croatian award for a scientific work (1971) and member (from 1983) and chairman of the Museum Council of Croatia (1988–90).

His publications are *Architect's Family Grahor* (1969), *Sisak – City and Architecture* (1970), *Present of Heritage* (1988) and *Introduction to Museology* (1993), along with over 200 articles in the fields of museology, conservation of cultural heritage, history and architecture.

Sandra Marwick is Keeper of Education and Outreach Services for Edinburgh city Museums and Galleries. This post was established in November 1992 to maximize the opportunities for life-long learning provided by the city's collections, and to make museum services accessible to all residents of the city.

The Keeper is responsible for developing education services for all age-groups; for co-ordinating both the planning and implementation of museum-related activities and the preparation and delivery of outreach services; and she participates in the publications, exhibitions and displays.

Sandra Marwick joined the museum service in 1987 as a volunteer member of the team working on the creation of the People's Story Museum which opened in 1989. Originally a teacher of history, she has wide experience of working with community groups. She has written several papers on aspects of Edinburgh's history, and on using museums as an educational resource.

Susan Pearce read History at Somerville College, Oxford, and then moved to National Museums on Merseyside, and City Museum, Exeter. She joined the Department of Museum Studies at the University of Leicester in 1984. She became Head of the Department in 1989, and Professor of Museum Studies in 1992. She is currently President of the Museums Association of Great Britain. She has travelled widely, including several study visits to the Arctic (Churchill Fellowship, 1975), and lectured in many parts of the world. Among her many publications are *Archaeological Curatorship* (1990), *Museum Studies in Material Culture* (1992) and *Museums, Objects and Collections* (1992). She is editor of the journal *New Research in Museum Studies*. She is currently engaged in a major research project on collecting practice in contemporary Britain.

Jane Peirson Jones studied Archaeology and Anthropology at Cambridge University and she joined the staff of Birmingham Museum and Art Gallery as an Assistant Keeper in 1975. She became Keeper of the Department of Archaeology and Ethnography in 1980. She has published on South American archaeology, ethnography and museum and interpretation. She was responsible for the development of the Gallery 33 project – a multicultural, multimedia anthropology gallery which opened in the Birmingham Museum and Art Gallery in October 1990.

From 1988 to 1989 Jane Peirson Jones was Lecturer in Heritage Management at the Ironbridge Institute, University of Birmingham. In 1990 she chaired the Museum Ethnographers' Group Working Party which prepared *Guidelines* on the curatorship of human remains. She was elected Fellow of the Museums Association in 1993 and is an Honorary Research Fellow, Centre of West African Studies, University of Birmingham and an Executive Board Member of ICOM, UK.

Kate Pontin is employed by the London Borough of Hillingdon as a Local Heritage Education Officer, helping the public to learn about and enjoy the natural and historical heritage of the Borough, through the use of sites, objects and archives. Previously she worked at Leicestershire Museums Service as a museum education officer specializing in the natural sciences. Kate is particularly interested in science learning in museums and having now completed her Masters Degree she is embarking on further research in the field.

Sanford Sivitz Shaman is Director of Fine Arts Exhibitions and Collections at the University of Haifa, where he also teaches in the University's graduate programme in Museology. Prior to assuming his current post in Israel, Sanford Shaman was Director of the Palmer Museum of Art at the Pennsylvania State University from 1984 to 1989. From 1980 to 1984 he was Director of the Museum of Art at Washington State University. A former National Endowment for the Arts Fellow in Arts Management (USA), he is a founding member of the Association of College and University Museums and Galleries, and he has served terms as that organization's Vice President and President. Sanford Shaman is also a former member of the Museum's Panel of the Pennsylvania Council for the Arts. His articles on contemporary art and museums have appeared in such publications as: *Art in America*, *Arts Magazine*, *The New Art Examiner*, *The International Journal of Museum Management and Curatorship*, *The Museologist*, *The Journal of Museum Education*, and *The Chronicle of Higher Education*.

Dr Bhargaviamma Venugopal gained a BSc from Kerala University, and an MSc from Calicut University, both in Zoology. He worked for several years as Educational Assistant in the National Museum of Natural History, New Delhi,

India, and has recently become Curator at the Natural History Museum at Mysore. Venugopal has followed courses in Museum Studies at the National Museum of Natural History, India (1984), and the University of Leicester (1990–1). He has been involved in visitor research since 1987, sometimes working with American colleagues. He has written several articles on this topic.

Mike Wallace is the author of a series of essays which explore the way history is presented to popular audiences. They will be collected in *Mickey Mouse History*, to be published by Temple University Press in 1995. He is working, with Edwin Burrows, on *A History of New York City*, to be published by Simon & Schuster. He teaches at John Jay College (City University of New York).

Andrea Weltzl-Fairchild is Associate Professor of Art Education, Concordia University. Her main interest is in museum education having worked in both schools and museums. Trained as an art historian, she taught art and art history in schools and university. Her current vocation is to encourage school teachers to make use of the museum as enrichment to their art pograms. Research interests focus on the aesthetic experiences of museum visitors of art museums.

1

Museums and communication: an introductory essay

Eilean Hooper-Greenhill

The third international conference in Museum Studies at the University of Leicester was held in April 1993. One hundred and twenty delegates attended from Britain, Sweden, Canada, Malta, Holland, South Africa, America, Switzerland, Taiwan, Croatia, New Zealand, France, Finland, Denmark, Greece, Portugal, India, West Indies and Malaysia.

The first and second international conferences were held in 1987 and 1990, resulting in Pearce, S. (ed.) (1989) *Museum Studies in Material Culture*, Leicester University Press, and Kavanagh, G. (ed.) (1991) *Museum Languages – Objects and Texts* and *The Museums Profession – Internal and External Relations*, Leicester University Press.

The third international conference took museum communication as its theme. This volume, which resulted, brings together a varied group of papers written by museum and university professionals from Britain, South Africa, Canada, America, Croatia, India, Israel and Austria. Four papers have been specially commissioned for the volume.

The papers include approaches to both theory and practice, with practical case-studies, and many of them address issues that have not been addressed before in any detail, such as adult education and museums, and the role of museums in a new South Africa.

This chapter has four main purposes: first, to outline the framework for the conference and hence for this volume; second, to review some aspects of museum communication in Britain, particularly issues relating to the museum audience; third, to relate audience research in museums to audience research in other cultural fields; and finally to describe the structure of this book.

A framework for the conference

I began to plan the conference 'Museum: Media: Message' in 1990. At that time, it was beginning to seem as though a conference three years later devoted to issues of communication in museums and galleries would probably be pretty topical. In 1990 we were witnessing in Britain the decline of public funding for the arts and museums, and were in the middle of a push by government to think of ourselves as an 'industry' with an economic role to play in social life, and with customers to satisfy. Marketing officers were being appointed in museums, and the concept of the 'audience' (all those people who might come to the museum) as opposed to merely the 'visitor' (those who did come to the museum) was beginning to take on considerable importance. It seemed reasonable to assume that the focus on audience would increase, and this has, indeed, proved to be the case.

Standards of management in general have come under scrutiny in both local and national museums, and standards of what has been called 'visitor satisfaction' (Office of Arts and Libraries 1991; National Audit Office 1993) and 'customer care' (Museums and Galleries Commission 1993) have been one important aspect of this. The Museums and Galleries Commission has issued guidelines on the quality of service for all visitors in museums (Museums and Galleries Commission 1993) and also guidelines specifically on provision for people with disabilities (Museums and Galleries Commission 1992). The Museums Association has established a working party whose work on equal opportunities in museums is well under way.

The assumption that attention to audiences would become of greater importance has been vindicated. From the chapters that follow, we will see how this has been reflected in practice in museums in Britain and in many other parts of the world.

It was more difficult to see in 1990 the severe recession that we have endured. Museums in Britain, and especially local authority museums, are now at a time of great crisis. Many museum people are losing their jobs, and many others are under threat. Nearly every local authority museum has been restructured, and some of the larger independent museums are on the verge of bankruptcy.

The reasons for this disruption are many, and it is not only museums that are suffering. Schools are losing teachers, and leisure facilities such as swimming pools are opening less frequently; many businesses have closed down, and very many people live in daily fear of losing their jobs. This context gives a particular poignancy to a book dealing with museums as communicators. It throws into high relief the past successes and failures of individual museums and galleries, and casts all our futures in a less than certain light. In my view, it tells us all too powerfully that if museums are not seen and felt to be part of the daily life of society, they will not survive.

Although survival is not automatically assured once social relevance is made clear, certainly without it closure is more than likely. The key to the development of well-understood social roles is the development of a better understanding of the tools with which we can work (collections, exhibitions, educational programmes) and the establishment and maintenance of qualitative relationships with audiences. Museums and galleries are fortunate in that there are many roles which they can play, there are many communicative methods to explore and many audiences with whom to work. For the future, development in all these areas will be vital.

This was the framework for the conference from which most of the chapters which follow were written; it is one of acute anxiety, but also one of immense opportunity. Change offers points for development and for new approaches. Survival demands this. Today museums must step forward to define for themselves a new future.

Museum communication in Britain

But what of the past? If the future for museums lies in the development of the communicative competence of the museum, what can the past offer us to help? I want to focus particularly here on what we know about museum audiences, because if we want to become better communicators we have to become very aware of our partners in the communication process.

What do we know about our audiences? I want to discuss this mainly in the British context, as this is the one I am most familiar with, but also because the nature of the field in Britain demonstrates some important points rather well. Let us consider audience studies in British museums.

Surveys of visitors to museums began in the 1960s. On the whole they were very small scale, and concentrated mainly on the demographic details of visitors such as age, sex, geographical location and so on. Mostly these small studies were carried out by museum staff, sometimes with the help of the local university or college. They were generally done with very limited resources, tended towards amateurism in methodology, and contented themselves with measuring a limited range of visitor characteristics. As public accountability increased, so the pace and the professionalism of visitor surveys has accelerated, with a particular urgency in the last eight years. It has been discovered that, with some exceptions, visitors to museums tend to be better educated and of a higher social class than the population in general. On the whole, it is the white population that sees museums as relevant, although specific exhibitions will attract specific audiences: in Leicester, for example, an exhibition of Afro-Caribbean history and art was visited by the Afro-Caribbean community, and exhibition called 'Vasna – an Indian village' was very popular with Leicester's large Asian population. This has taught us that museums attract the audiences they provide for.

Very few museum visitor studies looked at the museum visitor profile in the context of the profile of the local population, but gradually this too has become more frequent. Now, most museums know who their visitors are, how they reflect population patterns within a specific geographical area, how they relate to tourist movements and so on. Surveys in both local and national museums are carried out over time to monitor change and the effects of major policy shifts. Gathering basic data about visitors has become a necessary management tool.

During the 1980s a second type of analysis, which can be called participation studies, began. Government statistics such as Social Trends or Cultural Trends had already built up a small amount of not very helpful data on museum visitor patterns. During the 1980s, more specific studies commissioned by the tourist organizations (English Tourist Board 1982), central government agencies (Myerscough 1988) and some arts and museum bodies (Middleton 1990; Touche Ross 1989; RSGB 1991) began to look in more detail at what proportion of British adults visited museums, who they were, and, in outline, why they visited, generally looking at the last twelve (sometimes twenty-four) months. These studies were necessarily more broadly based than the museum visitor survey. They accelerated towards the end of the 1980s and the early 1990s.

Their conclusions are difficult to analyse as they variously report that 24 per cent, 33 per cent, 45 per cent and 56 per cent of the general population of Britain visit museums (Merriman 1991). Clearly we have to examine these data very carefully and ask questions about what definition of a museum has been used – whether, for example, this includes or excludes art galleries, or the built heritage. The time frame is also vital. The longer the time span, the greater the number of people who respond positively. In other words, if people are asked if they have visited a museum during the last two years, they are more likely to say yes than if they are asked about the last twelve months. The data suggest that a small proportion of people visit fairly frequently, but that a great many people visit rather irregularly over a longish period of time.

The most encouraging of these studies is one carried out for the Arts Council in 1991 (RSGB 1991) which used the time frame 'nowadays', which generally means 'in the last four weeks'. This showed that 48 per cent of the British population visited art galleries, museums and exhibitions, combined as a joint category, 'nowadays'. If 'nowadays' is a fairly short time span, and positive responses increase with longer time spans, a very large proportion of the British population is interested in museums and related institutions.

What do we know about what visitors do once they arrive in a museum or gallery? Research here is lamentably thin in Britain, although, under the title of evaluation, some work is beginning and some of the work that has been done is discussed in Part 3 of this volume. The pioneer in this area is, of course, the Natural History Museum in London.

The work that has been carried out at the Natural History Museum under the direction of Roger Miles is familiar to many. It is interesting that this work was carried out in a science museum, rather than in an art gallery. Science museums are often more aware of a specifically didactic purpose than other types of museum, and therefore have felt more strongly that they need to know what their visitors have learnt.

During the 1970s the Natural History Museum began to develop a series of new exhibitions. This was done as a very self-conscious process that was continuously monitored and documented. It was virtually unique at the time, although there was a glimmer of interest in exhibition theory at Liverpool Museum by the early 1980s, and further interesting evaluation work has been carried out there since.

Roger Miles and his colleagues concentrated on building an effective exhibition technology, using communication models from information technology, learning models from behaviourist psychology and sociological models from positivist

American mass communication theory (Miles and Tout 1979). The assumption of this research was that by perfecting the medium of communication (the exhibition), a successful transfer of messages would take place. It was assumed that if the exhibition was sufficiently expertly designed, visitors would automatically respond; in other words, that the medium itself was all-powerful and that the visitors were open to manipulation through its effects. Visitors were treated as a mass, a 'population'. After much trial and error and nearly two decades of work, it was admitted that this approach was not entirely successful, and that more attention needed be paid to the visitors and to their reasons for being in the museum in the first place (Miles and Tout 1991).

Other research into museum visitors at this time was virtually non-existent. Exhibitions were designed for 'the general public'. In the education department, with face-to-face teaching for identifiable groups with specific learning needs, the attention to audience was much more sharply focused, but this approach was not perceived as relevant to any other aspect of museum work. Now in the early 1990s, and specifically after the research carried out by Paulette McManus (see Peirson Jones, this volume), we are becoming more aware of the importance of the social context of museum visits, and of the fact that museum visitors do not become new-born beings as the enter the museum. People come to museums carrying with them the rest of their lives, their own reasons for visiting and their specific prior experience.

During the late 1980s and early 1990s the introduction of marketing methods to museums coincided with the rise to power of younger staff who frequently held strong convictions that museums should be more open and more democratic. These two forces both focused on audiences and their needs, and this resulted in the opening up of the issue for the first time of what people felt about museums. The combination of marketing and the move to democratize museums led to a pioneering study in London of the attitudes towards museums of people who were not regular visitors. A mass communications research firm, Mass Observation, was commissioned to do the work by the London Museums Service (which is a London-based museum advisory body, part of the Area Museum Service for South Eastern England). Earlier demographic surveys which had identified the main characteristics of typical museum visitors were used to construct a picture of those who were unlikely to visit. Discussion groups were then formed with, for example, men over 60, Asian women, and women with pre-school children. Together with an experienced and appropriate moderator, perceptions of museums were explored. For the first time in Britain, market research techniques were applied in the museum context to build a picture of perceptions and attitudes (Trevelyan 1991). Further work was carried out of a similar nature in Croydon (MacDonald, this volume).

In museums in North America, this approach to the collection of qualitative data is one aspect of what is known as naturalistic evaluation (see Hein, this volume), but in Britain this is still very unfamiliar. Marketing methods in British museums have, therefore, established the value of regular research into demographic profiles of visitors, and research such as the London studies are demonstrating how valuable qualitative work can be.

A further concept from marketing is that of 'target groups'. We now no longer design exhibitions for 'the general public'. We understand that different sections of the audience have different expectations and approach the museum for different reasons. We consider the needs of children, families, tourists, the elderly, schools, and people with a range of disabilities. This is becoming almost routine. However, our concept of 'need' is still at a very primitive and underdeveloped stage.

We have just about got to the point in museums in Britain now where we are asking what we can do to behave in a more sensitive way towards our audiences. We are beginning to wonder what 'evaluation' is and whether it can help us to do our job better. Finding very little qualitative work with audiences in museums, we are beginning to look outside to see what other people are doing. In the National Museums of Scotland, for example, an assessment of visitor responses to their Discovery Room in the summer of 1990 was organized jointly with the Open University in Scotland, and video techniques generally used for evaluating lecturers were adapted (Stevenson and Bryden 1991).

If we do look outside museums for helpful methods, where should we go? We can argue that museums work with two distinct models of communication. On the one hand, we can use interpersonal, face-to-face communication, and we see this in action in inquiry services for example, where the curator and an inquirer meet each other directly. Other examples might be found in some aspects of the educational work of museums, where museum teachers work directly with groups. On the other hand, museums can also be categorized as mass communicators, as, in addition to dealing with some people face to face, they also deal with a great number of people in a less personal way.

Many exhibitions share the major characteristic of most forms of mass communication in that they involve a one-way process, a single message source with a large group of receivers, and the messages themselves are in the public domain. Museums, when they communicate through exhibitions, publications, advertisements and other methods such as videos, can be characterized as mass communication media.

So museums can be seen as both mass communicators and interpersonal communicators. This means that there is a broad range of methods in other fields that might be relevant. Clearly work in the educational field is useful, and many papers in Parts 2 and 3 of this volume discuss examples of relevant educational theory and practice. I want, therefore, to go on to try to make some sense out of the great body of material that can be found in mass communication studies, and in the related fields of media studies and cultural studies.

Audience research in non-museum fields

The mass media have been studied since the beginning of the century, mainly but not exclusively in America. By the 1990s we are at a point in Britain where there are great numbers of courses in communication studies and in media studies.

There are now many overviews of approaches to the subject (for example, Gurevitch *et al.* 1982; Curran and Gurevitch 1991; McQuail 1987; Heath and Bryant 1992) and many accounts of specific projects which examine topics ranging from the political effects to the gender-specific uses made of the mass media. Museums are rarely, if ever, to be found in these accounts. Early mass communication theorists assumed the media audience to be an undifferentiated mass, widely dispersed, lacking in both self-awareness and self-identity, and incapable of acting together to secure objectives (McQuail 1987: 31). The mass audience did not act for itself, it was acted upon.

Media at the beginning of the century included the press, radio, cinema and advertising. During the 1920s and 1930s there was a broad consensus that the mass media exercised a powerful and persuasive influence on audiences susceptible to manipulation. This 'magic bullet' or 'hypodermic needle' theory proposed that the media 'worked' on the passive public and that the effects of this could be measured through the use of scientific techniques (Curran *et al.* 1982). Studies of 'audience effects' proliferated.

During the 1950s and 1960s, following these 'effects' studies, it became clear that the audience was not in fact as passive as had originally been thought and that people in many ways made their own use of media messages. Rather than being manipulated by the media, people manipulated the media. It was found that people expose themselves to, understand and remember communications selectively according to prior dispositions. The manipulative and persuasive effects of the media were therefore likely to be negated by the interpretations of the 'active audience'. Studies of 'uses and gratifications' were carried out.

The late 1960s saw the development of cultural studies in Britain, and the decisive rejection of the simplistic communications model and consensual model of society that American mass communication theorists had used (Turner 1990; McGuigan 1992). British cultural studies employed Marxist models of society, and saw the mass media as a site for ideological reproduction in the maintenance of social, economic and cultural power relations. Ideological 'work' was studied through semiotic analyses of texts; first, the literary text, and then later, other cultural artefacts such as film or, rarely, exhibitions.

Semiotic analysis studies the implicit ideological messages of texts achieved through representation and mediation; how, for example, are women portrayed in Bond movies, in coffee advertisements or in social history exhibitions? The analysis of the text is carried out at a theoretical level by the theorist and rarely tested. Where empirical studies were done, it was frequently shown that the theorist's analysis was mere assumption, and was not borne out by audience responses. Ideology did not in fact 'interpellate the subject' (to use Althusser's words), 'preferred readings' (in the terminology of Stuart Hall 1982) were not achieved; in contrast, the audience was actively deconstructing the message according to a whole range of complex factors that left the media message with a role little short of that of setting the agenda for thought. Media messages (and much of this work has been done in relation to television) could not tell people how to think, but could set the agenda as to what to think about. This

7

in itself is not insignificant, but it swings the focus back again to the audience, away from the text. A focus on the text alone does not tell us how audiences use it.

In the new focus on audiences that is developing, both mass communication studies and cultural studies theorists are united in their interest in the development of ethnographic methods. The older 'uses and gratifications' studies have been rejected, criticized for remaining at the level of individual psychology and failing to take account of larger social divisions and structures that in large part shape individual psychologies and responses. Ethnographic audience studies have used and adapted methods from anthropological fieldwork, where the researcher works very closely with the people she is studying, and the research is carried out in an open and reflexive way.

Recent TV audience studies are particularly interesting. It has been shown that gender, race and class have specific structuring effects in the reception of TV messages. To take just one example, which I found especially fascinating: *The Cosby Show* is an American comedy soap, which concerns, uniquely, an upper-middle-class black family and their daily doings (Lewis 1991). Unlike other black American TV shows, it has, in America, a very broad audience of both black and white middle- and lower-class viewers. Detailed ethnographic audience research was carried out in America through home-based discussions with different types of people, using class and race as structuring categories. It emerged that different categories of people interpreted the programme according to their own aspirations and understanding of self and that they failed to see those aspects of the programme that did not support their own world view. The interpretations were personal, but also depended strongly on race and class.

Middle-class white viewers, for example, saw the upper-middle-class American life-style and failed to accord any importance to the fact that the family was black. The family was perceived as so 'normal', so much in line with the everyday middle-class American as seen on TV, that their blackness 'just sort of drifted out of' the minds of viewers (Lewis 1991: 174). Working-class black people, on the other hand, were very aware of the blackness of the actors and found the positive black images all-important. They celebrated the small references to black culture that middle-class whites had failed to see, such as the naming of the grandchildren as Nelson and Winnie. Other groups responded in other ways.

The show is constructed around ambiguity. The family is both black and, through their life-style, like whites. The show presents a view of blacks that is both radical, in that most American blacks do not live as they do, and everyday, in that many American soap families do. This ambiguity allows people with radically different political views and social perceptions to accept the programme as appropriate and to find it sufficiently undisturbing to enjoy it.

The analysis of *The Cosby Show* focused on the nature of the text (the TV message) and also analysed, using ethnographic methods, the ways in which several different audience categories used the message to create pleasure for themselves. The way forward for communication studies and cultural studies is seen as the combination of textual and audience studies, with a sophisticated and complex model of both text and audience in place. This combination of models remains to be developed.

What can we in museums learn from this all too brief overview of audience studies in mass communication and cultural studies?

First, we can see that in terms of concept development, museums have not been in the forefront. Media studies in the 1950s proposed the active audience and the importance of social context in the reception of the message long before we had even begun to study our audiences in museums. Our methodology in museums has not paid attention to methods used by communication and cultural theorists, and an over-reliance on behaviourist, positivist methods has failed to reveal the importance of audience decoding. Up till now, we have had, in Britain, no ethnographic studies of museum visitors, and some of the chapters in this volume describe the new work in this field. We do need to begin to work in a more reflexive and more open way with audiences, to allow their descriptions of what museums mean to them to emerge during the research process.

A very important lesson from *The Cosby Show* example is the importance of the notion of polysemia, of plurality of meanings, that has been called in other contexts semiotic excess. *The Cosby Show* is carefully constructed to contain a range of meanings that are designed to appeal to the known different audience segments. The balance of appeal is carefully reviewed, in the knowledge that some people will see one thing and focus on one aspect, while others will pick up other messages. How much potential in museums is there for exactly this semiotic excess, this range of meanings, many of which will be invisible to many audiences, but which exist to be activated when someone with the experience to perceive and decode the message is present? I think the potential here is enormous and very exciting.

Mass communication research has thrown up other useful ideas, such as the rejection of the linear communications model in favour of a transactional model where messages are formulated, exchanged and interpreted in a continuous process.

We have, in Britain, learnt a great deal about audiences during the last decade. We know, for example, that we can to quite a large extent manipulate our audiences, by designing a product for a specific market. If we put on an exhibition about football, and market it appropriately, people who are interested in football will come to see it. We know also that people appear to respond very positively to the opportunity to handle objects and exhibits at discovery and interactive centres. At the National Museum of Scotland, for example, large numbers of people queue down the stairs and in front of the glass-cased exhibits in order to visit the Discovery Room.

What we do not really know is why people like to handle things, or why football (or other) memorabilia are important. Our learning has taken the form of trial and error. We observe large numbers of people queuing for the Discovery Room in Scotland and decide that we must have one too. The danger of learning in this

9

way is that we adopt the practices without understanding the principles. We go away and replicate the Scottish Discovery Room, and pretty soon there are little Scottish discovery rooms all over the place and everyone is bored to tears with them. Meanwhile the glass cases are still just as tedious as ever.

In order to develop truly we must look more deeply behind the successes and try to identify the principles of learning and of engagement that lie there. We need to know what the specific visitor finds meaningful, and we need to target individuals for our research according to specific structuring categories which include gender, race and class. Mass communications and cultural studies offer examples of work carried out in relation to other cultural fields. We can usefully learn from them.

The structure of the book

We live in dangerous times, times of constant change. Change is always different, and in museums we need to grasp and shape this difference to help us develop new ways of understanding our communicative potential. In order to do this we need to develop our knowledge, understanding and skills in several areas.

First, we need to work on the idea of the museum as a communicative medium. What does 'museums as media' mean? The chapters in the first part of the book go some way to address this issue, although the field is broad and deep, and the chapters presented here by no means exhaust what has become a very pressing area of professional study.

Museums are institutions based on objects. This is what makes them different from other social and cultural institutions. The first two chapters discuss approaches to the analysis of the object as a medium. Typically, in museums, objects are combined and presented to the public in exhibitions. Two chapters review the issues that this raises in terms of whom exhibitions are for, how they can be constructed, what models of good practice are available. How does the museum relate to external contemporary media? Two chapters examine this question, one in relation to nineteenth-century newspapers, and the other in response to the rapid development of new technologies today. Finally in this section, the moral role of the modern blockbuster art exhibition is questioned.

The second part of the book – 'Communication in action' – consists mainly of case-studies and examples of museums working with particular constituents. The first three chapters are more general: the first sets out the environment of the postmodern museum, describes some examples of the ways in which museums are responding to new demands and perceptions on the part of audiences and calls for the development of partnerships; the second chapter suggests guide-lines for meaningful partnerships; and the third chapter outlines a management structure for achieving successful relationships with visitors within the context of a specific museum service. The following five chapters discuss specific examples of partnerships with a range of audiences in Britain and South Africa. The importance of knowing the audience, researching their specific interests, attitudes and opinions, and the need to use this information in forward planning is demonstrated.

The third part of the book 'Evaluating the communication process', is concerned with theoretical approaches and specific case-studies of evaluation in museums and galleries. The first chapter presents a discussion of naturalistic or responsive evaluation based on the constructivist theory of education which is premised on the view that people construct their own realities. This is followed by two case-studies examining the relationship of schoolchildren and art galleries; the first explains the methods used to examine the museum/school interface, and the second discusses the meanings children made of paintings. The fourth chapter analyses the methods and findings of a comprehensive review of children's learning in a natural history gallery, and the fifth calls for the development of evaluative methods specific to historic sites. The sixth demands a review of the theory of adult education following some detailed research in Canadian museums and galleries. The final three chapters review aspects of gallery-based evaluation including: a report of a detailed review of the response of visitors to a new British ethnographic gallery; an analysis of the frequency of use of a natural history museum in India by families; and a review of the range of gallery evaluation and visitor research that is carried out at a large London national museum.

Museum communication is a new and growing area. We are rapidly developing theory and practice in the communicative methods that may be used in museums and galleries, and in assessing the use and value of these methods. But more, much more, needs to be done. In many ways, museums are only just beginning to consider themselves in relation to their visitors. For most of this century, museum work has gone on despite rather than because of visitors.

This book is the first in a new series *Museums: New Visions/New Approaches*. This series will be taking up some of the issues that are raised when museums begin to think of themselves as a part of the communication processes of society. There is much to learn, and the series aims to produce material that will help in this learning. The first few books will develop the area of how language works in museums, what evaluation methods are appropriate in museums, and how market research can be used to develop the communicative potential of museums. It is hoped that this volume and the volumes that follow will play their part as museums reinvent themselves for the new century.

References

Boyd-Barret, O. and Braham, P. (1987) *Media, Knowledge and Power*, London and Sydney: Croom Helm and the Open University.
Certeau, M. (1984) *The Practice of Everyday Life*, Berkeley: University of California Press.
Curran, J., and Gurevitch, M. (1991) *Mass Media and Society*, London and New York: Edward Arnold.
Curran, J., Gurevitch, M. and Woollacott, J. (1982) 'The study of the media: theoretical approaches', in M. Gurevitch, T. Bennett and J. Woollacott, *Culture, Society and the Media*, London: Routledge, 11–29.

English Tourist Board (1982) *Visitors to Museums Survey 1982*, Report by the English Tourist Board and NOP Market Research Limited, London.

Gurevitch, M., Bennett, T., Curran, J. and Woollacott, J. (eds) (1982) *Culture, Society and the Media*, London: Methuen.

Hall, S. (1982) 'The rediscovery of "ideology": the return of the "repressed" in media studies', in M. Gurevitch, T. Bennett, J. Curran and J. Woollacott (eds) *Culture, Society and the Media*, London: Methuen, 56–90.

Heath, R. and Bryant, J. (1992) *Human Communication Theory and Research: Concepts, Contexts and Challenges*, Hove and London: Lawrence Erlbaum and Associates.

Lewis, J. (1991) *The Ideological Octopus: an Exploration of Television and its Audience*, London and New York: Routledge.

McGuigan, J. (1992) *Cultural Populism*, London and New York: Routledge.

McQuail, D. (1987) *Mass Communication Theory: an Introduction*, London: Sage Publications, Ltd.

—— (1992) *Media Performance – Mass Communication and the Public Interest*, London and New Delhi: Sage Publications.

Merriman, N. (1991) *Beyond the Glass Case: the Past, the Heritage and the Public in Britain*, Leicester, London and New York: Leicester University Press.

Middleton, V. (1990) *New Visions for Independent Museums in the UK*, West Sussex: Association of Independent Museum.

Miles, R. and Tout, A. (1979) 'Outline of a technology for effective science exhibits', *Special Papers in Paleontology* 22: 209–24.

—— (1991) 'Impact of research on the approach to the visiting public at the Natural History Museum', *International Journal of Science Education* 13(5): 534–49.

Morley, D. (1992) *Television, Audiences and Cultural Studies*, London and New York: Routledge.

Museums and Galleries Commission (1992) *Guidelines on Disability for Museums and Galleries in the United Kingdom*, London: Museums and Galleries Commission.

—— (1993) *Quality of Service in Museums and Galleries: Customer Care in Museums – Guidelines on implementation*, London: Museums and Galleries Commission.

Myerscough, J. (1988) *The Economic Importance of the Arts in Britain*, London: Policy Studies Institute.

National Audit Office (1993) *Department of National Heritage, National Museums and Galleries: Quality of Service to the Public*, Report by the Comptroller and Auditor General, National Audit Office, London: HMSO.

Office of Arts and Libraries (1991) *Report on the Development of Performance Indicators for the National Museums and Galleries*, London: Office of Arts and Libraries.

RSGB Omnibus Arts Survey (1991) *Report on a Survey on Arts and Cultural Activities in G.B.*, London: Arts Council of Great Britain.

Stevenson, M. and Bryden, M. (1991) 'The National Museums of Scotland's 1900 Discovery Room: an evaluation', *Museum Management and Curatorship* 10: 24–36.

Susie Fisher Group (1990) *Bringing History and the Arts to a New Audience: Qualitative Research for the London Borough of Croydon*, London: Susie Fisher Group.

Touche Ross (1989) *Museum Funding and Services: the Visitor's Perspective*, London: Touche Ross Management Consultants.

Trevelyan, V. (1991) *'Dingy Places with Different Kinds of Bits' – an Attitudes Survey of London Museums amongst Non-visitors*, London: London Museums Service.

Turner, G. (1990) *British Cultural Studies: an Introduction*, Boston: Unwin Hyman.

Part 1

Museums as media

2

Collecting as medium and message

Susan Pearce

The notion that 'medium' and 'message' are identical, that what we say and how we say it are two halves of the same apple, is nowhere more evidently true than in the material world, the tangible and visible world of objects and the meaningful patterns which we make with them. Museums, of course, are the quintessential institutions, developed as a characteristic part of European culture, which exist to hold selected objects and specimens and in so doing give their own direct and distinctive messages from their object media through their exhibitions, education policies and so on; but in this chapter I shall be concerned to look below this to the material itself, to the ways in which we relate to it, and form it into those characteristic groups which we call collections, as which it normally arrives in a museum (see Pearce 1992). This will take us first to a brief analysis of our relationship with objects, and then to a notion of how collections are made from them. I shall go on to consider the open nature of collections as part of the political world of perceived value, and their hidden nature in the poetic universe of the individual. I shall then briefly describe the Leicester Contemporary Collecting Project which is intended to shed more light on our understanding of these matters, and finally draw together the threads.

Objects, like language and the manipulation of the natural world which gives living space, shelter and food, constitute one of the fundamental ways in which we construct ourselves, both as societies and as individual social animals. Objects are implicit in social action, which cannot happen without them, and explicit in that social practice can be 'read' from them. They are, therefore, always, both active and passive; we make them, and they influence us. Like all other human manifestations they are only significant in groups or sets to which meaning can be attached: a sentence needs all its words, a room all its things, for sense to be made and life to go on.

Collections, which derive from the object world but are, somehow, separate from it, are a special case of object grouping or setting, and much effort has been expended in attempts to define what a collection is. In 1968 Baudrillard suggested:

> Le stade inférieur est celui de l'accumulation de matières: entassement de vieux papiers, stockage de nourriture – à mi-chemin entre l'introjection

orale et la retention anale – puis l'accumulation sérielle d'objets identiques. La collection, elle, émerge vers la culture ... sans cesser de renvoyer les uns aux autres, ils incluent dans ce jeu une extériorité sociale, des relations humaines.

(Baudrillard 1968: 147–8)

Perhaps notions of anal retention are best taken with a large pinch of salt but the point about differential value is an important one, to which we shall return. Aristides offers:

collection [is] 'an obsession organized'. One of the distinctions between possessing and collecting is that the latter implies order, system, perhaps completion. The pure collector's interest is not bounded by the intrinsic worth of the objects of his desire; at whatever cost, he must have them.

(Aristides 1988: 330)

This draws our attention to the subjective nature of the activity. Alsop has offered a refreshingly simple approach. He says: 'To collect is to gather objects belonging to a particular category the collector happens to fancy ... and a collection is what has been gathered' (Alsop 1982: 70). This highlights two important aspect of collecting, its deliberateness and the idea that a collection is what somebody thinks it is.

However, all of this seems not to reach the heart of the matter. Rather than engage in the essentially arid and inadequate business of chopping definitions we should look at the actual collecting process, and try to see how it relates to the broader material world, and to ourselves collectively and severally.

Here, it is useful to make use of the basic principles of Saussurian semiotics, which can be set out in a diagram of the kind shown in Figure 2.1 where *langue*, meaning 'language', is the conventional term for fundamental structure of all kinds, including verbal language and other 'language' systems like objects, and *parole*, meaning 'speech', is the term for all concrete action whether in words or things. The world of ideas and raw materials offers a range of possibilities to each social group, and this it will structure into meaningful material culture in accordance with its social rules, themselves influenced by the surrounding material world. This, like all other social construction, takes place in the *langue* of the community concerned, a fount of social intention which lies somewhere between communal meaning and Jung's collective unconscious, both common to us all as community members and as individuals. Operation within the *langue* emerges as *parole*, social action in concrete form. For material culture this means actual objects organized in sets which embody genuine human social experience, and are capable of transmitting that experience to other people. We might, for example, see the range of possibilities of 1950s Britain as embracing both a need for many goods and the raw materials required to make plastics. These are structured into plastic objects against a social grammar which includes technical knowledge, and so gives us the sets of kitchen utensils, wireless cases and flower pots which give reality to our daily lives. These objects in

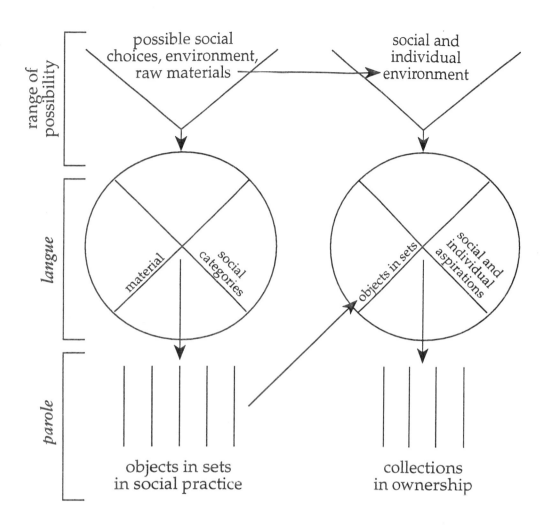

Figure 2.1 The collecting process expressed in terms of Saussurian semiotics

social practice then, as a second process, become part of the collecting *langue*, where they are restructured as collections in ownership.

We can see that the collection bears not a continuous or a one-to-one relationship to the source material, but rather a metaphorical relationship to this material, of which it can only be said to be representative in a very particular way. The notion of selection and of the selective process is crucial in the creation of a collection, because, although it may take a while for an individual to recognize his or her collection as such, the dawning of this recognition is the moment when the collection takes formal shape and the notion of deliberate selection is then projected both backwards and forwards.

The impulses against which this selective structuring is done, and from which collections result, are complex. They embrace both traditional social notions about what constitute 'proper' or 'valuable' or 'prestigious' material collections, and obscure but compelling movements in each individual's heart and mind which leads each one to collect. Both of these deserve our consideration.

How societies as a whole ascribe value to objects is a major area of political study in its own right. We are concerned here with those traditional European, and therefore curatorial, artefactual values against which all collecting is still likely to be judged, but towards which contemporary collecting may be adding a fresh dimension which may alter the balance of value, in museums and elsewhere. We can analyse how curators and collectors give value to material in terms of opposed pairs, including of course natural history material, which becomes 'artefactual' once it is labelled and brought into a classificatory system (Figure 2.2). The sets of pairs more or less write themselves, so 'obvious' are they, that is so deeply embedded are they in our inherited culture system of value creation, as described, for example, by Bourdieu (1977) in his notion of the cultural habitus, or Baudrillard (1968) in his system of objects.

authentic	:	non-authentic/ spurious
normal	:	odd
identifiable	:	unidentifiable
art	:	not-art
real	:	fake
scientifically recorded	:	no context
important	:	standard
interesting/ provocative	:	boring
culture/ within tradition	:	not-culture/ rootless
masterpiece	:	artefact

Figure 2.2 Analysis of the creation of value in material culture in terms of opposed pairs

Following Griemas and Rastier (1968) and Clifford (1988), but adapting their approach to the present purpose, we can discern a social plot structured around two axes about which object prestige and value are constructed: masterpiece/ artefact where 'masterpiece' means an accredited masterwork of man or nature, and 'artefact' means an ordinary thing; and authentic/non-authentic or spurious, where 'authentic' carries all the tones of genuine, sincere or culturally central and 'spurious' its opposite. A number of other pairs then find their appropriate places on the plot (Figure 2.3). These distinctions work across cultural systems. In the world of food, for example, *haute cuisine* belongs in the top left, meat

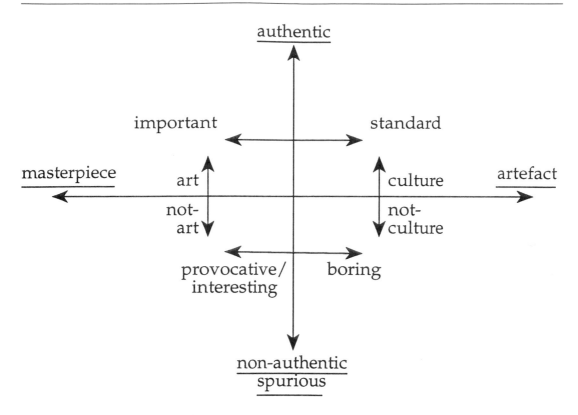

Figure 2.3 Social plot of the creation of value

and two veg on the right, in the upper or lower parts depending upon how well it is cooked, and in the bottom left come unsuitable confections with cream from a tube. We see that notions like tradition, purity or simplicity, and mainstream or normal are involved.

Translated into object terms, we can see that fine art, high applied art like silversmithing or traditional carpet weaving, together with 'fine' or 'important' (in Sotheby's sense) natural history specimens, and, also in Sotheby's words, 'primitive' art, that is non-western material to which Europeans have come to ascribe particular significance, belong within the 'authentic masterpiece' quadrant, while genuine hand-crafted material, which includes most archaeological and anthropological material, 'humble' applied art like patchwork and much social history material, together with most natural specimens, belong in the 'authentic artefact' quadrant. But in the 'non-authentic artefact' quarter belong commodities and utilities, the mass-produced material of our own time, together with Baudrillard's tins and heaps of paper, while in the 'non-authentic master-piece' quarter belong fakes, airport art, perhaps animals which have been unpleasantly taxidermed – stuffed cats playing with balls of wool, mice in trousers around tables and the like – garden gnomes, plastic flowers, 'pop' art before its elevation (Figure 2.4).

19

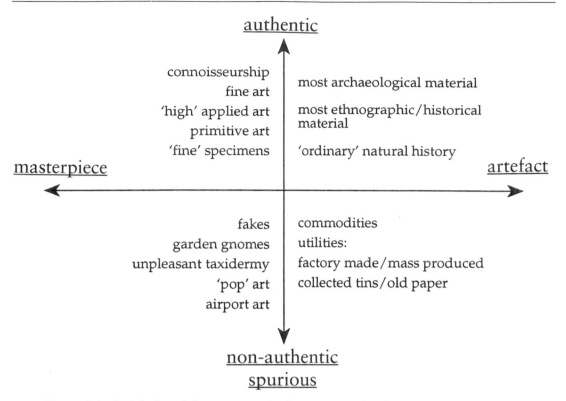

Figure 2.4 Social plot of the creation of value in material culture

It is obvious that most museum collections, and certainly those most on show, do, or have until very recently, belonged in the top half of the chart. Equally, we know from recent studies and projects that a great deal of popular contemporary collecting belongs in the bottom half. It would be easy to assume that this is purely a product of the class and education system as it has operated in Britain and in Europe over the last three centuries or so, and plainly this is a factor not to be ignored. Obviously access to capital bears an intimate relationship with the creation of cash value in objects to which great prestige is attached, and conversely prestige adheres to objects which are deemed valuable. But a moment's reflection upon the history of collecting suggests that this is an inadequate explanation. For one thing 'authentic' collections, especially in the natural history field, have, particularly in Britain, been created across the social range for at least two centuries. Thompson (1968) in his *Making of the English Working Class* cites the example of a young weaver in Luddenden, northern England, in the 1820s.

> I collected insects, in company with a number of young men in the village. We formed a library . . . I believe I and a companion of mine . . . collected twenty-two large boxes of insects; one hundred and twenty different sorts of British birds' eggs; besides a great quantity of shells (land and fresh water), fossils, minerals, ancient and modern coins.
>
> (Thompson 1968: 324)

Similarly 'non-authentic' collections have been made by members of the landed gentry; we may recall the great mass of miscellaneous collected material which has surfaced at Calke Abbey, now in the hands of the National Trust but once owned and filled by successive baronets and other members of the Harpur-Crewe family.

Arguments about class and capital, then, seem inadequate in the face of the great mass of collectors and collections. We sense that we are touching a universe, not wholly separate from, but distinct from, social or overt perceptions of value, a universe which matches that which we have already described, but is its opposing twin. If social values and political perceptions make up This World of intellectual argument and museum exhibition, then its twin is the Other World of the individual interior, where what is collected matters less than how and why it is collected.

Here we are in a poetic world of myth and metaphor where each of us can live with the chaos of experience and turn it into a little personal sense through the transforming power of collected objects (Figure 2.5). These offer us an enclosed and private world, where collections mirror and extend our bodies and souls. Collections take on the external reality of our passage through life: the objects in them sometimes come to us from the past as personal souvenirs or family heirlooms; we have material which belongs to important moments in our lives or perhaps, in its finding, created those important moments; we are anxious that our collections shall be kept intact, to be handed to our children or a museum, as our hope of a little immortality.

We love our collections, and yet exercise dominance over them by controlling choice and access. We tend, as a number of our studies are showing, to enhance our notions of gender through what we choose to collect. We create ordered space through our collections by arranging them on shelves, organizing their internal sequences and relationships, and putting them on display. We treat our collections as play, making out our own special ground, and playing within it to rules of our own devising. Games begin and end, and collections, too, can give us the satisfactions of completion and closure.

All of these fascinating areas, the politics and poetics of collecting, open up before us for exploration. The Chicago Project examined the way in which people relate to material in their own homes (Csikszentmihalyi and Rochberg-Halton 1981). Russell Belk and his colleagues in Utah (1991) carried out the Odyssey Project, a naturalistic evaluation of collecting across America. The People's Show Project in Walsall and now across the Midlands has produced much anecdotal evidence and interesting exhibitions as part of the extraordinary public response to this innovative idea.

In the Department of Museum Studies at Leicester, we are mounting two research projects which will focus on popular collecting in contemporary Britain. The first of these, the Leicester Collecting Project, will operate over the summer of 1993 and will involve the distribution of 1,500 questionnaires to randomly chosen individuals with the aim of discovering both quantitative and qualitative information about collecting habits and the nature of the material

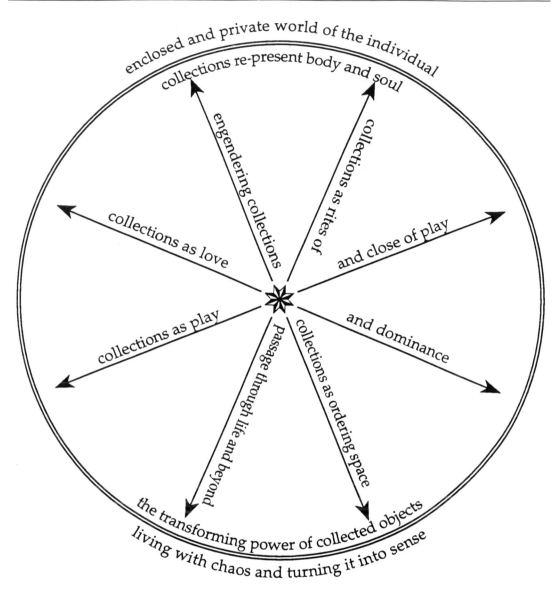

Figure 2.5 Collections and our passage through life

collected. The second will be the appointment to a three-year post of research student, who will work under the guidance of Kevin Moore and myself on an area of popular collecting, perhaps one which arises from the summer's work.

Probably one in three Americans collects something; and the figure is unlikely to be much less for contemporary Britain. Collecting is a major social phenomenon and needs to be understood in its own right and on its own terms. The politics and poetics of collecting are the politics and poetics of us all; and its messages are messages for us all.

References

Alsop, J. (1982) *The Rare Art Traditions: A History of Collecting and Its Linked Phenomena*, New York: Harper & Row.

Aristides, N. (1988) 'Calm and uncollected', *American Scholar* 53(3): 327–36.

Baudrillard, J. (1968) *Le systéme des objets*, Paris: Gallimard.

Belk, R. W., Wallendorf, M., Sherry, J., Holbrook, M. and Roberts, R. (1991) 'The history and development of the consumer behaviour odyssey', *Highways and Buyways: Association for Consumer Research*, 1991: 1–47.

Bourdieu, P. (1977) *Outline of a Theory in Practice*, Cambridge: Cambridge University Press.

Clifford, J. (1988) *The Predicament of Culture*, Cambridge, Mass: Harvard University Press.

Csikszentmihalyi, M. and Rochberg-Halton E. (1981) *The Meaning of Things: Domestic Symbols and the Self*, Cambridge: Cambridge University Press.

Griemas, A. J. and Rastier, F. (1968) 'The interaction of semiotic constraints', *Yale French Studies* 41: 86–105.

Pearce, S. (1992) *Museums, Objects and Collections*, Leicester: Leicester University Press.

Thompson, E. P. (1968) *The Making of the English Working Class*, London: Penguin Books.

3

The museum message: between the document and information

Ivo Maroević

Introduction: cultural heritage

Cultural heritage, materialized in the surrounding world, is one of the elements linking past and present in a given space. Cultural heritage establishes very close links with the space it lives in, so its cultural qualification is the result of various social processes through which it has acquired the designation 'cultural'. Culture is, among other things, 'the ability of a community to recognize, identify and produce symbols in identical ways' (Tuđman 1983: 137). Symbolic values obtained by objects of cultural heritage were established in the past and transferred to the new times; then new forms of life and meanings were created in a society which took old values and transformed them. Culture and the meaning of cultural heritage originated in a social environment, and their symbolic and other values accumulated in the material world that surrounds us. In that sense, the material world with its physical substance and the way it is shaped carries over all the layers of meaning deposited through time, many of which are illegible or incomprehensible because the cultural contexts of the objects' life have been changed.

Cultural heritage in space is considerably more stable in that sense, because it does not change its environment, but it has been changing together with the environment, and so part of the meaning is transferred to the space. Resistance and the long duration of communications in space or the existence of toponyms, the continuity of sacral spaces and their titulars are but examples which confirm that in space the continuity of material forms is not very often crucial or decisive for the continuity of symbolic values. The continuity of material forms is often covered by shells of new forms or functions. On the other hand, movable cultural heritage, including museum objects, has different characteristics. Here the stability is not so much linked with the given space, but rather with the material structure of objects. An object carries its symbolic and other semantic values within its structure, and the context of a new environment enables it to state these values or to have them settle as part of its own history, and reveal them to all those able to understand them.

Museum object

The museum object is an object of reality, a part of the movable cultural heritage. Transferred to the museum, the object becomes a document of that reality from which it was selected (Stransky 1970: 35). Thereby it becomes a document of those realities in which it lived earlier, but in a way which is not obvious or intelligible at first sight but only after closer study. The study shows the multiple layers of the museum object and its multilayered identities ranging from the conceptual, through the factual, the functional and the structural, to the actual identity (van Mensch 1989: 90). This multitlayered nature of meanings and symbolic values, which can be identified in the study of the museum object, constantly changes the field of its museal definiteness. The object can then be used to convey these multilayered values and meanings. The museality of a museum object as its basic museological determinant is increased by the widening of the field of its museal definiteness (see Figure 3.1). Delibašić says that

> in the process of the establishing of the meaning of a museum object the essential factor appears to be the individual and collective experience . . . as well as the relationship with other objects and with the space where the object is placed.
>
> (Delibašić 1991: 34)

This brings us to the conclusion that 'by establishing a number of different meanings of the same sign, the prejudice that museum objects can contain within themselves the objective truth of the extra semiotic universe is proved invalid' (Delibašić 1991: 34). Though Delibašić does not consider the existence of a communication pattern to be a framework for communication, he rightly claims that the significance of a museum object and its objectivity in reflecting reality are relative phcnomena. The museum thus never ceases to be a medium which uses objects as signs.

Document

When we speak about a museum object and its value as a document, it must be clear that in a museological context the object reflects one or several manifestations of its changeable primary context or, less frequently, of the archaeological context in which it appears as a discarded or socially used-up artefact. The documentary value of a museum object is manifested only in the museological context, while the subject-matter of the documenting process can be found either in other contexts or in the identities of a museum object or in the museological context itself. The documentary value of a museum object is expressed on the temporal axis, because during its lifetime the object accumulates the traces of time and events on its material and formal structure. At the same time, by its material structure and form it transfers the preserved values into the future. The continuation of the material structure as an expression of the documentary value of the object is shown on the axis of chronological time (see Figure 3.2).

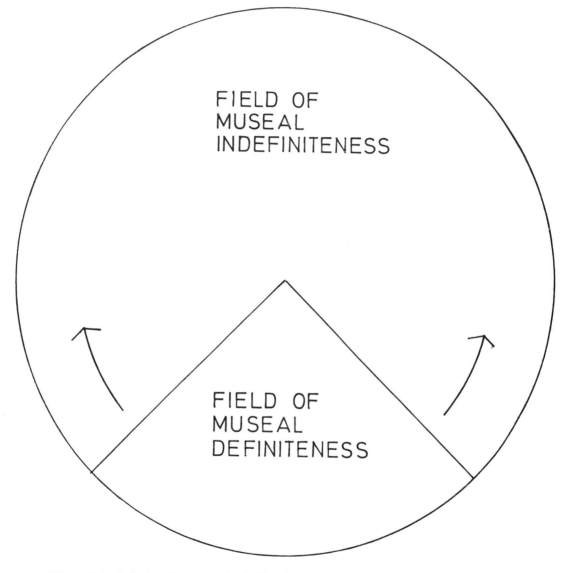

Figure 3.1 Relations between the fields of museal definiteness and indefiniteness

A museum collection is a multilayered set of museum objects. Most frequently, it acts as a unit composed of individual objects, so that it accumulates and transfers the documentary value of museum objects to a higher level. The collection is not a mere sum of museum objects, because by its very nature it may be enlarged or perhaps reduced in scope. It is a live organism, which in certain situations, when precisely defined subject-matter or related cultural and historical milieux are concerned, could play the role of a museum object, which viewed as a whole has the meaning and value of a document. In that case, the documentary values of the individual objects are accumulated together with the value of the collection as a whole.

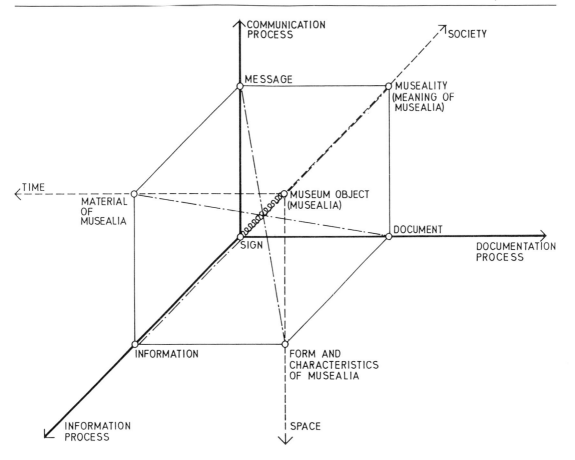

Figure 3.2 Overlapping of structural and functional analysis of a museum object (modification according to Tuđman 1983: 72)

The documentation processes evolving in museums are integrated with the other processes which contribute to establishing the documentary values of museum objects or collections. The perceived read-off values of the objects as documents are transferred to other media and so the documentary layer of the museum object is modified in media terms. The data on an object, its appearance and structure, its history and environment, its meaning and specificity are transferred to the medium of a text, a paper, an illustration, a film or a magnetic record. Thus documents on a museum object are established. They provide knowledge about the object, including its perceived characteristics and values in certain information and documentation systems. These systems will be able to operate and function independently of objects and museums, preserving part of the social consciousness about the object and its values, and contributing to the stabilization of knowledge about the heritage in museums and galleries. The documents cannot be substitutes for the museum object, but they can give us a definite notion about it. The wider the general knowledge about the object, the better our understanding of it.

Information

Information is a fundamental element of knowledge. It lives and is actualized as a result of communication processes between individuals and the world around them. It is not identical with the document (or object as document), because it is not a copy of the document (Tuđman 1983: 47–9). It contains both the perceived characteristics of the object and its interpretation. However, recorded information or data, i.e. sets of data, are inbuilt in human knowledge. In the museum world, especially in museological processes, information originates from various forms of communication between individual and object, the information being the articulation of what has been noticed or experienced during the communication process. This means that the information in museums is always revived, because with time conditions change as well as the people involved in communication processes with museum objects. It is therefore to be expected that information should appear on the axis of society just as the document appears on the axis of time (see Figure 3.2). Information, by its non-material quality, establishes a relationship between the object as a document and the society in which it is actualised. It makes its way into society and is the result of specific social relations.

Scientific and cultural information

The museum object and the collection are the sources of two kinds of information, scientific and cultural. In simple terms, the main scientific disciplines in museums (such as art history, archaeology, anthropology, ethnology or natural and technical sciences) deal with the consolidation of scientific (selective) information, while museology deals with the consolidation of cultural (structural) information. If information is the reaction of a user to the content of a message, then scientific information is more precise, and it tends towards greater objectivity and stricter verification. It is analytical because it proceeds from the user towards reality and discovers natural laws of regulation within the object. These laws are dealt with and regulated by the basic scientific disciplines. Together with ethical neutrality, the criterion of truth is of foremost significance for scientific information. Cultural or structural information has no strictly defined subject-matter. It is contained within the object and its meaning is determined by the context, by the physical or social environment. Cultural information is synthetic because it proceeds from reality towards the user. It discovers secondary meanings in the object such as value, importance, meaning or necessity. Cultural messages are those which produce cultural information structured on particular evaluation systems (ethical, aesthetic or political). It is difficult to format cultural information although it can be recorded and stored in an IN-DOC system (Tuđman 1983). Using this distinction between cultural information and cultural messages, we see that museology deals with cultural information, because it examines the reaction of the individual or society to museum messages or investigates the meaning of museum objects within a certain social or cultural context. It does not bring into question the truth of any scientific information. By interpreting this information, museology opens up new worlds of meaning in which even ideological manipulation is not excluded.

Scientific information is in a way selective as it can be formatted in accordance with precisely defined categories of data. It is possible to define the field of interest of such information and then to check it by applying formalized rules. The quantities of such information increase exponentially. Selective information does not allow subjective choice, but rather diminishes the amount of relevant information necessary for a particular purpose. Cultural information is of a structural type in that it enables the user to structure the fields of the subject-matter of the documents on the basis of experience if and when required. Whatever criteria the user requires are allowed for but it is difficult to format this information in such a way that it can be easily retrieved. Attempts are made to establish a relationship between structural and selective information in museum documentation systems, although by its nature this information resists consistent classifications between structural and selective systems.

The museum is a museological institution in which museum messages are created.

> One of the main museological determinants of the museum is that it represents a medium for transmitting certain messages and ideas. The medium could be defined as a manifold set of simultaneously used channels in which a system of signs is realized. The museum is, therefore, filled with signs or systems of signs, which are at the disposal of those who know how to interpret them.
>
> (Delibašić 1991: 28)

At the same time, Delibašić states that research in the museum could be carried out along two different lines. The first deals with the exhibition as the real form of the museum message, the second with the study of the structure of the museum message (Delibašić 1991: 28). A long time ago J. Glusberg said that 'the museum was a sign which contained in itself other signs' (Glusberg 1983: 27) and so he linked museology with semiology, considering the museum as being practically identical to the message.

Museum message

The museum message is a means by which the museum communicates the information contained in its collective resources and stimulates the production of new information within the museological context. The authentic museum message is expressed by the form of the object and it occurs within the given context, i.e. on the space axis. The first two axes, time and society, have already been explained: the time axis reflects the material quality of the object as a document, while the meaning of the object and the information derived from it are reflected on the axis of society (see Figure 3.2). Time and society are joined in space. The time, space and society axes determine museology as a symbolic activity defined by the sequential relation between the symbolic system of museality and the system of symbolic objects, i.e. museum objects (Tuđman 1990: 142). Only by the production of the museum message is the symbolic activity of museology manifested in the world around us. In other words, the full interrelationship between museum objects and the museality which they carry within them is expressed in space, especially at an exhibition. Thus museality enables the objects to express and convey various messages. At the same time, the new meanings of museality are stated through the relationship between the object and the space, with the active assistance of the audience. Museality exists and is always rediscovered in the numerous communication processes between the visitor and the cultural heritage.

The exhibition is a typical museum medium for expressing the museum message, though exhibitions may be set up outside museums and are not the only form used for expressing the museum message. It should be noted that there is a distinction between the museum and the museological message. The museum message is formulated and expressed within the museum as the most common form of a museological institution, therefore it is connected to the museum as a system. The museological message implies the formulation of messages of heritage as a cultural phenomenon. The interpreted or spontaneous message of an archaeological site, a ruin, a historic building or a historic town, produced by using museographical aids and appliances, has the meaning of a museological message as well as of the message created in the museum. The museological message is an organized one resulting from the interpretation or the statement of the values of the material objects' world of heritage.

Exhibition

An exhibition is an event where society and time meet and link in a defined space. Chronological time is transformed into communication time in the exhibition which thus becomes a closed system. Various heritage objects represent different chronological or historical times available at close quarters in the ambience of an exhibition reality. Thus completely new relations are established. Historical time has been changed into communication time due to the heritage objects which are documents of a past time and past events. At the same time they enable communication with the past in the present. Independent of the amount of knowledge and information existing on one side, and the objects as documents being inbuilt in the exhibition as a system on the other, they behave like an integrated entity. The museum message of the exhibition is realized only in the communication time and 'availability' of the exhibition to the audience. It is expressed by means of museum objects as documents and by organized representation of the scientific and partly cultural information. This information results from the earlier accumulated knowledge of the author of the exhibition and of the broader environment so that the exhibition is placed within a communication pattern. The exhibition thus becomes a creative act in which its space or ambience, the objects and knowledge of them are joined in a unique system, the final intention of which is to communicate defined messages and to discover new forms of museality of objects or groups of objects. Another aim is to enrich human knowledge and cultural awareness. Some authors make the act of creating an exhibition look like an artistic act. They consider the exhibition to be a specific work of art (Šola 1992).

From a semiological standpoint the exhibition fits with the chain of the communication process. In his linguistic analysis D. Škiljan suggests that the chain has six elements. On one side of the chain there is an emitter, on the other side a receiver. They are human beings who, individually or as a group, participate in the process. The emitter chooses the message from the common system and realizes it through a channel. The channel represents matter by which communication is transferred and it is necessary for both the emitter and the receiver to be acquainted with the organization of the channel. At an exhibition the museum objects and the museographical aids are the channel. The realized message always relates to a certain context which is copied into signs within a semiotic system (Delibašić 1991: 16; Škiljan 1985: 21). In the museological context this refers to the relation between museum objects and reality, or to the communication pattern in a wider sense which is defined by the ambience of the social environment in which the exhibition takes place. People as social beings have been closely connected with their physical environment. They are influenced by the experience of the social environment in which the exhibition takes place, as well as by the tradition, the culture and all other relevant social relations. The creation of the policy for museum exhibition politics becomes an extremely important factor in this context. Here the museum retains a certain independence from the social environment, as is obvious in the selection of exhibition themes or the definition of the dimension or content of particular exhibitions connected with the two basic motives of any exhibition, the social and the educational element of communication (Maroević 1991: 77, 78).

The individual creates the exhibition, emits the museum message and interprets the selected museum material. He/she articulates the exhibition space and contextualizes the museum reality. From the collective resources and from the world around us he/she selects objects as the carriers of museality according to the criteria of scientific truth and social importance, at the same time discovering common elements of knowledge concerning the objects selected for the theme of the exhibition. The exhibition is also designed by establishing relations among museum objects, and making them more readable with museographical aids and appliances. So the museum message is formulated through the conscious creative intention of the exhibition author. Nevertheless, the message reaches the visitor partly transformed by the numerous possible communication processes taking place between the museum objects and people. Beginning with the entire basic content and on to the specific features of particular details, the message depends on the levels of the social context of the environment in which the exhibition is installed.

E-T-Ac-S-A complex

If we try to elaborate this question, then we shall see that we can apply Težak's E-T-Ac-S-A complex model to it (Tuđman 1983: 196) (see Figure 3.3). Each exhibition contains a tension between emission and absorption. Creators of the exhibition who prepared the emission formulate the message and the goals of the exhibition, transmitting their own experience to their target audience. The exhibition as communication is by this fact limited to the public it is intended

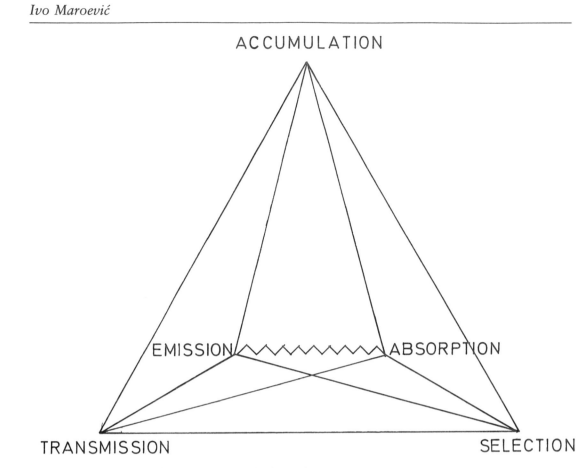

Figure 3.3 Double pyramid model of Težak's E-T-Ac-S-A complex

for. The larger the conception of the exhibition the wider the public intended, the more noise there is in the communication channel. The noise can be removed by such a conception of the communication appliance as will enable more versatile links on various levels. The public, who are in the absorption role, receive only what has been emitted; part of the audience receives perhaps insufficiently articulated messages that may emerge at the exhibition, messages which have been created by the context of the exhibition or by the capacity to understand, which depends on each individual visitor. In other words, in the exhibition everybody can find some special interest or special message, regardless of the intentions of the creator of the exhibition. The museum message therefore can be both an intentional target and a spontaneous one, the result of the receiver's individual inclinations.

What is meant by transmission, accumulation and selection, the basis of Težak's double pyramid model, the tops being emission and absorption? Accumulation is understood as the collecting of the relevant material for the exhibition. It has to support emission, because selection can be made only from the accumulated museum material, sorted and ordered in view of a possible message to be emitted.

The selection is a creative choice in which the goal of the exhibition becomes the dominant selection factor. Selecting objects for the exhibition we shall again confront scientific and cultural information systems and criteria. In the museum exhibition these two criteria are equal. The basic scientific background of the material (from the standpoint of the basic scientific discipline) is a *conditio sine qua non*, while the cultural component in a subjective interpretation, which depends on a set of elements of cultural evaluation of the museum activity in the environment concerned, is the factor which corrects the scientific requirement for an unambiguous interpretation. The selection procedure aims primarily to explain itself, and forms of communication will depend on how it does so. Finally, the transmission will respond to how the selection was made and it will do so by a series of museographical aids and means facilitating transmission of a complex message by the selected objects. The object, being a document, should play its role in the message, that of cumulative and individual information carrier. The object is a carrier and transmitter both of a common message and also of individual messages which will be disclosed only to those qualified or trained to receive them. The transmission will not deal with how the individual messages are formulated and transmitted. It will be an effort to encourage a statement (expression) of knowledge being originated at the exhibition. The statement should be clear but not predictable in all its elements. At the same time the transmission should be organized so as to explain the representation of knowledge by means of figurative, textual or multimedia instruments. The transmission should also be complementary to the museum objects and assist in their explanation of the target message.

Communication pattern

The exhibition is an event which is limited in time. It is also a space where the message is created and transmitted by the objects-documents and the information which they carry. The information has been actualized partly at the exhibition and partly during its preparation. It is then represented at the same exhibition as part of human knowledge. Can the exhibition become a set communication format? A communication format in a narrower sense is that for exchanging data. It is used to standardize the extent, number and quality of data in documentation centres and databases so as to ensure exchange of selective information. The exhibition is a more complex organism where the communication formats of particular elements can be noticed. For instance we can speak about the format of a caption or description of an object, about the format of catalogue data, or in a wider sense about the communication format of a synopsis or a scenario of the exhibition even if it does not serve a direct exchange of information. In its final form the exhibition surpasses the framework of a communication format and is transformed into a communication pattern. This follows from the fact that

> the relationship between the creators, the information and the users (i.e. the creators, the cultural heritage and the audience) is defined by the communication pattern. . . . [It] is the measure and the model of understanding between the creators (emitters) and the users. It is a model which

will be established by means of information as projection; it makes the common basis which provides the meaning and facilitates the function of information in society.

(Tuđman 1983: 173)

This means that the museum exhibition as a communication pattern of the museum message has united several factors whose parameters are changeable in relation to time and society. At different times and in different social relations the same museum material can therefore emit different museum messages and create different communication patterns of understanding by individual subjective creative acts. We must not forget the influence of different social spaces within which the different information 'topias' (from the Greek *topos*) have been developed. The museum exhibition as a communication pattern is brought about by the formal 'topia' of the information space represented by the museum as an institution. Consequently, the museum environment and the context influence the understanding of the message. The communication effect is not the same if the exhibition is organized in a museum or the town square, the street or at a café. An informal information 'topia' in the town creates a level of socio-cultural integration other than the museum with its own status and cultural meaning. Each subculture, culture or social community has its own ways of thinking which determine the rules within the communication pattern. Many different things are to be perceived in that context: the museo-logical communications of particular objects, zones or the ambience of cultural heritage in space. Integrated in the various information 'topias' they contribute to the humanization of life and to the permeation of consciousness by messages about the historical space around us emitted by the heritage. Though they are not museum exhibitions, they are nevertheless forms of museological interpretation of the heritage, which directly influence the (re)presentation of historical reality.

All the specific features of communication within a particular communication pattern determine the variety of extents to which the field defining museum objects of the heritage (i.e. museal definiteness) can spread. The layers of meaning of museum objects are extended, their museality is enriched and their information content expanded as well. Information about things and their mutual relationship is thus accumulated outside temporal relations. The information is a result of communication processes and messages received from various communication patterns.

The museum message is a concrete and actualized form of the content of a museum exhibition of any kind. The exhibition is an action which functions as a communication pattern with several messages composed as a logical unit. The character of the exhibition determines the specific structure of the messages and their forms. The museum message does not appear autonomously outside the document or the information because it is both information as a social fact (being actualized in society) and document as a material fact (Tuđman 1983: 108). This means that the museum message is based on those material objects selected as documents of a certain phenomenon. The product of the message is the informa-tion received and stored by those who visit the exhibition in order to participate in the communication. The objects functioning as documents belong to the inventory of the material culture. The information resulting from a communicated and actualized message belongs to the sphere of knowledge or non-material culture. This culture materializes in documentation (records, books, audiovisual means, etc.). The transformation of a document into knowledge, in order to be documented again, is performed by means of the communication patterns which reflect the phenomena of the social reality in which the communication takes place. Each society and every environment in which exhibitions take place, and where the museum message is formulated, is different and results in different information. Only the material side of the message is stable, i.e. the object functioning as a document. The message is generated in the object and it is actualized in the social environment which represents the communication pattern in a wider sense. This is to say it represents the framework and the distinctive features of the social environment in which the communication takes place. The communication pattern in a narrower sense is the exhibition itself as a form of the message. The instability of the social nature of the message and the information resulting from the communication process can be neutralized by recording the expressed message and by the creation of new documentation different from the object-document, but with recorded knowledge about it. Such steps extend the field of its scientific and museal definiteness.

Artistic exhibition

Artistic exhibitions are special phenomena, where meaning merges with the irrational, unreal and emotional. Eco said that objects with an aesthetic function play a complete and unreduced role. Museum messages with aesthetic functions have an ambiguous structure in relation to the system of expectations represented by the code. This ambiguity becomes productive at the very moment when it stimulates us to make interpretative efforts (Delibašić 1991: 5; Eco 1973: 72). Later it allows us to discover the direction of decoding. 'In the apparent disorder, which is contrary to the normal state of affairs, we can find a more essential order than the one that precedes the redundant messages' (Eco 1973: 2). This is why the message of artistic exhibitions is particularly individualized. It is different from those museum messages in which works of art do not have a part and it becomes a complex of parallel communications in which the speech of the museum exhibition is intertwined with the formal visual speech of particular works of art, groups or wholes. The receiver of such a message must be capable of receiving formal visual messages. Works of art can have a part in making other museological messages concrete but then their infinity is limited by the context of the exhibition in which they participate (for instance a work of art in a historical exhibition or as part of an exhibition of the natural sciences collection).

Conclusion

The exhibition is a complex museological information system and a specific communication pattern. The museum message, constituted in every individual visitor according to his/her interest, knowledge and imagination, is transferred at exhibitions to the users by means of museum objects/documents. Therefore all aids and appliances must be geared to the single objective of making the basic content of the exhibition readable (Maroević 1988: 91). The museum exhibition is an event which transforms reality, as well as being the place where the new reality is constituted and where new knowledge about the past is born in the clash of past and present time. Knowledge about the past is integrated in the present not only through the media, but through the actual witnesses and the participants of the past as well. The museum message which is created and communicated to the visitors represents a world of ideas which is hidden in the museum, captured within the physical structure of the objects functioning as documents. Such a world of ideas is expressed and represented by the information which is created and formulated as a message to be received by the visitors. The visitors then create their own world of meaning while the museums transfer the new information to the world of knowledge. The museum message thus brings the past world nearer to the present and refines the present world by suggesting new possibilities in the understanding of the future. At the same time it is deeply anchored between the document and the information, and inseparably connected with them. In this manner the museum message justifies the existence of museums.

References

Delibašić, E. (1991) 'Znak i muzej' ('Sign and museum') (diploma thesis, Faculty of Philosophy, University of Zagreb).

Eco, U. (1973) *Kultura, informacija, komunikacija* ('Culture, information, communication'), Belgrade: Nolit.

Glusberg, J. (1983) 'Hladni i vrući muzeji' ('Cool and hot museums'), *Muzeologija* 23.

Maroević, I. (1988) 'Komunikacijska uloga muzejske izložbe' ('The communication role of museum exhibitions'), *Informatica Museologica* 1–2(82–4): 90–1.

—— (1991) 'The exhibition as presentative communication', *ISS (ICOFOM Study Series)* 19: 73–9.

van Mensch, P. (1989) 'Museology as a scientific basis for the museum profession', in *Professionalising the Muses*, Amsterdam: AHA Books.

Stransky, Z. Z. (1970) 'Pojam muzeologije' ('The concept of museology'), *Muzeologija* 8: 40–73.

Škiljan, D. (1985) *U pozadini znaka* ('In the background of the sign'), Zagreb: Školska knjiga.

Šola, T. (1992) 'Za suvremeni muzei' ('For the contemporary museum') (manuscript, Institute for Information Studies, University of Zagreb).

Težak, B. (1969) 'Informaciono-dokumentaciono-komunicacioni (IN-DOK) sistem' ('Information-documentation-communication (IN-DOC) system'), *Informatologia Yuogoslavica* 1(1–4): 1–11.

Tuđman, M . (1983) *Struktura kulturne informacije* ('Structure of cultural information'), Zagreb: Zavod za kulturu Hrvatske.

—— (1990) *Obavijest i znanje* ('Information and knowledge'), Zagreb: Zavod za informacijske studije.

4

Exhibitions as communicative media

Flora E. S. Kaplan

Introduction

Museum exhibitions are products of research, organized and designed to convey ideas. They communicate through the senses, the primary sense being visual, by a process that is both cognitive and cultural. This process encompasses the way people think about what they see and the meanings they attach to it. Thus, within given historical and cultural contexts, exhibitions are kinds of public, secular rituals in the Durkheimian sense of social representation of collective 'self'. This view leads us to enquire about the nature of the collectivity being presented: who is presenting what? for whom? and why? The collectivity created and fostered by this process is also what is sometimes called 'a moral community', and finds national expression in museums (Anderson 1983; Kaplan 1981, 1994a, 1994b).

In recent years, in museums, the collective self being presented has come under increasing scrutiny with respect to both non-western 'others', whose objects are so often exhibited in western museums, and those 'ethnic others' within modern nations who claim recognition of a separate cultural heritage (sometimes as descendants of 'others' and sometimes not). In the past museums asserted a more singular vision. They organized and presented the results of scientific, technical and historical researches; and they interpreted an aesthetic and intellectual history rooted in the world view and interests of local political, economic and social elites. With the growth and downward spread of knowledge among increasingly diverse populations, especially in the nineteenth century, as part of a process I have called 'democratization' in emerging nation-states, new collective selves were created and recreated (Kaplan 1982, 1994a, 1994b).

The approach posited here grows out of long experience in the anthropology of art and material culture, and suggests a basis for looking at them in particular cultural, historical and political contexts in society. It is based on some seven years of curatorial experience with collections and exhibitions at the Department of Africa, Oceania and New World Art, at the Brooklyn Museum; on intensive anthropological fieldwork in art, in Africa (Nigeria) and the New World (Mexico); in conjunction with more than twenty years of university-based research and teaching in anthropology, art and museology. The approach, therefore, arises from an insider's view in the roles of anthropologist, professor, ethnographer, curator and museologist in New York and in Nigeria.[1]

I propose to look at museums as social institutions, as arenas in which political messages in the broadest sense are displayed, conveyed and converted into meaning by museum professionals and the audiences who view and review them. This approach, holistic and anthropological, was instituted in the 1970s at New York University, and underlay the graduate museological training programme begun at that time.[2] It is finding proponents among various disciplines now focusing on museums, in the United States and abroad, and it is reflected in a growing literature in the 1990s. A sample only is offered here (since this is not a review article) of some thought-provoking publications and comments that derive from comparable approaches: on museums and exhibitions (Cannizzo 1989, 1991; Karp and Lavine 1991; Mack 1990; Ottenberg 1991; Schildkrout 1991, 1992); on museums and audiences (Belcher 1992; Falk and Dierking 1992; Hooper-Greenhill 1992; Karp, Kreamer and Lavine 1992; Weil 1990); on museum collections, their formation and constituent objects (Berlo and Phillips 1992; Mack 1990; Pearce 1990; Price 1989; Schildkrout and Keim 1990).

Exhibitions are kinds of collective rituals, enacted to assert and perpetuate power; and they are based on objects and knowledge which, in these instances, are also secret and 'sacred', available only to those who 'know', and who have been initiated into the western notion of art and the world of academia. In post-colonial Africa, the diaspora and elsewhere, the objects, knowledge and rites of exhibitions are often inaccessible to those who were formerly dispossessed by governance, distance, and language. There is still a lack of mobility, resources, and ready access to western academia, its institutions and the related media outlets necessary for valid entry into the international museum arena, where, for example, Africans can present themselves to others.[3]

Curators may be seen as ritual specialists, people who are initiates and keepers of ritual knowledge (objects, labels, texts, display techniques, etc.). They are also mediators between two worlds. Cast as kinds of priests and priestesses, they sometimes perform privately – together with other initiated members and would-be initiates – in professional meetings, conferences and publications to refine and reinforce their knowledge of various subjects, objects and each other. On other occasions, they perform publicly for varied audiences and spectators – in exhibitions, lectures and catalogues – to reveal meaning, impart knowledge and convey values to be absorbed by the uninitiated. The messages of museum exhibitions are intended to connect those producing them and those receiving them. They make use of special spaces, museums, presumably neutral, where selected imagery, rhetoric and ideology may be joined emotionally and cognitively. In museums, however, those who own the spaces and those who serve them, elites and priests respectively, offer both sacred and profane knowledge in what are political arenas in the broadest sense. Museums are among the sites of competition for scarce resources in society, competition couched in metaphors of knowledge and display intended to resolve conflict. They are peopled with priests, performers, spectators and audiences, and underset with those elite groups holding power. Each is affected by the rituals enacted in museums, the representations made, the knowledge conveyed and not conveyed, and the perception of and response to them. Finally, some of the spectators may seek more active roles in like and unlike rituals, to represent themselves. In so doing they will assume new roles and challenge resident power groups, seeking change in an existing political hierarchy. When left unchallenged, such hierarchies persist.

Elites as well as competing mobile groups, vying for power, have always used objects, collections and public displays as a means of differentiating themselves, and legitimating themselves in a social hierarchy. Museums offer the opportunity to do just that – and exhibitions constitute a major method. The results, as noted above, are reflexive, eventually changing audiences by what they see and learn, audiences who reflect those changes back on to the institutions. This notion of reflexivity is integral to the Durkheimian view adopted here and applied to the western subculture of museums. It makes the approach offered dynamic, and provides a framework for interpreting museums and for analysing the communicative power of exhibitions.

Exhibitions originate with a curator or curatorial team responsible for the concept and content. They require architects, designers, museum craftsmen and various staff people to give ideas tangible form in three-dimensional space. The success of an exhibition is ultimately decided by the public, their attendance and word-of-mouth news of it. Exhibition reviews, another measure, have less import for the general public, but are of intense interest to some groups. These groups with special interests in museums and exhibitions, quite apart from the general public, may be divided into two broadly defined types: one, the *peer group*, is comprised of those elites who fund and control current cultural reproduction, including those affiliated through the established committees, organizations and units of the museum world, and those associated museum professionals and academics who fuel its intellectual engines. The second type is the *mobile group*, comprised of would-be elites seeking economic and political power and competing for prestige and the right to redefine themselves through control of cultural coin of the realm. To these ends mobile groups use knowledge of content and criticism of exhibitions as a means of ranking themselves in a commonly perceived social hierarchy graded towards elite status. Whereas the peer group ranks itself within parallel professional and social spheres at the top, the mobile group concerns itself primarily with social rank and its economic and political consequences. The Durkheimian view presented here will examine special exhibitions which, by definition, are of limited duration and most concerned with conveying their messages. There are also references to permanent exhibitions on view and temporary shows.

Exhibitions generally utilize the same basic elements to tell their stories: they employ objects either made and used by human beings or drawn from the natural world; they require texts, most often in the form of labels, wall panels, headlines and banners; and they incorporate other graphic elements, such as photographs, maps, charts and drawings. In addition, they use lighting, museum 'furniture' – cases, platforms, walls – and architectural elements that must protect the objects shown, enhance viewing and enclose exhibition space. Qualities of colour and texture attach to all these elements. Sound, seating and the media of film, video, slide projection, computers and simulation may also be added. Live elements often range from plantings to performance – dancers, actors and scholars, as well as lecturers and docents. In the galleries, museum guards function as unofficial guides. Budget permitting, print materials are prepared for the public in the form of free handouts, information sheets and brochures; guidebooks, and exhibition catalogues may be offered for sale.

Five African art exhibitions are considered here as communicative media. Four of them are drawn from the same culture, the Edo-speaking peoples of Benin, Nigeria. They utilize a traditional corpus of objects, most of which were looted at the time of the British conquest in 1897. This enhances comparison among them as communicative media. A fifth exhibition, 'Africa explores: 20th century African Art' (1991), is concerned with a wide spectrum of contemporary art, from 'extinct' to international. Each of the five shows has its own conceptual framework, selected objects, periods of time covered, locations, installations and audiences. All five shows have been well attended, with varied reviews and comments. I have curated two of them, and have seen the other three (the contemporary show, at more than one location). They are discussed, therefore, from two viewpoints: one is written as a participant-observer, the insider-organizer, and the second, primarily as an observer. However, I am more than an observer/spectator, being an anthropologist and a former museum curator. The first two Benin exhibitions to be discussed are presented from the insider's point of view and include as much data as are practicable in the space limits of this chapter.

The first show, 'Images of power: art of the royal court of Benin, Nigeria' (1981), opened at New York University; the second, 'Art of the royal court of Benin' (1985), was organized in Nigeria, on behalf of the University of Benin, in co-operation with the National Museum, Benin. Two other shows are discussed here, from the outsider's point of view: both comprised single, private collections of Benin art, each acquired by a major museum and placed on semi-permanent view. The first was acquired from the Joseph H. Hirshhorn collection (formerly in the Hirshhorn Museum and Sculpture Garden, Washington, DC). The collection is the basis of an installation and publication, *Royal Benin Art* (1987), at the National Museum of African Art, Washington, DC. The second collection was acquired from Mr and Mrs Klaus G. Perls; 'Royal art of Benin from the Perls Collection' (1992) was installed at the Metropolitan Museum of Art, New York. Finally, a more singular attempt to deal with contemporary African art was made in a special exhibition, 'Africa explores: 20th century African art' (1991), organized by the Center for African Art, New York. It represents renewed interest in contemporary art in Africa (Beier 1961; Brown 1966).

As detailed at the outset, the exhibition elements of all shows involve making difficult choices and enlisting the co-operation and participation of many people. It is crucial to recognize that an effective exhibition is more than simply an idea, the objects and the installation. And as the following discussion will show, it is more than a collection of great art or anything else for that matter. An exhibition that communicates must educate and excite the mind and the senses; when communication is optimal it creates an 'affect' among spectators and audiences. Affect happens when various exhibition elements combine in subtle and perhaps ultimately unpredictable ways for individual viewers, who are able then to cross an invisible 'threshold' of cumulative, personal and cultural experience. Thus, the viewer is an active participant in the communication process, not a passive observer. He or she brings unique experience, knowledge and perception into play, making affect and learning possible in particular historical and cultural contexts.

It should not be forgotten that the location of exhibitions in 'museums' – in those special historic, scientific, social and cultural institutions that arose in the western world – is also part of the process. Viewers are more likely to accept messages in the context of museums. This is even more important to consider in presenting non-western cultures, and the objects and art obtained from them, usually under colonial rule. The discussion of each of the five above-mentioned African art exhibitions will be prefaced with a brief overview of the historical contexts in which western museums gradually emerged as social institutions. It will illuminate the dynamics of collective social representation, outlined here.

Museums and beginnings

The roots of museums are conventionally traced back to the ancient western world, where art was first shown as the booty of conquest in the splendour of private villas. Seen also as objects of knowledge in the classical world, art and scientific specimens were used in a *mouseion*, or community of scholars, in the city of Alexandria. There, the muses of arts and science were studied (Kaplan 1983: 172–8). In the ensuing centuries – in palaces, churches, religious orders and noble residences – gold, jewels and objects of value continued to be amassed – to celebrate the power of gods and kings and to finance wars for the glory of spiritual and earthly kingdoms.

Fifteenth-century European exploration, conquest and trade filled Renaissance 'cabinets of curiosities', stimulating ideas and capturing the imagination of patrons, amateurs and scholars alike. Nineteenth-century rapid growth in scientific knowledge, and industrial and commercial expansion, heralded even more rapidly changing political boundaries. New nation-states that emerged in Europe itself, and later out of former colonial possessions around the world, made conscious efforts to weld together formerly separate ethnic groups within their arbitrarily divided, now centrally controlled, geographic boundaries. These nations, now led by new elites, with new ideologies, represented themselves with new and sometimes old reappropriated imagery (Kaplan 1994b). Foreign and former ruling elites, displaced by such groups, yielded their private collections and public institutions to national museums, especially in the early nineteenth to mid-twentieth centuries, to provide an overarching sense of 'self' in the process, and new bases for regional and national identity and for unity (Kaplan 1994a).

As the twentieth century now draws to a close, many of these nations and their ruling elites, in control of cultural patrimony and collective identity writ large, are coming under increasing scrutiny. Sudden shifts of political power in eastern and western Europe, the re-emergence of ethnic militancy, and the instant satellite and media coverage of events heighten tensions as well as expectations around the world.

Museums and their exhibitions are often harbingers of change. In the organization, interpretation and presentation of displays, competing power groups are often revealed, struggling to gain some measure of control in a public arena in which rituals of representation and self are enacted. In particular, this chapter looks at five African art exhibitions that shed light on the nature of exhibitions as communicative media. These exhibitions have special relevance for African-Americans – now 15 per cent of the US population and its largest minority population. Their emergence as mobile groups, seeking to control their own identities and destinies, can be usefully studied and some insights can be gained through this study and the framework it proposes as a model.

Exhibitions as communicative media: some African examples

The decision to do a Benin art exhibition at New York University in 1981 was based on the perceived needs, first, to increase the number of African art shows then offered in New York City, and second, to draw attention to the court art of sub-Saharan Africa, a hitherto neglected subject. The exhibition was intended to fill a void without duplicating the efforts of major museums. Its thesis was that the famed art of this ancient civilization emanated from the principle of divine kingship that informed the court and Benin society. Embodied in the person of the Oba, images of power were created to proclaim and record the achievements and continuity over some 800 years of this pre-European forest empire in West Africa.

Prior to 1981, there had not been a museum exhibition in New York devoted solely to Benin court art. 'Images of power: art of the royal court of Benin, Nigeria' (1981) filled that gap, and also gave emphasis to the living traditions. Before the New York University show, the last major Benin show in the United States had been mounted some twenty-five years earlier, at the Field Museum of Natural History, Chicago, when the Fuller Collection was acquired and exhibited (Dark 1962). The Metropolitan Museum of Art installation of the Perls collection (1992) resembles the Chicago show, as does the Benin installation (1987) at the National Museum of African Art, Smithsonian Institution, Washington, DC. Each museum exhibits the collection of an individual (the art dealer Klaus Perls and his wife, in the case of the Metropolitan Museum, and the collector Joseph H. Hirshhorn in the case of the National Museum of

African Art). After 'Images of power', in 1981, a small temporary student show, 'The art of power. The power of art', was set up at UCLA (1983); some Benin shows were mounted later, in Europe: 'Benin Kunst einer Königskultur' (1990) was shown in Vienna, Zurich and Paris; and 'Art royal du Benin' (1992) in Geneva. The Brooklyn Museum and the Center for African Art have endeavoured to include Benin art in many diverse shows in recent years. Thus, since 1981 the public has been exposed to a broad range of art and material culture that had not been widely seen before.

The NYU show was concerned with two main ideas that it wished to convey to the public about Africa: one was to demonstrate the remarkable durability of indigenous political systems. In Benin, for example, divine kingship has lasted over a period of 800 years, contrary to the west's popular view of African political systems as fragile. The second idea to be conveyed was that art in Benin had to be understood in its own terms: as technically skilled, stylistically assured, and steeped in cultural values as historical 'documents', aside from its renowned 'lost wax' casting and aesthetic qualities, recognized in the west. Rooted in antiquity, the art gives visual testimony to the longevity of Benin kingship, the glory of the Oba, the king, his court and retinue. It attests to the cultural depth and continuity of the belief systems that have been at the heart of the kingdom.

Exhibition texts and the catalogue (Kaplan 1981) placed this African kingdom and African royalty in world perspective, beyond European royalty, to address an audience of inclusion. Field photographs of living traditions, rituals and regalia were chosen deliberately and blown up to emphasize the people who inherited, created and used the art. These were carefully juxtaposed behind antique works of art from the sixteenth to nineteenth centuries, to show how objects were used, where and by whom. In installing the cases each piece was placed with attention to shape, size and detail to increase its 'readability', labels stressed function, and lighting was at moderate levels, spotting the cases and pieces in them. The natural linen covering case floors and bases helped to focus attention on the pieces in contextual settings.

Record numbers were attracted to the university's Grey Art Gallery, including unprecedented attendance by African-Americans from a wide spectrum of leadership among political, civic, economic and social groups, from middle- and working-class neighbourhoods, and from schools in and around the New York metropolitan area. Foreign visitors and others from various parts of the country included scholars and students, dealers, collectors, diplomats and museum people. There was no budget for advertising, and educational programming was accomplished with programme student volunteers in response to enquiries and requests from the public, special groups like the Urban League, and schools in the metropolitan area. Press and media coverage, recognition of the interpretative contribution of the exhibition by the National Endowment for the Humanities, and visitorship were a function of the effectiveness of word-of-mouth communication among the African-American communities and audiences drawn from a broad public. The show guest book as well as letters, on-site observation, and reports from participants made this clear. African-Americans were visible, vocal and positive about the show's dual messages. The exhibition, in emphasizing the presence of living Benins in context, engaged in the governance of their own venerable society, and drawing on their own words and view of the present-day world, was challenging stereotypical notions and popular media images of 'primitive' art and impoverished Africans that implied they were either too simple or too disorganized to be able to govern themselves. African-American commitment to the exhibition was also manifested in planning and financial support.

Benin was chosen as the subject of the programme's first exhibition because it is one of the great African art traditions, acknowledged for its technical excellence, naturalism and sophisticated style. It was organized to make the people prominent as well as the art – and in so doing, it crossed the then conventional, disciplinary boundaries between art history and anthropology that separated 'art' from 'ethnography' in presenting non-western cultures. Works were chosen for their technical skill, style definition, clarity and force of iconography, and range of available forms and functions relative to the exhibition themes and sections (Jarocki 1981). Rather than simply letting the art speak for itself, the labels succinctly informed readers about how the pieces were used in Benin, by whom and when (when known); and the pieces were installed to let the visitor study them closely, at approximately eye level, and in the round. Visual, visceral and intellectual affect was sought (Klein 1986).

'Images of power: art of the royal court of Benin, Nigeria' (1981) was cognizant of the rare opportunity to show privately held art in America, and to offer the works, concomitantly, as important political, historical and cultural 'texts' in a system of governance. Some reticent collectors who owned some of the most important Benin art in America fortunately felt the deep sense of responsibility entailed in such ownership, and willingly loaned the objects requested. The generosity of a number of dealers, several museums and other collectors, more than three dozen sources in all, are listed in the exhibition catalogue (Kaplan 1981).

Sixty-eight pieces were chosen, some never exhibited in the United States, and most shown together for the first time at NYU's Grey Art Gallery and Study Center, the site of the show, in January–February 1981. Through the co-operation of the insurers, Huntington Bloch, Washington, DC, a unique, high-value art show was installed. The art spanned the time from the first European contacts at the end of the fifteenth century to the present. The choices were guided by the precept that the best-executed works of art communicate best, in the service of a well-defined concept. They provided a goodly sample of the famed repertoire of Benin artisans and members of the palace guilds: 'lost wax' cast bronzes (leaded brasses were also glossed as 'bronze'); carved ivories and works in wood; modelled terracottas; wrought iron; cut and sewn hide; and woven cloth. These works were placed in cases, expensive hand-me-downs from a Peruvian gold show, grouped in thematic sections, and installed to allow full viewing in the round, directly; the cases were set out to enhance this kind of viewing in an orderly and accessible sequence.[4]

The exhibition script was divided into ten sections. The first, the 'Introduction', located Nigeria and Benin City on a map of Africa, set forth the show's concept and explicated its goals. The second section was preceded by a seventeenth-century Dutch engraving by Olfert Dapper, ubiquitous in virtually all Benin shows and publications. It shows the Oba (the king) and his entourage, heralded by chained leopards, in a procession outside the walled city, on a rare ceremonial occasion when he left his palace (Kaplan 1981: 78). This powerful visual image of the king, the court, the city and the palace is based on early visitor descriptions. In the second section, 'Ancestral heads', the visitor is offered a glimpse inside the palace. A blown-up field photograph of a royal ancestral altar goes straight to the heart of the culture and its central cult – ancestor worship. The display of ancestral heads of departed Obas, chiefs and bronze-casters which opened the show offered images of power emanating from the court, and illustrated the ranked hierarchy of birth, privilege and male ethos that underlies Benin society. The third section, 'Divine kingship, the Oba', addressed his roles, described palace organization, and presented Benin belief systems, embodied in their world view and religion, and centred on the person of the king. This section relied on text panels, labels, photographs of Oba Akenzua II, and works of art made exclusively for Obas.

The third section on divine kingship was followed by a fourth, 'Other altars', in which shrine furnishings used for chiefs, queen mothers and royal bronze-casters were displayed, showing the types of objects permitted non-royals, according to rank, generally in lesser media, and the replication of the ancestor cult throughout the society. 'Ivory treasures of the Oba', section five, highlighted the privileges and symbolism associated with the king's person and divine nature. Section six, 'Plaques of the Oba's court', attested to office holders, palace societies, conquests and other historic events. Like much other art, the plaques made possible comparison of past regalia with present, by using blown-up ethnographic field photographs taken at court rituals. Antiquities were shown in contrast with similar, contemporary objects in use, and the aforementioned photographs; oral tradition was included in labelling, in connection with the more tangible 'texts' – the works themselves. Section seven, 'Portuguese at the Oba's court', provided a record of early European contacts, trade and conquests, from the end of the fifteenth century, immortalized in court art. Afterwards, labels and wall texts note the Dutch, the French and miscellaneous others who traded with Benin, until the English conquered the Benin kingdom, at the end of the nineteenth century.

Section eight, 'Ornaments of person and dress', displayed objects of rank and status as defined in Benin. Because I wanted to give Benin women a visible presence in the show, and there were no photographs of queens at that time available in this country, I employed a graduate assistant, Valerie Griffith, to locate suitable photographs on her return home to England.[5] Some were found, taken by a British district officer in the 1950s, and I chose one of the Oba's wives for inclusion in the 'Ornaments' section. The queen was wearing rather elaborate jewellery in the photograph which made it suitable for this theme, although the association of women and ornaments was a rather conventional one. The lady was anonymous to all of us then, including the former district officer. I had not yet begun my research on the royal wives, and could not have accurately placed her elsewhere in the show at the time. This photograph did, in fact, spark my interest and helped stimulate the research undertaken the following year in Benin.

Section nine, 'Royal and chiefly furniture of the court', displayed yet another dimension of court life. Oil lamps that lit the palace, brass trays, boxes used to store personal ornaments and feathers, and chiefs' stools, pots, and staffs for home shrines were contextualized against blown-up ethnographic photographs. Section ten, 'Spirit cults of the Oba', was introduced by a text panel describing the spiritual and earthly worlds of the Benins, their religious beliefs and cosmos. Rare works of art used in palace rituals gave substance to the ideas: an Oduduwa bronze helmet mask, an idiophone recalling the 'bird of disaster' in the Ugie oro ceremony, as well as medicine horns and staffs belonging to native doctors, responsible for the health and wellbeing of the Oba. As a divine king, the state of the Oba's body and mind are, for the Benins, quite literally, the state of the 'state'.

The exhibition was concluded with a reprise of the events that marked the rise and later demise of the Benin kingdom under the firepower of a British military expedition in 1897. A wrenching photograph taken by a European after the expedition ended, shows Oba Ovonramnwen seated aboard the Protectorate yacht, *Ivy*, taking him into exile at Old Calabar in eastern Nigeria. But the concluding text panel does not end in 1897. It takes up the story of the restoration of the rightful heir, Oba Eweka, in 1917, when he ascended the throne; and it reaffirmed the vitality of Benin's living traditions.

The photograph of Oba Ovonramnwen going into exile, which appeared in the show and the catalogue, excited great interest in New York (and later in Benin), and illustrates the different meanings that can be attached to the same things by outside observers and culture bearers. One reviewer of the 'Images of power' exhibition was prompted to question the inclusion of this photograph, so prominently, in the exhibition. Initially, my decision was based on its indictment of colonialism and its historic importance in documenting a catastrophic event, quite apart from its rarity at that time in exhibits in the west. Beneath the long appliquéd velvet robe worn by the seated Oba, guarded by Niger Protectorate soldiers, and barely visible, one can make out the chains around his ankles. The reviewer thought the photograph was humiliating to the Oba, a perception that was at odds with the culture bearers' opinion. When asked to comment, Oba Erediauwa, the present Oba of Benin and great grandson of Oba Ovonramnwen, a number of his chiefs and other Benins simply stated the photograph was a historical fact. They were quite firm about this, and added that an Oba could not be humiliated because he *was* power. The Benin devotion to historical accuracy proved to be characteristic in later fieldwork as well (Kaplan 1990, 1991). African-American visitors to the New York show also accepted the photograph as history but for different reasons: the Oba's enslaved state resonated in their heritage.

Some thirty students researched labels and captions, and participated in the selection, installation and programming of 'Images of power' for a two-year period prior to the opening. They reported a refrain among visitors, especially the African-Americans at the show's opening and afterwards, that the objects were shown with so much love – a word that at first startled us all. The show clearly benefited from the input of other Africanists, especially from the suggestions of Sylvia H. Williams and the late Harry Bober; and from a close working relationship with the exhibition designer, Ralph Appelbaum, who still teaches in the NYU Museum Studies Program; from George Gardner, who taught then, and was the longtime director of exhibitions at the American Museum of Natural History. Gardner's gift of cases at the end of a museum tour in 1981 truly made it possible to show the Benin art in New York. The graphics designer, Sheldon Cotler, ensured a catalogue and poster commensurate with the messages of the show.[6]

Gallery design was simple, both to allow the art to stand out and to stay within the constraints of a budget that proved limited, despite National Endowment for the Arts and National Endowment for the Humanities and other funding. We had initially anticipated a more modest show, given the general reluctance of collectors and museums to lend important Benin works. We could afford neither an outside banner to announce the show nor the plants we would have liked to add depth to the space and to convey a feeling of the rainforest environment in which Benins lived. The brown formica cases were fitted with locked plexiglass vitrines, and provided the all-important security needed; the case interiors and object bases were wrapped with natural linen that gave texture and a neutral background to the rich darkling shades of bronze, brass, ivory, wood and terracotta objects. The blown-up and mounted (30 inches by 30 inches) black and white photographs on the grey gallery walls and in the large cases managed to provide some depth; the grey carpeting completed the neutral shell. The major piece of construction, an aesthetic and economical means of showing oversize pieces in the high-ceilinged, 2,500-square-foot gallery was a series of walls around some structural pillars. This accommodated a circular series of tall window cases that housed the 6-foot ivory tusks, iron staffs, wood rattlestaffs and varied palace furnishings. These tall circular cases served as a hub for the show, practically and symbolically. The remaining effects of rhythm and softly delineated sections were achieved by judicious placement of individual cases to maximize full viewing, and to direct traffic flow through the exhibition. Spot lighting helped to focus attention on the works in a generally softly lit atmosphere. A slide show ran continuously in a separate side room set with three dozen chairs; it dealt with the history of Benin, its technology in bronze casting, and the recent coronation (1979) of Omo N'Oba N'Edo Uku Akpolokpolo Erediauwa, thirty-eight in direct line of succession, in the second dynasty, dating back to the twelfth century.

All in all, twenty lenders, sixteen funding sources and contributors, twenty-two university and advisory committee members, thirty students, seven programme staff and support people, twelve photographic lenders, and seventeen designers and specialists, besides myself, contributed to the making of this exhibition – a total of 125 people. Given the size of the show, some sixty-eight objects, shown in 2,500 square feet of space, the number of human beings directly brought into relationship with each other (aside from anonymous printers and shippers) in this singular enterprise was, upon reflection, awesome.

The second Benin exhibition, 'Art of the royal court of Benin', was also a university show, organized at the behest of the University of Benin and CenSCER (Centre for Social, Cultural, and Environmental Research) as their first public exhibition, in Benin City.[7] Time constraints (there was only six weeks' lead time) and limited production facilities in Nigeria dictated a similar theme and that the same graphics be adopted from those previously used at NYU. The art and organization of the royal court in its manifold array must be understood through the Oba, who is the literal embodiment of the society, bound by the principle of divine kingship, and at the core of the Benin polity, throughout history. Using the same text panels, maps and blown-up photographs (the ones used in NYU's 'Images of power: art of the royal court of Benin', shipped to Benin), another exhibition was installed at the special exhibition gallery, Benin National Museum, February 1985. The same basic sections were used, in the same order, with one exception: a 'Modern works' section was substituted for the original section nine ('Royal and chiefly furniture of the court') and section ten ('Spirit cults of the Oba'). As expected, there were some significant changes in the overall size and dimension of the galleries – about half the NYU space was available, and about half the pieces, thirty-eight, all borrowed in Nigeria (74 per cent from museums and 26 per cent from private lenders).

The 'Modern works' section included traditional and commercial art inspired by court themes and oral history. This entirely new section was added because there were fewer antiquities available in Nigeria to support the original thematic sections. In the United States modern works of high quality have not been collected by individuals or museums, precluding a modern section in New York. The second show was seen by Nigerians, especially Benins, unlike the New York show; both had some foreign visitors from Europe and other parts of Africa and the USA. The Benin National Museum was located across the street from the Oba's Palace, in the centre of the city, in the middle of Ring Road. I had questioned whether such a show would be of interest to the local people. Fears that it might be redundant – a case of bringing coals to Newcastle – proved unfounded.

The Vice-Chancellor of Benin University, Professor Adamu Baikie, saw the exhibition as a kind of 'homecoming' for the art that had only been shown occasionally in the city of its origins. Indeed, the linchpins of this university show were the six major pieces bought back by Nigeria at the 1980 Sotheby's Benin sale in London. To mount 'Art of the royal court of Benin', cases had to be built, walls painted, and lighting installed. Plants, which were a luxury item we could not afford in New York, were now included, being loaned by Benin friends for the duration of the show. The blown-up historical and field photographs of Oba Ovonramnwen, Oba Akenzua II, the British military expedition, and of chiefs and palace ceremonies that had formed the background of the New York show, here were primary subjects of great excitement, many of the people being known through oral tradition but never before seen. The news spread quickly by word of mouth, and people who had never set foot in the Benin museum came to the show. Users of objects offered new interpretations, and private individuals made loans: Queen Ohan Akenzua, Prince Yemi Eweka, Priest O. Ebohon, a native doctor, Mr Samson Omoregie, an ebony woodcarver, and Mr Billy Omodamwen and Mr Osaize Omodamwen, royal bronze casters.

Local objects retrieved from museum storerooms in Benin and Lagos gave immediacy to the historic events shown: a ceremonial sword, an *ada*, taken at the time of the British military conquest, had meanwhile been returned by the family of Admiral Egerton; and a gun, said to be from the 'Oba's war canoe', came to the Benin museum from Australia where it had been sent as a gift to a friend by the commander of the 1897 expedition, Admiral Sir Henry Rawson. And the Benin ivory mask, carved when the original could not be borrowed back from England for the West African arts festival, FESTAC '77, was put on view. The Benin museum staff quickly made the show their own, bringing in audiotapes of Benin cultural groups as musical background for the galleries, and repairing the sound system, unasked, to make it possible. The exhibition came alive, fleshed out by the active participation of living people in Benin. The results were a different show in design and layout, and in objects; the messages altered. For the audiences the paucity of great art did not seem critical. History only heard and perhaps read became tangible; the events and art of the past were connected to the present by objects, photographs and famous personalities known and admired in the society. Intimacy replaced grandeur, history still in the memories of old people and passed on to their descendants came alive through photography and objects retrieved from the museum stores. Benins were less interested in the greatness of the past, they felt sure of their unique place among the cultures and courts of Nigeria and Africa. And they enjoyed the design, colours and mixture of photographs and objects, people and plants, in a complete environment. Music added immeasurably to the impact. 'Art of the royal court of Benin' recorded the highest attendance in the history of the Benin National Museum.

Two other Benin museum displays have been set up in the United States of America since 1981. The first is a handsome gallery of modest size in Washington, DC, befitting the twenty-one pieces shown, and illustrated in an accompanying catalogue, *Royal Benin Art, in the Collection of the National Museum of African Art* (Freyer 1987). The new African art museum in Washington, DC, was fortunate, in 1985, to receive the Benin collection begun in the 1950s by the late Joseph H. Hirshhorn, formerly part of the collections of the Smithsonian's Hirshhorn Museum and Sculpture Garden. The quality of the African pieces immediately established a window on to Benin art at the museum, where there had been little before for visitors to see of that great tradition. For example, a rare sculpture in the round of a fish shown at NYU had been in storage at the Hirshhorn Museum and is now on permanent display (Kaplan 1981: 26–7; cf. Freyer 1987: 30–1).

A small anteroom introduces the Benin gallery at the National Museum in Washington, DC. The art is installed in wall cases around the perimeter of the room, together with a number of field photographs. The largest splash of colour is the Oba's blown-up photograph in the anteroom. In both rooms a subdued atmosphere is created by the soft lighting and the neutral colours of the walls and floor, focusing attention on the pieces in the lighted cases. This reinforces the stated aim of the installation, to make these Benin objects accessible to scholars and public alike. The effect is monochromatic since, aside from an ivory spoon, the remaining twenty pieces are all bronzes and leaded brasses. Exhibited as art, the emphasis is on the pieces themselves; the labels draw on what existing sources available in the 1980s had to say about them. The catalogue by Bryna Freyer (1987) provides an informed, sensible and forthright introduction to the collection, with suitable illustrations, based on published sources. Together, the catalogue and exhibition give the public access to one of Black Africa's major art traditions in a tasteful and unpretentious way.

A second Benin collection was recently acquired from a major collector, and put on semi-permanent exhibition at the Metropolitan Museum of Art in time for the 80th birthday of the donor, Mr Klaus Perls. The installation remained in place for most of 1992, from 16 January to 13 September, before being sent off on a national tour by the American Federation of Arts (AFA). 'Royal art of Benin from the Perls Collection: treasures from an African kingdom' thus stated its mission clearly on museum banner, gallery introductory signage and catalogue. It calls attention to the generous gift of Mr and Mrs Klaus G. Perls (he is a leading modern art dealer) to the Metropolitan Museum of Art, numbering some 132 pieces. Together with the dozens of pieces the museum already owns, it is one of the largest repositories of Benin art in the United States, second only to the Field Museum of Natural History, Chicago.

With a connoisseur's eye, Perls collected works for their aesthetic value. And the quality of the collection is evident. But what was not evident in the way the collection was shown was either Perls's operative aesthetic or a sense of how these works came to be and constitute a collection – both subjects of considerable interest today to scholars and public alike. The catalogue makes some reference to these issues, and indeed one of its true pleasures is the photograph of Benin art in the Perls's home, displayed on a mantel beneath Modigliani's superb nude, *Nu Couché* (Metropolitan Museum of Art 1992: vi, Figure 1), accompanying Klaus Perls's Preface.

Regrettably, Mr Perls's ideas and reasons for choosing the objects he did and for making this collection were not utilized as a conceptual framework in organizing and installing the exhibition. The scheme adopted rested on grouping the collection into four sections, loosely based on types of objects. As a communicative medium the exhibition, 'Royal art of Benin from the Perls Collection', demonstrated that great art, in the absence of a well-defined idea, does not always make a great show. The catalogue, on the other hand, seems less confused, being neatly bound and inevitably linear. It is not experienced in the simultaneous visual field of three-dimensional space, variegated in depth and lighting, and offering unexpected as well as planned sensual stimuli, characteristics of exhibitions when well-thought-out ideas are implemented on the ground. The curator's simple typology, dividing the collection into four sections, were plagued by fuzzy boundaries, practically and conceptually, although they might have been acceptable, even interesting, and might have worked had they reflected something of the culture bearers' categories.

The organization of the Perls collection described in the catalogue and installed in the Michael Rockefeller Wing, yielded a pastiche of Benin works of art (Brawne 1982). The first of four sections making up the typological scheme for objects included all kinds of objects that would have been placed on royal ancestral altars and other types of altars; the second section was made up of plaques that would have been placed on palace pillars in the sixteenth and seventeenth centuries; the third section was devoted to many different kinds of Benin objects, some of which appear on the plaques; and the fourth section contained other objects from some associated groups like the Owo and Ijebu, other than Benins themselves (Metropolitan Museums of Art 1992: 26). Possibly, the curator's stated reliance for her ideas on other scholars who have followed their own research interest in Benin may also account for the uncertain viewpoint that marred the exhibition's communicative force (1992: x).

The resulting assemblage of cases in an open gallery, with nearby areas of other African and non-western art in full view, was intended to follow the four typological lines indicated above. This seemed to confuse visitors who had difficulty discerning the sections and intended paths. They would look up and about often, hesitating as to which way to go next, glancing at cases at either side and across the way. Some were seen searching for companions they had come with, now out of sight among the cases; some visitors asked guards for assistance and where to find certain pieces; and others reported being unable to find objects they had wanted to see again before leaving. It was not uncommon to observe visitors crossing and recrossing the main area of the special exhibition gallery and the subsidiary space opened up behind it. On the days when I was there, the audiences had few African-Americans or 'others' in evidence. However, special groups were invited to the Metropolitan; and the usual intensive efforts were made by the museum's large and active education divisions to bus in schoolchildren. When Mayor David M. Dinkins was invited to the Metropolitan Museum one such group was pictured with him.

The museum furniture – walls, piers, platform and cases – and the ceiling height often combined to minimize the art itself. The placement of small field photographs on walls and piers, evidently to suggest subtle comparison in size and placement with the bronze plaques (formerly displayed on palace pillars), were lost in the labyrinth of cases and dim lighting, and did little to provide focal points for locating objects and sections for visitors. These problems were identified by other reviewers, clearly well disposed to major acquisitions of high quality, and much room for improvement was found in the way things were shown (Freyer 1992). The warehouse look was surely not appropriate for the overall fine quality and comprehensiveness of the gift of the Perls collection. Dark (1993) comments on the cautious compilation of information in the catalogue drawn from now standard sources, and offers seasoned judgement on its limitations and uses in his overview.

51

All four of the Benin shows discussed here, whether temporary or permanent, relied on much of the same literature and sources in the field. None of the three curators had done original fieldwork, initially (Metropolitan Museum of Art 1992; Freyer 1987; Kaplan 1981, 1985 – my fieldwork began in 1982). These exhibitions were accepted by peer groups, and met with different degrees of enthusiasm and involvement among many audiences. All four shows had reference, in some way, to the Benin royal court: sometimes the ideas were vague and generalized, sometimes clear and well defined. The clarity of curatorial vision could be expressed in very different installations, but what seemed to impact most on communication and visitor experience was the visitors' own unique and personal backgrounds and experience in the communication process. The importance attributed to the royal court is consistent with the data: most of the extensive Benin art corpus was looted from the palace when the kingdom was conquered in 1897. Most of the art was originally collected by the royal court itself, over the centuries, to exalt and attest to events and persons associated with the history and succession of a complex and ancient polity. The Oba, a living divinity to his people, was and still is at the centre of Edo society. The continuing challenge of Benin art and its material record is to convey a clear sense of that polity from a miscellany of objects that reached the west out of context; and to seek out and contextualize the meanings and messages contained in those objects for living peoples – in Nigeria, in Africa, the diaspora and elsewhere.

Another kind of exhibition as a communicative medium

The fifth exhibition to be dealt with here as a communicative medium was a contemporary African art exhibition, 'Africa explores: 20th century African art' (1991). It was chosen for discussion because it poses new and subtle issues in African art in the maturing post-colonial world (Flam 1992; Fosu 1986; Hassan 1990; Oguibe 1993). This discussion is intended neither to apply to other similar exhibitions nor to be an exhaustive critique on the subject of contemporary art or this show. The latter is already fairly well covered (Cotter 1991; Flam 1992; Oguibe 1993; Pellizzi 1993). Quite simply, such shows are likely to increase in number in future, and will bear comparable burdens of proof. Contemporary modern art shows depart from established and well-known art canons of Africa, like Benin, considered here. Because the artists, critics, curators and art historians now working have a real stake in the future of contemporary shows (money and reputation) – and because modern art shows avoid the sticky problems posed by antiquities in collections – the issues raised by 'Africa explores' are both timely and troublesome. The problems of who represents what, to whom, and why cannot be avoided. They are inherent in the representation of self in exhibitions as rituals, and all the more so in post-colonial emerging nations and rapidly changing art traditions.

Any exhibition that purports to deal with (all) Africa, and even just contemporary artists from French-speaking Africa, will inevitably encounter problems.

The easel-map and printed handouts, thoughtfully added at the Corcoran Gallery site for the show in January 1993, made evident the show's limited sources of the art. Having seen this exhibition more than once, in New York and in Washington, DC (the opening and closing venues on the national tour), and having had the opportunity to weigh the cumulative effect of very different contexts – in terms of cities, museums, architectural settings, installations and audiences – provided an opportunity to rethink initial impressions and ideas.

The opening venues for 'Africa explores' were split at two locations: in the intimacy of the townhouse setting of the Center for African Art (1991) and in the minimalist space of the Soho loft building that houses the New Museum of Contemporary Art, in New York. The closing venue at the Corcoran Art Gallery and Art School, Washington, DC, was in a Beaux-arts setting. In between, the show was seen also in Dallas, St Louis, Charlotte, North Carolina, and Pittsburgh; these venues are not discussed here and the reviews conflicted. The show's aims, its geographic coverage and the categories used to organize the works into meaningful sections proved troublesome issues, even among exhibition enthusiasts. While categories, like typologies, are always arbitrary and can be debated, they must be able to bear scrutiny and make sense of the material. The five categories that sorted the art selected for 'Africa explores' were: 'traditional art', 'new functional art', urban art', international art' and 'extinct art'. The art itself ranged from kitsch to classics in its representation of the contemporary African scene, and the artists from traditional specialists who inherit or acquire rights to work, and self-taught carvers, painters and others, to those trained professionally in the west and/or its techniques. These eclectic works were themselves seen in wide-ranging architectural settings, museums and venues, by diverse audiences; they were accompanied by a catalogue written by a number of authors from diverse disciplines. Curiously, the catalogue's author is given as 'Susan Vogel assisted by Ima Ebong', in contrast to the usual appellation of 'editor' or 'editors'.

A leading art critic, writing in the journal *Art in America* (Cotter 1991), finds himself alternating between praise and perceptive questions about the many issues raised by both the catalogue and the exhibition. He points out that Vogel's aim to address 'the major themes and artistic innovations in African art of this century' if applied to 'an exhibition of American or European art would be unthinkable' . . . and all to be achieved within a modest New York townhouse and part of a Soho space (Cotter 1991: 104). He is admiring of her daring – but muses, and observes that it 'would be wonderful to know what thoughts African artists themselves have on such matters, but throughout the catalogue, as so often elsewhere, they are "spoken for" rather than given the chance to speak'. He, like Wahlman (1991), another reviewer, finds the catalogue 'crucial' to the exhibition itself (Cotter 1991: 110). Wahlman, a specialist in contemporary African art, along with Jean Kennedy, Frieda High-Tesfagoris and Marilyn Houlberg, whom she mentions, confesses to having needed the catalogue to understand Vogel's show, its contradictions and categories (1991: 30–1). It is clear there is something seriously wrong with an exhibition that cannot be understood when it is seen, especially by specialists. To the earlier questions posed – who organizes what, for whom and why? – the answer would seem to be: by and for elite and peer groups in power; and for those seeking to maintain that power in new markets for exhibition rituals – and attempting to define the collectivity in the western world and, perhaps, by extension, once again, in Africa.

The labelling in the show was in the art museum tradition, comprising brief identifications and title, the artist's name, and a line or two perhaps, as well as documentation of ownership and so on. A text panel usually provided background, opening a section. The signage throughout and for sections of the show was brief and unobtrusive. Occasional strong colours, red for instance, were used for background in a few of the rooms in New York, and a mustard yellow was favoured in most in Washington, DC. But the overall impression was one of sparseness in DC, with the paintings spread out and looking a bit lost on the walls of the spacious rooms (except for a few of the larger sculptures). In contrast, the several rooms on the three floors of the townhouse that was home to the Center for African Art offered no vistas, precluding a sense of the whole and contributing to the kaleidoscopic feel of the show. Viewing in the small-scale rooms, however, did allow things to be seen at close range and offered a feeling of intimacy with the works. This was not true at the New Museum of Contemporary Art in New York where some of the larger sculptures were shown at the same time.

Another art historian, Jack Flam, adds to the discussion on 'Africa explores'. He compares the show with its two most important predecessors: 'Primitivism in modern art' (1984), mounted at the Museum of Modem Art, New York, and the Centre Pompidou's 'Magiciens de la Terre' (1989) in Paris (Flam 1992: 88–90). Like Cotter and Flam, and some other reviewers, I, too, must confess to being visually seduced by some of the works in the show – and, also like them, to being disturbed. It was surprising to me, given the large African-American, African and Caribbean populations in New York and Washington, DC, that there were relatively few people from these communities in attendance when I visited the venues. Indeed, there were very few people in the galleries at all. The potentially mobile groups have not yet coalesced, it seems, and it is left to the initiates and would-be initiates to perform the rituals of exhibitions.

Nowadays, there are reviewers who are proposing to include 'everything' as part of the exhibition – the catalogue, symposia, educational programming, etc. (Berlo and Phillips 1992). Such propositions subvert the basic tenet of all exhibitions: they must suffice to communicate on their own as media, and must be coherent and accessible to the public and to the various groups they would address. Catalogues traditionally served as a permanent record of an exhibition, and always provided in-depth information and details for specialists and those willing and able to pursue the subject. Now the cost of catalogues is fast becoming prohibitive for most visitors, and educational programming, lectures, workshops and special events are necessarily limited by available funds, locations, time, space and scheduling – for museums, schools and individuals. Exhibitions open to the public are more important than ever before, and must make their ideas known directly, in the exhibition gallery, through means available and useful to it. An exhibition that fails to communicate as a medium, probably should not have been an exhibition in the first place – but a book, perhaps.

Conclusions

At the outset of this chapter, I stated that exhibitions and museums should be seen not only as places where rituals of collectivities are enacted, but more than that – they are political arenas in which the power of dominant groups is asserted, and where it may be challenged by new and emerging groups. The two Benin exhibitions, organized in 1979–81 in New York, and in 1984–5 in Nigeria, showed the active role played by visitors, even when the structure and elements of an exhibition remain intact. The intended messages of the first thematic show at NYU found ready response among African-Americans, peer groups and the public, each for different reasons.

The second thematic exhibition, in Nigeria in 1985, at the Benin National Museum, found the original messages of the show transformed into living history by the people themselves, as they readily assumed active roles in lending, implementing, interpreting and sharing their ideas, memories of events, knowledge of objects and their past, among themselves and with me. These people now included the queen whose photograph had been chosen five years earlier for the 'Images of power' show, Queen Ohan Akenzua; other participants included several of the princes, chiefs, their wives, royal bronze casters, wood carvers, ritual priests, carpenters, cleaning women, museum education officers, security men, designers, painters, members of a cultural group and personal friends, including an architect and the university driver, David Odia, and others who prefer to remain anonymous.

It remained for the most intellectually critical and probing review of 'Africa explores' to come from an African, Olu Oguibe (1993), a poet and artist, and winner of the All-Africa Okigbo Prize for Literature in 1992. He speaks with a sure voice, peeling the exhibition of its deeply layered messages with the same deftness and smoothness with which the Ghanaian sculptor, Kane Kwei, carved the onion-shaped coffin in the exhibit. Oguibe issues a call for Africans to 'narrate themselves and not be mere stagehands in a ventriloquist's show'. A true discourse will be achieved when Africans present themselves, and in their own voices (Oguibe 1993: 22).

It is no accident that a show which allowed contemporary African artists to speak in their own 'voices' (instead of being spoken for by an 'intimate outsider', as Vogel calls herself), was curated by an African-American, Grace Stanislaus. The show was a major loan exhibition from Africa, 'Contemporary African artists: changing tradition', that opened at the Studio Museum in Harlem in 1991. Ms Stanislaus is now the Director, Bronx Museum of the Arts, New York.

Responses to the exhibition, 'Africa explores: 20th century African art', expose the competitive, historical and political processes taking place among living peoples in former colonies and in the diaspora – no longer distant 'others' in need of intimate outsiders. Whereas mostly white controlled, western institutions and individuals have monopolized interpretation of African art in America, Europe and elsewhere, emerging mobile groups in Africa and the diaspora are entering the arena, demanding to be heard as well as seen. Like Oguibe, they are questioning those who have monopolized the communicative media of exhibitions and publications. They fear the spectre of cultural imperialism rising in Africa's modern post-colonial world. These are new 'voices' – portents of change (Hassan 1990), but also an opportunity for true discourse, as Oguibe suggests (1993: 22).

Notes

1 From late 1983 to 1985 as a Fulbright professor I taught at the University of Benin, Nigeria, Department of Sociology and Anthropology, and was affiliated with the university's Centre for Social, Cultural, and Environmental Research (CenSCER). Before leaving Nigeria in 1985, at the behest of the University of Benin and CenSCER, I organized and curated 'Art of the royal court of Benin' in co-operation with the Federal National Commission for Museums and Monuments (NCMM), at the Benin National Museum.

2 The NYU Program in Museum Studies, Graduate School of Arts and Science, was founded in 1977, at the Chancellor's initiative, to integrate the disparate offerings then in various departments and schools. The result was unified postgraduate, interdisciplinary training programme, within the Faculty of Arts and Science offered to those holding a Master's or earning a Master's or doctorate degree.

3 One of the first major travelling exhibitions from Africa was organized by Dr Ekpo Eyo, Director-General of the National Commission for Museums and Monuments (NCMM), in co-operation with Michael Kan, Curator, Detroit Institute of Art, Michigan, using the NCMM's collections and recent discoveries. 'Treasures of ancient Nigeria' (Eyo and Willet 1980) toured the United States and Europe, afterwards, for some five years, revising notions worldwide about the antiquity and achievements of some 2,000 years of African civilizations.

4 The customized cases from the travelling exhibition 'Gold of ancient Peru' were given at the end of its tour to the NYU Progam in Museum Studies by the American Museum of Natural History, for the Benin show.

5 Valerie Griffith, a native of England, a graduate student in the NYU programme, was invaluable in locating photographs in collections in England during her summer vacation. She was an assistant for the Benin exhibition, as were Barbo Freund, Kellen Haak and Stanley Tarver.

6 The poster and catalogue designed by Sheldon Cotler Associates, and photographed by Sheldan Collins, for the show 'Images of power: art of the royal court of Benin' won a national prize and honourable mention for museum publications at the first juried competition held by the American Association of Museums in 1981. Subsequently, it was among the 100 best exhibition interpretations, recognized in connection with the first twenty years of National Endowment for the Humanities awards, the only university show noted by both the AAM and the NEH.

7 The University of Benin and CenSCER were very keen to establish a presence in the city itself, never having had a public exhibition at the Benin National Museum. We were fortunate in having full co-operation from the NCMM for loans, staffing and transport of objects. In 1982 having been invited to give an intensive three-week seminar in Jos on exhibition development for senior staff of the NCMM I established close working relationships with the Director-General, Dr Ekpo Eyo, and the Director of the National Museum Michael Nkanta as well as various specialists. This made the show possible on short notice.

References

Anderson, B. (1983) *Imagined Communities: Reflections on the Origin and Spread of Nationalism*, London: Verso Press.

Baikie, A. (1985) 'Opening address', in *Art of the Royal Court of Benin*, Benin City: University of Benin.

Beier, U. (1961) 'Contemporary Nigerian art', *Nigerian Magazine* 60: 27–51.

Belcher, M. (1992) *Exhibitions in Museums*, Washington, DC: Smithsonian Institution Press.

Berlo, J. C. and Phillips, R. B. (1992) '"Vitalizing the things of the past": museum representations of Native North American art in the 1990s', *Museum Anthropology* 16(1): 29–43.

Brawne, M. (1982) *The Museum Interior*, New York: Architectural Book Publishing Co., Inc.

Brown, E. S. (1966) *Africa's Contemporary Art and Artists: A Review of Creative Activities in Painting, Sculpture, Ceramics, and Crafts for over 300 Artists Working in the Modern Industrialized Society of Some of the Countries of Sub-Saharan Africa*, New York: Harmon Foundation, Inc.

Cannizzo, J. (1989) *Into the Heart of Africa*, Ontario: Royal Ontario Museum.

—— (1991) 'Exhibiting cultures: "into the heart of Africa"', *Visual Anthropology Review* 7(1): 150–60.

Cotter, H. (1991) 'Under African eyes', *Art in America*, October, 104–11.

Dark, P. J. C. (1962) *The Art of Benin*, Chicago: Chicago Natural History Museum.

—— (1993) 'Royal art of Benin: the Perls collection in the Metropolitan Museum of Art', *African Arts* 26(1): 95–7.

Duchateau, A. (1989) *Benin Kunsteiner Königskultur. Die Benin Sammlung Des Museums für Volkerkunde Wien*, Zurich: Museum Rietberg.

Eyo, E. and Willett, F. (1980) *Treasures of Ancient Nigeria*, New York: Knopf.

Falk, J. H. and Dierking, L. D. (1992) *The Museum Experience*, Washington, DC: Whalesback Books.

Flam, J. (1992) 'Africa explores: 20th century African art', *African Arts* 25(2): 88–90.

Fosu, K. (1986) *20th Century Art of Africa, vol. 1*, Zaria, Nigeria: Gaskiya Press Corporation.

Freyer, B. M. (1987) *Royal Benin Art, in the Collection of the National Museum of African Art*, Washington, DC: Smithsonian Institution Press.

—— (1992) 'Royal art of Benin from the Perls collection: treasures from an African kingdom', *African Arts* 25(2): 90–1.

Hassan, S. (1990) 'Africans are talking to each other: towards a critical definition of contemporary African art', paper presented at the annual meeting of the African Studies Association, Baltimore, MD.

Hooper-Greenhill, E. (1992) *Museums and the Shaping of Knowledge*, New York: Routledge.

Jarocki, B. (1981) 'Images of power', *African Arts* 14(4): 72–4.

Kaplan, F. S. (1981) 'Introduction', in F. S. Kaplan (ed.) *Images of Power: Art of the Royal Court of Benin*, New York: New York University.

—— (1982) 'Towards a "science" of museology', *Museological Working Papers* 2/1981: 14–15.

—— (1983) 'Museum', in *Funk & Wagnalls New Encyclopedia*, revised 1989 edition, vol. 18: 172–8.

—— (1985) *Art of the Royal Court of Benin*, Benin City: University of Benin.

—— (1990) 'Some uses of photographs in recovering cultural history at the royal court of Benin, Nigeria', in J. C. Scherer (ed.) *Picturing Cultures: Historic Photographs in Anthropological Inquiry*, special double issue, *Visual Anthropology* 3: 317–41.

—— (1991) 'Fragile legacy: photographs as documents in recovering political and cultural history at the royal court of Benin', in *History in Africa*, vol. 18, Madison: University of Wisconsin, 205–37.

—— (1994a) 'Introduction', in F. S. Kaplan (ed.) *Museums and the Making of 'Ourselves': the Role of Objects in National Identity*, London: Leicester University Press.

—— (1994b) 'Mexican museums in the creation of a national image in world tourism', in June Nash (ed.) *Crafts in the World Market: the Impact of Global Exchange on Middle American Artisans*, Albany: State University of New York Press.

Karp, I. and Lavine, S. D. (eds) (1991) *Exhibiting Cultures: The Poetics and Politics of Museum Display*, Washington, DC: Smithsonian Institution Press.

Karp, I., Kreamer, C. M. and Lavine, S. D. (eds) (1992) *Museums and Communities: The Politics of Public Culture*, Washington, DC: Smithsonian Institution Press.

Klein, Larry (1986) *Exhibits Planning and Design*, New York: Madison Square Press, Inc.

Mack, J. (1990) *Emil Torday and the Art of the Congo 1900–1909*, London: British Museum Publications.

Metropolitan Museum of Art (1992) *Royal Art of Benin from the Perls Collection*, ed. Kate Ezra, New York: Metropolitan Museum of Art.

Oguibe, O. (1993) 'Africa explores: 20th century African art', *African Arts* 26(1): 16–22.

Ottenberg, S. (1991) 'Into the heart of Africa', *African Arts* 24(3): 79–82.

Pearce, S. (ed.) (1990) *Objects of Knowledge: New Research in Museum Studies*, London: Athlone Press.

Pellizzi, F. (1993) 'Africa explores: 20th century African art', *African Arts* 26(1): 22–9, 95.

Price, S. (1989) *Primitive Art in Civilized Places*, Chicago and London: University of Chicago Press.

Schildkrout, E. (1991) 'Ambiguous messages and ironic twists: into the heart of Africa and the other museum', *Museum Anthropology* 15(2): 16–23.

—— (1992) 'Revisiting Emil Torday's Congo: "Images of Africa" at the British Museum', *African Arts* 25(1): 60–9.

Schildkrout, E. and Keim, C. (1990) *African Reflections: Art from Northeastern Zaire*, New York and Seattle: The American Museum of Natural History and the University of Washington Press.

Stanislaus, G. (1991) *Contemporary African Artists: Changing Tradition*, New York: The Studio Museum in Harlem.

Vogel, S., assisted by Ebong, I. (1991) *Africa Explores: 20th Century African Art*, New York: The Center for African Art.

Wahlman, M. S. (1991) 'Exhibition review: Africa explores: 20th century African art', *Museum Anthropology* 15(4): 30–1.

Weil, S. (1990) *Rethinking the Museum and Other Meditations*, Washington, DC: Smithsonian Institution Press.

5

Observations on semiotic aspects in the museum work of Otto Neurath: reflections on the 'Bildpädagogische Schriften' (writings on visual education)[1]

Hadwig Kräutler

Introduction

The competent, reflective use of the possibilities of non-verbal, symbolic and holistic media has become increasingly important to counter shallow clichéd slogans and to enable people to move towards active participation and decision-making by offering positively inspiring and stimulating experiences. In this respect, museums with relevant messages and high-quality, eye-catching communication can be effective as public places for informal learning and entertainment. The decision-makers in these institutions, however, have to know how to use the museum's potential productively. For this there is no generally applicable formula. Not only does *the* museum not exist, but there are innumerable and very different institutions, each with histories and collections of its own, and with specific relations to its public.[2]

Newer research in museum communication is influenced by semiotics to the degree where concepts of a purely mechanistic transmission of information have been left behind. Societal conditions and possibilities of construction and transmission as well as production of 'meaning' (cf. Bruner 1990; Umiker-Sebeok 1991; Winner 1979) in the multidimensional diachronic and synchronic complexity of the interface 'museum–public' and its mass media qualities have been taken into account. Research regarding museums as socio-semiotic phenomena can yield valuable tools to improve and enhance the pertinence and meaning of their public-oriented activities.

The diverse forms and methods in which a museum deploys its public functions, and activates its partners, potential and actual, in its communicative efforts, can be termed the 'public language' of a museum (Belcher 1991: 43; Royal Ontario Museum 1976). The 'eloquence' of a museum, the occurrence and quality of these activities, especially in the form of permanent and temporary exhibitions which are the most readily perceived of its utterances, are indicators for performance and capacity.

Otto Neurath's museum and exhibition work[3] was primarily meant to serve communication. He developed specific theories and work methods on how to transmit information visually in order to educate and empower the wider population (e.g. Neurath: pp. 122–36). Although such stated goals may represent unattainable ideals, Neurath's achievements, seen in their historical context, can yield useful comparisons. His concepts of the design and media function of exhibitions, of exhibition and museum work as a social phenomenon, of a clear partnership with the public and, his central concern, the theme of communication through exhibition, will be examined in this chapter.[4]

The second part of the chapter deals with problems of communication through exhibition in general, with conditions and prerequisites within the museum institution, while the last part outlines the need for 'communication' to become a centrally and institutionally grounded work principle. This is argued in two ways. First, museums as public institutions have to maintain a clear relation to the public, and thus profile a specific place within the socially constituted and received cultural fields, and second, quality in exhibition design needs long-term traditions and institutional as well as public reflections. Neurath's principles and stringent work rules can be quoted as examples of these issues.

Otto Neurath

Otto Neurath (1882–1945) is best known for his achievements as a philosopher and social empiricist.[5] Within the 'Vienna Circle', of which he was a founder member, he served the cause of all those who were engaged in overcoming both the restrictions of the classical philosophical theorists and the limitations of the analytical theorists who dismissed as irrelevant any concern with the socio-political context in which science was practised (Uebel 1991: 9–16). Neurath's philosophical efforts in developing a metatheory, to be a critical theory of all knowledge, are paralleled by his other scientific and practical achievements. His contribution to visual education, the introduction of pictorial statistics,[6] and his work with museums and exhibitions are regarded as outstanding.

The museum and exhibition work of Otto Neurath had its practical beginnings in the 'Red Vienna' of the 1920s, a time when Utopian ideals of social change were plenteous, and political developments such as the crumbling of the European empires and the early results of the Russian Revolution made great advances seem possible. His aim, in line with his philosophical and social convictions, was to help democratically to produce universal knowledge, to develop theories operating at a high level of generality and to find ways for the general public, including the *Ungebildeten* (uneducated), to understand them. In the field of visual education Otto Neurath's work is hallmarked by the acronym ISOTYPE (International System of Typographic Picture Education) which stands for a methodological work principle centred on one clear goal: serving communication. This principle was developed by Otto Neurath and his team in the Viennese Gesellschafts- und Wirtschaftsmuseum (1925–1934) and perfected later in the two periods of emigration in Holland and England

(1934–40; 1940–5) (Neurath 1936/1980; Neurath: pp. 355–98). ISOTYPE[7] influenced all the work involved in exhibitions or museums, from the initial planning to the processes and structures needed for practical realization. It meant, above all, empathy with the future user. Neurath's principle offers an opportunity for reflection and comparison.

Otto Neurath's seemingly 'untroubled' or 'unafflicted' attitude[8] was based on and accompanied his visionary and strict methodological relations with the medium exhibition/museum as well as his phenomenological clarity. The influences of his manifold practical experiences with learners (cf. Dvorak 1982, 1991; Stadler 1991) and the stringency of his scientific treatment of philosophical and socio-logical questions (Neurath 1973; Stadler 1991a; Uebel 1991) had found concrete results in visual education projects such as exhibitions or museum work with schools (Neurath: pp. 403–9; Twyman 1975; Stadler 1982).

Neurath's conception of a museum began with the idea of communication, with the need for means to transmit information appropriate to the decision-making competencies which the visitors were to gain (Neurath: p. 56). He saw an exhi-bition as a medium which is both shaped and shaping, which is no less 'an object of practical use than tables or rooms' (Neurath: p. 133). With this clear goal, Neurath's museum concept (explicitly treated in 'Museums of the future' (Neurath: pp. 244–57) of course set out from a very different initial idea from that of the traditional, systematic and taxonomic museum collections.[9] There, objects are processed according to categories which the authors of the 'museum text' (the scientific personnel of the museum, the curators of exhibitions) as well as the visitors, conceive of as given and based on objectively generated facts (Porter 1991: 103–4; Pearce 1991: 150). Enhancing this institutional and historic image of proven 'validity' (cf. the concept of 'museality' used by Stránský 1991: 130–1), most temporary exhibitions only underline the more or less intended message. Since there is no means of control over the possible significance on either side, on the museum specialist's as little as on the museum visitor's, exhibitions represent very complex and rich perceptual situations, providing ample scope for diverse readings and approaches (Barretto 1991: 5–7; Pearce 1987: 181–6; Belcher 1991: 41–3) and remain preconditioned 'open texts'. Authors of exhibitions are very rarely asked to reflect on this situation of institutional preconception and to moderate its effects. The possi-bility of actively treating it, of working with this moment, therefore does not arise. Otto Neurath's comment, 'Most exhibitions suffer from the fact that they are not meant to inform the visitor systematically, but are meant as proof of the capabilities of the curators' (Neurath: p. 133) is still valid, for collecting and exhibiting are activities which are evidently used for 'peer group review' (Pearce 1991: 148–51).

The work of Otto Neurath and his collaborators yields contrasting material, since their concepts were not hampered by such traditional 'museal' stand-points.[10] One of the important aspects of ISOTYPE, for example, is that 'order and clear form are found for a given material to best enable the future user' (Kinross 1991: xiii; Neurath: pp. 355–98). This follows the statement,

'ISOTYPE rules are the rules for respecting the interests of the public (in a picture, in a museum or in all museums together)' (Neurath: p. 378). When designing the forms for intersubjectively valid information (which, it was stressed, was also to be understood by the uninformed visitor of an exhibition), the so-called process of 'Transforming' (Kinross 1982) was central. It meant, first, carefully selecting pertinent information, designing a three-dimensional realisation of the thematic concept, and aiming at an objective transformation, combining the views of specialists from different disciplines to create the composite medium 'exhibition' (Neurath: pp. 88–92, 180–206).

Using simple materials but the newest techniques, and working with the best artists,[11] Neurath's team produced sensationally attractive charts and posters, carefully and consciously designed pictorial statistics, three-dimensional models and reliefs as well as slide and magic lantern shows (Neurath: pp. 88–92, 150–3; 197–206). These were to serve as transmitters of practical information, conveying ideas to the exhibition visitors and enabling decision-making processes in the sense of democratic pluralities within a community (Neurath: pp. 56, 57–62) and, in very general terms, improving the *Lebenslage* (quality of life, cf. Nemeth 1981: 94–9).

Deliberately and in contrast to commonplace ideas about museums, Neurath negated the importance of the museum object (Neurath: p. 244). In most museum contexts care and attention for the objects dominate the work processes, explaining their qualities as originals or their specific singularities. Neurath, however, looked for generally valid comparative material and information which would be useful to all (Neurath: p. 2, 32, 244–6). In doing so, he underlined the priority of clear, factual 'communication', the importance of the 'legible' and meaningful visual message, which was to be tested out by visitors (Neurath: pp. 57–62, 355–98, 600–18). At the same time Neurath excluded both the auratic and quasi-religious 'metaphysical' qualities and the purely monetary values of 'precious' and unique things, which are often emphasized in the conventional museum (Neurath: pp. 636–45). Neurath, in contrast, was definitively interested in offering factual information, not dramatic or emotionally stimulating headlines or mystical experiences (Neurath: pp. 638–40).

Comparable to the work methods applied within ISOTYPE, the exhibition with a single author was replaced by a new communication model devised by an interdisciplinary team representing the interests of curator, designer, conservationist and public (Hooper-Greenhill 1991: 59). The visitors, in this model, are seen as active interpreters, with diverging levels and profiles of information, with previous knowledge, attitudes and values (Hooper-Greenhill 1991: 59), and different 'habitus' (Bourdieu and Darbel 1991: 15, 107) which define the possibilities of 'readings' (cf. for example Umiker-Sebeok 1991: 3–4).

The non-fixed 'medium' contains all the communicative elements of the museum, the building, people, staff, exhibitions, exhibits, objects, cafeteria and supporting installations, but also all extramural factors such as information prior to entering the museum building, media echo, topical factors. This non-fixed image is in a process of constant re- and de-constitution, and produces and reproduces different, diverging and sometimes even contradictory meanings (cf. Hooper-Greenhill 1991: 59).

Also in this sense, working with a comprehensive and open model of communication, as was characteristic of Neurath's methods and convictions, he enabled as many as possible unconventional, and thus inspirational moments. For example, he was convinced that a museum should have branch institutions (Neurath: p. 294) so as to shorten travelling times for visitors; and that museums should be located in everyday venues to make them approachable meeting points, or should be established in city council blocks to further the cause of decentralized education (Neurath: p. 199). It was of course clear that museums' opening hours should be adjusted to the leisure hours of the working class (Neurath: p. 37); and, above all, that a generally welcoming and accepting atmosphere was a prerequisite for any unoppressive learning and experience (Neurath: pp. 206, 252).

Central to Neurath's basic conception were the following deeply held underlying beliefs: access to education and information must be democratic (Neurath: pp. 78–84); complex and complicated issues can be presented and explained (Neurath: pp. 403–7); visitors must be accepted as equal partners, worthy of empathy and attention (Neurath: pp. 40–50, 51–6); verifiable rationality is preferable to priest-like mysticism (Neurath: pp. 2, 256); reality can be changed, but not by fatalism since only activities affecting the quality of life will improve it (Neurath: pp. 252, 258–64).

Such messages, even if only indirectly uttered by so-called 'indices', function as meaningful indicators for a basic tendency (cf. Hooper-Greenhill 1991: 53). Research in museum semiotics has recently taken to examining the possibilities of 'hidden' relevance (Mounin 1985, quoted in Hooper-Greenhill 1991: 58), a means of identifying certain determining connections and connotations within a communication process. The signalling elements are chosen in such a way as to ensure the greatest possible congruence between the intended message, given by the communicator in the designed medium 'exhibition', and its expected 'readings' by the receiver (Hooper-Greenhill 1991: 59).

Exhibition as a composite medium

To exhibit means to show or expose something, and in so doing put it in an eye-catching light. The design elements of exhibitions can include spatial, optical, acoustic, haptic and olfactory experiences, all of which can be used to their full extent. Sensory stimulation, time and space categories, as well as movement, can be used to attract the viewer's attention to a specific message (Belcher 1991: 37–9). In spite of the very highly developed technical possibilities of media transmission, the exhibition medium is used in presentations and representational acts in the sciences as well as in art, politics or religion, and to a similar extent in commercially oriented enterprises. 'As a medium, exhibition has always been such that the novel and new have found immediate application, and that the rapid pace of technological developments assures exhibitions an exciting future' (Belcher 1991: 37). All these 'experience' environments are designed with the well-known goal of influencing the viewers. Exhibitions in this sense are therefore intended at least to inform, but also sometimes to communicate. They are expressive manifestations which play an important role within the mass media (Treinen 1981).

Semiotic studies have treated museums and exhibitions like any other observable socio-cultural phenomena, as signifying systems, as forming and formed (shaping and shaped) hidden social logic (Umiker-Sebeok 1991; Hooper-Greenhill 1991). The basic and important meaning is thereby defined by the selection, arrangement and framing of the objects, the contexts of the visits, the images and public relations work produced for a specific presentation; and all this has to be seen within the complex and 'tradition-bound conditions of the language of museum presentations' (Stránský 1991: 130), i.e. within museum work as a whole. In this sense, it is certainly valid that 'exhibition is also subject to the various vicissitudes inherent in a dynamic, evolving medium which has its roots in historical, social, economic, educational, political structures of society' (Belcher 1991: 42). It is also true that 'the artistically composed museum display becomes . . . a cultural creation which (implying authorship) . . . acts not only through its scientific content, but also through its aesthetic eloquence' (Jerzy Swiecimski in Belcher 1991: 42), through the construction of a 'dreamland'. At best, an exhibition can also satisfy the most generally accepted criteria of an art form and 'can elate, excite, arouse, satisfy, anger, shock, depress' (Belcher 1991: 41).

Pearce states, 'as normally conceived by their originators, exhibitions are works of art in the traditional European sense . . . like a novel or a play, [addressing] themselves to a chosen set of human circumstances' and

> set out to convey intelligible messages. Doing this by selecting elements from the flux . . . of life, then composing these into a pattern . . . to the satisfaction of the originator. They depend on shared educational experience and cast of mind, on internal integrity and compelling perceptions.
>
> (Pearce 1987: 182)

All material elements of an exhibition and the respective framings (building, specific location within a certain type of architecture, style of announcements) define the ways in which an exhibition becomes meaningful for the individual visitors, connecting the intended message with their specific repertoires of associations and connotations, and the pertinent and relevant social facts. Thus meaning and information for an exhibition visitor can only be produced within the complex and necessarily positive interaction of his/her own categories of thinking and experiencing and the forms offered in the exhibition (Umiker-Sebeok 1991). The visitor will 'see' what is shown, and will see and interpret whatever is there within his/her own background of experiences and pre-knowledge. If the basic conceptual plan cannot be recognized, the complexity of the exhibition message and the diffuseness of the visual-spatial material continuum will constitute a 'total' receiver situation, not compatible with the exhibition competency of the visitors.

The idea that everything in a museum, all artefacts or object elements in the museum surrounding, exert sign functions is basic to an understanding of the museum as a semiotic communications system (Stránský 1991). In an article on the exhibition 'Die neue Zeit' (Neurath: pp. 133–6) Otto Neurath stated that the organizer (der Deutsche Werkbund) was responsible to the public for ensuring 'that systematic completeness is achieved. ... not only a fairground-type accumulation', for as Neurath continued, 'once the notion of deliberate exhibition didacticism has been accepted, a set of ideas for reform follow automatically' (Neurath: p. 133). Every possibility for pre-informing, grouping, mainstreaming, and providing overviews, comparisons, headlines and explanatory texts, as well as recapitulating information already given, has to be used (Neurath: pp. 135–6). Among other things he listed providing an overview, for confusion 'is amiss' and 'the visitor is happy with what is to be taken in in one look: selected and carefully treated pertinent examples; planned integrated design' (Neurath: pp. 135–6). In the sense that 'exhibitions are pieces of functional design with the purpose of doing a specific task' (Belcher 1991: 41), it may still not be possible 'to attribute specific "meaning" to everything in the design, even to the width of the columns which are used to present the information', as Neurath wrote in the article 'Design methods of the Social and Economic Museum' (Neurath: p. 19).

Thus, according to the communicative competencies of the intended actual or potential partners, semantic possibilities and aspects of 'empathic' exhibition design will be applied. Decisions on how to make the message clearly 'legible', for whom, on which level of speech, in which specific jargon, with which pictorial images, and with how much technical refinement, clearly depend on the intentions of the exhibition designer. Use of complicated exhibition- or stage-design elements will only be understood by the public with the 'right' education and a certain training in abstract thinking: for the uninitiated it can exert an alienating effect which is not only symbolically excluding (Heinisch 1989: 24–5). Still, suspense and coding can clearly become productive elements, so that in this context, the argument runs against a didactic approach which would force itself on the learner, killing curiosity and critical attitudes and arousing resistance.

Although systematic research of the exhibition as a medium has made progress since Neurath's time,[12] only a limited number of scientific projects have treated this cultural phenomenon in its dynamic social context (Stránský 1991: 130; Umiker-Sebeok 1991: 2; Merriman 1989, 1991). Neurath's statement 'a technique and tradition in museum and exhibition design which can make use of secured and proven experiences [are evolving] only very slowly' still remains valid as far as the effects of certain techniques are concerned (Neurath: p. 40; cf. Belcher 1991: 197–209). Unanimously, however, it is stated that early acquaintance in a family context provides a seemingly inherent, self-reliant and therefore most effective exhibition competency (Bourdieu and Darbel 1991: 107; Dimaggio and Useem 1978: 149–58).

In this context the advantages of exhibitions are defined as including opportunities for very personal 'firsthand' experiences offered by original theatrical and authentic three-dimensional effects exploiting multi-sensory possibilities, the contrast of real sizes, the dramatization of tiny elements if needed, with all the possibilities of theatre (Barretto 1991: 5; Belcher 1991: 42). Furthermore, several facets of a topic can be presented at different levels of pre-knowledge, in varying degrees of scientific treatment, enabling visitors to choose, to organize their information retrieval, and to consume the exhibition as they please (Belcher 1991: 38–9). All these advantages and possibilities are indeed appreciated by visitors and confirmed in various visitor surveys (cf. e.g. Bitgood *et al.* 1989: 40–50).

It has to be kept in mind that even in the 'purest' exhibition form, an originator (with a particular set of values etc.) is still there; even to the extent of individual idiosyncrasy becoming 'unintelligible' (Pearce 1987: 183). But on the other hand, since strict disciplinary specialization does not show everyday contexts either, here too 'the outcome is not outright falsification, for this implies intention, but certainly a systematically erroneous simulation' (Neurath: pp. 101, 175; cf. Porter 1991: 109–10). For an exhibition to be successful, the fact of qualified subjective selection is a necessity. But it has 'to remain within objectivity', and an exhibition must have a beginning, a main body and an end, as well as offer basic structural and decipherable experiences (Pearce 1987: 182). The more exhibition competency visitors have at their disposal – and this is certainly not the same for visitors at an agricultural show as for those at an art exhibition – the less visitor motivation, the fewer signalling posts, 'threads' and structures throughout the exhibition are needed to make the intended messages clear; and the greater the probability of congruence between intended and decoded message.

For Otto Neurath 'complete' does not mean thrilling, and 'it is just as impossible to do exhibition work as it is to paint a poster by formula' (Neurath: p. 3). 'It has to do with artistic expressive qualities and sensitivity in their use in both the early design stages and in the final production, in order to find an enthralling and functioning language' (Neurath: pp. 118–25).

Public exhibiting in museums

In public museums, exhibitions are arranged according to the tenets of public service institutions which are clearly centred on objects, i.e. collecting, categorizing, preserving and interpreting artefacts (Belcher 1991: 38) in the service of society as a whole (ICOM 1990: 3). Otto Neurath's statement of 1933[13] is still valid sixty years later: 'museums and exhibitions are gaining steadily increasing attention, because they exert an especially strong and many-faceted influence' (Neurath: p. 198). It is evident that enormous unused potential is to be found in the possibilities of diverse interpersonal activities within exhibitions, in the 'museum environment as interactive milieu' (Screven 1974), using the group dynamics of visits and encouraging 'conversational' interaction with visitors (cf.

McManus 1991: 40–6), for 'while the book serves the individual learner, the museum can serve both the individual and the group if there is empathic and scientific guidance' (Neurath: p. 198).

From this potential for more visitor-oriented and visitor-engaging activties, a mandate to relate to these findings clearly evolves. Neither communication nor 'culture' is passively or mechanically passed from one generation to the next. Both are conditioned by socially construed and socially defined strategies and rules for the transference and generation of meanings (cf. Winner and Umiker-Sebeok 1979; Bruner 1990). Uncoordinated, haphazard museum education or public relations work which function as empty formulas and do not touch vital interests, as for example mass-tourist attractions, do not serve to build up relations with the public. Ready-made programmes of this kind, or on the other hand rare and exclusive insider-events for the initiated few, turn museums into ivory towers, accessible to many but truly meaningful only for a small segment of society. Thus, museum visiting patterns will remain socially stabilizing measures, in which discipline systematics may have to be seen as representing and reinforcing social hierarchies (Bourdieu 1974; Bourdieu and Darbel 1991).

Insufficient representation of the interests of the public within the museum leads to a marginalization of publicly oriented work, instead of its integration as a central concern. Clearly, the tasks of the museologist in this context comprise the so-called classical museum functions which have to be dealt with and treated in a well-balanced harmony (ROM 1976: 240; ICOM 1990: 16; AAM 1992). Among others, one duty is to make sure that the 'language' of object-oriented museum work becomes clear and understandable, and that it does not become the exclusive territory of museologists as sole 'owners' (De la Torre and Monreal 1982: 18).

Some museums have a document at their disposal which clearly states institutional goals and asks for clarity as to what, when, why, for whom, and by whom material culture is collected and exhibited. However, how all the costly and time-consuming museum work relates to the financing public is not usually reflected. It is usually only expressed in the naive and uninformed question as to whether or not an exhibition will be popular with the public, in other words whether enough paying patrons can be statistically proven. Strategic planning for the attainment of these goals, 'a policy, policy-statements to develop better, more effective professional categories than visitor-figures' (Hooper-Greenhill 1988: 230), has to be demanded for future planning. Such a theoretical framework must be seen as a counter-measure against sometimes overweight developments and pressures in the context of the collections and must develop the visitor services role of museums, especially in relation to the political decision-making representatives and bodies.

If 'communication' is truly the aim, it can only be achieved by active and genuine empathy with the public as partner, through continuous efforts and an institutionally reflected 'language'. The argument goes that it may not be possible to develop a generally valid set of rules, but that it is essential 'to develop a kind of exhibition tradition. Long-lasting institutions such as museums' (Neurath: p. 67) are needed for this, since with their help, 'improvisation will be replaced by method which allows more perfection' (Neurath: p. 71) and which will minimize any random staff idiosyncrasies.

The necessary clarity in this respect, as recognized by Otto Neurath and his collaborators, first in the goals and thereafter in the steps to be taken, needs the institutional concept, which prescribes binding guidelines. In his long article 'Museums of the future', Otto Neurath stated, 'The museums of the future should certainly not be as I would have them, but as the visitors and users would want them to be' adding the important clause which put this statement into context: 'if they knew what a museum is' (Neurath: p. 244). The 'transformer' or 'trustee' whom he wished for and who, in his view, is involved in all processes, representing the interests of the museum public and shaping the museum 'utterances' accordingly, has not yet become commonplace (Ames 1991: 55–6; Hooper-Greenhill 1991: 58–9).

Notes

All translations are by the author.

1 All quotations referenced as: (Neurath: pp.) are from: *Otto Neurath Band 3: Gesammelte bildpädagogische Schriften* ('Otto Neurath, Volume 3: Collected writings on visual education') ed. Rudolf Haller and Robin Kinross, Vienna: Verlag Hölder-Pichler-Tempsky, 1991.
2 In this chapter the International Council of Museums' definition of 'museum' is used, not only because it is the most widely accepted and internationally best known but also because it identifies the museum as a public service institution with a clear communicative function. It covers many different institutions, including, for example, conservation institutes, exhibition galleries, monuments and sites, botanical and zoological gardens, nature reserves and science centres. Of special importance, however, is the statement that a museum is 'in the service of society and of its development . . . [and carries out its activities] . . . for purposes of study, education and enjoyment' (International Council of Museums 1990: 3).
3 A first evaluative account of Otto Neurath's museum and exhibition work is in preparation as a Ph.D. dissertation by this author, at the Department of Museum Studies, University of Leicester.
4 Besides the collection of writings on visual education (see Note 1), further material used for this chapter – documents, writings, personal correspondence of Otto Neurath – is held at the Department of Typography and Graphic Communication, University of Reading, Great Britain.
5 Born in 1882 in Vienna, Otto Neurath studied physics, mathematics, history, political economy and philosophy in Vienna and Berlin. He was to have started a university career with Max Weber in Heidelberg, but was caught up in revolutionary action in 1919 in early days of Germany's Weimar Republic. He was imprisoned in Munich and after being released was not allowed back into the country.
   In Vienna, besides his work and involvement in the so-called Wiener Kreis (Vienna Circle) of philosophers, he took an active part in the workers' movement, in adult education, and in the 'Red Vienna' city housing programme. In this connection he founded the Social and Economic Museum in 1925. Otto Neurath, politically and racially persecuted, was not able to continue his work in Austria after 1934. He fled to the Netherlands, which he had to leave in 1940, this time for England, where he died in 1945.
6 The widest application of Neurath's work is found in pictorial signposting, as used in traffic signals in international airports, for example. A first study on Otto Neurath's

contribution to visual communication was completed in 1979 as an M.Phil. thesis by Robin Kinross (Kinross 1979).

7 This article, referring to semiotic aspects of Otto Neurath's museum and exhibition work, treats ISOTYPE as a methodological principle. It is not concerned with linguistic aspects of the pictorial statistics as, for example Karl Müller's paper, 'Neurath's theory of pictorial statistical representation' (K. H. Müller in Uebel 1991: 223–51).

8 Cf. the title of the recent film *Otto Neurath – the Unafflicted Thinker*, produced by Österreichischer Rundfunk, Vienna, 1990, and directed by Caro Wolm; or in the same vein: 'this man founded socialism with only a pencil at his disposal' (Brunngraber, in Stadler 1982: 3). This impression may have been based on Otto Neurath's unaltered optimism and his own 'will for hope' concerning fundamental changes and developments in society (Nemeth 1981: 94).

9 All the various definitions of 'museum' agree that the specific quality of the institution 'museum' which differentiates it from other educational or scientific institutions is the fact that all the diverse work basically revolves around authentic, original objects.

10 This image of the institution 'museum' is confirmed by many visitor studies and surveys (cf. ROM 1976: 87–8; Belcher 1991: 38; Merriman 1991: 60–8).

11 Co-operation with excellent modern artists as, for example, Gerd Arntz, responsible for the graphics at the Gesellschafts- und Wirtschaftsmuseum in Vienna, contacts with the avant-garde, with the Bauhaus in Dessau and with El Lissitzky, were decisive in the practical form-giving process of realizing Neurath's ideas (cf. Kinross 1991: ix–xii).

12 Starting from early research employing behaviouristic methods (e.g. Melton 1933) and questions of learning theories and psychological problems, museums in the USA have made progress in visit evaluation and evaluation of the relevance of exhibitions to visitors (cf. Screven 1974; Shettel 1973; Wolff and Tymitz 1979; Bitgood *et al.* 1989). In the 1970s a comparable tradition was started in Europe, but with a clearer orientation towards a socially critical approach (cf. in France: Bourdieu 1974; Bourdieu and Darbel 1966; Bourdieu 1984; Bourdieu and Darbel 1991; Barthes 1973; in Germany: Treinen 1981; in Austria: mainly at the institute of sociology, University of Vienna, cf. Majce 1982).

13 As Neurath was a prolific writer and advocate of his museum work, it is surprising how little direct influence is found in contemporary museum developments. Neurath's 1933 contribution to the German *Museumskunde*, for example, met with no obvious response (Neurath: pp. 197–206). But of course there were other people also interested in organizing museums and exhibitions as educational media; comparable, for example, is the work of Paul Otlet at the Palais Mondial in Brussels (Neurath: p. 244), or the museum design of Alfred Lichtwark in Hamburg (cf. Lichtwark 1908) and the work of Alexander Dorner in Hanover (Cauman 1958), but these writers take their starting points from existing object collections.

References

American Association of Museums (1992) *Excellence and Equity*, Washington, DC.

Ames, P. (1991) 'Measures of merit?', *Museum News* 70 (5) September/October, 55–6.

Barretto, M. Horta (1991) 'Museum language and exhibitions' speeches', unpublished paper delivered at the Annual Meeting 1991 of the ICOM International Council, Committee for Museology, Vevey.

Barthes, R. (1973) 'The great family of man', in *Mythologies*, St Albans: Paladin.

Belcher, M. (1991) *Exhibition in Museums*, Leicester, London and New York: Leicester University Press.

Bitgood, S., Roper, J. T. Jr and Bonefield, A. (eds) (1989) *Visitor Studies – 1988: Theory, Research and Practice*, Jacksonville, Ala: Center for Social Design.

Bourdieu, P. (1974) *Zur Soziologie der symbolischen Form*, Frankfurt/Main: Suhrkamp.

—— (1984) *Distinction*, London: Routledge & Kegan Paul.

Bourdieu, P. and Darbel, A. (1966) *L'Amour de l'art, les musées et leurs public*, Paris: Editions Minuit.

—— (1991) *The Love of Art. European Art Museums and Their Public*, London: Polity Press.

Bruner, J. (1990) *Acts of Meaning*, Cambridge, Mass.: Harvard University Press.

Cauman, S. (1958) *The Living Museum*, New York.

De la Torre, M. and Monreal, L. (1982) *Museums: an Investment for Development*, Paris: International Council of Museums, Unesco.

Dimaggio, P. and Useem, M. (1978) 'Social class and arts consumption: the origin and consequences of class differences in exposure to the arts in America', *Theory and Society* 5: 141–61.

Dvorak, J. (1982) 'Otto Neurath und die Volksbildung. Einheit der Wissenschaft, Materialismus und umfaßende Aufklärung', in F. Stadler (ed.) *Arbeiterbildung in der Zwischenkriegszeit. Otto Neurath – Gerd Arntz*, Munich and Vienna: Löcker Verlag.

—— (1991) 'Otto Neurath and adult education: unity of science, materialism and comprehensive enlightenment', in T. E. Uebel (ed.) *Rediscovering the Forgotten Vienna Circle*, Dordrecht, Boston and London: Kluwer Academic Publishers.

Heinisch, S. (1989) 'Museale Rekonstruktion von Geschichte', in Museumspädagogischer Dienst (eds) *Reproduzierbare Verhältnisse – Bericht Museumspädagogische Fachtagung*, Vienna and Dornbirn.

Hooper-Greenhill, E. (1988) 'Counting visitors who count', in R. Lumley (ed.) *The Museum Time-Machine: Putting Cultures on Display*, London: Routledge.

—— (1991) 'A new communication model for museums', in G. Kavanagh (ed.) *Museum Languages : Objects and Texts*, Leicester, London and New York: Leicester University Press.

International Council of Museums (ICOM) (1990) *Statutes. Code of Professional Ethics*, Paris.

Kavanagh, G. (ed.) (1991) *Museum Languages: Objects and Texts*, Leicester, London and New York: Leicester University Press.

Kinross, R. (1979) 'Otto Neurath's contribution to visual communication, 1925–1945: the history, graphic language and theory of Isotype', unpublished M.Phil. thesis, University of Reading.

—— (1982) 'Die Aufgabe der Transformation', in F. Stadler (ed.) *Arbeiterbildung in der Zwischenkriegszeit. Otto Neurath – Gerd Arntz*, Munich and Vienna: Löcker Verlag.

—— (1991) 'Einleitung', in Rudolf Haller and Robin Kinross (eds) *Otto Neurath, Gesammelte bildpädagogische Schriften Band 3*, Vienna: Verlag Hölder-Pichler-Tempsky.

Lichtwark, A. (1908) 'Über Museumsarchitektur', *Museumskunde* 25 (4): 270.

McManus, P. (1991) 'Making sense of exhibits', in G. Kavanagh (ed.) *Museum Languages: Objects and Texts*, Leicester, London and New York: Leicester University Press.

Majce, G. (1982) 'Kulturhistorische Großausstellungen; Wer kommt warum (nicht)?', in Verlag für Gesellschaftskritik (eds), *Kulturjahrbuch 1*, Vienna.

Melton, A. (1933) 'Studies of installation at the Pennsylvania Museum of Art', *Museum News*, 10 (15): 6–8.

Merriman, N. (1989) 'The social basis of museum and heritage visiting', in S. M. Pearce (ed.) *Museum Studies in Material Culture*, Leicester: Leicester University Press.

—— (1991) *Beyond the Glass Case. The Past, the Heritage and the Public in Britain*, Leicester, London and New York: Leicester University Press.

Mounin, G. (1985) *Semiotic Praxis: Studies in Pertinence and in the Means and Expression of Communication*, New York and London: Plenum Press.

Nemeth, E. (1981) 'Otto Neuraths Utopien – Der Wille zur Hoffnung', in F. Stadler (ed.) *Arbeiterbildung in der Zwischenkriegszeit: Otto Neurath – Gerd Arntz*, Munich and Vienna: Löcker Verlag.

Neurath, O. (1936/1980) *International Picture Language*, The Orthological Institute, London. *International Picture Language/Internationale Bildersprache* (A facsimile reprint of the English edition with a German translation by Marie Neurath), Department of Typography and Graphic Communication (ed.) Reading: University of Reading.

—— (1973), *Empiricism and Sociology*, ed. M. Neurath and R. S. Cohen, Dordrecht and Boston: D. Reidel Publishing Company.

—— (1981) *Gesammelte philosophische und methodologische Schriften*, ed. R. Haller and H. Rutte, 2 volumes, Vienna: Verlag Hölder-Pichler-Tempsky.

—— (1991) *Gesammelte bildpädagogische Schriften Band 3*, (ed.) R. Haller and R. Kinross, Vienna: Verlag Hölder-Pichler-Tempsky.

Pearce, S. M. (1987) 'Exhibiting material culture. Some thoughts on interpretation and legitimacy', *The International Journal of Museum Management and Curatorship* 6: 181–6.

—— (1991) 'Collecting reconsidered', in G. Kavanagh (ed.) *Museum Languages: Objects and Texts*, Leicester, London and New York: Leicester University Press.

Porter, G. (1991) 'Partial truths', in G. Kavanagh (ed.) *Museum Languages: Objects and Texts*, Leicester, London and New York: Leicester University Press.

Royal Ontario Museum (ROM) (1976) *Communicating with the Museum Visitor – Guidelines for Planning*, Toronto.

Screven, C. G. (1974) *The Measurement and Facilitation of Learning in the Museum Environment*, Washington, DC: Smithsonian Institution Press.

Shettel, H. H. (1973) 'Exhibit: art form or educational medium', *Museum News* 52: 33–41.

Stadler, F. (ed.) (1982) *Arbeiterbildung in der Zwischenkriegszeit: Otto Neurath – Gerd Arntz*, Munich and Vienna: Löcker Verlag.

Stadler, F. (1991) 'Enzyklopädie und Einheitswissenschaft – Bausteine eines wissenschaftlichen Weltbildes', *Erwachsenenbildung in Österreich* 42(1): 26–32.

—— (1991a) 'Otto Neurath: encyclopedist, adult educationalist and school reformer', in T. E. Uebel (ed.) *Rediscovering the Forgotten Vienna Circle*, Dordrecht, Boston and London: Kluwer Academic Publishers.

Stránský, Z. Z. (1991) 'The language of exhibitions', in ICOM-International Committee for Museology (ed.) *The Language of Exhibitions – Basic Papers, ICOFOM Study Series 19*, Symposium, Vevey, Switzerland.

Treinen, H. (1981) 'Das Museum als Massenmedium – Besucherstrukturen, Besucherinteresse und Museumsgestaltung', in ICOM Committee for Education and Cultural Action (ed.) *Museumspädagogik Museumsarchitektur für den Besucher – Hanover 1980*, Hanover.

Twyman, M. (1975) 'The significance of Isotype', in Department of Typography and Graphic Communication, University of Reading (ed.) *Graphic Communication through ISOTYPE*, Reading.

Uebel, Thomas E. (ed.) (1991) *Rediscovering the Forgotten Vienna Circle, Austrian Studies on Otto Neurath and the Vienna Circle*, Dordrecht, Boston and London: Kluwer Academic Publishers.

Umiker-Sebeok, J. (1991) 'Shaping identity in a children's museum: a sociosemiotic study of consumption experiences in a cultural gallery', unpublished paper for a conference at Indiana University.

Van Mensch, P. (1991) 'New directions in museology: New directions in museum education', in ICOM-CECA (ed.) *Education and Research, Education 12/13*, Paris, 63–4.

Winner, I. P. (1979) 'Ethnicity, modernity, and theory of culture text', in I. P. Winner and J. Umiker-Sebeok (eds) *Semiotics of Culture*, The Hague: Mouton Publishers, 103–47.

Winner, I. P. and Umiker-Sebeok, J. (eds) (1979) *Semiotics of Culture*, The Hague: Mouton Publishers.

Wolff, R. L. and Tymitz, B. C. (1979) '*Do Giraffes Ever Sit? A Study of Visitor Perception at the National Zoological Park*', Washington, DC: Smithsonian Institute.

6

Early museums and nineteenth-century media

Rosemary Flanders

In Britain in the nineteenth century the creation of a new museum culture, from South Kensington to Glasgow, inevitably gave rise to a new communicative relationship between museums and their civic audience.

The general public was gripped by the emergence of these centres of learning. Museum evolution was closely tied to the concept of civic pride and a motivated Victorian public was receptive to – indeed, at times positively craved – information about developments. One natural and key link between museums and their audience was newspaper and journal coverage, which spread the message of cultural expansion. Journals devoted much space to the fortunes of institutions, from learned editorials to gossipy titbits. Museums and art galleries were a 'media event', new, vibrant and challenging, and the role of newspapers in reporting this 'event' cannot be ignored. This communication process was not always uncritical: journalistic or editorial advice was offered on matters of taste and administrative prudence, sometimes to the point of waging a campaign. Museums became increasingly central to the debate about all things cultural and a public record of this role is to be found in the press. It is important to note that museums were actively participating in this means of communication, supplying up-to-date information for publication. Regular museum going by the general public was a relatively new pastime and the facilities and their visitor numbers were of great interest. Statistics featured large in the press and with astounding speed.

This chapter takes for granted a general understanding of the development of museum culture in the nineteenth century and of Victorian socio-cultural concepts and concentrates on the actual way in which issues concerned with museums and art galleries were reported in a cross-section of newspapers and journals. For the purposes of this study it is necessary to limit consideration to a small range of institutions and a small selection of newspapers. The latter includes two regional papers published in Liverpool – *The Daily Post* (first published in 1855) and *The Daily Courier* (in that format from 1863) – *The Times* (published in London from 1788) and three weekly journals – *The Literary Gazette and Journal of Belles Lettres, Science and Art* (from 1817; hereafter called *Lit. Gaz.*), *The Athenaeum Journal of Literature, Science and the Fine Arts* (from 1828; hereafter called *Athenaeum*) and *The Illustrated London News* (from 1842; hereafter called *ILN*).

Today, as one passes the silver casket presented to Andrew Barclay Walker, Mayor of Liverpool, to mark the benefaction of the art gallery in his name, it is easy to overlook the importance attached at that time to the public display of progress – the Victorian devotion to the commemoration of good works. Here is a visible symbol acknowledging a goodly deed and it was a natural choice for *The Illustrated London News* of 8 September 1877 to illustrate the said casket. The accompanying article notes:

> The ceremony of presenting to the Corporation of Liverpool, and opening for the public enjoyment, a new building erected there by Mr Andrew Barclay Walker, the Mayor of Liverpool, at his sole cost, for a gallery of fine art, took place on Thursday afternoon. It is nearly four years since Mr Walker, entering upon the first year of his mayorality [*sic*], announced this munificent gift to his fellow-townsmen. . . . The address of thanks to the Mayor, voted by the Corporation, in the name of the town of Liverpool, is inclosed [*sic*] in an ornamental casket, manufactured by Messrs Elkington and Co., the design of which includes a representation of the building.
>
> (*ILN*, 8 September 1877, 234)

In December 1873, *The Illustrated London News* had recorded 'the munificent act of liberality' and further noted that Walker's offer

> to provide at his own cost for the erection of a Gallery of Fine Arts, the probable outlay upon which is estimated at £20,000, is worthy of the position he holds in that great commercial town, and it will be cherished in the memory of future generations.
>
> (*ILN*, 20 December 1873, 606)

Perhaps Walker himself was influenced by an article in the *Athenaeum* six years earlier under the title 'Art and antiquities in Liverpool' which praised Joseph Mayer for giving his great collection to Liverpool rather than London, one option he had seriously considered:

> May this example of patriotism and a love of Art for its own sake induce other wealthy possessors to do likewise in their respective industrial centres. For the manufacturing taste of the country, if it would compete successfully with that of foreigners, needs the culture which the study of Art in collections of this character can alone bestow.
>
> (*Athenaeum*, 15 June 1867, 791)

Whatever the events leading up to it, coverage of the actual opening of the Walker Art Gallery was extensive, both in London and local papers. *The Illustrated London News* had the visual edge, by the nature of its devotion to sketches of people and events. It is of passing interest to note that a full right-hand page of views relating to the opening of the Gallery had opposite on the left-hand page battlefield sketches of the war between Russia and Turkey (*ILN*, 8 September 1877, 253). *The Illustrated London News* wrote

> In recognition of the generosity of the Mayor, it was resolved that the opening of the gallery should be accompanied by a demonstration as

widely representative as possible. With this view, a procession of artisans
employed in twenty different trades was organized. This assembled in the
Volunteer drill-ground ... and paraded the streets till the Townhall was
reached, when it was joined by a second procession, representing the
Town Council, and including Lord Derby and other invited guests. A
grand muster of volunteers also took place. The weather, though rain at
first threatened, proved fine and sunny. After passing along the leading
streets, all thickly lined with enthusiastic spectators, who repeatedly
cheered and waved their hats, the procession arrived at the Art Gallery ...
Lord Derby then declared the building open, amidst flourishes of trumpets
and loud and hearty cheering. The scene in front of the gallery was highly
imposing. Bands of volunteers were marching up and down into position
with drums beating; bodies of artisans, with colours flying and bands playing, were filing past in an apparently endless stream.

(*ILN*, 15 September 1877, 254)

The journal went on to note that in his opening address Lord Derby said he
'did not know that any man who had money to spend could do better than
follow the noble example of the Mayor of Liverpool; and he hoped it would be
followed in all the leading towns' (*ILN*, 15 September 1877, 254).

To say this was a 'media event' would be an understatement. It literally brought
Liverpool to a halt. Where the London papers gave generous and proud coverage to the regional success, it is in the Liverpool dailies one finds the nitty-gritty
of the gallery opening. *The Daily Courier* (4 September 1877) carried letters
to the editor about the poor sales of post-opening banquet tickets, the general
view being that individuals had preferred to put their donation towards the
testimonial gift to the Mayor. There was also a letter of complaint that the
Procession Committee had almost overlooked working men in the planned
event. The same day the front page of the *Courier* was covered with advertisements announcing the closure of shops and businesses and details of traffic
restrictions for the opening. Editorials supported debate on 'Art in Liverpool':
'It is not good that all artistic influence should be concentrated in the metropolis. This is an intellectual centralization which it is possible to carry too far,
and which is to be deprecated in the interests of the provinces' (*Daily Courier*,
6 September 1877, 4).

In the same edition, under the heading 'The public and the art gallery', a short
item stated emphatically that 'the people of Liverpool will be on their best
behaviour today' and called on all to act with decorum when allowed into the
new building, concluding 'we have no doubt the Art Gallery will be none the
worse for being visited by the multitude'.

The familiar high moral tone is further evident in the *Courier*'s editorial the
morning after the opening:

When half a million persons every year read books in the Library, and
when another half million persons annually inspect the refining ... treasures of the Museum, there can be no question that a multitude of visitors

will throng the Art Gallery to drink in the inspiration of genius and to be imbued with the lessons the paintings and marbles silently teach.

(*Daily Courier*, 17 September 1877, 4)

The message was definitely that a visit to the museum or gallery was good for your spiritual, moral and intellectual health. *The Daily Courier* had earlier noted the inspirational nature of the occasion on the muse of Mr John McLaughlin, local poet, 'whose poems are always characterised by taste, gentleness and melody'. His work 'The story of the Walker Art Gallery', the paper continues, 'is in six cantos, and contains local allusions to men and things' (*Daily Courier*, 1 September 1877, 7).

The final word on the Walker Art Gallery opening comes from the *Athenaeum* and lives up to the title of the column, 'Fine art gossip': 'One happy result may be anticipated by means of the Mayor's munificent gift, that is, a lasting cessation of the bickerings which have endured so long, and have so greatly retarded the progress of art in Liverpool' (*Athenaeum*, 15 September 1877, 344).

Not all local coverage of museum activities concentrated on 'grand events'. There was genuine debate about the shape and role of museum collections. *The Daily Post* had, in 1859, set out in an editorial about the imminent completion of the New Free Public Library and Museum, Liverpool, suggestions on display and collecting policy. The writer acknowledges that 'the two easiest things in the world are the giving of advice and the spending of other people's money' (*Daily Post*, 26 November 1859, 3), and goes on to do the former and suggest on the latter. The article continues with a vote of confidence perhaps enviable in today's climate:

> with regard to the plans suggested for the interior arrangement, the report of the curator, Mr T. J. Moore, as to the museum, is the most important. He speaks from an extensive practical knowledge, and his opinions, of course, are worthy of every attention.

The writer, acting as a voice on behalf of the public, does strike one warning note:

> There is one mistake . . . which seems to act like the wet blanket in most museums, intended to be of a popular character, – it is the crowding together [*sic*] species and objects in which there are shades of difference, but no striking contrasts. These things are valuable to students; but museums, unless of a special class, cannot hope to become so complete in every department; so that by seeking quantity rather than a rich and suggestive variety, they are occupying room and limiting the interest in other respects.

(*Daily Post*, 26 November 1859, 3)

In December 1859 *The Daily Post* carried over two issues a lengthy analysis entitled 'The town museum additional report' by the Reverend Hume. Considering all the official reports put forward, he calls for a wide-ranging collecting policy and rejection of a static museum centred on the natural history collection bequeathed to the town in 1851 by the Earl of Derby:

> In this town we seem to have invited and encouraged a mistake by our abuse of terms. The Public Museum or Town Museum is nowhere spoken of; the Derby Museum is extensively known. In Slater-street the title of the whole collection is 'Derby Museum' a part being put for the whole. . . . We must, therefore, hold any one excused who falls into the error of assuming that a general collection is a secondary matter; while we remark, in passing, how readily a verbal mistake may be converted into a permanent and almost incurable injury.
>
> (*Daily Post*, 2 December 1859, 7)

He continues in a subsequent issue of the newspaper: 'It must not be said of us by persons at a distance that Liverpool has only one idea, or that there is any lesson valuable to mankind which our rulers prohibit us from learning' (*Daily Post*, 3 December 1859, 3).

The public debate about the nature of museums, their format, collecting policy and priorities was aired, in this way, in both the regional and metropolitan press during these formative years.

News stories were not always about progress and success. As early as 1852 *The Literary Gazette* took up a cause, and wrote:

> We learn with much regret that the Ipswich Museum, to which we have at various times called attention, is in a very unprosperous condition, the Committee having intimated to the Town Corporation that unless it is adopted as a public institution . . . they must reluctantly yield up their trust and, we presume, sell off. . . . It was not to be expected that a comparatively small provincial town could keep up a museum establishment . . . without assistance from the borough rates, and we trust that no time will be lost in making this a municipal institution.
>
> (*Lit. Gaz.*, 4 December 1852, 893)

Press communication about advancement, however, was by far the order of the day. In 1857 *The Illustrated London News* concentrated attention on the regions, with news of the Lichfield Museum and Free Library:

> The laying of the foundation-stone of this institution was performed with great ceremony and éclat on Monday last. Lichfield was one of the first cities in England to avail itself of Mr Ewart's Act for the establishment of a museum and free library. A very large procession was formed at the Guildhall at noon, headed by the Mayor and Corporation, magistrates, dignitaries of the cathedral, and a large number of the citizens. The magnificent band of the King's Own Staffordshire Militia was in attendance, the inauguration being closed by the performance of the grand chorus from 'The Creation' by the band, and by cheers of the vast multitude.
>
> (*ILN*, 24 October 1857, 419)

It happens that on the same page as this article a note appears on the 'Close of the Art-Treasures Exhibition at Manchester'. The report appears to imply the regions' disappointment that the Queen was at neither the opening nor the closure of this great cultural event. As the Great Exhibition of 1851 in London, so the Exhibition of 1857 in Manchester has a valid place in consideration of the subject under review. Their importance in focusing debate about the nature of collections is clear, and both were consistently reported on in the capital and other centres.

The Times was one newspaper which regularly published visitor figures during the Manchester exhibition: 'On Thursday, the fashionable day, 4,262 persons entered with season tickets, and 3,553 on payment of half-a-crown each. Of these 2,537 arrived by railway' (*The Times*, 20 June 1857, 12). It is fascinating to note that these statistics appear in a national newspaper two days after the event. The channels of communication were indeed open. *The Times* gave constant updates of news from the Art Treasures Exhibition, which vied with the ongoing mutiny in the Indian Army for column space.

Despite the sour grapes about her timing, the Queen did visit the Manchester exhibition and *The Illustrated London News* gave much coverage to this in July 1857:

> The Queen and Royal Visitors were received enthusiastically by the Executive Committee, the Manchester and Salford Corporation, and nearly 70,000 visitors. The weather was showery, and interfered considerably with the comfort of the hundreds of thousands of outside spectators who lined every street through which the Royal cortège passed.
>
> (*ILN*, 11 July 1857, 42)

If this report confirms royal interest in a regional exhibition, the same year saw public display of the royal seal of approval on a great metropolitan museum initiative. The role of Victoria and especially Albert in the development of the various South Kensington projects is well known. It was unthinkable that this cultural achievement would not be opened in the presence of Their Majesties. The Court Circular in *The Times* on 22 June 1857 begins: 'The Queen and Prince Albert, accompanied by the Princess Royal, the Archduke Maximilian of Austria, and Prince Frederick William of Prussia, went in the evening to Brompton to be present at the opening of the South Kensington Museum' (*The Times*, 22 June 1857, 9).

There were fourteen others in her party and the event was reported in *The Illustrated London News*: 'the entire suite of buildings was lighted for the occasion, it being a recommendatory aim of the establishment of its national purpose, to afford evening exhibitions' (*ILN*, 27 June 1857, 636).

The following Tuesday evening the buildings were again lit and visited 'by a large assemblage, including a great number of persons distinguished in the various walks of art, science, literature, political and social economy; and the attendance of ladies gave unusual brilliancy to the soirée' (*ILN*, 27 June 1857, 636).

The museum as social as well as cultural venue is further confirmed in the *Athenaeum*'s column 'Our weekly gossip':

> The novelty of lighting up the New Museum at South Kensington is not restricted to nights for the public only, but the Committee of Council on Education have established a regulation by which any society for promoting science and art may have either the whole or only portions of the Museum, or the lecture theatre, lighted and open upon payment of a fee which covers the cost of the gas and the attendants. Accordingly, during the past week, the Fine Arts Club have held their June meeting in the Hall of Ornamental Art, and the Chemical Society a meeting in the Museum, which was entirely lighted for the purpose.
>
> (*Athenaeum*, 4 July 1857, 854)

The importance and drawing power of this new institution is not lost on the press. *The Illustrated London News* devoted much column space to the Educational Collections in the South Kensington Museum. The layout of the rooms and nature of their contents is covered with minute attention to detail:

> entering from the south end of the building, the first division is the mechanical – including hydraulics, pneumatics, hydro-statics etc. .... The two next recesses contain physical and chemical apparatus and diagrams. The first exhibits microscopes ... and the second a large collection of apparatus for galvanic, voltaic, and frictional electricity. ... In the next recess, geography and astronomy, is a large collection of maps and astronomical diagrams, some globes, and some orreries by Newton. In the nave, opposite, stands the Astronomer Royal's model of the Greenwich transit circle.
>
> (*ILN*, 4 July 1857, 5)

This same edition quoted visitor figures for the South Kensington Museum for the prior week: 14,000 persons viewed the collections which, from the paper's description, required a certain degree of sophistication of the spectator. The front page of the *Athenaeum* on 18 July confirmed the success of the museum with an advertisement placed by the administrators:

> To accommodate the crowds attending this Museum in the Evenings, the Museum will be open three Evenings a week till further notice. The admission will be *free* on Monday and Tuesday Evenings, and by payment of 6d on Wednesday Evenings. The hours are from 7 till 10.
>
> (*Athenaeum*, 18 July 1857, 893)

It would appear from this impressive visitor interest that reports of unease about the actual site of the new development were unfounded. *The Illustrated London News* carried, in August 1857, an article about the removal of the Architectural Museum from Westminster to the new museum complex at South Kensington. The article notes this move as 'a subject for congratulation among architectural students and the frequenters of the museum generally' but notes 'the change of location was at first greatly objected to' as 'a student has further to go' (*ILN*, 22 August 1857, 189).The article goes on:

> At the annual conversazione recently held at the museum, the chairman, the Earl de Grey, president of the [Architectural] society, successfully combated the objections which had been raised to the change of locality.

Mr George Gilbert Scott, the treasurer (to whose indefatigable exertions the success of the museum is mainly due), announced the additions which had been made to the collection. The determination of the committee to persevere in the task which they had undertaken in establishing the museum was being constantly strengthened by practical results; and any misgivings which might have been entertained as to the prudence of the removal of their museum had been entirely set at rest by a comparison of the number of visitors which had been increased twentyfold.

Referring to the South Kensington site as a whole, there was a certain wistful note struck in *The Illustrated London News*:

Upon no spot in the suburbs of the metropolis has the hand of improvement been busier than upon this locality. Thirty years ago the site of Brompton Church was a nursery-ground. . . . Adjoining were some villas, with charming grounds, the scene of many a gay fête; and beyond were the retreats of two or three favourite actors, who must have enjoyed this rural seclusion after the sickening glare of the theatre and the town. Brompton Park has been broken up, and groves and gardens have been cleared away, perchance for the site of some future art-town; but, with all the advantages of the change, one cannot help regretting the sweeping away of so many memorials of interesting persons, events, and circumstances, as were associated with this once rural spot.

(*ILN*, 27 June 1857, 636)

Here was progress at a price, but *what* progress . . . 'This Museum, containing Pictures, Sculpture, Architecture, Building Materials, Ornamental Art, Educational Collections, Patented Inventions and Products of the Animal, will be OPENED to the Public on Wednesday, the 24th June' (*Athenaeum*, 20 June 1857, 773). This front-page advertisement in the *Athenaeum* must have excited keen interest. In a quite separate advertisement further down the same page someone had thought to add, as an afterthought, 'The South Kensington Museum is situate near to Old Brompton Church.'

Visitor figures for 1856, noted in the *Athenaeum*, show that the public had no trouble in finding the British Museum. In all 361,714 visitors had been recorded in 1856, although this was somewhat of a decline from the 2,527,216 in 1851, the year of the Great Exhibition (*Athenaeum*, 27 June 1857, 828).

At almost the same moment as the South Kensington evening openings, *The Times* made editorial comment on the Friday night parliamentary debate wherein:

Sir J. Trelawny inquired why the British Museum should not be opened in the evening, so that working men might share more largely in the advantages of the institution. The Chancellor of the Exchequer replied, that the matter had been under consideration, and especially as regarded the reading-room, but that the danger arising from lights was too serious to be encountered – justifiable ground of objection, beyond all doubt.

(*The Times*, 22 June 1857, 8)

79

The *Athenaeum* was full of praise for the British Museum in the last months of 1857 on changes to physical access, with the opening of a previously unused staircase and the public display of more museum items in this new viewing area:

> We cannot but hail with pleasure this new proof of the new desire which has recently been so strikingly manifested by the Museum authorities to make the treasures of our great national storehouse more and more available for the instruction and gratification of the public.
>
> (*Athenaeum*, 7 November 1857, 1393)

A few weeks on the museum was further praised in the 'Fine-art gossip' column for adopting a 'richer mode' of display (*Athenaeum*, 26 December 1857, 1627). Only months earlier the paper had reported a charge that officers at the British Museum were open to fees. A *Times* correspondent had evidently asserted that he paid a fee to a museum officer for 'a courtesy denied to others more scrupulous than himself'. *The Athenaeum* called for him to prove the accusation and clear up the sorry scandal (*Athenaeum*, 29 August 1857, 1091).

The year 1852 had seen other 'scandal' in the press concerning the British Museum. *The Literary Gazette* had reported, in a heated article, on a senior appointment of a man thought not to be up to the job. The journal does not mince words:

> the choice made by the principal trustees, and virtually by the Archbishop of Canterbury, is likely to place the working of the present system in such a point of view before the country at large, as may materially hasten its downfall.
>
> (*Lit. Gaz.*, 17 January 1852, 64)

Later in the year, the *Gazette* was reporting another 'outrage' concerning the British Museum. The Louvre had requested permission to take casts of certain Greek statues in the British Museum and was refused. The issue appeared under 'Topics of the week' in the *Gazette*, which again was unreservedly forthright in its opinion:

> This lack of liberality and of courtesy is only another proof of the incompetency of the present managers of our great national institution to discharge their functions in a manner fitted to advance the interests of learning and science, or to sustain the honour of the country.
>
> (*Lit. Gaz.*, 25 September 1852, 734)

This example of the press as public watchdog was further in evidence from 1852 in the ongoing debate over the appropriate site for the National Gallery. Again *The Literary Gazette* called on the public press to 'direct attention to what is going on in a matter of so much national importance' (*Lit. Gaz.*, 30 October 1852, 812). Arguments throughout the newspapers were divided between backing the proposed move to South Kensington and leaving the collection where it was at Charing Cross. One letter to the editor of *The Times* in June 1857 put a rather convincing argument for St James's Palace as the site for the National Gallery: '[The Palace] being open in the rear to the St James's Park there is a free circulation of air, which is of such paramount importance to prevent the varnish of pictures from becoming chilled' (*The Times*, 22 June 1857, 9).

It is clear from the review in this chapter that in the nineteenth century museums were a powerful force at the forefront of cultural debate. The press was a forum for this debate on all levels, a record of public opinion as well as editorial preferences. The message clearly communicated in nineteenth-century newspapers and journals by, and on behalf of, museums and art galleries was that of a new cultural movement which aroused great passions and pride. It is clear that this message was being communicated to a receptive and appreciative audience.

Sources

The Athenaeum Journal of Literature, Science and the Fine Arts
The Daily Courier (Liverpool)
The Daily Post (Liverpool)
The Illustrated London News
The Literary Gazette and Journal of Belles Lettres, Science and Art
The Times

7

New technologies for museum communication

Anne Fahy

Museums have traditionally communicated collections-based and associated information through a variety of media, but the advent of new technologies now presents them with the opportunity to develop new ways of communication which allow the visitor to explore the richness and diversity of collections at their own pace and to their own requirements. Sophisticated computer-based applications now and in the future may completely change the ways in which museums communicate internally and with external bodies. This chapter will discuss the nature of museums' information and documentation systems and consider some of the technological options currently available in the commercial sector.

Information is an important commodity in the business world. In the United Kingdom alone, it has been estimated that nearly 8 million people were employed in information activities in the mid-1980s (Angell 1987). In 1989, the Confederation of Information Communication Industries stated, 'the British information industries represent, in terms of gross output, at least 7.5 per cent of the national product'. One estimate of the value of the electronic information services in 1988–9 was about £600 million with a forecast that this figure would have doubled by 1993 (Moore and Steele 1991).

Moore and Steele (1991) divide up the information sector into two discrete groups focusing on services and on technology. The services sector is made up of those which produce and disseminate information products, such as database services, library services, research services, books, journals or video. Museums can be placed quite firmly into this first category.

The information technology group produces technology-based goods and services, primarily telecommunications and computers. This chapter will not consider the technological aspects of the information sector, except where they have an impact upon museum practice.

In the public sector, there has been an increasing recognition of the importance of information goods to the empowerment of the community and also to the local economy. Moore and Steele (1991) include an estimate from the Society of Information Technology Managers that local authorities will invest over £880 million on information technology. Some local authorities have invested in the enhanced provision of information about the services they offer as a means of increasing public awareness of their activities and their quality. Museums would appear to be on the periphery of such developments, having focused upon the provision of the more traditional museum services, such as exhibitions, public programmes and publications. Although information has underpinned the work of museums, the provision of a wide range of information services has not been recognized as a major activity.

Museums and information

This chapter has concentrated upon information as a broad concept, but what information goods does the museum produce? The public perception of the museum is based upon the services provided by museums, which have tended to be object-based activities (exhibitions, public programmes based on the collections, catalogues). Such activities, which involve curatorial judgements about the 'importance' and 'value' of objects and the control of information given to the visitor, have, in the view of writers such as Ames (1985), disempowered visitors and left them as passive receivers of curatorial wisdom, rather than positively interacting with the museum environment. More recently, the museum profession has realized that museums are not and have never been objective in their world view, but reflect the socio-political ideologies of those who run and support them (Merriman 1991; Tawadros 1990).

Furthermore, objects have traditionally been placed at the heart of the museum by curators and this view finds expression in the definition of a museum produced by the Museums Association (Museums Association 1992). While it is true that objects are central to the museum, indeed they are what sets the museum apart from other leisure and educational attractions, the importance of the objects lies in their cultural or environmental significance. Axiomatic to this is the need to record the significance of the object in a manner which is usable and can be protected for the future. Taking this view further, MacDonald and Alsford (1991) question the primacy of the object, arguing that the real value of the museum is in the preservation not so much of the objects themselves, but of the information relating to them.

Information about an object is fleeting. It is easily lost if it is not captured at the time the object is acquired by the museum. Without it, it is difficult to make decisions and judgements about the importance of the object to the museum and cultural history. Indeed, most museums would now hesitate to collect objects without adequate documentation about their past history, while objects with limited information may be vulnerable to deaccessioning if the museum comes under pressure to rationalize collections.

From this information, the museum is able to establish title to the object, record the history of its manufacture, use and ownership, all of which will influence any decision relating to its acquisition and to its use within the museum collection.

After the initial stage of recording, other information may be kept as the result of physical and scientific examination of the object and of research – field-based, literature and comparative – which is incorporated into the museum's documentation system.

In addition to the traditional object-based information stored by museums, other categories of information may be retained. These include lists of the location and nature of archaeological sites, sites of environmental interest, industrial sites and places of local historical importance. Information of this nature may be used to enhance collections information, and can be used to plot changes in environments over time (Pettit 1991). Planning authorities consult museums and other organizations about the environmental impact of proposed land developments or the archaeological implications of new building projects. Museums, with their long-term aims and historic collections, are ideal repositories for this kind of information, particularly as it can feed back into existing collections information.

Museums also hold information about people – biographical information about artists, makers, users and local worthies, or about industrial and other processes. Museums will also record what has happened to objects once they have become part of the collections. This information is essential for the effective care of the collections and for future planning.

Increasingly, museums are faced with difficult decisions relating to collecting, as purchase grants diminish and stores fill. More museums are now limited in their collecting activities and, particularly in the area of social history, collecting has focused upon acquiring information rather than objects (Kenyon 1992).

Increased emphasis upon the cost elements of collecting has also meant that museums must justify the funds spent upon collecting and the use made of collections for the public benefit (Audit Commission 1991; Lord, Lord and Nicks 1989). One way of improving access to collections is by making information about collections more widely available. The ability of the museum to do this successfully depends upon the effectiveness of the documentation system and the extent of senior management commitment to develop the system and allow greater public access to the information and, thus, the collections.

The importance of museums' documentation systems is well documented in the literature and in professional circles. Yet documentation has been one of the most problematic areas of the museum's activities, as surveys carried out by the Museum Documentation Association and the Association for State and Local History have demonstrated (Roberts 1986; American Association for State and Local History 1991).

Within the United Kingdom, the National Registration Scheme has made an impact by setting minimum standards for documentation which must be met by all registered museums (Museums and Galleries Commission 1988).

One key area has been the introduction of automated documentation systems using the computer to store and access collections records. Automation presents distinct advantages for museums: information entered once can be used in many different ways; access to sensitive information can be limited through the creation of levels of access on a 'need to know' basis; back-up copies can be easily made (unlike manual systems); changes can be made automatically (unlike with manual systems when you have to change all the cards); many different indexes can be created which it would be time-consuming and cumbersome to do on a manual system; levels of validation and terminology control can be built in to the system; many users can access information through the creation of networks or through copies on single-user systems.

On an intellectual level, computers can provide curators with the opportunity to interrogate their collections' information in more innovative ways, making connections which could not have been made easily with a manual system. However, to get information out of the system, someone has to enter it into the computer. Museum computerization projects are major undertakings and require human, space and time resources on a large scale. For example, the Documentation Unit at the National Museums of Scotland has spent the past five years working full-time on the automation of their collection records (Burnett 1988).

Good project management is essential, along with a clear view of the ultimate aims of the documentation system. Once completed, automation should make the day-to-day business of the museum easier and faster (provided that the system is user-friendly). Through the creation of local area networks, it becomes possible for museums to share their collections information between departments, which may all use the same information in different ways.

Management information should be easier to access and should aid decision-making at all levels throughout the museum. Enquiries from members of the public and other groups should be answered faster and more thoroughly. In terms of exhibition development and research, the system should permit the databases to be searched in more diverse ways, allowing greater connectivity.

Decisions relating to data storage will depend upon how the system is to be used. The different storage media available for digital information should allow museums to package information in different formats to meet the requirements of their varying user-groups. Local area networks will allow more than one user to the same access stored in a central fileserver; stand-alone systems may make use of diskettes; optical reflective disks are capable of storing 55,000 still images or 36 minutes of moving video. They provide the means for storing images of objects and may assist in collections management and research by allowing access to images of light-sensitive material and fragile materials without the need to handle them physically. CD-ROM which was designed to store text and is capable of storing the equivalent of 150,000 pages of text is an ideal mass storage device for collections information and, in its extended form (CDXA), digital images and audio (Bayard-White 1991).

Each storage medium has its own advantages and disadvantages, and decisions must be made at managerial level as to the most appropriate format to suit the museum's existing and future information requirements.

Beyond museum documentation systems, computers are increasingly used to monitor and control environmental conditions, for commercial activities such as points of sale, for general administrative purposes, building management, desktop publishing, exhibition design and for project management (Brite 1988; Cassedy 1992; Eiteljorg 1991; Garfield 1992; Roth 1992). All of these applications have had a profound effect upon the ways in which museums work, in human and operational terms. They may require new skill sets from employees and the introduction of different modes of working with new contractual arrangements which have to be incorporated into the museum's own culture. Such developments will have their own implications in the management of change and how employees cope with it (Defries 1993).

The introduction of automated collections documentation systems and other computer-based applications should aid the communication channels within organizations, permitting the increased exchange of data between departments. However, looking beyond the walls of the museum, new technologies can also expand and enhance communication with other museums, the academic community and the public.

Museum information and user networks

Museums already have many different user groups: educational establishments such as schools and universities, planning authorities and other departments within central and local government, scholars, and other museum professionals requiring information for exhibition work or comparative material for research purposes. Each group may require the same information, packaged in slightly different ways and with varying layers of interpretation. At present, most communication is still carried out using more traditional formats such as publications, teachers' packs and correspondence.

Computers and computer-controlled technologies are ideal tools for this purpose, having the ability to store large amounts of information (within the museum context, we are always talking about large amounts of complex information), which can be accessed and manipulated in a variety of forms.

Linked to the wide range of technological options, developments in the field of telecommunications have also created opportunities for museums. The increasing use and importance of wide area networking has made the world much smaller, and accessible to anyone with a computer and a modem. The increased use of fibre optic cabling and the introduction of digital telecommunication systems will make wide area networks even more accessible as well as faster and cheaper. Existing networks such as JANET (Joint Academic Network) and the many international networks, such as INTERNET, already provide researchers with the means to read academic papers and respond to them much faster than the traditional route of publication in journals. The proposed SUPERJANET network will incorporate museums and include images.

Individuals in different cities and countries, using the international and national networks, are now able to exchange information much faster than had hitherto been possible. Some organizations are now accessing the international networks to spread information about their activities, using bulletin boards such as that on INTERNET. The Conservation Information Network is a good example of the potential of wide area networks within the museums community. An international network for the dissemination of information relating to conservation, it is a joint project between the Canadian Heritage Information Network, the Getty Conservation Institute, the Smithsonian, the Canadian Conservation Institute, ICOM, ICOMOS and ICRROM, providing access to databases containing information on conservation.

The most notable museums network is the Canadian Heritage Information Network (CHIN) which demonstrates what can be achieved if there is real commitment to taking advantage of the technology available and a willingness to share information between museums.

Established in 1972, the network acts as a national clearing-house for museums and collections information and as a focus for the development of standards and systems in support of information sharing. CHIN currently maintains over 100 separate institutional databases from museums in Canada. The databases are accessed through CHIN's mainframe computer in Ottawa using terminals or microcomputers. From the databases, the users have selected certain fields of non-confidential information which is shared through three national databases for the humanities, natural history and archaeological sites. The humanities and natural history databases are available to all CHIN clients, by other museums on request and by the general public through their local museum. It is intended that the same levels of access will be allowed to the archaeological sites database (Sutherland 1991).

In addition to the databases maintained directly by CHIN, collections information from other museums is also stored, with the long-term aim of creating a Canadian National Inventory which will serve as an index to museum collections across Canada.

Museums are faced with a unique opportunity to share information with each other and with the wider public, as a result of technological development. However, to reap the benefits, museums have to take into account a number of important factors.

First, museums must agree upon a common structure for their records which can be internationally understood, at least for a core group of information. Organizations such as CIDOC (the international documentation committee of ICOM), the Museum Documentation Association and the American Association of Museums are already working towards such an end (American Association for State and Local History 1991; Museum Documentation Association 1992). Second, they have to agree upon a protocol for the exchange of electronic information and this work is currently being carried out by CIMI, a working party consisting of representatives from a number of international organizations concerned with museums documentation (CIMI 1991).

Third, they must agree upon a common terminology for the description of objects. Some subject disciplines have made major advances in this area, notably the fine and decorative arts with the publication of the Getty-sponsored *Art and Architecture Thesaurus*. Originally published in Anglo-American, versions in other languages are now under consideration.

Finally, and perhaps most importantly, museums have to commit themselves to the principle of sharing information and to consider how shared information can be maximized. Linked to this final point is the question of quality of records and also the fact that many museums are still some distance away from having fully automated collections documentation. This may well be the most serious stumbling block to sharing information.

Future resolution of these issues should make it possible for museums to operate within a truly international network of ideas and information exchange. In particular, this should assist the research process, making it quicker and simpler to locate objects of interest and assess the information associated with it.

A researcher working in one country could retrieve information and images of objects in the collections of museums elsewhere without having to travel. The researcher can then use this information as the means to decide which objects should be examined in detail and filter out inappropriate material. In terms of collections care, the objects will be protected against handling and the possibility of damage.

Older collections which have been dismantled and dispersed may be reunited electronically and this may be of particular value to those states which have lost significant parts of their cultural heritage to museums in other countries. Where restitution of material is not possible, the country of origin would still have some access to material.

In a time when there is a thriving market in stolen cultural material, information about stolen objects can be transmitted worldwide via networks. This idea may be realized; the Canadian Heritage Information Network has proposed the formation of an international register of stolen works of art, which will combine text and images, whilst in the commercial world, the International Loss Register fulfils a similar function.

Increased use of electronic media may also make it easier for curators to adopt a more multidisciplinary approach to collections interpretation, as well as making museums more open and democratic through increased public access to non-sensitive information. Of course, curators will still have a responsibility to protect objects from potential sources of harm and deterioration and 'sensitive' information will, by its nature, remain restricted. However, the time has come for curators to build bridges and partnerships with other museums and the wider academic community. This point is particularly pertinent, given that museums are under increasing pressure to justify the relevance of themselves as institutions and of their collections, whilst museum-based research is increasingly suffering in the face of other priorities.

Enhanced communication networks between museums, universities and other research organizations will be of benefit to all groups and to the generation of new knowledge. The general public, who are the paymasters of museums, should also benefit from new technologies. In broad terms, museums must take advantage of the different mass storage media available to develop information products for the public. Already bibliographic databases and other sorts of information are available to the public in libraries in the form of CD-ROM and on-line access. This is an obvious area where museums could make collections catalogues available on a commercial basis. Indeed, some museums are already involved with the publication of collections information and images in an electronic format, such as the videodiscs produced by the Smithsonian Institution, the *World of the Vikings* videodisc published by York Archaeological Trust and the National Museum of Denmark and the proposal to make available the collections of the National Gallery, London, on line and CD-ROM.

New technologies and exhibitions

Within the context of the museum, what role have new technologies for enhanced communication, particularly in the sphere of exhibitions? Hooper-Greenhill (1991) identifies the provision of interactive experiences which provide the opportunity for further learning and deeper experiences as one way of improving exhibition management.

Interactive devices have an active and important role to play in the communication process. This is emphasized by research carried out by the British Audio Visual Society which showed that whilst we only remember 10 per cent of what we read, we remember 90 per cent of what we say and do (Bayard-White 1991).

There are many different types of interactive devices. Some are high-tech and others of a more simple nature. It is important to remember that there is a range of technological choices and that they will be influenced by the nature of the exhibition, the duration of the exhibition (whether the interactive can be reused) and the finance and expertise available within the organization.

Much has already been written about interactive multimedia in museums (for example, Freedman-Hardy 1991; Hoffos 1992; Prochnak 1990). For the purposes of this chapter the term 'multimedia' is used to describe 'a set of tools and technologies which can be used to create new applications or perhaps even enrich existing ones' (Prochnak 1990: 25) through the merging of sound, moving images, graphics, animation and computing, under the control of the user.

Interactive video technology has largely been used by the commercial market for the development of training packages and marketing, though an increasing number of museums have used the technology to introduce applications within exhibitions. There are two approaches to the use of interactive video: the use of commercially available (generic) videodiscs and custom-made programmes designed for a specific purpose.

Interactive video generally utilizes a microcomputer and monitor with a reflective optical disc. An input device will normally be used, and may be a keyboard, joystick, mouse or, most commonly in museums, a touch screen. The computer controls the interaction of still and moving images (stored on the videodisc) with text and graphics (stored on the computer) and allows the user to interact with the programme. The data on the videodisc are stored in analogue form, which is tied to the differing and incompatible broadcast standards between countries (Bayard-White 1991).

The National Museums on Merseyside have made use of two generic videodiscs in the Activity Room at the Natural History Resource Centre, Liverpool Museum. *British Garden Birds*, published by the BBC, provides moving film footage of birds, which is linked to the mounted specimens on display in the room. Visitors can select a bird and are then shown a short film clip, with a commentary by David Attenborough. A second videodisc contains footage of volcanoes.

The same approach has been adopted in the Collections Room using a generic videodisc to provide images of minerals which are linked to information from the collections database (Foster and Phillips 1988). Museums with limited financial resources for interactives of this nature may find the use of existing videodiscs a viable option as they need only find the funds to purchase the hardware and software to run and control the system, along with the cost of the videodisc. Compared to the cost of mastering a disk, which can be in excess of £45,000, these are low-cost options within the reach of many museums.

In the main, museums have tended to produce their own videodiscs which have a limited use beyond the purpose for which they were produced. Amongst the many interactive video discs now used in museums, the interactive videodisc at the Bank of England Museum uses the format of a game to test the visitor's knowledge about the work of the Bank of England and as a means of showing the visitor some of the Bank's high-security activities, such as the manufacturing of money (Hoffos 1992). The Imperial War Museum uses videodiscs to show original moving film footage, photographs and sound archives about the various campaigns of the Second World War within the exhibitions, bringing them greater immediacy and poignancy. They have also placed images of their art collection on to videodisc to allow visitors to view items which are not on display (Davidson 1990). At the Design Museum, visitors can design a toothbrush.

Digital storage of data will also permit museums to integrate text and images within one application. At one end of the spectrum there is the simple text-based application, typified by the personal comment application included in 'The art of the potter' exhibition at the National Museums and Galleries on Merseyside (Foster and Phillips 1988). Using two stand-alone BBC computers, the visitor is able to look up information about specific objects on display, and via two other databases, biographical details about the makers represented in the exhibition and a glossary of terms relating to ceramics. The system is simple and easy to use, though it is limited in its use as the hierarchical structure of the software does not readily permit users to browse within the system, according to their own interests.

Hypertext and hypermedia (which include images and sound) allow non-linear access to information, and provide the possibility for users to explore databases in ways more akin to human thought through the creation of links. Alsford (1991) sees hypermedia's 'main advantage over conventional databases in the way it allows users to access information and to learn about a subject – that is, as an interpretive tool' (Alsford 1991: 1). Within museums, hypertext-based applications have been developed at the National Museums of Scotland and the Design Museum, London. The National Museums of Scotland have developed a series of applications, specifically for inclusion in temporary and permanent exhibitions (Buchanan and Burnett 1990), while the Design Museum Collections Database allows the visitor to explore the collections in more detail through the provision of additional information about objects, makers and design movements.

The National Gallery's Micro Gallery utilizes specially written software to present a hypermedia interactive about the collections and related themes. Set apart from the main displays, the Micro Gallery uses Apple Macs to provide high-quality digital images of the collections linked to pages of art-historical information. Visitors are free to select from five menus, which are linked: the Paintings Catalogue, which provides a complete illustrated catalogue of the collections; the Artists Section which contains biographical information and a visual index of the National Gallery's holdings of works by each artist; a General Reference to allow visitors to find general information and explanations of art terms; a Pictures Types section, giving a classification of the collections by type and a Historical Atlas to present the collections by place of production and time period. Users are able to jump between the sections, allowing them to explore related entries in the other sections. A gallery tour is also provided, so that users can plot their movement around the gallery. A copy of the personalized tour is printed out free of charge and a Micro Gallery chargecard allows users to print out pages from the system, subject to copyright restrictions (National Gallery 1991).

The Micro Gallery is impressive in the quality and range of images. It is regarded as a facility to help visitors explore the collections through the provision of additional information, but the siting of the Micro Gallery apart from the collections means that it does not detract from the pictures, and visitors must make a conscious decision to visit it.

A more recent application has been the introduction of CD-I (Compact Disc Interactive) into museums, namely at the British Golf Museum in St Andrews. Using compact disc technology, CD-I can be regarded as an extension of the audio compact disk and the CD-ROM, in that one disk will incorporate text, sound and still and moving images. The British Golf CD-I takes the user along a journey through time to trace the origins of golf, and includes a game and quiz. CD-I presents a real commercial opportunity for museums as it has been specifically marketed for use in the home (Phillips Electronics UK Ltd 1992).

Indeed the British Golf Museum CD-I is commercially available for domestic users from Phillips.

DVI (Digital Video Interactive), on the other hand, has been developed for the professional computing market. DVI uses similar technology to CD-I, but unlike CD-I, it does not specify the hardware, operating system and storage media for multimedia delivery. DVI is a software-based process which provides compression and decompression of digital data on any IBM compatible computer, regardless of storage medium. Few museums as yet have used DVI, though Jersey Museum has a DVI system to store eight hours of film, information and images for its 'Story of Jersey' exhibition. The system gives the visitor access to other collections on Jersey and shows parts of the island's heritage which cannot be brought to the museum (Carter 1992).

It is clear that with the development of ever more sophisticated decompression and compression techniques for the storage of digital information, and as full-screen moving images can be stored digitally without problems of space, the museums sector will move towards digital storage. Digital storage has advantages over analogue in that it can be easily moved between networks, there already exist international standards for storage and in the long term it will be cheaper than analogue formats. Owing to their limited resources, museums tend not to be leaders in the developmental field. It is far more likely that they will adapt existing technologies as they become accepted in the commercial sector.

Issues

Four major issues stand out when considering the use of interactive multimedia in museum exhibitions. First, central to the success of each application is a well-defined concept of the aims and objectives of the application, how it interacts with the rest of the exhibition and a view of its target audience. Like any exhibition, the application will be doomed to failure if it does not take these factors into account at the planning stage (Mintz 1991). Their role should be considered during the initial planning of the exhibition to ensure that the finished interactive is appropriate for its purpose (McLean 1992). Failure to do so may condemn the interactive to the place of a gimmick with limited value to the overall aims of the exhibition.

The second issue is the importance of evaluation to measure the effectiveness of the application. Front-end, formative and summative evaluation are all essential to monitor the public reaction to interactives. The use of computerized inter-actives within museum displays is still relatively new and the introduction of each new application can provide important lessons for other museums. There is a need to publish this information to the museums community so that we can learn from each other's mistakes and successes. Taking into consideration the cost of many computer-driven interactives, dissemination of information may prevent others from making costly mistakes.

Traditional exhibition design already has well-documented evaluation techniques to measure the success of exhibits. Such methods are of equal value to computer-based applications and institutions such as the National Museums and Galleries on Merseyside, and Birmingham City Museums and Art Gallery have already used them to measure the success of interactives (Peirson Jones 1993).

Consideration must be given to the robustness of hardware and software. Touch-sensitive screens, whilst user-friendly, sometimes fail, or become dirty and insufficiently sensitive when pressed, causing failure and user frustration. Mice, keyboards, joysticks and other similar devices are also prone to failure, particularly if they are not strong enough to cope with heavy usage from enthusiastic visitors (Oker 1991). Malfunctioning interactives can frustrate the visitor, affecting the quality of the visit and leaving a poor impression of the museum.

Software must be user-friendly, yet provide the visitor with the freedom to explore information to a level appropriate to their needs (McLean 1992). Visitors must always be able to escape from applications and they must not feel threatened it. Curators devising interactives must 'guard against information overload' (Alsford 1991: 10) or run the risk of failing to achieve their aims. The success of the videodiscs at the Bank of England is partly due to the design of the system which echoes the commercially available quiz machines.

Finally, there is the question of curatorial control of information. Museum displays are the product of a selection process during which the curator decides what information and viewpoint will be conveyed to the visitor. Writers such as Ames (1985) have questioned the validity of the predominance of the curatorial viewpoint and have argued for a more democratic approach to museum information and objects, as well as to the general control of museums. Computerized interactives could, in theory, be an ideal tool for allowing the public access to information which has not been 'processed' by the curator. In practice, however, they perpetuate curatorial dominance and control, as it is time-consuming and costly to create applications which are broad and deep enough to allow the user to depart from curatorial judgements. In addition, there is the dilemma that all museum information has been subjected to curatorial influence as to the validity of some parts over others. Museum documentation, by its very nature, forces the curator to balance the 'value' of different types of information, and judgements are likely to be made according to criteria set by formal academic training in subject disciplines. Thus, whilst applications may allow users to explore information in a less structured way according to their own interests, the information they are exploring will have been 'processed' to meet accepted curatorial values.

The future

In the future, improved telecommunications systems, such as the conversion of all telephone exchanges from analogue to digital and the replacement of existing telephone lines with fibre optic wiring will make it easier to transmit very large amounts of digital information quickly between museums (Pring 1992).

This may precipitate an explosion in networking on a national and international level, which may make it easier for all museums to participate.

Satellite technology, well established in the commercial world, has had a limited impact upon museums. However, projects such as the Jason Project at the National Museums and Galleries on Merseyside, which took place on 1–13 March 1993 is a good example of what is possible, given the right resources. The project established a live satellite link with an underwater research project in the Bahia Bay. The aim of the project was to bring scientific enquiry live to children and adults and to tie it in with the other activities of the museum. On a less ambitious scale, the Monterey Bay Aquarium used microwave transmission to convey live pictures of underwater exploration in the Monterey Canyon back to an audience at the Aquarium (Connor 1991). Choice of project is crucial and careful thought must be given to ensure that the project is exciting enough to capture the imagination of the visitor as well as educate.

Within the context of multimedia, the commercial sector has been primarily concerned with bringing full-screen, full-motion moving images in a digital format (which has been difficult because of the large amounts of memory required). Increased sophistication in the development of compression and decompression techniques, probably through DVI, will soon make it possible for museums to use images but without the problems and cost of having to master disks.

Virtual reality may also become significant within the museum context. Through computer-created worlds, visitors may be able to experience through their senses exploration of the sea bed, a Roman colosseum or the museum stores (security considerations taken into account). Virtual reality may also become a useful planning tool for building projects and exhibition development, by allowing the project team to visualize the finished product before it has been built (Eiteljorg 1991; Tsichritzis and Gibbs 1991).

The technology is developing, and for museums the challenge will be harnessing the most appropriate technologies for their specific needs. Underpinning these exciting developments will be the need for accurate, scholarly information which can be converted for other uses. We must never lose sight of the fact that to communicate, we must have something to say, some information we want to transmit, and to do this, we need to return to the heart and lifeblood of the museum, the object and its associated information.

References

Alsford, S. (1991) 'Museums as hypermedia. Interactivity on a museum-wide scale', in D. Bearman (ed.) *Hypermedia and Interactivity in Museums: Proceedings of an International Conference*, Pittsburgh, Pa.: Archives & Museum Informatics, 1991, 7–16.

American Association for State and Local History (1991) *Documentation Practices in Historical Collections. A Report from the Common Agenda*, AASLH Technical Leaflet 176, Washington, DC.

Ames, M. (1985) 'De-schooling the museum: a proposal to increase public access to museums and their resources', *Museum* 145: 25–31.

Angell, C. (1987) *Information, New Technology and Manpower: The Impact of New Technology on the Demand for Information Specialists*, Library and Information Research Report No. 52, London: The British Library.

Audit Commission (1991) *The Road to Wigan Pier? Managing Local Authority Museums and Galleries*, London: HMSO.

Bayard-White, C. (1991) *Multimedia Notes*, London: Chrysalis Interactive Services.

Brite, R. (1988) 'Parlez-vous computer?', *Museum News*, July/August, 12–14.

Buchanan, S. and Burnett, J. (1990) 'Where do you come from?', *Museums Journal* 90(8): 28.

Burnett, J. (1988) 'Computerisation in the National Museums: some prospects', *Scottish Museum News*, Winter, 4–5.

Carter, J. (1992) 'Switching on to an island's history', *Museum Development*, October, 26–8.

Cassedy, S. (1992) 'The high-tech museum: exhibits', *Museum News* 71(4), July/August, 40–1.

CIMI (1991) *A Primer on CIMI*, Halifax: CIMI.

Connor, J. (1991) 'Promoting deeper interest in science', *Curator* 34(4): 245–60.

Davidson, E. (1990) 'Interactive videos at the Imperial War Museum', *Audiovisual Librarian* 16(2): 70–3.

Defries, J. (1993) 'Managing change with confidence', in D. A. Roberts (ed.) *Staff Development and Training: Meeting the Needs of Museum Documentation. Proceedings of an International Conference*, Cambridge: Museum Documentation Association.

Eiteljorg, H. (1991) 'Computer-assisted drafting and design. Programs for presenting architectural history and archaeology', in D. Bearman (ed.) *Hypermedia and Interactivity in Museums: Proceedings of an International Conference*, Pittsburgh, Pa.: Archives & Museum Informatics, 114–17.

Foster, R. and Phillips, P. (1988) 'New applications for computers in the National Museums and Galleries on Merseyside', in A. D. Roberts (ed.) *Collections Management for Museums*, Cambridge: Museum Documentation Association, 127–32.

Freedman-Hardy, G. (1991) 'Mulling interactive multimedia? Consider these three options', *Museum News*, September/October, 85–6.

Garfield, D. (1992) 'The high tech museum: conservation', *Museum News* 71(4), July/August, 38–9.

Hoffos, S. (1992) 'Multimedia in museums and galleries', *Museum Development*, October, 21–5.

Hooper-Greenhill, E. (1991) *Museum and Gallery Education*, Leicester: Leicester University Press.

Kenyon, J. (1992) *Collecting for the 21st Century*, Leeds: Yorkshire and Humberside Museums Council.

Lord, B., Lord, G. D. and Nicks, J. (1989) *The Cost of Collecting. Collection Management in UK Museums – a Report Commissioned by the Office of Arts and Libraries*, London: HMSO.

MacDonald, G. F. and Alsford, S. (1991) 'The museum as information utility', *Museum Management and Curatorship*, 10: 305–11.

MacDonald, S. (1990) 'Telling white lies', *Museums Journal* 90(9): 32–3.

McLean, K. (1992) 'Computers in exhibits: what are they good for?', *Curator* 35: 246–8.

Merriman, N. (1991) *Beyond the Glass Case. The Past, the Heritage and the Public in Britain*, Leicester: Leicester University Press.

Mintz, A. (1991) 'Moving target', *Museum News*, May–June, 65–8.

Moore, N. and Steele, J. (1991) *Information Intensive Britain. A Critical Analysis of the Policy Issues*, London: Policy Studies Institute.

Museums Association (1992) 'Code of practice for museum authorities', *Museum Yearbook*, London: Rhinegold Publishing.

Museums Documentation Association (1992) *Why We Need a Standard*, Cambridge: Museum Documentation Association.

Museums and Galleries Commission (1988) *Guidelines for a Registration Scheme for Museums in the United Kindgom*, London: Museums and Galleries Commission.

National Gallery(1991) *Micro Gallery Press Release*, London: National Gallery.

Oker, J. (1991) 'Reliability of interactive computer exhibits or, why doesn't this @$!!$& thing work?', in D. Bearman (ed.) *Hypermedia and Interactivity in Museums: Proceedings of an International Conference*, Pittsburgh, Pa.: Archives & Museum Informatics.

Peirson Jones, J. (ed.) (1993) *Gallery 33. A Visitor Study*. Birmingham: Birmingham Museums & Art Gallery.

Pettit, C. (1991) 'Putting "bloody mice" to good use', *Museums Journal* 9(8): 25–31.

Phillips Electronics UK Ltd (1992) *Introducing CD-I*, Suffolk: Phillips.

Pring, I. (1992) 'Notes on the major platforms', in Arts Council, *Very Spaghetti. The Potential of Interactive Multimedia in Art Galleries*, London: Arts Council.

Prochnak, M. (1990) 'Multimedia is the message', *Museums Journal* 90(8): 25–7.

Roberts, D. A. (ed.) (1986) *The State of Documentation in Non-National Museums in Southeast England*, MDA Occasional Paper No. 9, Cambridge: Museum Documentation Association.

Roth, E. (1992) 'The high-tech museum: security and information management', *Museum News* 71(4), July/August: 42–7.

Sutherland, I. (1991) 'CHIN: a computerized information resource for Canadian Museums', *History News* 46(4): 16–18.

Tawadros, G. (1990) 'Is the past a foreign country?', *Museums Journal*, 90(9): 30–1.

Tsichritzis, D. and Gibbs, S. (1991) 'Virtual museums and virtual realities', in D. Bearman (ed.) *Hypermedia and Interactivity in Museums: Proceedings of an International Conference*, Pittsburgh, Pa.: Archives & Museum Informatics.

8

Education, sunflowers and the new vulgarity in art museums

Sanford Sivitz Shaman

When Van Gogh's *Sunflowers* was auctioned in April 1987 to a Japanese industrialist for $39,900,000 fuel was added to a growing concern that museums were being shut out of the art market. The prices fetched for works by Mantegna, Rembrandt, Manet, Turner and more recently Van Gogh have increasingly placed masterpieces further out of the reach of most museums. Three months after the sale of *Sunflowers* an anonymous telephone bidder acquired Van Gogh's *Bridge of Trinquetaille* for $20,200,000. Then in November 1987, John Payson retracted his longstanding 'permanent loan' of Van Gogh's *Irises* to the Joan Whitney Payson Memorial Art Gallery at Maine's Westbrooke College, to auction the painting for a staggering $53,900,000. Yet another Van Gogh, *Portrait of Adeline Ravoux*, completed what Van Gogh specialist Carol Zemel called the 'Quadruple Crown' (Zemel 1988: 88), when it fetched $13,750,000 on Christie's auction block. Three years later, and still expanding, the 'Crown' claimed yet another prize when *Portrait of Dr Gachet* was removed from permanent loan to the Metropolitan and auctioned at Christie's for $82,500,000.

Redefining the cliché, astronomical, these figures prompted Met Director Philippe de Montebello to comment that he 'felt like a fossil awakened from another era' (Philippe de Montebello quoted in Zemel 1988: 88). Noting that, 'Gone are the days when the Metropolitan Museum could bring home a Rembrandt ... for $2,300,000,' Zemel contended in her *Art in America* article that 'the purchasing power of the new collectors ... virtually eliminates museums (save the Getty) as players in this game' (Zemel 1988: 88). Precisely the same sentiments were expressed by *Time* Magazine's art critic Robert Hughes. Following the *Sunflowers* sale, Hughes characterized 'the multi-million dollar marvel' as 'commonplace' in today's art market, as he expressed what is a growing concern that private collectors and speculators are pushing museums out of it. Hughes fears that 'no museum in the world can compete with the private sector for paintings like *Sunflowers*' (Hughes 1987: 46).

To be sure $82,500,000, $39,900,00, $20,000,000 and even $13,750,000 are hefty sums for any muscum. Such figures are more appropriate as the bottom line of a budget for a new building than the cost of a single acquisition. According to Zemel, 'the $3,000,000 commission paid on *Sunflowers* alone exceeded the Met's 1987 purchase budget' (Zemel 1988: 92). In spite of what this could mean to the fate of masterpieces for research, study and public appreciation, as long as there are buyers who are willing to pay, auction houses will always welcome the highest bid. Further, according to some observers, among those in the bidding are collectors 'intent on buying a price tag'. *Barron's*, for example, reported just prior to the sale of the *Bridge of Trinquetaille*, that 'auctioneers say, when an object or category of art has crossed the million dollar barrier it becomes all the more popular.' Describing a Van Gogh as 'money mounted on the wall', Maggie Mahar of *Barron's* observed that some collectors pay unprecedented prices simply 'to relish the role of record breaker at a public auction' (Mahar 1987: 6; Shaman 1987: 13; Shaman and Prakash 1989: 6).

While soaring price tags increase interest in art, Van Gogh's paintings metamorphose into 'money mounted on the wall', and some collectors aspire to the role of record breakers, art museums seem to be left behind in the dust. Consider, for example, Zemel's commentary on John Payson's decision to retract his loan of *Irises* from the Joan Whitney Payson Memorial Art Gallery in order to place the painting on the auction block:

> The rewards and punishments of this kind of art marketing were felt most keenly with the *Irises* sale. The Joan Whitney Payson Memorial Art Gallery at Westbrooke College lost what art critic Edgar Allen Beem called 'the only world-class painting in the entire state of Maine.'
> ... [John] Payson chose, moreover, to liquidate an asset already provisionally installed in the public domain. No matter how much the college gallery will receive, the loss to the state and its public is not recuperable.
>
> (Zemel 1988: 92)

Irises had been purchased by Australian businessman Alan Bond, who ultimately was unable to pay the loan Sotheby's made to him on the $53,900,000. As a result the painting has come to hang in the Getty Museum; but at the time Zemel wrote her article, out of the four Van Goghs comprising the 'Quadruple Crown', only the whereabouts of *Sunflowers* was known. She also reported that Ronald de Leeuw, director of Amsterdam's Rijksmuseum, expressed concern regarding soaring insurance values and premiums and their effect upon loans to the 1990 Van Gogh retrospective (Zemel 1988: 88–93, 151). Today we know that many of these fears have been overcome. Nevertheless it is clear that auctioning works from public collections can potentially make them obscure from research, study and public appreciation.

It may seem that it is the museums and their audiences who are the victims of this 'new vulgarity' (Hughes 1987: 46), but perhaps there is even a deeper wound. The fine collections that our museums have built are likely to remain intact, and are likely to continue to grow. (Many collectors still adhere to the ethic that they are not 'owners' of a work of art, but rather temporary 'caretakers' with a responsibility to promote preservation and study. Such collectors are generally very interested in the welfare of art museums, and basically are to be thanked for the development of public collections and exhibitions.) Moreover, in spite of the art market ripple effect that could result from the drama at the auction block, museums will continue to discover 'affordable' new artists and re-evaluate and rediscover 'affordable' forgotten artists and art forms. It is in fact this phenomenon that renders the art world a vibrant changing and growing community where research and scholarship stimulate new exhibitions and new collections.

I would contend that the wound inflicted by the 'new vulgarity' goes well beyond our concern for increasing public collections to the very core of the educational role of the art museum. In a world where 35,000 people die each day as a consequence of hunger (twenty-four people – eighteen of them children – die every minute as a consequence of hunger), seven-figure price tags for paintings by an artist who himself was no stranger to hunger is not only vulgar and deca-dent, but is demonstrative of an art world out of touch with the rest of the world, and out of touch with the very art that gives it substance (Shaman 1987: 13). As critic Douglas Davis wrote in *Art in America*:

> Art has never been more vulgar than now . . . because life has never been so vulgar, so poised on the edge of self-destruction. *And this is precisely why the price of art has no end: vulgarity whets the desire for its opposite.* We bid for art, more of us than ever before, to escape real life. Failing time and again, we keep on paying, in pursuit of a goal that is clearly beyond price.
>
> (Davis 1988: 23)

But how are our public art institutions – art museums – responding to this situation that Robert Hughes has described as 'demeaning to the public sense of art?' (Hughes 1987: 47). In her book, *Selling Culture*, Debora Silverman notes that art museums, as public educational institutions, should be educating the public 'to put the moral brake on conspicuous consumption' (Silverman 1986: 18; Shaman 1987: 13; Shaman and Prakash 1989: 6). But as Silverman and others point out, while the auction houses and wallet-flexing fat cats set new records in spending, museums seem to be dancing as fast as they can to keep in step with the new consumerist aesthetic (Shaman 1987: 13).

Reinforcing this point of view, Jan Adlmann, director of the Vassar College Art Gallery, addressed the Association of College and University Museums and Gal-leries shortly after the *Sunflowers* sale in June 1987. As one of the speakers on a panel entitled 'Balancing the ivory tower and discotheque', Adlmann cited the auctioning of *Sunflowers* and similar sales as a major factor contributing to the public's present 'perception of art as a commodity.' He painted a picture of a growing materialism which has manifested itself in consumerist attitudes preva-lent in our art museums (Shaman 1987: 15).

Adlmann and Silverman's assertions give credence to the argument that art museums have played just as large a role in the development of a consumerist aesthetic as the highrollers and auction houses. Critic Douglas Davis goes a step further and charges that museums have been key in the very situation that is forcing them out of the art market:

> the art-marketing system now in place is anchored in the center, not the margins of society, and therefore is secure. The buyers are in the first

place trained by an educational system that seems as permanent, in a postindustrial society, as agriculture – or as the stars. Their product is nourished by the same system, and validated by an institution unknown in the seventeenth century and certainly not common until this century: the art museum. Through exhibitions and publications, the museum provides food stamps, in effect, for a voracious marketplace that splits and diversifies as it expands, adding stars and schools more rapidly than it drops or ignores old ones. Collectors beget collectors who beget, indeed often invent, new art movements to buy.

(Davis 1988: 22)

These critics suggest that the consumerist aesthetic is winning out over conscientious education in our museums. Moreover, many of our major museums have in recent decades embraced the role of entertainers through proliferation of the blockbuster, which has come to assume a profile closer to that of a well-marketed broadway musical than that of a forum for educational activity and spiritual refreshment. But this phenomenon seems to be the result of a broader societal symptom closely connected to a distressing emphasis upon consumerism. People consume for entertainment. And the art museum (perhaps inevitably) is becoming part of the complex and highly sophisticated – albeit overexaggerated – system of consumerism that surrounds us. Douglas Davis writes:

The destiny, then, of the museum in our time is contemporaneity, extended far beyond the boundaries even of the prolix fine-art marketing system. . . . Not even that system, with its roots in the collector–gallery–auction circle, can provide a stream of artists and events large enough to slake the burgeoning appetite of a world now swollen with middle-class consumers. We are becoming a society committed to collecting and historicizing ourselves day in, day out.

(Davis 1988: 23)

These conditions are not isolated. Nor is their meaning only for the art world and the museum world. But rather such conditions are reflective of a greater societal situation. To illustrate this, one need only compare the above passage from an essay by Douglas Davis, *Newsweek*'s architecture critic, to a passage from a paper by the great 'authority of rabbinic learning', Joseph Dov Soloveitchik, who in 1965 described our society as a:

society which is technically minded, self-centered, and self-loving, almost in a sickly narcissistic fashion, scoring honor upon honor, piling up victory on victory, reaching for the distant galaxies, and seeing in the here-and-now sensible world the only manifestation of being.

(Soloveitchik 1977: 201)

Among the ways in which we narcissistically 'score honor upon honor' is our obsession with 'historicizing ourselves'. To see this obsession in action one needs only to observe the blockbuster exhibition. Highly controversial among museum professionals, the blockbuster is viewed by some as the great achievement of today's museums. Albert Elsen of Stanford University, for example, contends that blockbusters represent a 'dramatic' method for museums that meet their 'obligation to educate the public and justify taxpayer support'. Asserting that blockbusters have greater outreach and public relations capabilities than other museum programming, he refers to the blockbuster as a 'quintessentially democratic museum undertaking'. Elsen asks, 'Is it not the goal of the big exhibition to make important, if esoteric, knowledge intelligible, and to make beautiful and significant art accessible in a meaningful context?' And he concludes that the blockbuster 'is our most dramatic gesture of thanks to the same public that pays for our enterprise' (Elsen 1986: 26–7; Prakash and Shaman 1988: 22).

There is, however, another aspect of the blockbuster. Superproductions designed to attract millions, the commercialized, sensationalized blockbusters can be seen as having played a key role in furthering the public's 'perception of art as a commodity'. Designed to be consumed by the public, these mega-exhibitions with their mobbed galleries leave little room for getting much of a glimpse of a work of art let alone contemplation and spiritual refreshment. As Jan Adlmann put it:

> Anyone who has spent ten minutes in stunned silence before the Apollo Belvedere (as I did in the Vatican show), only to find it once again on view a hundred-fold in the museum shop – in miniature, in soapstone, and 'coffee table size' – must ask themselves, 'ivory tower or discotheque?' Indeed, anyone who has fought their way through a typical Met blockbuster and then discovered that, upon being bodily propelled from the show, they are plunged into a boutique of replicas, 'Madonna and Child' jig-saw puzzles, poster and catalogues, must ask themselves – 'ivory tower or discotheque?'[1]

But is there a relationship between the blockbuster and soaring prices of the art market? Zemel believes there is. She writes: 'Payson's profits were doubtless enhanced by the *Irises*' featured position at the entrance to the 1896 "Van Gogh in Saint-Remy and Auvers" exhibition at the Metropolitan, and its reproduction on a popular poster for the show' (Zemel 1988: 92,151). It is an accepted fact that exhibitions . . . and better yet reproducing a work in an exhibition catalogue . . . and better yet reproducing it in colour . . . and better yet the right exhibition at the right museum . . . raise the value of a work of art. This is clearly a motivating factor for many collectors who lend works to travelling exhibitions. Indeed were it not for this fact of life, museums would have difficulty borrowing works of art and organizing loan exhibitions. But perhaps a question worthy of exploration is whether in our zeal to present greater and greater exhibitions with thicker and thicker publications we may not in the end cut ourselves off from the very collections which are the lifeblood of a museum.

Zemel's observation, 'There is little doubt that . . . the pictures' exhibition record and the degree to which they were seen often enough to become "classics" within Van Gogh's oeuvre substantially increased both the *Sunflowers*' and the *Irises*' value' (Zemel 1988: 92), conjures up a situation not unlike what it takes to make a Top Forty hit. This places museums, their exhibitions, exhibition catalogues and the whole public relations network in a position akin to the music industry's commercial radio station, the juke box, and MTV video. Let us hope that 'payola' never comes to art museums.

Or has it? Debora Silverman's book *Selling Culture*, makes one wonder, as she reveals how the Met's Costume Institute, headed by Diana Vreeland, aligned its exhibitions with vast international sales campaigns at Bloomingdales to promote a new consumerist elite in line with prevailing consumerist attitudes. *Selling Culture* further describes how the Costume Institute made a shift from 'cultural education' to 'commercial manipulation', using exhibitions like 'Man and the Horse' as elaborate advertisements for Ralph Lauren/Polo, and 'Chinese Imperial Robes' for promoting Yves Saint Laurent's perfume, Opium (Silverman 1986: 18; Prakash and Shaman 1988: 18–20; Shaman 1987: 14; Shaman and Prakash 1989: 6).

With the growing emphasis upon consumerism, the public is systematically taught to view art 'as a commodity', and this commodification of art is ironically symbolized by the Van Gogh sales. As evidence of this we need only turn to such references as 'money mounted on the wall' (Mahar 1987: 6) and *Time*'s reporting the sale of *The Bridge of Trinquetaille* by announcing that 'Van Gogh is still hot', appropriately not under 'Art', but 'Business' ('Van Gogh is still hot' 1987: 51; Shaman 1987: 13). It seems that Theodore F. Wolff of *The Christian Science Monitor* was justified in fearing that after the sale of *Irises*, the public importance of Van Gogh 'will henceforth hinge primarily on that $53.9 million figure. Little else will matter.' 'Sadly,' as Wolff goes on to say, 'that is bitterly ironic, for such blatant commercialism of art is the exact opposite of everything Van Gogh lived and worked for' (Wolff 1987: 23; Shaman and Prakash 1989: 6).

An explanation for this 'blatant commercialism' in the world of art is offered by Dr Ravi Batra. In his book *The Great Depression of 1990*, Batra explains economic phenomena according to P. R. Sarkar's law of social cycles which asserts that society is cyclically dominated by one of four social classes: labourers, warriors, intellectuals or acquisitors. According to Batra, currently we are in an era of acquisitors, whose promotion of commercialism some critics see in the art world as well as in our museums. Regarding the commercialization of art, Batra writes:

> One distressing feature of the epoch of the acquisitor is that the acquisitive mentality eventually infects all sections of society. Attitudes of the ruling class do not spread so much, do not become so pervasive, in other eras; but in the age dominated by the wealthy, other groups ultimately submit to the allure of money. Everything is commercialized as a result – music, art, literature [and] sports.
>
> (Batra 1987: 47; Shaman and Prakash 1989: 6)

This commercialization underscores the necessity to remind ourselves that art museums are public educational institutions, and their emphasis should be upon meaningful educational activities for the public. The question asked by Dr Alice

Carnes, Director of the Willamette Science Center, has pertinence for all museums and cultural institutions: 'If an institution sells science, promotes technology and solicits the support and good will of industry with no hint of question or critique, in what sense is that institution scientific, or a museum?' (Carnes 1986: 30; Shaman 1987: 14). Likewise, art museums must continually ask themselves in what sense they contribute to the art world and in what sense they are museums? In other words, as public educational institutions, art museums have an obligation to assess constantly how effectively, ethically and morally they assume a role among that world populated by artists, scholars, art dealers and collectors. This must be balanced with constant self-assessment as to how effectively, ethically and morally art museums teach the public about art and art issues.

In 1878, while working as a lay evangelist in the south of Belgium, Vincent Van Gogh was so moved by the poverty around him that he gave away his clothes and other belongings. How bitterly ironic it is that Christie's celebrated the sale of his *Sunflowers* for $39,900,000 with 'a savory cake in the form of *Sunflowers*, the frame made of flaky pastry, the colors rendered "impasto furioso" in various hues of saffron-tinted cream cheese, the green bits done in spinach, and detail added with studdings of seed' (Hughes 1987: 46). It is hard to believe that an artist like Van Gogh could ever approve of the realization of his paintings as objects of extreme conspicuous consumption. To say that the sales of five Van Gogh canvases for a collective $210,250,000 is a dramatic departure from the intent and values of the artist is a gross understatement. The sales, and the excessiveness they represent, render these paintings simply objects of competition for acquirers. The sensitivity, the struggle and the compassion of Van Gogh have been deadened by a distorted price tag, which is what has captured our attention and our imagination. In the words of Robert Hughes, '*Sunflowers* was once alive, and now it is dead – as dead as bullion' (Hughes 1987: 47).

If it is not the responsibility of museums to preserve the soul as well as the body of art, then, as Alice Carnes might ask, in what sense are art museums truly devoted to art, and in what sense are they museums (Shaman 1987: 14)? A topic that suggests extensive debate is whether or not art museums have the power, the ability and the courage to reverse the situation that motivated Hughes to write in *Time*: 'The big auction as transformed by Sotheby's and Christie's, is now the natural home of all that is most demeaning to the public sense of art' (Hughes 1987: 47). But even if art museums are incapable of having any impact upon their unfortunate situation, clearly the time has come for those of us who work in art museums to look deep within ourselves to see how much we are part of the consumerist aesthetic.

Note

1 Quoted from Jan Adlmann's comments during a panel discussion entitled 'Balancing the ivory tower and the discotheque', at the 1987 annual conference of the Association of College and University Museums and Galleries, held at the University of California, Berkeley. (See Shaman 1987: 13, 14.)

References

Batra, R. (1987) *The Great Depression of 1990*, New York: Simon & Schuster.

Carnes, A. (1986) 'Showplace playground, or forum? Choice point for science museums', *Museum News* 64(4): 29–35.

Davis, D. (1988) 'The billion dollar picture?', *Art in America* 76(7): 21–3.

Elsen, A. (1986) 'Assessing the pros and cons', *Art in America* 74(6): 24–7.

Hughes, R. (1987) 'Of Vincent and Eanum Pig', *Time* 129, 15: 46–7.

Mahar, M. (1987) 'What price art?', *Barron's* 67(26): 6–7, 29–32.

Prakash, M. S. and Shaman, S. S. (1988) 'Museum programs: public escapism or education for public responsibility?', *Art Education* 41(4): 16–24, 41–3.

Shaman, S. S. (1987) 'Speakeasy, in step with the new vulgarity', *New Art Examiner* 15(4): 13–14.

Shaman, S. S. and Prakash, M. S. (1989) 'The duty of art: museums and social consciousness', *The Journal of Museum Education* 14(1): 5–8.

Silverman, D. (1986) *Selling Culture*, New York: Pantheon.

Soloveitchik, J. D. (1977) 'The lonely man of faith', in N. Glatzer (ed.) *Modern Jewish Thought*, New York: Schocken.

'Van Gogh is Still Hot', *Time* 130(2), 1987: 51.

Wolff, T. F. (1987) 'The art of selling a $53.9 million van Gogh', *Christian Science Monitor* 80(3): 23.

Zemel, C. (1988) 'What become a legend most', *Art in America* 76(7): 88–93, 151.

Part 2

Communication in action

9

Changing media, changing messages

Mike Wallace

Changing media

Museum professionals are certainly aware that as we creep toward the twenty-first century, people, particularly children, are increasingly media savvy. But I wonder if curators have fully grappled with the future consequences for their institutions. As today's tots will be tomorrow's visitors, it's worth a quick assessment of the possible impact of growing up in an electronic era on historical sensibilities. Experiences will of course differ according to country, class, race, culture and gender, so I will keep my examples close to home.

My granddaughter Khendum experienced her first postmodern confusion the other day. Her father had videocammed her and her mother exchanging coos. When my wife and I came to visit, he played back the tape for the assembled family. Six-month-old Khendum's eyes shuttled back and forth in puzzlement between her real and her simulated mummy. She also contemplated her instant-replay self with intermittent fascination and discombobulation. The stack of videotapes chronicling her life will no doubt grow as tall as she does (as once my parents inserted countless Brownie shots of me into leatherette black-paper albums). Should Khendum later edit her tapes into a video diary, or incorporate them into an autobiographical school 'paper' (perhaps using software already available for helping to write personal histories), will these electronic *aide-mémoires* give her a different understanding of her own transformation than my fragmentary snapshots gave me? Will our understanding of change change over time?

In a few years Khendum and her peers will probably be playing with computer history games (at home for those whose families can afford the hardware; at arcades for those who can't). There's already a bumper crop to choose from. One is Merchant Colony, a 'fun-packed, high resolution video game that the whole family will enjoy!' You begin in London during the eighteenth century (the time 'when Britain became Great'). Picking up an electronic ship, you proceed to 'hire troops and tradesmen to protect and maintain your fleet, establish colonies, develop industries and battle native uprisings while you import and export products to exotic destinations, selling your goods for profits that you reinvest back into your empire'. (In a nice touch you can also stock up on teachers, who 'build schools adjacent to native huts, helping to prevent uprisings there'.) Hopefully Khendum will prefer more benign games, like Where in America's Past is Carmen Sandiego, in which players chase bandits back in time, with the computer disbursing clues as to their current whenabouts, and providing lifts to various eras via chronoscanner. This game is wildly popular with 10-year-olds (interestingly, with girls as much as boys).

In her teens, Khendum will no doubt be reading (viewing?) electronic history books. Friends of mine at the Center for Media and Learning just finished reformatting their textbook on working-class history into hypermedia. Lying in bed, with Powerbook on tummy, or seated in a school computer lab, readers – viewers? – can branch off from conventional text and swing from medium to medium, summoning up film snippets of factory sites in the 1910s, or listening to reminiscences by Triangle Fire survivors. Khendum and her classmates will be able to write papers – construct presentations? – on compact disk, assembling bits of film, sound, narrative and document to bolster their arguments. As a writer and teacher I remain committed to books. Will the next generation or two be? There are already 2.5 million CD-ROM drives in active use in the US, a figure expected to jump to 10 million in three years.

For after-school entertainment, Khendum might go to an Interfilm. One played recently in New York. It was a thriller in which characters got into difficulties and turned to the audience for advice; we all pushed buttons, our votes were tallied, and in seconds the character (and plot line) responded to the will of the majority. Will we become accustomed to rewriting the script of history films, sending Wellington down to defeat at Waterloo, granting Lee victory at Gettysburg?

But all such pastimes are likely to pall with the advent of virtual reality. I recently went to a VR gallery. Popping on my helmet I was launched into a three-dimensional world of enemies-behind-pillars with whom I exchanged electronic rifle fire. As I moved my head, my angle of vision moved – 360 degrees; as my real hands moved, so did my simulated ones; as my feet paced, I seemed to race through hyperspace. The possibilities of this for the historically inclined are mind-boggling – more on this anon – though for now innovators mainly seem to be working feverishly towards building better war games, and achieving breakthroughs in 'teledildonics', the science of simulated sex.

With such delights to occupy her, will Khendum be likely to visit a museum (apart from being shepherded through on obligatory school convoys)? Certainly many people are figuring out how to entice her there.

You all know the outlines of this debate. So let's quickly rehearse the polar positions some have staked out, each with its associated possibilities and perils.

One camp seeks digital salvation, urging us to plunge joyously into the new world of interactive videos, compact disks and high-definition TV. 'Intelligent' museums in Japan, Ottawa's Canadian Museum of Civilization, London's

Museum of the Moving Image, and heritage operations such as Dover's 'White cliffs experience' are alive with gleaming control rooms linked by fibre optic channels to omnipresent computer terminals and interactive stations. These multimedia museums have the advantage of speaking the lingua franca of tomorrow ('I'm designing for the television generation', says the Dover creator). They provide the possibility of individually tailored visitor experiences. They are not tied down in their interpretative strategies by objects (in some cases having none at all).

These outfits are well positioned to explore the possibilities of virtual reality. Though still in its infancy, the technology is already capable of amazing feats. Experts recently 'reconstructed' the original eleventh-century Cluny Abbey – which had been destroyed after the French Revolution – and allowed tele-virtuality viewers to wander about inside its hallways. Imagine what's coming! Donning a helmet and seeing oneself in the Acropolis listening to a Platonic dialogue. Or being seated behind Orville Wright as he skims the air over Kitty Hawk. Or being trapped inside the flaming Triangle Shirtwaist Factory. Or being a Vietcong guerrilla under fire from an American helicopter gunship. Or being a slave and having the option of talking back to an overseer and discovering the consequences (having your electronic hide whipped).

There are drawbacks, of course. The mammoth expense of all this puts you at the mercy of funders – which politically delimits the issues you can explore, the interpretations you can advance. Nor, despite techno-determinist fantasies, does fancy equipment guarantee interesting ideas. The First Law of Computing remains in effect: garbage in, garbage out. There's a lot of gaudy banality out there. There is also the dissolution danger. Cutting loose from objects might put an end to museums; even theme parks might melt into air. Right now the new technology is costly; it demands collective viewing procedures. For a time people will use virtual reality as they once used telephones (and now faxes) – in neighbourhood centres or centralized galleries. But if prices tumble far enough, why not just stay at home and plug into the information grid? (We're already within inches of being able to dial up a museum and tour it electronically without getting out of bed.) Writ large, the social consequences could be significant: another erosion of public space. Remember that crowds used to assemble in front of the great newspapers' bulletin boards on election night, or during wartime battles; now they tune to CNN.

All of this is why some worried museologists advocate the opposite reaction to mediatization – insisting on the absolute primacy of objects. Some believe that in an era of infinite reproducibility people will become repulsed by inauthenticity, wary of endless fraud; that they will be drawn inexorably to the aura of artefacts which provide tunnels in time back to actual human actors; that they will thirst for old objects which, blessedly, were not made and 'patinaed' last week. That they will seek the *frisson* of contact with museum-certified originality.

Walter Benjamin and all that.

At the extreme, museums might become zoos for the real, an endangered species; or shrines – tranquil, sacred spaces for the unmachine-mediated savouring of relics.

But here, too, drawbacks abound. Speaking Latin when all about are into the vernacular invites disaster. A heightened exclusivity might well widen the existing gulf between those who feel comfortable with museum culture codes and those who – failing to crack them – opt to stay away.

Also, relics only have meaning if they are invested with it by the host culture. I find the low-tech Churchill War Rooms in London, frozen in mid-VE moment, to be enormously evocative; but will they resonate equally with generations for whom the Battle of Britain is as temporally remote as the Punic Wars?

And how to present subjects for which you have no objects? The poor, notoriously, leave little detritus behind. Nor have museums collected history's leftovers with an even hand: until quite recently the Smithsonian's National Museum of American History in Washington, DC, had forty silk top hats but not a single snap-brim cap.

Besides, romancing the 'real' takes you only so far. Focusing on objects can foster empiricism, make you forget that artefacts don't speak loudly to untutored ears, and lead to the fetishization of things: industrial machines become lovely *objets* when presented in gleaming isolation from their original man-eating context.

But these are false choices. At most museums, the outlines of a coming *détente* with media seem clear enough. Most museums will use hardware and software to elucidate objects, explicate contexts, and involve visitors. Examples abound.

Smithsonian 'Engines of change' videos set static machine-tools into absorbing motion. In Richmond, Virginia, videotaped actor-workers at the Valentine's 'Working people of Richmond' demonstrate the use of rolling mills and talk heatedly about the social relations of factory life. At Ellis Island, mangle boards and prayer books, ouds and clogs are accompanied by audiotaped donor descriptions. Computer installations at the Art Gallery of Ontario afford micro-inspections of paintings while the Getty offers mini-movies on the techniques of medieval scribes. A consortium of American art museums has produced an ingenious interactive programme which allows users to explore four Impressionist artists, clicking on icons which bring up details of paintings, present points of view from commentators (who also interrogate each other), and offer mini-biographies and oodles of contextual information.

Other devices stray a bit further from objects. At the Lowell Mills, Massachusetts, voiceovers simulate dinner-table talk among operative manikins. Interactives at Boston's Museum of Science put visitors in the shoes of the mayor of a town confronting a water shortage, and the Smithsonian's tropical rain forest show allows interactive strategic planning about preservation versus development issues. The South Australian Maritime Museum affords computer access to passenger lists, letting visitors track ancestral arrivals and take away a printout record. The National Museum of American History's 'Information age: people, information and technology' gives you a bar code for inputting and taking out personalized data at various scanner stations. The Holocaust Museum in Washington matches each visitor with a victim of the same age and sex, letting one follow the fate of a temporary twin.

The list goes on and on and will continue to exfoliate as imaginative curators get ever more conversant with the possibilities of the new technologies. Nor will new capabilities require shedding old ones. Museum-makers need not opt automatically for a high-tech solution when, as is often the case, a (cheaper) low-tech approach will do just as well, if not better. At a glitzy science museum in New Jersey schoolchildren scoot by interactive computer modules and scurry over to tunnels they can crawl through or rock faces they can climb.

Museums need not limit themselves to borrowing tools and techniques from the media world. They can also become places that interpret the media world itself.

This task can be approached in two different ways: first, by examining the history of that world – explaining developments in image and information production, and transformations in the political, cultural and social contexts of such production; second, museums can assess the impact of media on society by investigating the construction of consciousness in a media-enmeshed world. Forays have been made into both fields.

In the first category, the Museum of the Moving Image (MOMI) presents a social history of the film and television industries, offering visitors a look behind the screens. Portions of the Smithsonian's 'Information age' – the parts which treat older technologies like the telegraph and telephone – actually raise critical questions about context and impact. (The latter half, alas, fades into a celebratory display of products offered by the computer and communications industries – by no coincidence the show's sponsors.) The Strong Museum's 'Selling the goods: origins of American advertising' (in Rochester, NY) and the Valentine's 'Smoke signals: cigarettes, advertising and the American way of life' both examine the cultural impact of the persuasion industry, though they shy away from tackling some of the tougher questions – such as the influence of sponsors on content.

Shows in the second, deconstructionist, category often begin with the recognition that visitors now enter museums with well-stocked mental film banks. In particular, a vast amount of media history is being produced and consumed. People carry in their heads both raw footage (video clips culled from endless replays on TV) and narrative sequences (recalled from movies, docudramas and documentaries).

This media history is highly variegated. Responding to the world around it, it changes over time: it has its own history. There's quite a distance between *Gone with the Wind* and *Roots*. Indeed there is such a bewildering array of different interpretations available that it's conceivable that the plethora of media narratives has fostered a peculiarly malleable sense of the past. Where once the critical iconic images were graven in stone on church walls, now they are subject to instant revision as we flip from channel to channel. (Or – and here's a question for analysts of historical sensibilities in the media age – do some images gain an indelible primacy of place? Will the encircled wagon train revolve for ever in our cinematic brain, protecting the women and children as their menfolk fend off the howling redskins while awaiting the Seventh Cavalry, despite the valiant revisionism of Arthur Penn and many others?)

Whatever their impact, the mass media are unquestionably major players in the history biz – perhaps the single most critical source of popular historical imagination. For many, because cinematic modes of perception seem so real, moviepast *is* the past. So much so that it's perhaps not surprising that when curators at the Alamo erected a mural depicting their site's historic events they decided to substitute the faces of Hollywood actors from a 1960 movie for the original heroes: Davy Crockett became John Wayne. Certainly for Ronald Reagan, who portrayed General Custer in the *Santa Fe Trail*, the line between movie America and historical reality was notoriously blurred.

As images and narratives together constitute a goodly (and growing) portion of most people's historical capital why shouldn't museums turn media into artefacts? Why not mount shows that deconstruct for visitors the kinds of historical messages embedded in Hollywood movies or TV docudramas? How about exhibits which use morsels of film, along with other objects, to raise questions about the narratives people carry in their craniums? Why not demonstrate that film, like written history, conveys not an unequivocal 'truth' but a narrative interpretation? Again, some pioneers have pointed the way forward.

The rain forest show had a nice example of what's possible in its *Reel Jungle* video. By presenting clips that display the way Hollywood has distorted the jungle – excerpts from Tarzan movies, scenes of drunken natives cooking missionaries, safari expeditions seeking King Solomon's Mines – the exhibit confronted our clichés and laid bare their sources.

The London National Maritime Museum's recent show on pirates began not with historical 'reality' but historical fiction. The exhibition started with literary images (Byron and Stevenson), moved to portraits drawn from the stage (*Pirates of Penzance*, *Peter Pan*'s Captain Hook), and then presented snippets from cinematic treatments like Errol Flynn's swashbuckler *Captain Blood*. Only then, when people had a better sense of how the stereotypes in their heads got there, were they ushered towards a historical recounting. By making it plain to people that their misconceptions were the result of media-promulgated myths, not personal stupidity, the process defused resistance to reconsideration.

A current National Museum of American History exhibit, 'American encounters', examines the roots of stereotypes that litter the minds of visitors to the south-west. It does so by analysing how the nineteenth-century tourist industry manufactured and marketed exotic and romanticized images of Indian and Hispanic cultures.

And MOMI has a penetrating corner where it runs, on adjacent monitors, two news accounts covering the same anti-war demonstration. One is a snotty putdown, the other earnest and empathetic. It's an instantly transparent lesson in the way putatively objective accounts are heavily value-laden in their selection, emphasis and explication of images.

Given that so many museums are now heavily into oral and video history work, it might be interesting to go a step farther, by pitting memory-as-artefact against media-as-artefact. Imagine an exhibit that contrasted clips from *Rambo* and *Apocalypse Now* with filmed interviews done with veterans and anti-war activists. Or exhibits could present mini-assessments of popular movies and TV series, perhaps asking 'What did Ken Burns's *Civil War* leave out?' (answer: 'Slavery'), or exploring John Kennedy's assassination by branching off from Oliver Stone's *JFK*. Again, the point would be to strengthen visitors' historical skills by raising consciousness about how people learn about the past.

But museums needn't look far afield for media constructions to deconstruct. They can (and increasingly do) start with themselves. Gallery 33 at the Birmingham Museum is one such self-reflexive show (see Chapter 23 in this volume). It examines the lives and motives of its founding collectors, and situates the institution in the context of British colonialism. An interactive video underscores this for visitors, demonstrating that who you are helps shape how you see, and that a single object can mean different things in different surroundings. In the US, a similar enterprise at the Washington Project for the Arts – 'The other museum' by Fred Wilson – forces visitors to confront the imperialist roots of western ethnography and nineteenth-century museum display. (It might also be fun to examine the images of museums which crop up in contemporary popular culture, such as the recent portrayals in *Batman*, *Ghostbusters II* and *When Harry Met Sally*.)

More generally, there seems to be a trend towards acknowledging publicly that exhibitions are particular interpretations rather than universal truths. Here again computers can be helpful, as at the Smithonian's 'Information age', where the curator offers videotaped comments on the background and intentions of the show. It's worth noting, however, that interactive displays can also undercut this promulgation of authorial responsibility. They can foster the illusion that a machine is providing value-free interpretations when of course it's presenting pre-programmed perspectives. (The same potential for projecting a sham objectivity exists in electronic books.) This might be offset by building a critical component into the system; touch-screen users could select a box labelled 'A different view' to bring up a short commentary from someone outside the museum who argues against the exhibition's central premises.

An even more dramatic way to demonstrate that museum messages are interpretations, shaped in part by broader social figurations, would be to compare the transformation of history museums in 'east bloc' countries today with the changes wrought in United States institutions over the past two decades.

In what remains, I will explore this question of changing museum messages in the east and west, though about the former I know very little, and can only pose questions for others to answer.

Changing messages

A massive turnabout in public historiography appears to be underway in Eastern Europe.

The German Historical Museum, which was set up in West Berlin to counter the interpretative narrative embedded in East Berlin's Museum of German History, has now taken over its former rival and replaced every Marxist-oriented exhibit. Budapest's Hungarian National Agricultural Museum has covered over with flowered panels the cases of its Marxist presentation on 'The history of Hungarian agriculture in the twentieth century'. Bulgaria's Communist Party history museums, through which schoolchildren and visiting east bloc tourists once trooped, are now shut down. Bucharest's National History Museum has removed the hundreds of portraits of Ceausescu – looking eerily like Liberace – which once graced its galleries. They are stored, together with Communist Party memorabilia from the now defunct Museum of Communist Party History, in a locked room – number 44 – to which the equivalent of a month's salary will purchase admission. And in Russia, the Central Lenin Museum in St Petersburg (formerly Leningrad), which had admitted photos of Trotsky, Kamenev and Bukharin into their galleries after Gorbachev's speech extending glasnost to Soviet history, now faces, along with two score more Lenin museums, the possibility of Lenin himself becoming a non-person.

A great deal of this is to the good. Parts of these enterprises were dreadful, particularly when it came to acknowledging unpleasant truths about a domestic regime or its relations with the Soviet Union. At the Czech party museum which I visited in 1988, a panel gestured at the Prague Spring, but overshadowed its few newsclippings of Russian tanks with outsize portraits of smiling Soviet soldiers dandling Czech children. A new Hungarian exhibit on agriculture after 1945 is able, as the old was not, to make a critique of collectivization and deal with the fate of the kulaks.

Nevertheless, it is interesting and salutary to watch some of the same people who used to talk caustically about the Soviet Union's Orwellian penchant for rewriting history with each twist of the party line now applaud vigorously the abrupt volte-face which appears to be in motion. The regnant assumption seems to be that ideological hacks are being replaced by 'objective' scholars. But were the old presentations so unmitigatedly propagandistic and bereft of any redeeming historical insight? In addition to their blind spots (or, better, blind regions), were there some areas – like antagonistic class relations – which a Marxist perspective was able to highlight, and which might now go un-addressed with a different set of assumptions and values in power? Certainly the Museum of German History retailed a plethora of regime-coddling mythologies

– particularly about the post-1945 era – but observers from Kenneth Hudson to *The Economist* found much of value in its exhibitry. One East European museum professional has cautioned that: 'What happened in the Communist period to museums was by no means all bad, nor is what may follow all good.' Indeed, some curators fear that 'freemarket ideology may become the test of appropriateness of exhibit schemes'. Or, worse, that their institutions might get caught up in the revival of hypernationalism and be required to generate patriotic displays, or push territorial pedigrees. The deliberate demolition of museums, archives and monuments in Bosnia is a chilling portent of the extremes to which 'historical cleansing' can go.

It will be fascinating, indeed, to see if the end of the cold war generates a host of retrospective readjustments elsewhere on the planet. Will the National Museum of Intervention in Mexico City, a 1981 operation recounting Yankee imperialisms past and present, survive the Salinas government's opening to North American capital? (Mexican textbooks have already rehabilitated dictator Porfirio Diaz as a pioneer who attracted foreign investment.) Will the Chinese museum devoted to American-backed Kuomintang torture of Red revolutionaries be shut down by officials luring investors? What will be the fate of Nicaragua's Museum of the Revolution under the Chamorro regime? Will the Tuol Sleng Museum of Genocidal Crime, a horrifying memorial to Khmer Rouge mass murders (set up by the Vietnamese), survive new governmental reshufflings?

It's too soon for us – or at any rate me – to say much about these contemporary rewrites. But abundant testimony exists about another museum metamorphosis – that which has taken place in the United States over the last thirty years.

Let me spin you a Whiggish narrative. In the 1940s and 1950s, America's historic museums and sites drowsed happily on the margins of a go-ahead culture, tending their genteel artefacts, perpetuating regnant myths. Blacks, women, immigrants and workers figured as supporting actors, as offstage voices, or not at all.

Then: rude poundings at the door. In the 1960s and 1970s a new generation of curators – inspired by movements in the streets and leagued with youthful colleagues in the academy – marched into these institutions and revamped their agendas. Issues of race, gender, class, imperialism and ecology were opened to exploration. In the 1980s, Reaganites attempted to reverse these developments. But social history and multiculturalism grew stronger in universities and museums, facilitated by government-financed (by the National Endowment for the Humanities) bridges between scholars and curators.

The results can be read in the current museum landscape. Setting aside cavils about the way particular exhibits have been executed, a quick survey suggests the scope of transformation. Consider race. Colonial Williamsburg, which long elided even the existence of black slaves, now has uncostumed African-American guides interpreting lives of the once 1,000-strong slave labour force at Carter's Grove plantation. In the old Capitol Building in Jackson, where 1950s lawmakers once yahooed segregation bills into law, now the Mississippi State Historical Museum displays Klan paraphernalia of intimidation to tell the story of 'Reconstruction and its aftermath'. In Richmond, former capital of the Confederacy, the Valentine museum has switched from loving arrangements of genteel artefacts to shows like 'Jim Crow: racism and reaction in the new South', and the same city's Museum of the Confederacy, long a sanctum of the Lost Cause, has mounted 'Before freedom come: African-American life in the antebellum South'. Explorations of America's racial experience have become almost routine, from the Chicago Historical Society's 'A house divided: America in the age of Lincoln', featuring living history performances about black abolitionist Frederick Douglass, to such Smithsonian shows as 'Field to factory: black migration 1915–1940' and 'A more perfect union: Japanese Americans and World War II', which recounts the story of the internment camps.

Turning to imperial expansion, which in the US took the form of conquering the continent, we find the National Museum of American Art (in 'The West as America') indicting painters of iconic frontier scenes for complicity in the region's appropriation. At historic sites (like the former Custer battlefield, now renamed Little Bighorn), and at institutions like the new Indian Museum in New York, indigenous peoples contribute to their own representation. Hidatsa Indians helped to create the Minnesota Historical Society's complex portrait of their forebears' response to invasion, 'The way to independence', while Cherokees welcome a planned Hopkinsville museum on the Trail of Tears, the forced deportation march in which 4,000 died. And shows like the NMAH's 'American encounters' replace celebratory sagas about winning the West with complex stories of Native Americans, Africans, Asians and Europeans clashing with and changing one another, a story presented as ongoing.

Perhaps most amazing is the way the Columbus myth was vanquished. It's hard to convey the stunning obduracy in the US of Washington Irving's fairy tale of flat earth, hocked jewels and benign 'discovery'. Museum shows like the National Museum of Natural History's 'Seeds of change' helped put forward the perspective of those for whom his advent prefigured pestilence, servitude and death. So did objections by American Indian Movement activists against shows like 'First encounters: Spanish explorations in the Caribbean and the United States' at the Florida Museum of Natural History. When it went on the road, the Albuquerque Museum offered a handout providing Indian perspectives on the exhibit. And these US protests were only a faint echo of those in South America, where indigenous peoples demonstrated from Alaska to Peru. Even at the Seville World's Fair and the Barcelona Olympic Games, Columbus proved an embarrassment. As the *New York Times* noted, Christopher Columbus's fall from grace in 1992 was even steeper than that of George Bush.

Or consider museological treatments of class. In abandoned factories across the country, museums address the lives of vanished labourers, recall their skills and sacrifices, confront management–labour conflicts. Lowell, Massachusetts, interprets mill girls' lives. The Valentine's exploration of tobacco and iron workers treats issues of race and ethnicity, examines Knights of Labor organizing, and connects home life with work life. At Homestead, the Historical Society of Western Pennsylvania laid out the context of the great 1892 strike. The Essex Institute presented 'Life and times in Shoe City'; the South Street Seaport looked at urban craftworkers; Ellis Island surveyed the movement of immigrants into the national workplace; NMAH's 'Symbols and images of American labor' compared worker self-representations with public perceptions, and a travelling SITES (Smithsonian Institution Traveling Exhibition Service) show, 'Who's in charge', examines management–labour relations past and present. The vogue for class analysis is not limited to workers: Rochester's Strong Museum put on 'Neither rich nor poor: searching for the American middle class'. Oddly, after being the solitary focus of attention for so many years, upper-class lives are now scanted.

Or consider gender issues. The National Women's Hall of Fame, which opened in Seneca Falls in 1968, has been joined by the National Park Service's Women's Rights National Historical Park in chronicling feminist history. Institutions devoted specifically to women's history are still rare – apart from local galleries and historic houses – but major institutions have produced substantial exhibits incorporating new historiography. NMAH curators have put up 'Men and women: a history of costume, gender, and power', and 'Parlor to politics: women and reform, 1890–1925', but perhaps most remarkable is their redoing of the First Ladies' gowns exhibit. This long-time semi-sacred site, to which Hillary's violet confection will soon be whisked and embalmed, has been completely remodelled. Now the dress graveyard is preceded by rooms which present the women as political and cultural actors, and interpret presidential couples as symbolizing the gender relations of their era. It's hugely popular. I heard one woman remarking to her 12-year-old daughter: 'You know, dear, the last time I was here they only had the gowns. They said nothing about the First Ladies themselves. It was *so* insulting.'

Turning to the ecological front, we find substantial departures from the Gee Whiz School's rhapsodizing of technology. Recent exhibits promulgate more qualified accounts, admitting the ambiguous impact of Progress on human and natural ecology. NMAH's 'Engines of change' salts its portrayal of an essentially beneficial industrialization with accounts of worker setbacks and environmental destruction. The State Historical Society of Iowa explores the impact of expanding agricultural productivity on forest, wetlands and prairie. 'Seeds of change' compares the 1492 and 1992 ecoscape, brings the Mexico City story down to its festering present, and argues for renewable resources. The rain forest show not only describes their decimation over the past century, but ascribes responsibility to specific agents – developers, loggers, ranchers, agribusiness, international banks and consumers of rainforest commodities; it also explains how visitors inclined to help can actually do something to help solve the problem. (Follow-up studies have found the presentation extremely effective.)

Consider, also, the willingness of this generation of curators, scholars, funders and audiences to survey recent history, much of it grim. Museums-cum-memorials dot the public landscape.

In Memphis's former Lorraine Motel, the National Civil Rights Museum places Martin Luther King's assassination in broader context, setting portions of a charred freedom rider bus and a replica of King's Birmingham jail cell right next to the balcony where he was felled. Interactively inclined visitors can board a 1950s-era segregated bus, and get told by a driver-mannequin to 'Go to the back'; or sit down next to sculpted protesters at a lunch counter sit-in. The Birmingham Civil Rights Institute displays King's actual cell along with segregation artefacts like separate water fountains against an audio backdrop of gospel and crowd sounds, sirens and speeches. And a Civil Rights Memorial in Montgomery, Alabama, honouring forty victims of the movement killed. (Malcolm X's legacy has proved tougher to museographize, and major battles have been fought over whether or not to preserve his assassination site, New York's Audubon Ballroom.)

In the former Texas state schoolbook depository, the Dallas County Historical Foundation offers 'The sixth floor: John F. Kennedy and the memory of a nation'. It introduces the various assassination theories and commission reports, and includes audioaccounts by witnesses. And Kent State University plans a memorial to the students shot down there.

More official versions of recent events can be found at the presidential mausoleums which are rapidly blanketing the land, including those of Eisenhower and Nixon, Kennedy and Johnson (the Lyndon Baines Johnson Library and Museum is the second most popular tourist attraction in Texas after the Alamo). Bush was hard at work on his the first day out of office.

What does it all mean? Is unabashed applause the appropriate response to this Whiggish presentation?

Yes and no.

On the no side, there are still lots of places doing business in the old way. There are also questions about what difference the changes make. A Marxist analysis – Groucho Marxist that is – suggests if blacks *et al.* have got into museums they can't be much worth getting into. The cynical might say that museological alterations are sops – substitutes for changes in power relations. That blacks, women and Indians have fared far better in exhibits than at workplaces, in homes, or on the streets. And that while the new historians were restocking museums and colleges, Reagan was restocking the judiciary and bureaucracy.

I disagree. While it is true that transformations in representation have outstripped those in reality, curators and scholars have made real contributions to shifting the terms of America's public discourse. And language counts. Proof comes from opponents. The 'West as America' show's challenge to mythic pieties provoked a furore of complaints from conservatives incensed at its deconstruction of fables. The *Wall Street Journal* called it 'an entirely hostile ideological assault on the nation's founding and history'. To be sure, some of the exhibit's captions were humourless and bludgeoning, affording tempting targets. But the real objections were to its having advanced critical theses amidst the yellow-ribboned frenzy of Operation Desert Storm, an exercise President Bush had explicitly cast as an opportunity to get beyond the historical self-doubts engendered by Vietnam. Critics had already attacked schools and universities which dared revise the traditional canon, and fashion multicultural curricula. Now museums, too, were accused of imposing stifling standards of 'political correctness'.

To a degree these outcries merely reflect impotence. But they also remind us of the fragility of these gains, of their potential reversibility. Still, it is worth noting that even institutions like Disneyworld's EPCOT have recognized that old verities don't fly – not just with blacks and women but with the burgeoning upper-middle-class ranks of college graduates who have been exposed to social and historiographical upheavals. The producers of EPCOT's US history pavilion – the 'American adventure' (presented jointly by American Express and Coca Cola) – felt impelled to feature prominently Susan B. Anthony, Frederick Douglass and John Muir robots in their story.

Yet for all the changes, distinct limits remain on what can be said in museums. Certain issues – usually those that remain politically volatile – can be addressed only if the discussion is not brought down to the present; others are entirely taboo. Let us finish by looking quickly at messages which cannot be uttered.

Forty years after America began its intervention in Indochina and nearly twenty years after the last helicopters lifted off from the roof of the Saigon Embassy, there has not yet been a single substantial museum exhibition on the causes, course or consequences of the war in Vietnam. To say nothing, literally, of the anti-war movement. Despite a huge and burgeoning body of reflection by participants, historians, novelists, moviemakers and playwrights – and the erection of hundreds of memorials – the closest is the Smithsonian's Vietnam Veterans Memorial Collection. This is a fascinating collation of objects left at the Memorial, ranging from personal memorabilia of the fallen, through memorials to gay soldiers, to rejected Congressional Medals of Honor accompanied by letters protesting Reagan's support for the contras in Nicaragua. It is poignant, and powerful, but eschews any commentary whatever.

Other countries, of course, have not done much better. The French are still wrestling with Algeria. And many participants still find the Second World War too hot to handle. The Hiroshima Peace Memorial Museum rejected Japanese peace organizations' calls to depict the country's prewar aggressions – bowing to right-wing groups who refuse to apologize for Japan's behaviour. Indeed the soft-pedalling of wartime brutalities in Japanese schoolbooks (and the comments of occasional cabinet ministers) have provoked diplomatic protests from China, South Korea, and other Asian countries. And not until Professor Yoshiaki Yoshimi irrefutably proved that Korean 'comfort women' were forced to service the Imperial Army did the government reverse its denial of responsibility.

Sexuality is another toughie. The story of homosexuality has been addressed in underground and guerrilla history institutions generated by the gay and lesbian community. It has been treated in a vast scholarly literature. But accessing mainstream museums has so far proved impossible. A group of major institutions (the Museum of the City of New York, the Brooklyn Historical Society, the New York Public Library and the potentially defunct New York Historical Society) has launched an ambitious attempt to treat the history of homosexuals in New York City, but so far potential funders in the corporate, public and private world have refused to touch it, and it may well yet collapse.

On gender issues, one could imagine fascinating exhibitions on the history of birth control (including abortion); on the disjunction between idealized 'family values' and realities such as wife beating and child abuse; on the history of prostitution; or simply a museum on the history of women. But despite the stupendous scholarly output on all these issues, and their front-page salience to people's lives, they remain in the realm of the undoable.

In the arena of labour and the economy, for all the particular studies of nineteenth-century artisanal and industrial workers, we still lack any major museum exhibit covering the history of organized labour, or shows that treat twentieth-century white-collar or public employees. A few pioneering exhibits have tackled homelessness in historical perspective, but for all the debates over welfare recipients and the 'underclass' nothing treats such populations historically in a museum setting. (Andrew West's English-based suggestions about the need to collect the material culture of the poor – including not only cardboard boxes that shelter the homeless but the government forms that govern their lives – are equally telling in the American context.) More to the point, we never discuss the production of poverty and unemployment. Most Americans are well aware of the current hard times, and the crises of the 1970s, and the Great Depression of the 1930s, but few have a clue that busts have alternated with booms on virtually a clockwork basis since the early 1800s.

Nor for all the defunct mines and mills recycled into museums is there ever much attention paid to what many visitors want to know most when they enter these spaces: where did the jobs go? An exhibit presenting a global perspective on 'deindustrialization', perhaps arranged by a multinational museum collaboration, might track the flight of factories from New England to North Carolina to Singapore and China – noting the simultaneous impact on American towns and cities, and on Asian countrysides. Indeed, the connections between 'deindustrialization' and 'immigration' demand exploration in their own right. Ellis Island does a wonderful job on the earlier twentieth-century but, despite some nods towards recent arrivals, it fails to remind us that 'immigration' is hardly finished business, that the political battles which animated earlier Americans are ongoing today.

Ecological concerns have clearly made great strides in museums, but we seem more comfortable talking about tropical rain forests elsewhere than toxic dumpsites in our own backyard. And why not integrate a green perspective into other areas? At the Henry Ford Museum and Greenfield Village in Dearborn, Michigan, the 'Automobile in American life' exhibition is a spectacular improvement over earlier formulations. But the show still shies away from exploring the decision to opt for gasoline-based private cars rather than mass transit, or from reckoning with the social and ecological consequences of that decision.

And how about having some of our living history farms take up the question of the transition from family farming to agribusiness? Most agricultural museums end their stories in the 1870s. They concentrate more on sowing and reaping than they do on those developments – tenantry, migrant labour, foreclosures, world markets, commodity exchanges, and agrarian movements – that might explain how the old farms, whose values they celebrate, succumbed to the corporate agribusinessmen who today dominate American agriculture and account for much of the damage done to the countryside.

Had I the time and the knowledge, I would stir some English examples into this analysis. But it is hard (not to say presumptuous) for a flimsily informed out-sider to evaluate the English explosion of interest in the past, as evidenced by the rapid – not to say fantastic – growth of museums and what gets called the heritage industry.

I don't really grasp what is driving this development. Some say the turn to the past is a function of England's global decline; it supposedly generated a desire to retreat into a fantasized past, which entrepreneurs quickly provided, for a profit. Others suggest the history boom is a mere epiphenomenon of embourgeoise-ment: more people, with more time and money, do what middle-class people do, which is go to museums. But I also see (and read of) quite different tendencies – associated more with institutions like Glasgow's People's Palace or the urgings of the Social History Curators Group and WHAM (Women's Heritage and Museums). These initiatives seem to be reaching out, with new messages, to new constituencies, as in the work of the museums of labour history in Edinburgh, Manchester and Liverpool; Gallery 33 at Birmingham; Hull's Old Grammar School Museum; and even (to some degree) the Imperial War Museum. So I'm puzzled.

Nor do I know what can and can't be said today in England. My untutored eye finds suggestive the absence of an institution devoted to the history of the British Empire, especially as a place of this kind might help to contextualize multicultural immigration. I know there were serious discussions about creating one in the mid-1980s, and a host of objective problems stood in the way, but I wonder how important political constraints (such as, perhaps, the difficulties of confronting the issue of Northern Ireland) have been in blocking its emergence.

In any event, I am not saying – let me be clear – that 'controversial' subjects are the only ones worth talking about. But I do think it's worthwhile expend-ing considerable energy in tackling such issues, because they are important to people. Given that studies show non-museum goers find museums irrelevant as well as intimidating, dealing with issues germane to people's lives might help overcome their resistance.

It's obviously a risky strategy. Funders, certainly in the corporate sector, prefer to avoid controversial subjects and critical treatments. The National Museum of American History tried for five years to get support for its women's history shows, but failed, and when they did get vast sums for 'Information age' and the forthcoming 'Science in American life', they found themselves embroiled in battles over interpretative content. Piper-payers like calling tunes.

An alternative strategy seeks to generate public sources of support. This is not the same thing as expanding 'market share'. It is obviously important to adopt such ideas from market proponents as can improve museum attractiveness (though without buying into their notions of consumer sovereignty). But commodity producers, divorced from principle and passion are as unlikely as corporate sponsors to tackle difficult but interesting issues. And one lesson I draw from the past decades in the US is the usefulness of new messages in reaching new audiences.

The post-1960s transformations were not 'market-driven' but ultimately political phenomena. Black (and many white) parents wanted representations in schools and museums that broke with racist stereotypes; committed curators pushed for these transformations; in turn they were able to pull in new audiences and generate political support from elected officials. The Valentine was a moribund institution; but after five years of 'controversial' shows, visits quadrupled (thanks in part to a substantial increase in the number of African-Americans) and the budget quadrupled as well (thanks in part to black elected officials). The Dallas and Memphis museums both got backing from state and localities which supported their agenda and presentation. The Japanese camps show pulled new audiences and was defended against attack by powerful Senators responding to those constituencies.

I applaud efforts to demystify and democratize museums by sharing authority with communities, involving them in planning, collecting and evaluating, and helping non-professionals to mount displays, as in the exemplary work of the Brooklyn Historical Society with Latinos, AIDs victims and others; the Chinatown History Museum's neighbourhood collaborations; the Valentine's meetings with community spokespeople to plan and then criticize shows (including video excerpts of their opinions in the exhibition); the extensive consultations with local reminiscence groups and the incorporation of oral histories and volunteers at Hull, the People's Story in Edinburgh (see Chapter 12 in this volume) and Springburn Museum in Glasgow, and the Museum of London's 'Peopling of London'.

I part company, however, with those who propose that curators deprofessionalize themselves and transfer power to 'the community'. Aside from being utopian, the American experience suggests that abuse is not inevitable. In the US, activist curators, linked to committed scholars, were vital agents of change. And the strong professional communities they forged have been crucial in protecting those gains, in raising issues that transcend (but involve) particular communities, and in establishing an apparatus of critical commentary (notably the scores of journals that now review exhibits) which is indispensable to future progress.

We need more of this kind of professionalization, not less. Forging a community of public discourse about museum exhibits provides individual curators some degree of leverage against funders who would use their purses to impose their interpretations. Professional associations of academics made some progress towards curbing the once commonly assumed right of trustees to fire professors whose ideas they didn't like. The proposal from Al Young, professor of history and adviser to the Chicago Historical Society, for a Museum Bill of Rights which would put 'curatorial freedom' on a par with 'academic freedom' is worth some exploration. In addition, institutions should videotape their presentations and make them available to the curatorial community on a much more regular basis.

In conclusion, I urge museums to seek not simply customers but constituents, to become partners with communities in effecting change; to serve as centres of civic debate and organization (with modest expectations about how much such forums can achieve); and, finally, to continue to think imaginatively about new ways of saying things, and boldly about new things that are worth saying.

10

Museums in partnership

Gaynor Kavanagh

Much discussion about museums and museum developments in the 1990s has centred on the word 'partnership'. The purpose of this chapter is to explore both the meaning and spirit of partnerships in museums and to identify the different ways in which partnerships work in practice. From this, a set of ground rules for partnership arrangements will be extrapolated and presented by way of a conclusion. The approach adopted is very much a British one, although some of the case-studies and ideas are bound to have parallels in other countries.

But first some definitions: a 'partner' is one who has a share or part with another or others; that person is a sharer or a partaker. A 'partnership' is the fact or condition of being a partner, with all that implies. To be in a partnership means the establishment of role relationships, with codes and expected forms of behaviour. Expressed like this, partnership sounds a positive and potentially rewarding arrangement. However, these are surface meanings. A partnership is a social contract and is never fixed: it is in a continuous state of evolution. All individuals choose to begin, define, negotiate, develop, enable, thwart, end or redefine partnerships according to needs and circumstances; so do museums. So too do politicians and policy makers, who have extended their vocabulary to include the word 'partnership' whenever the 'feel good' factor is required. It joins a neat stock of convenient words such as: community, network, enablement, devolution, culture, local initiative and empowerment, which in sum usually mean: 'there is not enough money (or will) to go round'. This is especially true when anything to do with Europe, social provision, research or the arts is concerned, and is a fact of life that most museum people work with every day. The words trickle into the vocabulary and are happily passed on. For example, this is a heading from a piece in the December edition (1992) of the *Museums Journal*: 'Working in partnership: or networking in action'.

Museums enter into partnerships as a result of many different circumstances: political pressure, preconditions of fund applications, planning and management necessity, public spirit, personal disposition, or professional preferences. Some partnership arrangements work: others do not. For some the rhetoric is stronger than the reality, for others the spirit is stronger than the letter. But who are the real and likely partners in museum provision? Who are the sharers and partakers? Some seem, at first, fairly evident: established audiences, donors, scholars, trustees and funders. But what about others: the museum staff, suppliers and contractors, users with special needs, schools, other museums, the trainers, the universities, the press, associated or related commercial and service industries, such as tourism? And of course, there are the potential partners: current non-users, social and other services, artists and arts providers, scientists, technologists, heavy industry, the unemployed and public utilities. The list could go on and on. In a sense, what matters is not just with whom a museum enters into a partnership arrangement, but why, with what objectives and with what kind of commitment. This has underpinned the quality of museum provision for more than one century, although perception of who or what is 'partnership worthy' has changed.

There are so many areas where the museum enters into a partnership that it is difficult to know where to begin: certainly a comprehensive list is not possible. The problem is made more complex by the languages the museum world adopts. One museum's partner is another's visitor, client, governing body, customer, colleague, informant, researcher, neighbour or subordinate. In some museums, the word 'partner' might not be used at all, but the quality and spirit of partnerships – sharing and partaking – are well in evidence. Equally, a museum might be glibly referring to its 'partners', yet there would be little to indicate their true or generous existence in its work. Again, we are back to the spirit of the thing rather than the letter.

I would like to deal with five very broad areas of partnership in museum provision, in respect of audiences, collections, joint museum initiatives, and development.

Museum visitors as partners

In spite of all the research and discussion generated on the subject of museum visitors, it has to be faced that many museums still perceive visitors in the gallery as a homogeneous group, unaffected by factors such as socio- or political circumstances, cultural backgrounds and personal interests. Such museums still believe in exhibitions communicating directly on a dry head-to-head basis, with all the (lengthy) script read and consumed, and every nuance caught and devoured with relish. Others believe the visitor to be of no importance whatsoever, and therefore direct their exhibitions at what and whom they know: friends and fellow scholars. In such instances, the 'collective self' of the exhibition begins and ends with the curator's own mind and personality: such work becomes easy to identify. These exhibitions leave the visitor with the feeling that they are walking uninvited around someone else's space and are at best unwelcome and at worst trespassing. All but the curator concerned appear to recognize, in some part, the self indulgence of such exhibition forms. But such approaches have been undergoing tremendous challenge and are being up-ended.

For those ready for a more constructive approach, research and greater under-standing are to hand. Much more is now known about the experiences of visiting museums and visitors' abilities and preparedness to choose the areas of knowledge they wish to address and share. People engage with museums on many different levels, and each person to some degree will have a unique set of priorities, which can be enabled or restricted by what the museum has to offer. The initial reason for visiting will have a significant impact on the 'shape' of the experience. People have a whole host of objectives for their visit, many not necessarily conscious. They might including some of the following:

- to enhance the bonds of relationships and family;
- to partake in and enjoy joint experiences;
- to find out about things;
- to provoke discussion;
- to explore thoughts and feelings;
- to look and listen;
- to escape and think;
- to escape and not to think.

Visiting a museum with small children in a family group will be different from visiting with fellow members of an adult education class or alone. The priorities and therefore agendas will alter according to defined and dominant needs. Every person will use the space the museum provides in his or her own way, but in the context of their immediate circumstances. Further, they are most likely to meet the museum's interpretation principally where their feelings, memories and curiosity are joined or provoked. People feel secure and learn best when they can move comfortably from what they know to new areas of knowledge. And indeed we all learn when our emotions are involved, moving from the affective to the cognitive. However, this area is extremely problematic, because it is both very British and very professional not to talk about feelings, even good ones like humour and affection, which is perhaps why so many museums are devoid of both.

The meeting of the museum with the visitor is a site of extraordinary possibilities. Developing provision, in partnership, allows for recognition of the capacities, priorities and needs people naturally bring with them. The days of the take-it-or-leave-it museum are numbered.

- People expect to be respected.
- They expect to be interested.
- They expect to be expected.

Museums have been getting better all the time at provision for social comforts, for example better rest areas and cafés. The greatest need now lies in develop-ment of the exhibitions and indeed the whole communication strategy of the exhibition spaces. Thinking of visitors as partners in a learning experience is one way of proceeding.

But developing museums as environments in which people can feel, think, look and respond requires a great deal of learning on the part of the museum. It also requires a capacity to recognize the nature of the 'contract' it is entering into with the public. For example, if a history museum is willing and able to make the kind of provision which offers the histories it makes, not as rigid 'story-lines', but as open-ended discussions, then it must expect (and indeed welcome) the challenges that result. The rejection of restricting chronological narratives, in preference for more thought-provoking approaches, has meant that, not before time, content and historiographic style are at last getting on to the museum agenda.

To take one example: in Annapolis, Maryland, in the United States, comments of visitors were recorded following a tour of an eighteenth-century formal garden and a discussion on the relationship of landscape to political authority (quoted in Potter and Leone 1992). Among the comments received was one which read: 'You've read too much Foucault and Girouard and not enough on eighteenth-century garden design. I recommend Maynard Mack, *The Garden and the City* and numerous books by John Dixon Hunt.'

Another read, 'Interesting (but as far as I can see unfounded) theorising and rather pretentious intellectually.'

These are not easy comments to receive, especially if the project leaders had a personal attachment to the way things were being approached. But they are evidence that there was enough in the programme to encourage people to think about what they were seeing and hearing and make a response. If that was a conscious aim, then the programme must have been both highly stimulating and effective.

If museums equip visitors to look at the histories on offer, if partnerships are entered into where ideas and views are provoked and exchanged, if the aim is to make things that much more interesting, then some adjustments on the part of the museum have to take place. It has to be much more aware of itself and its audiences. It also has to be aware of the mechanisms and philosophies of its own subject. But particularly, it has to be willing to enter into the spirit of experiment and exchange. Of central importance, this requires that the museum should be able to laugh at itself and enjoy the partnership. As with all things in life, one gets what one gives.

Partnerships in collecting

Of course, museum provision is far more than the sum of the displays. The quality of the facilities (who wants to encounter a filthy café and grumpy museum staff?) and the standards aimed for throughout the museum's services say a great deal about how much respect it accords its audiences, funders and, of course, of prime importance, itself.

This extends to the energy with which a museum pursues its collecting, recording and research, and the degree of care devoted to the long-term well-being of the collections. It should be remembered that although the museum exists in the context of present-day service, it has a central responsibility which has been delegated to it: the long-term care of fundamentally important material. However, the definition of this material and exactly to whom it is, or will be, 'fundamentally' important, can only be arrived at through careful thought and consultation. The deadening hand of the concept of 'museum worthiness' (or is the ghastly word 'museality' to be used here?) has got a fair amount to answer for, including: partial and often tediously repetitive collections, the omissions of those objects – and therefore histories – that fail to conform and the perpetuation of damaging stereotypes. Scholars, politicians, fieldworkers and everyday people all have views about what is important. The huge gaps in our collections, especially in the field of social and industrial history, bear witness to some curatorial inability to question, look and, above all, ask.

Of course, there are many useful precedents of where museums have worked in partnership to create collections which now serve as detailed records of human experience. To take just one: the Imperial War Museum, established in 1917, chose to bring together collections of material reflective of all aspects of the war and did so by setting up specialist sub-committees, each dedicated to forming collections within their areas of interest. The sub-committees were constituted not of curators but of people working within or connected to the field their committee represented, such as the Admiralty, Munitions, the War Office and the Air Services. A Women's Work Sub-Committee was also established.

The women who served voluntarily on this sub-committee were either aristocratic or connected with figures prominent at the time. Agnes Conway, the daughter of the museum's director Martin Conway, acted as secretary. The women set themselves an objective: the collection of exhibits, and the formation of a record of the war activities of women by means of photographs, pamphlets and manuscript reports from all women's organizations. They divided up the responsibilities between themselves, and took every initiative to expand the collection and to make the case for women's work to be remembered through the museum. Within eighteen months, they had accumulated sufficient material to mount an exhibition at the Whitechapel Art Gallery. Opened in October 1918, this attracted 82,000 visitors in the six weeks it was open.

The record of the Women's Work Sub-Committee is impressive. Between 1917 and 1920, it commissioned paintings and models, and brought together a collection of documents and uniforms, badges, books and photographs. The main part of this is now held by the Department of Printed Books at the Imperial War Museum (IWM) and amounts to 189 boxes of papers, 20 albums of press cuttings and 100 books. It covers the record of 1,200 war charities and 6,000 home hospitals (Wilkinson 1991: 31). Further, the sub-committee attempted to put together a record of all the women who had lost their lives during the war, either on service, on the Home Front in munitions work or on the land. They wrote to the nearest relatives of the deceased and asked for photographs. The letters written in reply, now held in the IWM archive, are a painful record of lives lost. The grief contained therein draws a razor blade across the heart. In April 1920, the Women's Work Sub-Committee had compiled a Roll of Honour of 800 names and the albums of photographs were ready to be mounted.

This is an example of women, with an agreed common aim, in partnership. They were prepared to work together, in the creation of a collection which now stands as an unrivalled research archive and monument. In doing so they drew respectfully on the partnership of others, especially other women.

Partnerships between museums

To come back to today, there are many precedents for museums working together to maximize resources and to learn from shared experiences. In Britain, much of this is promoted and facilitated by the Area Museum Councils (AMC) and supported by the Museums and Galleries Commission, which exist to monitor and promote museum standards. The spirit of co-operation found between many museums in Britain is further aided by the fact that the profession is a comparatively small one and, through conferences, specialist group work and training opportunities, many people establish strong professional contacts which see them through their careers. Many museums do work together, sharing facilities and equipment, experience and expertise. Such arrangements as joint promotional schemes, shared on-site training, merchandising agreements and the commissioning of regional-based research, help museums to help themselves and each other.

The Middleton Report, published in 1990, on the future of independent museums, identified a number of different arrangements small and medium-sized museums in Britain could enter into as a means of maximizing their oppor-tunities and minimizing their costs. Middleton argued that in the 1990s museums would need to work much more closely with each other and with commercial and other operators. Perhaps, not foreseeing the potential impact of the Local Government Review and the contracting out of services, or the effects of the current recession on all businesses and services, some of his ideas now sound out-dated and, for many types of museum, inappropriate; for example, the leasing of collections to commercial organizations. The omission of two fundamentally important points were, however, glaring: the development of genuine equal opportunities in museums and the improvement of museum provision to accommodate and celebrate our plural society are vital components of future success. Nevertheless, Middleton had much to say, especially about visitors, that was helpful and his support for more joint ventures between museums was well received.

In the 1992–3 financial year, the Museums and Galleries Commission, in response to the Middleton Report, set aside grant aid for joint initiatives, that is partnership or networking arrangements. Yet few applications of substance were made. Of the six projects funded, four highlighted marketing in some way, two had a training element, and one involved the purchase of computer hardware and software which would be shared by three museums. One of the successful applications was towards a joint education project, involving ten museums (all without full-time education officers) in one county, surely just the kind of project at which the scheme was originally aimed. Of the six successful applications, three were from museums acting in consort, two were from related bodies and one from a heritage enterprise. It would seem from this evidence that although museums may be prepared to act together informally, formal arrangements are much harder to strike. As museums become ever less certain of their central means of funding, initiative and flexibility in management will become ever more important. Whether museums will be willing or able to spot the benefits of joint initiatives remains open to question. The Museums and Galleries Commission's funding of such projects has now been discontinued.

Partnerships with museum authorities

Even when museum professionals have sparkling ideas, great collections and good contacts, things go wrong. Sometimes museum development is blighted because of a failure to see or respond to the need to work with people within the political and commercial contexts of provision. Further, for a museum to make an effective case for itself, it must have worked out what its case actually is. The 'museums-are-by-definition-good-and-noble-things' line of argument, will convince no one, and will fall on the stoniest of ground when it comes to fund-raising. People want evidence, persuasive argument backed up by relevant case-studies and a strong sense of well-placed purpose. Then they might wish to be associated, and to work in partnership to agreed ends. It matters that museums can strike a chord that sounds right.

Woodhorn Colliery Museum, a museum devoted to the social and industrial history of mining communities in Northumberland, is doing just that. At first glance, it might seem that this is just the kind of museum that would be under-going budget cuts and experiencing unspoken civic disillusionment and the demoralization of all staff members. It is a local authority-run museum, in an area of economic decline where levels of tourism are hard to sustain. It is also the kind of site that soaks up capital.

So what is different here? The museum, which opened in 1989, has been developed by Wansbeck District Council, who see it as part of an economic strategy to regenerate the area which has been severely hit by the consequences of the decline of the coal industry. The Council has strongly supported the museum's expansion, investing in excess of £500,000 at a time when the capital spending of most local authorities has been rigorously controlled. Wansbeck's commitment to the museum and to continued investment in it is due not to its success as a tourist attraction, which is as yet limited, but to its place as a symbol both of the district's pride in its past and the Council's achievements in creating a new purpose and direction for the area.

The museum has thus become synonymous with the image of the area. In no small measure, the success of this museum has to be ascribed to the energy and convictions of those who run it, who were prepared and willing to listen to all interested parties and to offer their governing body something very positive. In the words of the Museums and Cultural Services Officer for Wansbeck, Penny Wilkinson:

> a museum must become a means for a community to retain its identity and build a new direction. . . . The rights of communities which have lost their economic base is a political issue, but by becoming associated with a community's struggle, a museum is not necessarily taking a political role. Aligning its purpose and practice with the strategies and objectives of its governing body can be seen as a pragmatic move. . . . If museums follow the thinking out there, local authorities might consider that the museum is something that they cannot afford to give up.
>
> (Wilkinson 1993)

Surely, such a philosophy and approach are only possible where the museum is prepared to see people as potential sharers and partakers in the museum experience; where – in turn – the museum is prepared to share its strong sense of purpose with others; and where museum professionals are prepared to take note of 'the thinking out there'.

Partnerships with others

Many museums in inner-city areas have been given excellent opportunities to work with other bodies, both public and private. Underpinning many of the initiatives undertaken have been the twin necessities of urban regeneration and improvement of the environment. Of great benefit to museum development, provision for local leisure needs and regional-based tourism have been distinct elements of the projects created and joint-funded.

Perhaps the best example of this is the Museum of Science and Industry in Manchester. The Castlefield area of the city, in which the museum is situated, has been described by the museum's director as once being 'a forgotten part of the city', into which few people ventured. Now it is a Conservation Area, a thriving and highly regarded part of the city, the regeneration of which has been led by the museum, working in partnership with a host of other agencies. These have included local councils, Central Manchester Development Corporation, the Department of the Environment, the European Community and the English Tourist Board.

The interpretation of the Castlefield area as a whole is now invested in a management company, organized by the Central Manchester Development Corporation, which operates a ranger service. The success and popularity of the museum and the careful development of the Castlefield's environment have encouraged private sector companies to invest in housing, office and leisure projects. In sum, the area has become a fine and balanced sector of the city specializing in arts and leisure provision. And this is largely because people have been prepared to dream dreams, recognize genuine opportunities and work open-mindedly with others towards agreed ends.

131

Sometimes partnerships fail

A measurement of the true success of any project or development is the knowledge that nothing is guaranteed and often even good ideas fail. It would be both false and insensitive to claim that partnerships are the answer for all museums in all situations: they are not. Things go wrong, people or organizations can let the museum down, fail to reach targets or fulfil commitments. Museums can misread situations, put too much faith in arrangements that are not propitious, and choose partners who are not sufficiently equipped or prepared. Most of the partnership arrangements engaged in are calculations, and are based on an expectation of goodwill, which sometimes evaporates. Most museums have found themselves in such circumstances, at some time. The best that can be expected is that they are prepared to learn from the experience in such a way that it cannot be repeated.

There are many illustrations which could be given here, but the most topical at the time of writing is the inability of a small number of provincial museums in Britain to match grants awarded by Area Museum Councils (*Museums Journal*, May 1993, 12). The funding of specific projects on a partnership basis between museums and Area Museum Councils is a well-established practice. Hitherto, the only uncertainties have been whether the project suits the criteria for the funding scheme and if the AMC concerned has sufficient funds to go round. The pressure on AMC funding still exists, but now the situation appears to be beginning to change. Although an agreement may be drawn up, a museum may not be able to secure its matching half of the funds and thus keep its part of the bargain. Cheques have been returned and projects scaled down or abandoned. In such instances, the partnership between museum authority and AMC has, in effect, failed. It is important not to exaggerate the scale of this problem: many museums have been managing their resources very well and have been able to rely upon the full support of their funding authorities. But in a period of recession, when there has been considerable uncertainty about the future of local government, no museum in this sector has been totally secure. However, this experience indicates that museums now and in the future cannot afford to have only one option in their funding schemes; a back-up arrangement has to be identified and prepared. It also shows, most graphically, that museums have to be demonstrably and energetically providing a service which has a range of positive values and which is linked, in partnerships, to a variety of interests. This will be the surest route to continued funding.

The ground rules for partnerships in museums

In conclusion, a set of ground rules might be suggested:

- A museum should not use the word 'partnership', if it is not able or willing to enter into a spirit of compromise, shared responsibilities and mutual tolerance. It is not a game or a management exercise. Feelings are engaged, expectations are raised, and self-esteem is often at stake.

- A museum must have its objectives realistically defined and explained with clarity. It must be certain of what it wants to achieve and should be prepared to leave room enough for it to happen, even in ways that might not have been considered, as yet.
- Mutual understanding should be a genuine aim from the outset. The museum needs to explain itself and be prepared both to listen and hear its partner or partnership group explain themselves. People know remarkably little about museums and what it takes to make a good one. Equally museums often know remarkably little about local groups, other organizations and new enterprises.
- It is important that the right of the other party to have an individual approach and agenda different to the museum's is respected.
- There has to be room for disagreement and for the mutual acceptance of areas where compromise is not possible. Other people have the right not to agree with the museum. Sometimes this is an indication that the museum has not listened in the past. At other times, it may indicate an inappropriate choice of partner.
- A museum must know where the boundaries are, and where compromises cannot be made. In all appropriate circumstances, museum processes and principles have to be absolutely clear and totally adhered to.
- A museum should allow sufficient scope and flexibility for both parties to change either their agenda or their approach in the light of discussion or experience.
- There is a definite need to be businesslike, but not officious. All areas of understanding and agreement should be set out in writing.
- Contingency plans need to be mapped out in the event of things not going according to plan.
- Finally, a review and acknowledgement of the processes, the losses and the gains are essential. Always celebrate the successes. Chalk up the rest to experience.

Partnerships are entered into and maintained as long as some form of mutual benefit exists. This chapter has largely been about the benefits museums gain from partnership arrangements: in this respect it has been rather one-sided. An equally profitable line of research would now be to investigate how other bodies and individuals view and measure their involvement with museums. Such a study could add to the learning and perhaps lead to more profitable partnerships all round.

Note

I am grateful to Dr J. Patrick Greene for permitting me to quote from his unpublished paper on 'Leisure in urban regeneration - the Manchester experience', given in Portsmouth in March 1993.

References

Middleton, V. (1990) *New Visions for Independent Museums in the UK*, West Sussex: Association of Independent Museums.

Potter, P. B. and Leone, M. P. (1992) 'Establishing the roots of historical consciousness in Modern Annapolis, Maryland', in I. Karp, C. Mullen and S. D. Lacine (eds) *Museums and Communities. The Politics of Public Culture*, Washington, DC: Smithsonian Institute.

Wilkinson, M. (1991) 'Patriotism and duty: the Women's Work collection at the Imperial War Museum', *Imperial War Museum Review* 6: 31–8.

Wilkinson, P. (1993) 'Speaking with authority', *Museums Journal*, February, 20.

11

A museum manager discusses museum communication

Stephen Locke

This chapter is concerned with the issues of managing two types of communication: the communication of the museum's purpose to its public and communication between museum colleagues. If the former is to be achieved, the latter is crucial. I describe the experience of Hampshire County Council Museums Service in the hope that, suitably considered and interpreted, it will be relevant to others.

Setting the scene: introduction to Hampshire County Council Museums Service

The public face of Hampshire County Council Museums Service is a network of thirteen museums, eight of which are local museums based on a particular model. The other museums differ in various respects, chiefly being more specialized or site-specific. The Service as a whole is supported by a headquarters and collection management centre. This account is concerned with the eight local museums which have been deliberately planned and developed to communicate a particular role.

The fundamental basis for our communication is our Statement of Purpose: 'We aim to inspire and satisfy a deeper level of interest, enjoyment and understanding of Hampshire's heritage and environment, by developing the full potential of the museum collections in our care, and assisting other organizations with similar aims.'

This Statement is clearly founded on communication of the attributes of museum collections; the provision of assistance to other organizations, although a vital function of the Service, is not relevant to this chapter.

Each of our local museums embraces four elements:

1 'permanent' displays which relate to the environment and history of the community they serve. The theme of these displays can be thought of as telling 'the story of (e.g.) Andover'. Indeed, in a number of our museums this is the formal title of the displays and in all of them it is an internal 'working' title used by the people who created them;

2 a room or space in each museum providing more resources and information. These include literature, indices, information about relevant material elsewhere (e.g. the County Library Service), copies of less accessible material (for example from the County Record Office), databases, videos and local photographs;

3 a temporary exhibition gallery, which provides space for exhibitions which extend the scope of the Service (for example, for material not represented in our collections), provides access to parts of our collections not otherwise on display, or provides facilities for community generated displays;

4 'permanent' displays of parts of the County Council Museums Service's collections which are not local to any one museum. This is material, of which costume, ceramics, firearms, and horology are examples, of particular quality, and of regional or national significance.

Who are we communicating with?

Hampshire has the greatest population of any English shire county (approximately 1.6 million). The towns in which our museums are located are perhaps bigger than you might think (Fareham 104,000, Basingstoke 147,000, Eastleigh 110,000). These figures are for 1993, rounded to the nearest 1,000, and are for the district area, but they may be taken as approximating to the natural catchment area of the museums concerned, and indicate the significance of the populations we are aiming to serve. We know, reliably, that between 45 and 63 per cent of our visitors to local museums live in the district, a proportion that rises to between 68 and 77 per cent for people living in Hampshire as a whole. For the museums I am considering, our visitors are overwhelmingly local. This is not the place to record a variety of other data about our visitors or measures of relative use of our museums, which we believe we have reliably ascertained, but one point is worth emphasizing because I suspect it is true for other local museum services: that is, compared with the socio-economic profile of Hampshire's population, we attract relatively more people in groups C2, D and E than AB and C1. This view is contrary to repeated surveys at other UK museums, but I believe that most surveys have, for obvious reasons, been at what you might term 'high status' museums (national museums, large independent museums and regional museums, especially those that charge for admission or require their visitor to spend significant time and effort to reach them). Very broadly speaking, and leaving aside the question of how popular our museums are, they are visited by increasing numbers of the kind of people they are planned for.

How are we communicating?

Our 'permanent' local displays (in practice nowhere older than ten years and mostly more recent) focus on the natural environment and human history of the area served by the museum, and together they may be said to describe the County of Hampshire as a whole. The Service has some twenty years of experience providing these displays, which means many opportunities for making mistakes and, hopefully, learning from them. Because our adoption of a marketing philosophy is relatively recent, and our plan is still fairly basic, it is difficult to speak very sensibly of success or failure of the harmonization of displays and related services with the requirements of the public we seek to serve. Nevertheless, in my personal experience, interpretation of museum collections has been planned as thoughtfully and coherently as in many museums, and perhaps more so than some. This makes it possible to attempt to evaluate them against fairly well-established aims.

As our Statement of Purpose emphasizes, we see our role as educational and interpretative, however entertaining we try to be, and our displays are always some sort of compromise between telling a story and presenting collections we happen to have. We find it difficult to appreciate the more extreme points of view about the role of objects versus their interpretation through other media, and about education versus entertainment. Crudely put, we believe our visitors expect to learn something when they come to our museums, but they naturally expect us to stimulate and interest them, and I think they recognize when we try to do this, whatever the method, and are pleased to see the effort, whatever the result.

In our more recent displays we have increasingly discriminated between displays of objects, the setting of scenes and the provision of information. Thus we display objects in a simple and flexible, sometimes crowded manner. We provide for local material to be replaced, rotated and in some cases taken out for handling sessions. Displays which tightly integrate objects, text, graphics and other media on an individual basis are inherently inflexible; we want to make it possible to reorganize a case without devaluing the supporting interpretation.

We have increasingly created simple scenes to illustrate local themes, such as conditions in a workhouse, a local industry, environments and so on. In some cases these incorporate museum collections but the prime intention is to set a scene. We think people like these, not at the expense of other forms of inter-pretation, but as part of a balanced communication of our aims.

The provision of textual information beyond brief sentences on graphics and object labels is increasingly being provided by methods which give more infor-mation to those who want it without putting off people who don't (handouts, for example). Information is provided in displays in the form of 'page devices' – relatively robustly mounted information in a form of static ring-binder.

Much more intensive sources of information are provided in resource rooms/areas. The overall philosophy is to use museum collections to stimulate interest in a balanced and attractive interpretation, and provide supporting information in specific locations. A probable future development will be to allow people to 'take the information home with them' using the opportunities of information technology.

Creating communication within the Service

A brief account of one aspect of our Service necessarily simplifies a complex situation. Among the important issues which are involved in the creation of the public face of the Service are integrating the participation of specialists within the Museums Service, and harmonizing local objectives with countywide aims. The expertise which I am particularly concerned with here is:

- the local museum management, led by an experienced professional curator with the support of two or three museum assistants (attendants);
- the education officer who has a specific brief to develop a coherent county-wide education policy to support the national curriculum;
- the marketing officer, who has an analogous brief to develop a service-wide marketing plan;
- the exhibitions officer, who co-ordinates the provision of temporary exhibitions to the museums;
- senior management, who are responsible for the provision of an integrated county museums service which fulfils all its aims.

For all the elements of the Service I have described so far, countywide policies are expressed through the services provided by local museums. Even though the staff mentioned above share a common purpose, they will have significantly different, and valid, perceptions about priorities and how to achieve them. We aim to make these differences creative, harmonize them, and communicate them through the medium of our Local Museum Service Plans. We do not approach these issues in a hierarchical way as I believe line management and staff structures, as I have argued elsewhere (Locke 1992), do not provide appropriate solutions.

The Local Museum Service Plan

The roles of the Local Museum Service Plan are:

1 *Negotiation and harmonization of local, countywide and specialist concerns*: production is achieved through a working party of the local curator, with the education officer, marketing officer and exhibitions officer, supported if necessary by the senior manager with overall responsibility for Hampshire history.
2 *Defining the resources required for the management and development of museums*: Local Museum Service Plans are the basis for both devolved budgets for museums and any countywide budgets which will support the plans.
3 *Statements of standard and performance*: the Local Museum Service Plan includes descriptions of current standards of service and performance indicators.
4 *Ownership by staff*: the statements of standard and performance encourage staff to identify with the plan in a realistic fashion.

5 *Communication of museum aims to community*: the statements of standard and performance are a basis for discussion with local joint management committees of county and district councils and of service level agreements should this be required.

It is likely that to many staff, especially those concerned with the operation of museums, the Local Museum Service Plans will become the only formal plans of which they need be aware in detail. Relevant elements of central plans (collections management, acquisitions, marketing, education, the budget) can all be expressed through Local Museum Service Plans. In this sense they can be seen as an outcome of devolved management and a solution to the problem of encouraging local creativity at the same time as maintaining overall standards and benefiting from strategic support. Indeed, the approach was first conceived as a method by which a countywide education policy could be expressed through a network of different local museums; as the process has developed, more uses for the plans have become apparent.

I hope that museum assistants (attendants) will benefit from Local Museum Service Plans. Because of their level of detail, timescale and immediate local relevance, museum assistants can identify with them, criticize and influence them and of course help implement them.

No museum manager with any significant experience should be naive enough to rest too much faith in any process of planning or structural approach. Because we are so reliant on the skills and knowledge of specialist staff, ordinary human interactions soon affect the achievement of any plan. The challenge is to mediate and harmonize these interactions within a framework which recognizes both long-term strategic values and standards and allows a flexible response to local circumstances. This can only be done at a certain level of detail, and may seem to be an onerous process, but when achieved, it provides a rigorous definition of the role of the museum and the work required to fulfil that role, both of which are essential for effective communication between colleagues and, most importantly of all, with the communities we serve.

Reference

Locke, S. (1992) 'The County Team' in 'Curatorial Identity', *Museums Journal*, October, 29–30.

12

Learning from each other: museums and older members of the community – the People's Story

Sandra Marwick

It is 2.45 p.m. on Wednesday, 9 December 1992. A woman sits holding a brightly coloured cardboard Easter egg in her hands and she talks vividly about an incident in her life when she was seven or eight. Several other people listen intently to her. Surrounding them are cases of brightly coloured pottery which somehow add an extra dimension to the scene.

The woman was me, and the occasion a training day for social and community workers, organized jointly by the Living Memory Association, the Social History and Education sections of Edinburgh City Museums and Galleries, and held in the pot gallery of Huntly House museum.

Why? What were a museum curator and a museum educator doing running a course for which one might have expected social services to be responsible?

In part, the answer lies in the manner in which the People's Story Museum was created and developed, and its operational philosophy – a philosophy inspired by the criteria set by Edinburgh District Council's Recreation Department in its Leisure Plan, and the priorities established there with regard to target areas and social groups. In part, the answer lies in the recent creation of a new post within the museum service, that of Keeper of Education and Outreach Services, the main purpose of which is to 'maximize the opportunities for life-long learning provided by the collections of Edinburgh City Museums and Galleries, together with the development of access to museum services for all residents of the city'. One of the ways in which this is to be achieved is by developing and fostering links with community and social workers, and co-operating with them in offering specialized projects and programmes. In part the answer lies in the vivid phrase coined many years ago by John Cotton Dana: 'Learn what aid the community needs: fit the museum to those needs' (Allen 1981: 112).

The People's Story was created primarily to tell the story of the life and work of Edinburgh people, from the late eighteenth century to the present day. At the outset, the decision was made to involve Edinburgh people in the presentation of their own history, and that oral testimony would provide the basis of much of the research and displays.

> The term 'The People's Story' was taken literally, as the story was to be told as far as possible in their own words and in this way the museum may be seen to be returning history to those who created it . . . in effect a handing over of some of the power from the Curator to the public. Instead of the Curator's expert opinion being stated on a label the words of the person associated with the subject were used.

> (Clark and Marwick 1992: 54, 55)

Here was one answer to the question posed in 1986 by Lalage Bown, then Professor and Director of the Department of Adult and Continuing Education at Glasgow University: 'How can ordinary people acquire a sense that they have a stake in a museum and how can they see museums as places of both learning and enjoyment?' (Bown 1987: 8). In essence, what was established before the museum opened in July 1989 and what has remained ever since is a partnership between museum staff and members of the community, especially older members, which has proved mutually beneficial.

What is the definition of older? Nowadays 50+ is considered the starting point of the third age, but our groups of older people tend to consist more of those of pensionable age, of whom there are 51,686 in Edinburgh (1991 census).

A wealth of experience, knowledge and practical assistance became available through the creation, with the Edinburgh branch of the Workers' Education Association, of a project entitled 'Memories and things'. The objective was

> to develop ways in which the city museums could be used to stimulate older people to reminisce about the past and to explore ways in which memories could be integrated with the collections of The People's Story to give an added dimension to the presentation of history.

> (Clark and Coutts 1989: 30)

The 'Memories and things' project has been well documented in a book of that name and elsewhere (Beevers *et al.* 1988; Clark 1987–8: 25–7). Suffice it to say that the practical results were considerable: taped reminiscences, two books, two calendars, a slide tape show, two exhibitions and contributions to exhibitions put together by Lothian Health Board Education Department, and collaboration with the playwright Alan Spence for his play *Changed Days* (Clark *et al.* 1989: 35–43). Older people advised on displays, layout of text on information panels, wrote dialogue for a sound track and cleaned up objects. In so doing, they learned something of the organization required in creating a museum from scratch; but more importantly, they came to appreciate how much they had to contribute. Confidence grew, as did a sense of pride in past and present achievements, and the realization that the People's Story was indeed to be *their* museum.

Here is Annie Scott, one time fifth housemaid at Carberry Tower, writing in her church magazine:

> at least I'm losing the inferiority complex I've had all these years about my menial job. . . . They have an effigy of me dressed in the uniform

I wore at Carberry, in a glass cabinet, on my knees, cleaning a steel grate. There is a video of me and three other people talking about our jobs. After I've gone, at least I'll be there for posterity, a museum piece!

Museum staff learned a story of Edinburgh's people which is not recorded in the usual historical sources. Objects gained new meaning when placed beside the words of the people who used or owned them. 'Some of us wore brats, what y'd cry an apron. This is a kind of coarse one . . . see the rough bit round the neck. Mostly, you got a soft bit there' (Tam Morton, docker, born 1909).

Work experience and leisure time became more vivid, immediate and personal: 'Every Saturday night we went to the theatre – Lyceum or the Empire. 7.30 every night. It cost you 6d – for the gods' (Jean Hay, born 1914).

And, as the thirty-three figures on display in the museum are all based on real people, it was great fun to have Peggy Livingston in 1989, photographed standing beside Peggy Livingston as a fishwife in 1957; and Mary Gillon recorded alongside herself as tram clippie in 1918.

In the period since the opening of the People's Story, collaboration between museum service and older people has developed in three directions: partnership with the members of the People's Story reminiscence groups and with other older people individually; partnership with agencies working with older people; the provision of training.

Members of the reminiscence groups felt that they wished to continue their involvement with the People's Story, and several suggested that they should act as museum guides, not in the sense of conducting tours, but simply to be in the galleries at specified times, to talk to visitors, listen to their reminiscences, answer questions and report any relevant information to museum staff. Another group member borrows the slide tape presentations *She Was Aye Working* and *Memories and Things* and shows them to community and local groups.

The People's Story Roadshow was a week's outreach programme undertaken to celebrate the museum's first birthday. Five separate venues were identified in different parts of the city, and a day was spent in each, with the aim of publicizing the People's Story, and encouraging local people to think about the history of their area. The programme consisted of exhibitions and videos, hands-on sessions, demonstrations, children's activities and reminiscence with maps, photos and newspaper cuttings, relating to the areas, to act as trigger material. Among the people who assisted were members of our reminiscence group who especially enjoyed demonstrating the games they played in their youth, using replica toys. Diabolos were thrown in the air, tops spun and peevers (hopscotch) played by old and young together.

Old and young together, or cross-generational work, is hardly a new concept. I do not remember a time when I did not talk to older people, whether as a small child pestering my grandmother for stories about her apprenticeship as a dressmaker; or as a student anxious to hear about the First World War from my grandfather. However, the use of oral history as a formal source of learning is a relatively new development in schools. As we are keen to support this, in December 1990 a competition entitled 'Capture the spirit of Christmas Past' was organized.

Participants, aged from 10 to 14 years (upper primary, lower secondary), were invited to find out from a relative, neighbour, friend, what Christmas was like before 1950. (In Scotland, traditionally Christmas was not a holiday, the main celebration taking place at New Year.) The entries received included many verbatim interview transcripts which provide a source of original archive material for us, while participants were given a real appreciation of the value of talking to older members of the community. As Billy Kay, broadcaster and writer, said in his address to a Scottish Local History Forum conference, 'oral history is a partnership between old and young' (October 1991).

This lesson was reinforced by a similar project organized several months later to complement the temporary exhibition on health which was the museum's contribution to the Edinburgh International Science Festival. Primary school pupils uncovered a wealth of information on health care before the creation of the National Health Service and on home cures and illnesses, by interviewing grandparents, older neighbours and the school lollipop man.

An extra dimension was added to the Health Exhibition by the series of 'home cures' activity sessions. Members of the reminiscence group had a marvellous time working with pupils, teachers, parents and museum staff, to demonstrate the remedies of the 1920s and 1930s – bread poultices, a sweaty sock (for a sore throat), menthyl crystals, butter balls. The older people loved being with the children, while one teacher said she had never seen her pupils so stimulated and interested.

Yes, it *was* fun, but behind all the vinegar and brown paper lay a serious purpose, namely to make the point that, not so long ago, people relied on home cures because they could not afford to consult a doctor. 'It cost 2/6d to visit the doctor; 7/6d to call him out,' said Betty Hepburn who went on to relate that as a child she didn't go to the dentist, but to the chemist round the corner 'who pulled your teeth for 6d'. What was important for Betty and her friends was that *their* experience, *their* history was seen as meaningful and interesting to young people. A 10-year-old girl summed up the whole ethos by pointing to Betty and Joan and saying, 'See these two ladies over there? They're great.'

This combination of oral reminiscence and practical help, which has been the basis of our partnership with older people, continued throughout 1991–2. Text for the temporary exhibition 'Headlines', which looked at hair care in Edinburgh during the past 200 years, used extracts from taped interviews with all age groups and many interviewees gave or lent objects. Older people were particularly helpful when describing working practice, fashion styles or how hair was looked after in the home. One hairdrying machine from the 1920s proved to be something of a puzzle. In spite of research into trade catalogues and much discussion, no one could fathom the purpose of a lever at the side. A former hairdresser, now in his nineties, who visited the exhibition came up with the answer: 'That was just for pulling the machine round the salon!'

In a Roundtable Report entitled 'Unhanding the visitor', Ken Yellis wrote, 'Hands-off museum education means equipping visitors to establish their own relationships with objects, collections and disciplines of the museum world' (Yellis 1984: 23). This positive statement seems especially relevant to an assessment of how far the People's Story partnership had developed by the beginning of 1992 when Helen Clark, in tandem with a company called Needleworks, decided to undertake a community banner project.

A wide range of community groups, from an Asian girls' sewing club to Adult Training Centres, to primary schoolchildren helped cut out and stitch, but the main input came from the reminiscence group who chose the theme and contributed to the design. In the process, new skills were learned and one lady of over 70 tackled a sewing machine for the first time in her life.

The banner is very object-based and features a number of contemporary people sharing their history with each other, surrounded by the objects, photographs and words which hold most meaning for those individuals who have created this work of art. Yet, although much of what is shown relates to people's past lives, equally, much that is there is about the museum, its collections and what it represents.

So far, the emphasis of this chapter has been on partnership with older members of the community who are active and mobile; but from the outset it was recognized that there were many others for whom the museum collections remain inaccessible. How could contact be made with people in hospitals, day-care centres, community education venues, residential homes and sheltered housing schemes? One solution seemed to be the creation of a number of handling boxes, each containing about six objects from the reserve collections, plus photographs and advice for prospective box borrowers on how to plan a session. Themes with a popular appeal were chosen – heating, lighting and cooking; leisure and going out; work.

These one-person portable boxes (and those created by the Museum of Childhood), have proved enormously popular with agencies who work with older people. Responsibility for collecting and returning boxes lies with the users who book in advance. Further boxes were created following two evaluation meetings where feedback was received and suggestions made; both the therapeutic and the stimulative value of the objects was stressed, especially by those who work with dementia sufferers.

Another means of reaching older people – taking the People's Story to them – is the long-established medium of the slide show. All manner of community groups write or phone to ask if someone will come and speak, but many of the most lively sessions have been those with people well beyond 50+. A number of pensioners' societies and retired folks' clubs meet in a variety of venues throughout the area covered by Edinburgh District, from the Prudential Pensioners meeting in the Royal Abbey Hotel to the St Anne's Old Folks Club assembling in their church hall, to branches of the Probus Club (retired business and professional men) using bowling clubhouses and local meeting rooms. All these groups organize themselves, with structured meetings and planned programmes of speakers.

In addition, all over the city are many more, informal morning clubs, lunchtime clubs and afternoon clubs, often run by volunteers or community care workers. Transport is provided for members who would not otherwise be able to enjoy the conviviality that such groups provide. Periodically, a request is made for a member of the museum's staff to do a session. There are men and women with hearing problems, impaired sight, lack of mobility, but what vivacity and humour emerges after a few slides showing the 1940s kitchen or washhouse sets, or after asking the question 'what was your mother's store (co-op) number?' Controlling a school class is nothing when compared with attempting to restore order among excited 80-year-olds who have been trying out the People's Story quiz. So much is given back at these sessions; sometimes materially by donations to the collections, sometimes physically by a visit to the People's Story by those able to travel, but always as a gaining of knowledge from the sharing of people's experience. Malcolm Knowles has written that 'Experience is a resource for learning and when experience is ignored, the adult perceives it as a rejection of him or herself as a person' (Sharpe 1984: 263). It is the philosophy of the People's Story that people's life experience should be valued, and that a renewed sense of worth be felt by the communication of that experience.

Participation in these activities is of course very demanding of staff time, and regrettably it is not always possible to meet demand. Partnership can often be maintained simply by the supply of information to a group leader. One organizer of activities for a retirement home wanted to consult over an idea she had to do several 'then and now' sessions relating to prices. Photocopies of archive material – wartime price regulations, early twentieth-century co-operative adverts – provided the basis for a small but stimulating project.

Objects from the handling boxes are most commonly used as trigger material, but a tin bath, soap, washboards and dollies provided a follow-on link to a performance of *Soapsud Island* by the Questors Theatre Company. During the period of the 1992 Edinburgh Festival, Age Concern organized, in a number of community venues, a series of performances of this play which was based on the reminiscences of former Acton laundry workers. As a continuation of one afternoon presentation, members of the audience of older people joined with the cast of the play and staff from the People's Story for an informal reminiscence session. The actors were delighted to have spontaneous feedback from the audience, and to discover from one ex-laundry worker that her working life in a prewar Edinburgh laundry was not very different from Soapsud Island. The People's Story subsequently ran an afternoon seminar which was attended by some of the actors and by the organizers of the older people's groups who had seen the play.

Another agency which has established a partnership with the museum service is the Department of Continuing Education in Edinburgh University. Here a 50+ Network has been set up with the purpose of encouraging older learners back into education. With the assistance of Continuing Education staff, the 50+ Network has its own committee and a variety of courses is offered.

Creative writing is especially popular and during the session 1991–2, a project entitled 'Hands up for new jotters' was undertaken, based on people's experiences of school days. Objects from the Museum of Childhood handling boxes were used as trigger material and visits were paid to the museum. As an end-product of the course, readings of the participants' plays were given by professional actors at the Traverse Theatre.

The course tutor, wishing to extend the scope of the work achieved, then contacted the People's Story to see if further progress could be made. One immediate result was participation in a lunchtime session of the 50+ Network, to demonstrate how reminiscence and oral history had been used in the production of exhibitions, publications, slide tapes, video and the setting up of a museum. A more significant step for the museum service came in the summer term of 1992, but this will be described later. For the 1992–3 session, a creative writing course entitled 'Life's work' is in progress, this time looking at experiences of work and using the People's Story collections as inspiration.

The cornerstone of the 50+ Network philosophy, and indeed of all adult education, is that adults bring their own experiences to new situations, and that adults are responsible for their own learning. This may seem very obvious, but anyone involved in working with, in particular, older adults, will agree that taking personal responsibility is not always easy. We have all been influenced or scarred by our own childhood learning experiences, and for generations to whom education meant sitting in serried ranks being fed 'knowledge' – 'Teach these boys and girls nothing but Facts' (Dickens 1854: 1) – the person-centred approach can be extremely uncomfortable.

An adult education tutor recently described the difficulty she had in gaining the confidence of one particular group she was leading, until she 'proved her competency' by giving a straightforward lecture. Thereupon the class breathed a collective sigh of relief and allowed her to adopt other approaches. During the People's Story banner project, I observed with interest the reluctance of the older women to take decisions, and their instinctive appeal to the project organizer, Helen Clark, who transferred the responsibility back to them, with positive results.

Decision making and first-hand involvement with museum collections was part of the enabling process demonstrated during the 'Headlines' community con-sultation project. 'Headlines' originated in the 1991 temporary exhibition of that name mentioned previously. From the outset the intention was that the exhibition would be the first in a series of what are to be known as exhibition starter packs (ESPs) – loan kits consisting of portable exhibition boards, display cases, a box of objects and photographs.

'Headlines' was piloted during a six-week partnership with a community educa-tion worker, a group of elderly women from the Craigroyston Reminiscence group, a group of young mothers and two members of museum staff (Brace 1992). The older and younger women selected objects and photographs, wrote captions based on their tape-recorded sessions and contributed objects of their own to the final exhibition which was displayed in the community centre, attracting much local interest.

Following the success of the 'Headlines pilot', an ESP launch was held to inform community education workers and other interested parties of the availability of 'Headlines', and to receive suggestions for themes for further ESPs. Guidelines accompany the pack but borrowers can develop their own ideas, according to the needs of their groups. Although any community group can book 'Headlines' interestingly the first users were Edinburgh and Leith Old People's Welfare Council.

Mention of the production of guidelines leads to the third area of partnership – the provision of training. The idea of the museum service making available some form of training for users of handling collections was established during the 'Memories and things' project, when two sessions were held for potential borrowers of the handling boxes. However, during the hectic prelude to the opening of the People's Story and the months of consolidation afterwards, no further training was offered, until the need for establishing guidelines for good practice in another, related area was forcibly brought to our attention.

Helen Clark and I were invited to attend a teachers' in-service training session on the Standard Grade History examination. In this examination 30 per cent of the marks are awarded for an investigation carried out by each candidate, with the minimum of teacher guidance. During the course of the in-service, several examples of bad practice by pupils in the undertaking of oral history interviews in residential homes came to light. As the People's Story promotes the use of oral history, and has built up a wealth of expertise in the carrying out of oral history interviews, the decision was made to produce guidelines both for students intending to interview older people and for those in charge of residential homes.

At this stage, the involvement and sponsorship of the Living Memory Association was sought. The LMA is an umbrella organization for anyone interested in or working with reminiscence and oral history in Lothian Region, and museum staff are prominent in committee and ordinary membership. The guidelines have now been published, and it is appropriate to mention that while the benefits of oral history to both younger and older people are stressed, difficulties are not glossed over. This chapter emphasizes the positive benefits of partnerships with older people, but it would be foolish to pretend that it is sweetness and light all the time. To quote from the guidelines:

> If expectations are too high, disappointment or disillusionment can ensue. Young people should be made aware that interviewing an older person is not always easy or straightforward. Some older people have hearing problems, or have difficulty remembering: some repeat the same stories several times or digress before reaching the conclusion. Patience, tact and clear communication are essential. Personality clashes can occur between people regardless of age. Oral history is a partnership and it is wise to remember that both participants bring their needs and perhaps divergent aims and objectives to that partnership.
>
> (Living Memory Association 1993)

147

These guidelines are for teachers, pupils and those in charge of residential homes. Practical training workshops have also been arranged at Huntly House museum for members of the Living Memory Association, and museum staff have trained their own volunteers who then undertake interviews on behalf of the social history section.

In a recent article entitled 'Whose museum is it anyway?' Jocelyn Dodd wrote: 'The process of first meeting the community and then working with it, requires many skills different from those traditionally used in formal museum education. Such skills are less concerned with systematic learning, but more about negotiating, networking and confidence building' (Dodd 1992: 31).

'Negotiating, networking and confidence building': these words sum up our response to the request from the 50+ Network to which reference was made earlier. As an extension of the 'Hands up for new jotters' course, the tutor approached Helen Clark and me with the proposal that we offer a six-week training course in oral history for any member of the 50+ Network who might be interested. One of the ideas which the Director of the Centre for Continuing Education is pursuing is that of volunteer tutors and housebound learners; namely that people taking a course of study at the centre should then share what they have learned with those who are unable to leave their homes. Oral history was seen as perhaps being a variant of this.

Accordingly, six one-and-a-half-hour training sessions (two in the Centre, four in Huntly House) were organized for five members of the 50+ group and one young woman from another class who expressed interest. Interview techniques were taught, and objects from the handling boxes used. It was a learning experience for all, and we quickly realized, among other things, that one and a half hours was not long enough! Evaluation of the course was very positive, and the young woman has now gone on to undertake a reminiscence project among older people.

Museum educators working with young people will be familiar with that excellent publication, *Learning from Objects* (Durbin *et al.* 1990). (Fifty ways with a Big Mac box and all that!) Museum educators are even supposed to know about using objects with adults. But how many opportunities for learning are lost when our handling collections are not used to maximum effect? A number of valuable lessons were learned in the summer of 1991 when, at rather short notice, a colleague was asked if a group of older blind and partially sighted people could handle a couple of objects on display, during a visit to Huntly House museum.

Instead, objects from the People's Story and Museum of Childhood boxes were laid out on tables in the lecture room, to which the blind people and their sighted volunteer helpers were conducted. Watching what happened was illuminating. Helpers tended to hand objects to their blind companions as though they could see, rather than place them in their hands; then, with great enthusiasm, say what the object was, rather than allow individuals to touch and explore first. All but one of the group had become blind later in life. The exception was a lady who had been blind from birth She was a revelation, both in the confidence with which she handled stone piggy, diabolo, satin shoes, and the descriptions she gave. At the beginning of the afternoon, the group organizer had been sceptical about having such an object-handling session. By the end, she had no doubts. Her group left animated, sighted and non-sighted alike enthusiastically swapping experiences.

But objects can evoke painful memories too. Whenever we have held workshops and follow-up sessions, such as that after *Soapsud Island*, the question has recurred, 'How do you deal with painful memories?' along with 'How do you stop one person dominating a group, and how do you ensure that everyone contributes?'

After much discussion and thought, it was decided to offer a series of training days, through the Living Memory Association, and to invite a specialist to take charge of each session. The first of these dealt with painful memories and was held in Huntly House museum under the direction of a family therapy counsellor. And that is how I came to be delving into memories of my past, for the whole purpose of this particular course was 'learning by doing'. In order to understand what happens to the people in your group, you must have personal experience. Numbers were limited to ten on this occasion – two museum staff and six women and two men involved in community care or reminiscence work. We all found the experience powerful, exhausting, extremely useful and not long enough. Everyone expressed a wish for future sessions.

So where do we go from here? How will our partnership with older people develop and grow? More training sessions for those working with older people will be offered – there is certainly a market; every course, so far, has been over-subscribed, and when museum collections are being used, we feel a certain responsibility to ensure that maximum benefits are gained. There will be more outreach projects undertaken in the community, using established groups and networks.

As part of the museum division's contribution to the Edinburgh Fling (April/May 1993), a joint project with members of Edinburgh District Council's Arts Outreach team is to be undertaken in a community centre in a part of the city not previously targeted.

On the completion of the Children and Young People's Strategy – a policy document about to be formulated by Edinburgh District's Recreation Department, after an ambitious consultation process with children and young people – work will begin on a strategy for older people. Older people will also be involved in the creation, in the autumn of 1993, of a new community museum at Newhaven, formerly a fishing village, but now incorporated into the City of Edinburgh.

Part of my remit as Keeper of Education and Outreach Services is to work with older members of the community. There is so much potential, so much to do, but resources are limited. Two themes alternatively inspire and haunt me. One is a remark made by a local church minister – 'All those people sitting in their rooms all day doing nothing: can't we *do* something?' The other is the example of the

Heights and Hill Community Council described in *Museums, Adults and the Humanities* (Collins 1981: 354–6). This project was breathtakingly simple but immensely effective, and involved the more active residents of a New York single-room occupancy hotel bringing learning to the less mobile.

Learning, lifelong learning, is what the partnership process is all about. The message is learning from each other: the medium, museums, collections and people. If through museum collections, people can be encouraged to move beyond reminiscence into reassessment and revaluation of their own lives; to advance from reflecting about the past to examining the present and to questioning the future, then we can agree that the museum is 'a site where people learn about people (including themselves) primarily through objects that people have made, used or found meaningful' (Schlereth 1984: 5).

References

Allen, L.(1981) 'Community involvement', in Z. Collins (ed.) *Museums, Adults and the Humanities*, Washington, DC: American Association of Museums.

Beevers, L., Moffat, S., Clark, H. and Griffiths, S. *Memories and Things*, Worker's Educational Association, South East Scotland District.

Bertram, S. (1981) 'Use of a cultural voucher system to stimulate adult learning', in Z. Collins (ed.) *Museums, Adults and the Humanities*, Washington, DC: American Association of Museums.

Bown, L. (1987) 'New needs in adult and community education', in T. Ambrose (ed.) *Museums in Education: Education in Museums*, Edinburgh: Scottish Museums Council.

Brace, D. (1992) 'The headlines project', *Living Memory Association Newsletter*, August.

Clark, H. (1987–8) 'Reminiscence work and Edinburgh city museums', *Journal of the Social History Curators Group* 15: 25–7.

Clark, H. and Coutts, H. (1989) 'Telling the story', *Museums Journal*, November 1989, 30.

Clark, H. and Marwick, S. (1992) 'The People's Story – moving on', *Journal of the Social History Curators Group* 19: 54–5.

Clark, H., Ineson, A., Moreton, G. and Sim, J. (1989) 'Oral history and reminiscence in Lothian', *Journal of the Oral History Society* 17(2): 35–43.

Collins, Z. (ed.) (1981) *Museums, Adults and the Humanities*, Washington, DC: American Association of Museums.

Dickens, C. (1854) *Hard Times*, London: Collins.

Dodd, J. (1992) 'Whose museum is it anyway?', *Journal of Education in Museums* 13: 31.

Durbin, G., Morris, S. and Wilkinson, S. (1990) *Learning from Objects*, London: English Heritage.

Knowles, M. (1973) *The Adult Learner: A Neglected Species*, Houston, Tex.: Gulf Publishing Company. (Quoted in S. Nichols (ed.) *Patterns in Practice*, Washington, DC: Museum Education Roundtable, 126.)

Living Memory Association (1993) *Guidelines for Collecting Oral History by Young People*, Edinburgh: Living Memory Association.

Schlereth, T. (1984) 'Object knowledge: every museum visitor an interpreter', Roundtable Reports 9(1), in S. Nichols (ed.) *Patterns in Practice*, Washington, DC: Museum Education Roundtable, 102.

Sharpe, E. (1984) 'Education programmes for older adults', Roundtable Reports 9(4), in S. Nichols (ed.) *Patterns in Practice*, Washington, DC: Museum Education Roundtable, 102.

Yellis, K. (1984) 'Unhanding the visitor', in Roundtable Reports 1 in S. Nichols (ed.) *Patterns in Practice*, Washington, DC: Museum Education Roundtable, 126.

13

Disabled people and museums: the case for partnership and collaboration

Eleanor Hartley

The ideas expressed in this chapter are based on the experience of the Richard Attenborough Centre for Disability and the Arts at Leicester University (RAC). The Centre has its roots in the Adult Education Department and has been working for some ten years to create and develop arts courses for people with a wide range of disabilities, including blindness and visual impairment, motor impairment, learning difficulties and various forms of mental illness. The research and teaching programme that has been built up by the Centre over these years has been based on the principle of partnership, whereby student and teacher together explore new pathways to the arts and alternative ways of learning.

In practice, this has meant that each student working with a member of staff has examined, often by a process of trial and error, a range of methods and techniques which might successfully provide a route into the arts for him or her. All those who come to the Centre do so because they have not been able to satisfy their interest in the arts as participators, observers or through traditional channels. The discovery of possibilities, which takes place between staff and students, and between students, must be essentially collaborative for the work of the Centre to have any meaning.

During these years the Centre has regularly contributed to museum exhibitions, workshops and seminars which have directly related to the needs of disabled visitors. Our endeavours at the Centre have many parallels with those of colleagues in the museum service who are working in the area of special needs. There are, of course, differences in our situations, and thus my comments on the concepts of partnership and collaboration will need to be interpreted in the light of the experience of each individual museum and gallery.

It is difficult to make an honest assessment about our attempts at collaboration. Most of us working in an education context assume we are fostering good relationships with our client or student groups and that collaboration is one of the foundation stones on which this relationship is built. But to work from a basis of partnership implies an understanding of the equality which exists between the provider and those for whom provision is being made. Where establishments have been traditionally seen as the guardians, interpreters and dispensers of knowledge, the real processes of partnership, involving at least two-way communication between all parties concerned, have not been encouraged. This is particularly so where people with disabilities are concerned.

But circumstances have changed, both in my place of work and in yours. We are being forced to address the interests of new client groups, to look for new markets and to respond to social and political pressures, and much of this pressure has been very healthy in terms of the development of ideas and practice. The impact of this change may be most obviously illustrated by the emphasis now being placed on the need for physical access to museums and art galleries. Although it could be argued that not enough is being done to make buildings accessible to people with disabilities, there is no doubt that considerable improvements are taking place. Many old buildings, and not a few new ones, have had serious access problems and have tried to solve them, often partially, occasionally absurdly, sometimes imaginatively. Beacons of good practice in the museum sector stand out. Greenwich Citizens' Gallery has been a trail-blazer; the Harris Museum at Preston and the Horniman Museum, London, have both shown what can be done when the needs of disabled people are seriously considered, and Stoke City Museum and Art Gallery have similarly given consideration to provisions which will make the disabled visitor's experience as 'normal' as possible. However, there are many more examples of buildings concerned with the arts, and museums in particular, which are still not negotiable in a wheelchair, where deaf people and those with visual impairments can feel very alienated, and where people with learning difficulties are treated with suspicion. The Arts Council Report of 1992 reminds us that of the 200 galleries surveyed, only 30 per cent had taken active measures to improve their facilities for disabled visitors. Much of this inadequacy was put down to a tendency simply not to think things through (Earnscliffe 1992).

In cases where issues of physical access have not been addressed, it is very possible that effective communication between the museum and the disabled community is hampered by the financial implications of adaptation and change. A policy of carefully planned development which provides access by stages is feasible even within budgetary constraints and much can be done to make people with disabilities feel that they are valued visitors who are worthy of the same respect as everyone else. Indeed, some of these measures involve little or no financial investment. Despite this, there has been a reluctance on the part of some establishments to embark upon a programme of access provision, perhaps because it was thought that conceding to even a small change, a ramp to a main door for example, would open a floodgate of demand that, even with grants for adaptation, could not be met in the present economic climate. This concern has been fuelled by some recent reports which highlight the anomalies of buildings with partial access and which on the whole have been less than sympathetic to the attempts of some museums. But a policy of phased access provision can be agreed upon through negotiation involving policy makers and disabled users: both parties have good reasons for collaboration.

Access, however, means much more than getting in through the doors and moving relatively freely inside. Educational access is of equal importance and often receives far less attention, although it is widely understood that making information more relevant and more easily obtainable is essential if new groups of visitors are to be reached. Again there has been a major shift in the last ten years with some landmarks, particularly in the United States and in France. Outreach staff with special responsibility for disabled visitors, tactile exhibitions and workshops, handling sessions, signed tours, braille labelling, relief maps and audio guides are much more in evidence and some museums manifest a high degree of collaborative effort between staff and disabled users. The appointment of at least one member of museum staff who has responsibility for disability issues has been particularly successful, especially where the member of staff has a disability, although there is always a danger that too much is invested in one person or in one under-resourced section (often the education department).

Disability issues need to be part of our mainstream cultural provision rather than the occasional special conference or exhibition. There is undoubtedly an oddness about special disability events at museums, particularly exhibitions of paintings by blind and visually impaired painters for example, if they are not integrated into a programme where disabled people are given equal regard. These occasional events at their worst can be patronizing, particularly when exhibitors need to be recognized for their art, not for their disability. They have also, in some cases, served to reinforce the exclusion of disabled people from mainstream provision within the museum service.

At best, however, 'special' exhibitions can serve to illustrate the contribution which art can make to the lives of people with disabilities. Furthermore, they can inform and contribute to the world of the arts to the benefit of us all. This was one of the intentions, for example, which guided 'An eye for art' at the Gunnersbury Park Museum in 1988, an exhibition of paintings by blind and visually impaired artists which explored, among other things, the aesthetic of low vision.

Despite these reservations, exhibitions have been one of the Richard Attenborough Centre's major forms of publication. They have given direct evidence of the processes which lead to finished work and are statements about what is possible. The fact, for example, that someone without sight can produce an eloquent self-portrait head offers irrefutable evidence to other students and teachers. It may also demonstrate that following a less familiar path imposed initially by a disability can produce unique insights. The Centre has developed and mounted a number of special exhibitions over the last ten years. The latest of these, 'Finding form – an exhibition of sculpture to touch', was designed as a travelling exhibition which during the period 1998–91 followed a nationwide route which included Milton Keynes, Coventry, Nottingham, Cleveland, Portsmouth, Swindon, Derby, York and Middlesborough. At each location workshops and seminars were organized to run in parallel with the exhibition and participants and visitors included children from mainstream and special schools, adults and young people from day centres and residential homes, and a cross-section of the public, a small percentage of whom had disabilities. The seminars attracted a great many teachers and other professional groups as well as trainees from art schools and colleges of education.

153

This exhibition was certainly not without its flaws. It was very difficult, for example, to design stands which were a suitable height for all abilities and disabilities. It was, however, a brave attempt at collaborative work involving a mix of professional and amateur artists with and without disabilities. It provided a positive and active image of people with disabilities and at the same time encouraged the visitor to consider the development of the artists' ideas by the inclusion of statements from all the participating artists about their work. Although designed for visually impaired people, it opened up opportunities for everyone to learn through touch, and we hope that the able-bodied enjoyed it as much as disabled visitors did.

At the planning stage of this exhibition four professional artists were each asked to create works of sculpture which could be touched: they were also asked to supply their source material. A number of visually impaired students were invited to produce individual and group projects which again could be touched and were asked to explore the process of translating ideas taken from forms in nature into works of sculpture. There were two major points to the exhibition: the first was to illustrate that works of sculpture developed from sources; the second was to show that sculpture in its various stages could be explored and understood through touch as well as through sight, and that touch was a form of exploration and expression whose boundaries were very wide. Above all, the exhibition was intended to reinforce the essential philosophy and practice of the RAC, namely that our exploration of the theory and method of the learning process must be based on collaboration and partnership.

Attempts at collaboration such as the one described above are of course only small drops in the ocean and there is always a possibility that they will remain occasional events which pay lip-service to the interests of minority groups. Realistically, the number of disabled visitors to museums and galleries remains very small, even at these special exhibitions. This must cause us to question, yet again, not only how accessible and welcoming museums are, but how relevant they are in terms of the cultural experiences of disabled people. Certainly for people who are visually impaired, the overwhelmingly visual world of the museum and gallery may remain largely inaccessible, however good the *aides-mémoire*, braille labelling or audiotapes. It is, perhaps, too easy to forget that even among people with full vision works of art are not always simply and easily understood.

It remains to be seen if, in the future, disabled people will find more reasons to participate in the experiences of our common culture as interpreted by today's museum services. Some of the signs are promising: there is at one level a huge commitment that 'in Europe and elsewhere, disabled people must have the opportunity to share our common cultural heritage. Only in this way will they be truly full members of society.' Other indications are less hopeful. A true partnership between disabled and non-disabled people in any context requires not only new resourcing, but a shift in power structures which gives disabled people some role to play in deciding how money is spent. These are possibilities which have become politically sensitized at a time when resources have been limited and commitment to social changes which are not led by market forces is thin on the ground. In a political and economic climate where collaboration is difficult to achieve, there is evidence of increasing polarization between some organizations for disabled people and some of the traditional providers of information, services and resources. The 'disability arts' culture is one such example of polarization which in its most extreme form has denied the relevance of collaboration and partnership between disabled and non-disabled people in the arts. This growing perception of cultural divide has as many ramifications for museums as it has for the performing arts and arts education, denying as it does the unifying language of shared cultural experience.

In terms of widening our experiences of life and our perception of the arts, there is everything to be gained from the fostering of collaboration between disabled and non-disabled people and between people with differing disabilities and different insights. In the museum context, as elsewhere, there is a great deal to be lost by not meeting the real challenges of true partnership.

References

Breitenbach, N. (1992) 'Afterword', in *Museums without Barriers: a New Deal for Disabled People*, Paris, London and New York: Fondation de France, in conjunction with Routledge.
Earnscliffe, J. (1992) *In Through the Front Door*, London: Arts Council of Great Britain.

14

Integrating school visits, tourists and the community at the Archaeological Resource Centre, York, UK

Andrew Jones

Introduction

This chapter is divided into three unequal parts. First, there is a description of the development of the Archaeological Resource Centre (ARC) with an account of its present layout and exhibits. Second, there are examples of special events run at the ARC to give some indication of the variety of activities arranged and how links are being made between archaeology and aspects of the arts and science. Third, there is a brief assessment of the Centre's achievements in the first three years of operation.

The Archaeological Resource Centre: history and development

In 1977 the York Archaeological Trust (YAT) began to use the redundant medieval parish church of St Saviour in central York for the storage of bulk finds from excavations. Several decades of neglect had left the building barely secure. The roof leaked copiously, the interior was home for countless pigeons and the stonework had deteriorated badly. However, as a store for archaeological finds – pottery, bone, tile and soil samples – the building was an improvement on a riverside warehouse subject to periodic flooding. Thus, finds were placed on racking and protected from rain and pigeon excrement by plastic sheeting.

At that time plans were drawn up to transform the building into an archaeological research centre by installing a mezzanine floor provided with facilities for research and curatorial staff. The ground floor would continue to be used for storage. Sadly, in those days lack of funds precluded this development.

In 1984 the Jorvik Viking Centre (JVC) opened and instantly proved to be hugely successful at communicating with a mass audience about the Vikings in York and archaeology in general. The enormous number of visitors to the Centre rapidly began to provide the York Archaeological Trust with the financial resources that allowed a dramatic increase in its staff. In addition, the Trust began to explore new ways of achieving its charitable objective – educating the public in archaeology.

Comments from visitors to the JVC, including archaeologists, school teachers and members of the general public, made it clear that there was a need for another archaeological centre in York. Was it possible to look again at the plans for St Saviour's church and integrate public archaeology, finds research and curation? Much work was necessary to transform the building into a centre for research and visitors. A fund-raising campaign was initiated, the building was renamed St Saviour's Archaeological Resource Centre, and a phased pro-gramme of refurbishment and improvements began. The roof was renewed, a mezzanine floor was constructed with offices and work benches, a new heating system was installed, intruder alarms and other security equipment were fitted. By improving the standard of storage (using roller racking) it was possible to use the nave as an area for public display and still store most of the small finds from excavations and a considerable quantity of bulk finds at the church. This work was carried out over the period 1986–9.

The ARC is located on what is now a quiet, largely residential, side street and occluded by a monstrous modern building, The Stonebow, which houses a betting shop, the Job Centre and a subterranean snooker hall. The impression of the street is not inviting to casual visitors. It was necessary to see if visitors could be attracted along St Saviourgate. In the summers of 1987 and 1988 a temporary exhibition, 'Viking ships', was mounted at the building to attract visitors the 100 yards from one of the main tourist areas of York, The Shambles. This exper-iment proved a success and was followed by an exhibition of holograms in 1989.

During this time plans were made for permanent displays at the ARC. A team of researchers, designers, computing staff and others was assembled from the Trust's own staff, with specialist advice from researchers in the University of York, to develop displays. The brief was to design interactive exhibits that were accessible and interesting to visitors of all ages and backgrounds. Each display had to be safe, engage visitors' attention for approximately seven minutes and be easily reset. The aim was to design an academically sound yet exciting place for anyone interested in archaeology and what archaeologists do.

The ARC opened experimentally in February 1990, free of charge, and began charging on 1 April 1990. Visitors are encouraged to participate in a wide variety of absorbing activities in which they handle archaeological finds, experiment with replicas to investigate early technology, and discover how computers are used by today's archaeologists.

The ARC is the main flagship for the Trust's educational activities, a place for York residents, families, tourists, and school and college parties. It is also used for seminars, lectures, day schools and evening classes.

Unlike the Jorvik Viking Centre which is a magnificent spectacle, the ARC actively encourages the visitor to participate.

The Resource Centre is also the main home of the YAT Finds Administration Department, whose staff package and catalogue the thousands of finds recovered

157

during excavations. In addition, finds researchers, some staff of the York Archaeological Trust, and other visitors from museums and universities around the world study and report on objects at the ARC.

Visitors spend most time in the nave of the church in the Archaeological Activity Area (AAA) but the mezzanine is also open. Here other facets of the ARC, the architecture of the building and the work of researchers on anything from Roman glass to Neolithic fish bones, can be viewed. The area beneath the tower with its fine reset twelfth-century corbels is an ideal venue for lectures, video shows and other presentations. There are often temporary exhibitions in the tower area of the mezzanine and there is a general archaeological information point where visitors can learn about excavations and sites open to the public. Outside in the graveyard there is an archaeological garden growing dye plants, cereals and other plants known to have been exploited in York in the past. There is also a collection of architectural fragments, mainly from York's medieval buildings, and a pleasant informal garden.

A host of local historical and archaeological groups use the building, including the York Excavation Group, the York Branch of the Young Archaeologists Club and the York Oral History Project. Day schools and evening classes are also held at the ARC.

Almost all aspects of the ARC are suitable for visitors with special needs. Wheelchair access to the Archaeological Activity Area is excellent; however, it is not yet possible for visitors in wheelchairs to visit the upper floor.

The Archaeological Activity Area

The prime object of the AAA is to allow visitors of all ages and all abilities to find out more about how people lived in the past by investigating archaeological materials and experimenting with a range of crafts and technologies. Information technology, from pictograms to interactive video, plays an important part in the display. Friendly trained staff, clearly identifiable in bright red jumpers, are on hand to help visitors explore the displays and the building. Most of the staff are students on work experience placement or volunteers who come regularly.

Visitors are encouraged to handle and sort ancient finds, unlock replica Viking Age padlocks, learn to spin and weave, and stitch together copies of one-piece Roman leather shoes. Viking Age and later writing can be explored by arranging magnetic hand-carved runes on a picture of a Viking Age grave marker. In addition, some resources are available on request. For example, visitors can write in beeswax on replica Roman writing tablets.

The last section of the AAA is a display of micro-computers which demonstrate their potential to handle archaeological plans and distribution maps. In addition, they show which data are recorded for the many objects recovered by excavation. An interactive video allows visitors, by simply touching the screen, to examine an archive of captioned colour photographs taken during the excavations at 16–22 Coppergate, York. Most recently we have installed a computer system that allows visitors to interrogate the 1851 census returns for St Saviour's parish.

The ARC shop contains a wide variety of carefully selected educational and other academic publications, and souvenirs including high-quality replica pottery.

Operational details

In its present form the ARC can accommodate a recommended maximum of thirty visitors every thirty minutes when running at full capacity. Already we are fully booked for most weeks during term time. We recommend that parties be no larger than thirty pupils plus accompanying adults. Parties of adults are best limited to fifteen. We recommend that visitors allow an hour and a half for a visit to the ARC.

A video giving a brief introduction to the archaeology of York and showing several of the activities at the ARC is available free of charge for short-term loan. In addition, we have produced 'Notes for teachers: primary and lower secondary' (Binns 1990), which includes a description of the activities and ideas for preparatory work, and an education pack full of ideas for activities that can be done in preparation for a visit or as follow-up. An illustrated booklet giving details of four archaeological walks was published in 1992 (Kemp and Jones 1992). Each walk begins at the ARC and visitors to the city are encouraged to explore the Roman Fortress, Viking, Norman and medieval York.

Examples of special events at the ARC

Special events are organized throughout the year. These include food tastings, demonstrations of ancient technology, holiday activity mornings for children, art exhibitions and other archaeologically related events. Below are details of three events which illustrate how the ARC is making links with other aspects of human material culture.

Music and theatre discovery workshops

The ARC has held two series of music and theatre discovery workshops for children aged roughly 7–11 years. Each workshop lasted for two hours on successive Saturday mornings when the Centre is usually closed. The workshops are designed for anyone wishing to explore sound and theatre – they are not just for children who have developed performance skills.

The workshops were led by a local contemporary composer based at the University of York. He has recently been resident composer at the Banff Centre, Canada, and his work has been performed at the Norwich, Leeds and Brighton festivals, 'Island to island' at the South Bank, London, and Musica Nova, Glasgow. He based the workshops on 'Rituals and relics', the title of an exhibition of landscapes held at the ARC during the summer.

Those taking part created their own rituals using materials available at the ARC – bones, pottery and other suitable objects. Each person was encouraged to contribute to the workshop so that the final piece was the product of all those involved. This was performed to parents and friends.

The events were grant-aided by Yorkshire Arts.

From lamps to lasers

'From lamps to lasers' was a collaborative pilot project between the Department of Physics of the University of York and the ARC. The event took place on a very windy and wet Saturday and Sunday in November 1991. The concept behind the project was to integrate hands-on demonstrations showing some of the properties of light (visible and invisible) with displays of ancient lamps, other equipment and materials used to generate light from prehistoric times to the present day. It was also an experiment to see how the ARC could be used at weekends when much academic work in the building ceases.

Visitors were greeted by a hologram of a friendly young lady who blew a kiss and winked at them. Coloured shadows, revolving disks, a laser making symmetrical patterns and a display on polarized light were demonstrated by physicists from the University of York in place of the usual slide show.

Moving on to the displays, visitors were confronted with a huge lump of beef suet taken from a beast killed earlier in the week. This caused some consternation, particularly to vegetarians. Some of the suet had been rendered down and clarified, and was used to make tallow candles and rush lights. Visitors were encouraged to have a go. This display provided a natural link to the ARC's display on bones – a comparison of the size of modern and ancient cattle leg bones.

Members of YAT staff kindly displayed their personal collections of lamps and lights dating from 2000 BC to the twentieth century. A genuine Roman lamp was filled with olive oil and lit. More recent lamps included Edwardian bicycle lamps, oil and acetylene, early battery lamps, a 1960s architect-designed table lamp, a camping gas light, a modern battery-operated torch and a replica Roman lamp. Many of these were displayed working.

A bendy mirror, diffraction gratings, a display of microwaves (not strictly light but part of the electromagnetic spectrum) and a giant kaleidoscope, normally displayed in the concourse of the Physics Department at the University of York, entertained young and old alike as visitors clambered inside the kaleidoscope to find hundreds of reflections of themselves.

The Yorkshire Branch of the British Association for the Advancement of Science provided materials for a range of hands-on activities. Visitors made brightly coloured spinners and investigated colour mixing. In addition, the British Association team devised an electronic problem-solving activity where visitors were able to make a working model of a lighthouse, or disco lights, from everyday recyclable materials such as pop bottles, yoghurt pots, sweet wrappers, kitchen foil and scrap paper.

Archaeological textile specialists from Textile Research Associates showed how fragments of brown cloth, often recovered from ancient latrine pits, were in fact once brightly coloured pieces of clothing dyed with plant and animal extracts.

Transparencies from the *Bradford Telegraph and Argus* showed how inks are over-printed to bring colour to newspapers. Computer monitors illustrated fluorescence and gave insights into the use of computers in archaeology to record finds and examine their distributions. Interactive video, a laser-based technology, beautifully linked archaeology and physics.

Upstairs a bench showed a selection of archaeological finds from York: Roman pottery lamps, Viking Age stone lamps and beeswax, medieval prickets (spikes to hold rush lights and candles), a fine pair of eighteenth-century candle snuffers and part of a piano candle-holder. Displays of medieval stained glass and lighting showed stunning colours of the past. In addition, the displays explored the links between light, glass and the spirit of God in the Middle Ages. In the Christian tradition, St Bernard of Clairvaux wrote, 'As the glorious sun penetrates glass breaking it . . . so the word of God, the Light of the Father, passes through the body of the Virgin, and then leaves without undergoing any change.'

People in the Middle Ages relied on oil lamps, candles and rush lights to light their houses and places of worship. Only four chandeliers are known to have survived in Britain from the Middle Ages, and they are all in churches or cathedrals. Three have a figure of the Virgin at the centre. The Mother of God was the symbolic channel for the Light of the World, Jesus Christ. She was also identified as the radiant woman in St John's Revelation, 'clothed with the sun, with the moon under her feet, and on her head a crown of twelve stars' (Rev. 12:1).

Judaism still requires the kindling of lights in the home to inaugurate the Sabbath and festivals. The hanging lamp with spouts radiating in the form of a star was often depicted suspended above festive tables in Hebrew manuscripts of the Middle Ages. Most of today's other religions also use light to focus worshippers' attention.

A selection of medieval stained and painted glass was placed on a light box. Stained glass windows are made out of shaped and coloured pieces of glass held together in mosaic patterns, rather like a jigsaw. To begin with, stained glass windows were only found in churches and monasteries. Stories from the Bible, the life and work of Jesus and the saints could be shown in these glass mosaics, helping those who could not read books to understand the lessons the church wanted to teach them. As the light shone through the windows, they were not only beautiful but instructive.

By using a magnifying glass visitors could examine the edge of the red glass and see, first of all, that half the glass is colourless, or slightly green, and that only the top half is red. Looking even closer at the red half it was clear that there were lots of very thin layers of red with thin layers of colourless glass in between.

Visitors were also encouraged to compare pieces of red glass. The red layer on top of one piece was not as thick as it appeared to be on another. This is because, later in the Middle Ages, at the time of Bannockburn and the Black

Death, glassmakers managed to colour the glass with a single layer of red which would let light through very easily. This is called flashed red. Some of the pieces on display had very thin flash – yet it was still possible to see the colourless glass where the red has been chipped off. Red glass like this can be seen in the nave of York Minster.

Hands-on displays from 'Xperiment', part of the Manchester Museum of Science and Industry, were borrowed in order to demonstrate characteristics of ultra-violet light, and reflection. A laser was used to transmit sound waves and fibre optics used to transmit video signals.

Although the displays were extremely well designed and interesting in their own right, there can be no doubt that the most important contribution to the event was the large number of demonstrators who gave their time to explore light with the public.

The Beatles: the tangible evidence. An exhibition of Beatles memorabilia

As Paul McCartney was about to celebrate his fiftieth birthday during the York Festival in June 1992, the ARC decided to hold a temporary exhibition of Beatles memorabilia. This was the first ARC community archaeology project involving York residents.

The exhibition made the link between today's material culture and finds recovered from excavations in the city. For example, medieval pilgrim badges were purchased by pilgrims at holy sites and taken home to be cherished for many generations. These mass-produced objects can be seen as forerunners of today's souvenir trade.

The Beatles memorabilia loaned by York residents illustrated the range of material evidence in people's houses in 1992. Not surprisingly it was dominated by records, but also included magazines, tickets, cushions, badges, tin trays, posters and newspapers from many countries.

Many of the objects in the exhibition were of little financial value when they first appeared. By 1992 they were worthy of public exhibition and some are highly sought after by collectors.

The importance of the objects in the exhibition comes from the significance people place on them, and is closely linked to memories of times past. Significance cannot easily be measured and so the importance of an object cannot readily be assessed unless the background of the owner is known. The display made the point that when we know little of the culture or society that produced objects, it is more difficult to assess the significance of those objects.

The care archaeologists take excavating, storing and studying fragmentary and often insignificant-looking remains enables us to look more systematically at the evidence and to build a more complete picture of the past. As archaeologists we acknowledge, however, that we will never really know the full significance of many of the finds we dig up. This is only apparent to the individuals who used and, sometimes, treasured them.

162

Assessment of the first three years of the ARC

The three years since opening have witnessed considerable success. The ARC has won three major awards: the British Archaeological Award for 1990 as the Best Archaeological Presentation to the Public; the Best Museum of Archaeological or Historical Interest in the 1991 Museum of the Year Awards; the Gulbenkian Award for Museums and Galleries for Best Imaginative Education Work for 1991.

The ARC has been visited by museum designers, curators, directors and academic archaeologists from all over the world. The ARC's influence is now visible in displays in places as far flung as Japan and as close as Lincoln and Carlisle.

The number of visitors per year has grown from 33,000 in 1990 to over 60,000 in 1992/3 (see Table 14.1). It is particularly pleasing to report that the anticipated problems of integrating school visits with those of other sectors of the community proved unfounded. The ARC is of most interest to adults accompanying children, whether they are teachers, parents or grandparents. The majority of adults who visit the Centre alone enjoy watching younger visitors take part in the activities when it is busy and are happy to move around the building to avoid the worst congestion. During term time we are most busy with school and college groups, at holidays we have most general public visitors. Figures 14.1 and 14.2 dramatically show the pattern of visitor attendance throughout 1992–3.

Table 14.1 Admission price and visitor numbers at the ARC, 1990–2

Year	Admission charges		Number of visitors	
	adult	child	schoolchildren	total for year
1990	£2.00	£1.00	23,017	33,233
1991	£2.20	£1.10	29,356	55,932
1992	£2.75	£1.75	31,413	60,287

Note: The number of schoolchildren includes primary, secondary and tertiary students in pre-booked parties.

We have provided work experience opportunities for over 200 students from York and elsewhere. Many are as young as 15 years of age and gain their first experience of archaeology at the ARC as they study travel and tourism. A large number are postgraduate students of archaeology and heritage management who have been able to conduct visitor surveys and help develop displays and temporary exhibitions.

The future also looks bright. We are now busy planning to modify the displays so that we can allow even more visitors to explore archaeology actively.

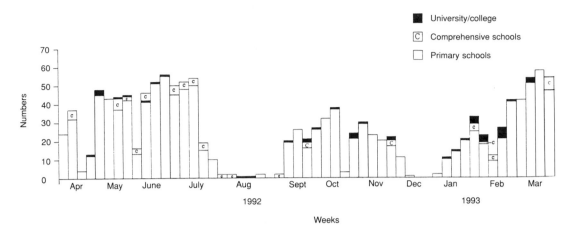

Figure 14.1 Graph to show numbers of school/university/college parties at the Archaeological Resource Centre 1992–3

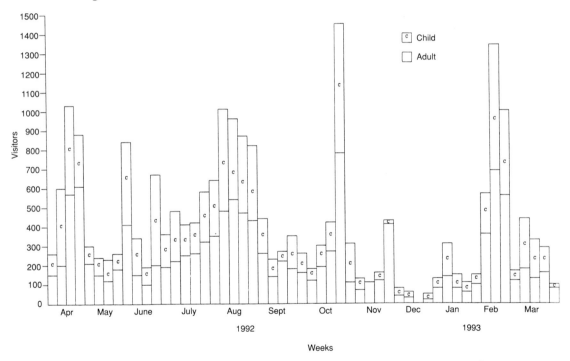

Figure 14.2 Graph of independent visitors for the period 1 April 1992 to 31 March 1993

References

Binns, G. (1990) *Notes for Teachers (Primary and Lower Secondary)*, York: Archaeological Resource Centre.

Kemp, R. L. and Jones, M. W. (1992) *The Time Traveller's Guide to York*, York: Archaeological Resource Centre.

15

Changing our minds: planning a responsive museum service

Sally MacDonald

Croydon is building a new museum and a new museum service. Its aims are 'To encourage creativity, communication and a critical awareness of history', and 'To be relevant, responsive and accessible to everyone'.

We hope to create a dynamic and flexible museum facility, a people-centred (as opposed to a place-centred) local history service and a museum which empowers local people, attracts visitors from London and the south-east and gives Croydon a sense of place.

I started work in 1989 and the museum is due to open in 1994; it is a luxury to have had five years to develop the service. We are also lucky in having been able to start almost from scratch. But I cannot claim that we have planned in a systematic way from the start. Planning a responsive service in Croydon has been a haphazard, often ill-considered and sometimes enlightening process, which I try here to present as coherently as I can. But we do not have all the answers. And maybe the thing about trying to be responsive is that you never do; you have to keep asking and you have to keep changing your mind.

This chapter is about the various types of market research we have carried out, both formal and informal, expensive and cheap. The service has not yet opened to the public, and so most of this research has been formative evaluation or concept development. But we are also looking at ways of trying to structure our service to make it more responsive long-term.

Who is it for?

Croydon's popular image is that of a grey suburban wasteland: mock Tudor on the outside, faceless offices at the centre; acres of chain-store shopping; somewhere you have to go through to get from London to Gatwick airport. It was described in *GQ Magazine* as 'the monolithic mirror glass headstone to the life that none of us wants' (Coster 1992) and by the London *Evening Standard* as 'the Steve Davis of southern towns' (Cotton 1991).

And the people who live there get a bad press too. The *Evening Standard* described 'Croydon man' as follows:

He is definitely not homosexual; he spends his weekends building loft extensions to prove it. He met his wife at a Chris de Burgh concert at Fairfield Halls, the only place in England where you can still see The Strawbs. Since then he has been fenced in with baby equipment. He is happy though, because his house and garden are full to the brim with stuff, all bought in Croydon, the Great American Hinterland of England, where there is nothing much to do but shop.

(Cotton 1991)

That is a powerful image, and one which deeply affects people who live and work there – both of these journalists were brought up in the Croydon area – but it is a little more complicated than that.

Croydon is London's most populous borough – over 317,000 people live there. Around 17 per cent are of African, Caribbean or Asian origin. The north of the borough is densely built up, while the south is greener – it includes a lot of land in the Green Belt – and much more affluent. As many people commute into Croydon as commute out of it to work – over 100,000 a week – and even more go to shop in the centre. It is, despite its image, a diverse and fascinating place.

Is it a museum?

In 1987, for a variety of reasons connected with urban regeneration and local pressure, the Council decided to build a major new cultural complex in the centre of Croydon, incorporating a new library, cinema, arts facilities, shop, café, exhibition galleries and a museum.

It would have been quite easy to set up a traditional and easily recognizable museum. Some ACORN research we commissioned in 1989 suggested that Croydon had a strong base of traditional museum-goers. But these would still only represent a small proportion of the local community. Starting a new service seemed to present an opportunity to shape, or position, the museum in a non-traditional way; to build a service that was more relevant and more accessible to more people than most museums are.

What sort of museum?

We commissioned the Susie Fisher Group to carry out qualitative research on attitudes to history and the arts among local people (Fisher 1990). They talked, in focus groups, to a range of types of people we felt were unlikely to visit a traditional museum, together with two control groups of museum users. To start with, the researchers were uncomfortable with our choice of groups. To market a commercial product, one talks to the people most, or more, likely to buy. But we believed that if we were serious about empowerment and access we had to approach the research in a different way. The results of this research have already been published (MacDonald 1992). There follow a few examples only of how plans changed as a result of the findings; of how it changed our minds.

'They're just smelly old relics. Security guards saying, "Shut up".'

(young white adult)

'I don't think you look forward to museums, but you enjoy them once you've made the trog.'

(family museum-goer)

We expected the non-users to feel differently from the control groups, but we found that the differences were not that great. Almost everyone thought most museums were pretty boring. The museum-goers go there through a sense of duty. This was reassuring for us because we had been worried that traditional users might be deterred by something different.

'Croydon – what history?'

(museum-goer)

'If the museum was just what Croydon was I don't think I'd really bother.'

(black teenager)

'You can't say you're off to the museum to your mates, can you?'

(white teenager)

We discovered that somehow we had to find a way of marketing Croydon Museum Service without using the word Croydon or the word museum. The research suggested that we promote ourselves around concepts like fun, discovery, creativity and world links. We changed the name of the museum to Lifetimes and will probably promote it along the lines of 'a unique living history game'. Very briefly, Lifetimes will be an object-based display aiming to cover a whole range of aspects of human experience – food, crime, transport, sex – from 1840 to the present. The exhibits will be linked via an interactive computer that activates the displays and connects objects with people, pictures, sounds and film, and puts them in a variety of contexts.

'Black artists? Our country's culture shouldn't be changed for them.'

(white museum-goer)

'We'd be lost without family history.'

(Asian retired)

'I'm not interested in an ethnic museum. I don't know anyone who would be.'

(black teenager)

The research confirmed our feeling that it was vital for us to achieve good representation of different cultures in Croydon, and that the best way to do this and to combat racism was not to have a black history section or a women's history section but to integrate histories and make connections wherever possible. I believe that representation – in collections and displays – is absolutely fundamental to achieving a relevant and accessible service.

Our methods of collecting, which have evolved over the last three years, are fully discussed elsewhere (Fussell, forthcoming). But we constantly monitor our collections as they grow, in the light of information we have from contemporary censuses and census summaries, in order to identify where gaps and weaknesses lie. We collect in a very personal and collaborative way, through oral history, often borrowing rather than taking objects from their owners, copying photographs rather than acquiring them. Our local contributors are recorded for the interactive and they check and edit the scripts for those sections that apply to them. It is a lengthy process of building up trust, but it is very rewarding.

We still have a lot of gaps in our representation. As a result we have employed an Irish researcher (the Irish are Croydon's largest ethnic group) and an Asian researcher, both on short-term contracts, to build up our collections and links with individuals and communities we found we were not reaching; in order to achieve fair representation we need to make special efforts in particular areas.

'Museums are boring. They should have the future.'

(Asian teenager)

'I like seeing how things were then. Something you can relate to your parents. Say up to 100 years ago.'

(family museum-goer)

'They should take you out of yourself – holograms, moving models.'

(young white adult)

'It would be good if you could take part in plays.'

(white teenager)

'You've got to have fantasy if you want people to go.'

(family museum-goer)

The early research suggested many things we would never have thought of ourselves. We had been going to concentrate on the recent past anyway, but as a result of the research we introduced a 'Future' section. We cannot afford holograms and moving models, but partly as a result of local people's suggestions our education work and interpretation will incorporate drama and role play. We shall also be designing in a special display area for individuals and groups to make their own displays with staff help.

So the research changed our plans for marketing the museum, it affected our collecting strategy, our plans for the content and shape of the displays and for the way in which we interpret them. It was expensive, though – it cost £12,000 in 1991 – and we had to build on it using much cheaper methods.

How can we make this interesting?

I have said that we are almost starting from scratch; but we do have some collections. The Riesco collection of Chinese pottery and porcelain was collected by a local solicitor and founder member of the Oriental Ceramic Society who bequeathed it to Croydon. It is a very traditional museum collection, which is currently on display in the Fairfield Halls, a concert hall and theatre in Croydon. It is very interesting pottery but it is a very boring display.

We shall be rehousing the collection in the new complex and we wanted to get suggestions for improving the displays. This time we did employ a consultant, but we did the recruiting ourselves, through schools, community groups and work contacts. We recruited teenagers, schoolchildren and adults, including Chinese people and people with special needs. Doing the recruiting yourself is time-consuming and it can mean that you are talking to people who already know you and who feel obliged to be polite about your ideas. But it is cheap.

We recorded the groups talking. People told us what they found most interesting about the pots – the fact that some of them had been buried, the significance of the glaze colours, the value of the pieces – and this will help us to develop themes for the displays. We asked everyone to fill in a cartoon speech bubble giving advice about the displays. This piece of work took a couple of days and cost us £700 for the consultant's fees. Once again it has helped us in practical ways such as designing the lighting and casework, sorting out themes for the gallery, and planning activity programmes.

Like this?

One of the simplest and most significant ways in which we seek feedback is by giving talks to groups in Croydon. We use slides of what we are doing, along with slides of other people and places to show what we are planning, to start discussions and to find out what people think. We do not reach a representative audience in this way; in Croydon the groups wanting speakers tend to consist mainly of elderly, white women. And there are major limitations on what you can do with a large group – people cannot be expected to talk openly about difficult subjects, like racism for instance. But it is possible to get useful feedback and ideas. If we were more proactive and organized about whom we talked to, we might achieve more in this way.

We have also held exhibitions to try out ideas. The 'Living memories show' took place in a gallery in Croydon's main shopping centre in 1990. In many ways it was a trial run for Lifetimes; it had similar content but without the interactive element. We evaluated it via the exhibition attendants and using a touch-screen questionnaire. The qualitative feedback via the attendants told us a lot about which areas of the exhibition people liked. It cost us nothing. The touch-screen questionnaire – which cost around £400 – told us that it was only people under 20 who felt comfortable using it, and that some of them used it many times, and enjoyed giving us several different answers.

How can we make it better?

Lifetimes is built around an interactive computer, and in designing and developing the software we built in several stages where we could test and adjust it. We tested the second prototype by inviting along two groups to have a look at it. One group was of local teachers – clearly schools are a big potential market – and the other was a group of the Croydon people who had been involved in contributing to the programme; they had been recorded on tape and had contributed objects for the displays.

Both groups were quite frank and told us practical things about using the interactive. Teachers would need copies of the programme to show their classes before a visit. Contributors felt that the interactive would be so popular we would need other forms of information and interaction for people who could not get to use it. We had been planning cassette guides but they insisted we should have ordinary labels as well; we had been going to be daring and do without them.

That was very simple testing; it took organization but only lasted an afternoon and evening and cost us nothing but our time and some tea and cakes. As a result, we changed our minds and our plans again.

How can we make it even better?

We have recently tested the third prototype of Lifetimes. This was a critical point in the development of the interactive programme, and we decided to use professional researchers. The brief was to answer the following questions:

- Is the subject matter interesting? too difficult or too shallow? If not interesting, how could it be improved?
- Does the style – voiceovers, text, images – work? Do people find it entertaining or off-putting? How could it be improved?
- Are there any practical improvements users can think of?
- Will people come to it? How much would they pay to get in? Would they come more than once?

We decided that we needed to test these ideas with particular groups, rather than simply with a random sample of people. We felt that we could organize sessions with Lifetimes contributors and with Council members ourselves. The session with councillors was held last of all, so that if necessary we could feed back to them what everyone else had said. Had we not carried out the formal testing, the views of colleagues, contributors and councillors would have been the only views considered, and the changes we made as a result would have been quite different.

This prototype was tested using something called a hall test, carried out in an empty shop in the shopping centre over three days. Shoppers outside were recruited by the Susie Fisher Group working to agreed quotas. They were invited to come and use the prototype, which was set up alongside a model of part of the displays and some objects. Researchers watched and chatted to people about their response to it. During the three days, 120 people tested the prototype. Museum staff acted as helpers in the testing process so that they could see how it was done.

This testing gave us all sorts of practical help in making the interactive easier to use; people suggested many alterations to the programme. We were told that black people were inadequately represented on it; that there should be more material obviously aimed at children and about children's lives; that clearer instructions were needed; and that there should be a 'bored' button for stopping the programme.

Older and younger people used the interactive in different ways; older people liked to have a human guide beside them to help them get started, whereas younger people found out how to use it by themselves. We found it did stimulate discussion and interaction in the way we hoped it would. But it raised problems we do not yet know how to solve; people with arthritis in their hands may have real difficulty using the touch screen, and we seem to need a volume control.

But most of the findings have been easy to implement. We had planned to introduce systems of scoring and prizes as part of using Lifetimes. However, the research showed us that people might want to score but were not very concerned with winning prizes. Abandoning this option will save us at least £5,000 immediately in programming costs – much more in the long term, with the cost of administering a scheme of prizes. The research cost us £4,500; so in this instance it is possible to demonstrate that research can save you money as well as improve your service.

What exhibitions should we show?

We are currently testing ideas for our exhibitions programme. Museum staff had brainstormed a long list of ideas for exhibitions, but we wanted to know if any of them were at all appealing to other people. Again this is being carried out through focus groups led by facilitators from the Susie Fisher Group. The three focus groups were mixed ethnically, grouped by lifestage: teenagers and young adults, people with young families, older people. They were not museum-goers, but had each watched some 'cultural' programme on the television within the previous year, so they were broadly receptive to the kind of discussion taking place.

We gave the researchers our initial concepts for the exhibitions – titles and subtitles, key words and ideas, and photocopies and postcards as illustrations or stimulus material. Our exhibition officer and I sat in, as anonymous observers, on two of the discussions. Each group sorted the exhibition ideas into those they liked, those they disliked and those they were not sure about, just on the basis of title and subtitle. They then discussed each subject in turn, the facilitator drawing out key themes and areas of interest. The groups then looked at the illustrations we had chosen. Frequently these images seemed to be a turn-off or a disappointment; sometimes they helped get to the root of people's interest.

The second stage of this work is to test the ten most popular exhibition ideas on a much wider group of people. The researchers have designed a semi-structured questionnaire designed to elicit responses to one particular exhibition idea, with a question at the end asking for suggestions for exhibitions. These questionnaires are being used by leisure and marketing students from local colleges. Each student has to interview five people of different ages about one exhibition idea, and the overall quota is designed to test ten proposals on a range of people of different ages and ethnic groups, male and female. We do not have the final results yet, but we do know that some of the shows we thought would be wonderful may in fact have very limited appeal.

This research is costing just over £4,000. It is a lot of money, but it is defining our exhibitions programme for the next two to three years, and if it means that we put on better and more popular exhibitions then it should, in the long term, save us money, as well as helping us to do what we set out to do. No commercial company would dream of launching a new product without substantial research. Museum products may have more to do with knowledge, power, creativity than with money, but they are still products which need to be marketed and sold if we want people to have them.

How can we go on getting better?

At the moment I am not sure whether we should be planning to commission more research work like this from outside companies on a regular basis, or whether to concentrate on developing skills in-house in a responsive structure. Probably we should try to do both.

We will soon have a small annual budget for research, and each exhibition budget will have a sum built in for evaluation. In theory, the more thought and research that goes into concept testing, the less will need to be altered after opening, but I still think our longer-term displays will need a contingency sum for putting problems right.

Finding time for review and reassessment is even more difficult than finding money. At Croydon we have had the real luxury of a long lead time for developing the service; without it we could have done very little of this research. It will be more difficult to build in research time while running a service to the public.

The area I think is most important, but which I understand least, is how we can achieve a responsive staff. We are planning that all museum staff work front-of-house on a rota basis. That way everyone gets to meet the public and sees how they respond to displays and exhibitions. Everyone will also spend some time working behind the scenes. We will not have attendants or warders, only museum assistants.

Until now – with the exception of our administrative assistant and our Irish and Asian freelance researchers – we have only appointed people with museum experience and training. This is because in developing a new service people need to work on their own initiative a lot and we felt we needed people with a certain level of confidence and experience. But it seems to me that one of the drawbacks of this is that all our established curatorial staff are middle-class white graduates and six out of seven of us live outside Croydon. As staff we are quite unrepresentative of our target audiences and I do feel that this is a problem.

We plan, before we open in 1994 to appoint five more museum assistants. These people will be recruited locally and appointed without museum training or experience. Degrees will not be necessary. We will be looking for lots of other qualities though, such as good communication skills, experience in working with the public, open-mindedness and a very organized approach to work.

We then aim to train these people, mostly in-service, in every aspect of museum work; cataloguing, preparing exhibitions, carrying out research, and doing administrative work. We shall all, including those of us with museum qualifications, need training in front-of-house duties such as evaluation, enquiry work, customer care, security and guiding. We hope that we can organize this to tie in with National Vocational Qualifications so that people in Croydon can gain qualifications that will be recognized elsewhere. It seems to me that the current state of museum training with its emphasis on a certain type of academic qualification is one of the biggest barriers to achieving a responsive service. I have absolutely no idea whether our training plan will work but I am sure that it is worth trying.

It is hard to find the money and it is hard to find the time for evaluation. We have a long way to go. We shall not be able to evaluate our service fully for at least another two years. But I do think it is the right way. I believe in empowerment and access and accountability. And I think it is possible to argue for greater responsiveness on all sorts of levels and using different words. You can argue for charterism or democracy, access or choice. You can use your findings to support bids for more money, or to improve or prioritize your services when money is tight.

It does take some courage to start, though. If you are used to thinking that you know best – after all, you're a museum professional – it's unpleasant when you find you don't. On a personal level it seems to me that being responsive means learning to listen, learning to love failure, and learning to change your mind. And here's a suggestion from a real Croydon man: 'Be flexible and open to criticism' (black retired).

Note

My thanks to all my colleagues at Croydon for their ideas, commitment and hard work, to Susie Fisher and Jo Jarrett who did most of the research, and to everyone in Croydon who has participated in it.

References

Coster, G. (1992) 'City of The Damned', *GQ Magazine*, July.

Cotton, I. (1991) 'In defence of Croydon man', *Evening Standard*, 22 May 1991, p. 9.

Fisher, S. (1990) *Bringing History and the Arts to a New Audience*, research undertaken for London Borough of Croydon.

Fussell, A. (forthcoming) 'Politics with a small "p": collecting with that personal touch', paper delivered at the Walsall Conference, 'The politics of collecting', 1992.

MacDonald, S. (1992) 'Your place or mine?', *Social History Curators Group Journal*.

16

Museums, myths and missionaries: redressing the past for a new South Africa

Janet Hall

Social and cultural changes

This chapter seeks to outline the position in South African museums after years of apartheid government, and to comment on the effects this has had on the cultural traditions and attitudes to cultural heritage in our country. It will also include examples of innovative partnerships which have been formed between some South African museums and their local communities, that demonstrate a spirit of genuine co-operation and trust.

In 1990, with the final dissolution of apartheid, the government opened the formerly 'white' state schools to all races. This move has brought a sharply increased awareness of the importance of an education that will prepare children for the multicultural contacts that are now part of their everyday lives.

It is no longer acceptable educational practice to judge and label people, and new perspectives are being sought which will teach that despite the many differences between us we all share a heritage that needs to be acknowledged and commemorated.

Many teachers have turned to museums for help with multicultural, multiethnic perspectives on the school curriculum, and as the Education Officer I find myself directly on the interface between museum, teachers and expectant school groups. As museums we owe our visitors a greater understanding of, and a broader perspective on, the people we claim to serve. There is a compelling need for us to look at comprehensive multiethnic provision very soon.

There is an African proverb which says, 'Until the lions have their historians, tales of history will always glorify the hunter.' Within this proverb lies the essence of South Africa, a country deeply rooted in the ancestral traditions of thousands of years, and at the same time one deeply divided and degraded through the ignorance and cultural arrogance of successive waves of colonists, missionaries and an apartheid government, all of whom have failed to recognize the richness and complexity of the African peoples they met and subjugated.

Largely as a result of missionary zeal and their aim to 'convert' the heathen and teach them to adopt a lifestyle similar to that of nineteenth-century Britain, traditional religious beliefs and customs of blacks have been disrupted by western Christian ethics; the western money economy and system of taxation have severely damaged the traditional kinship system which formerly provided for all one's needs; and traditional clothing, music, foods, arts, crafts and skills have largely been subsumed by the more robust but not necessarily appropriate European culture, leaving most black South Africans living as second-class copies of their white compatriots.

At the same time the voices of these people have also been excluded from the political structure of the country, thereby reinforcing the dominance of a white minority. This also served to justify the notion that blacks have a status that is inferior to whites and not worthy of a place in history. For many years, therefore, white South Africans have learned a one-sided and distorted history of the multicultural land they live in.

In the new South Africa it is very clear that if all population groups are to gain a realistic sense of their own identity and cultural heritage, and live together in a truly multiracial society, these imbalances will have to be redressed immediately and a new approach to cultural heritage found.

Museums are by definition repositories of the past – keepers of the collective story – but as Dr John Kinnard of the Anacostia Neighbourhood Museum in Washington, DC, said on his visit to South Africa in 1987, and as was repeated by the eminent British museologist, Dr Kenneth Hudson, during his visit during 1991, 'unless South African museums make serious efforts to balance their portrayal of the country's history, they will remain monuments to white supremacy, fossilised in a biased past and utterly irrelevant' (Dr Hudson quoted in Kahn 1992: 9).

Museums in South Africa are a legacy of the British colonial era, and are by their very origin a western Eurocentric concept. As pointed out by Dr Brian Stuckenberg at the 1987 Annual Museums' Conference, 'We are *in* Africa, but not yet *of* Africa. It is time to outgrow our European prototypes' (Stuckenberg 1987: 297).

Ill-prepared by their upbringing, museums in South Africa may be tempted to shrink from the challenge of a new nation and pretend that their rightful place is in the past, but they cannot afford to make this mistake: our glory is not in our past track record but rather in our future. Our glory will be in the unbiased interpretation of a nation in change.

We cannot afford for the word museum to be one of outmoded, static, insulting and degrading connotations deeply rooted in a divided past. If this were to happen it would remain a word of abuse rather than celebration. The need for an authentic African approach to museums is urgent, and will require unique creativity if museums are to be able to claim a right to existence.

Because of racial superiority and Eurocentric perceptions and values it is an unfortunate fact that the richness and diversity of South African cultural history has not been given the recognition and attention it deserves – least of all in museums where collections are heavily biased towards whites, while records of black cultural traditions are at best fragmentary and at worst non-existent. Yet as pointed out by Rhoda Levinsohn in her book *Art and Craft of Southern Africa: Treasures in Transition,*

> Among the Tribal people of Southern Africa today there exists a rich and varied centuries-old artistic tradition. . . . Little known in the West . . . the treasure of material arts that expresses the physical and spiritual requirements of indigenous Southern Africans is threatened, experiencing a decline so precipitous in the last ten years, that urgency must now characterize the need to document what remains before its disappearance is complete.
>
> (Levinsohn 1984: 5)

Museums should never underestimate the contribution that they could make towards preserving the cultural heritage of those societies that are buffeted by more dominant cultures and peoples.

I recently watched a fascinating National Geographic film on Japan where, acknowledging the need to safeguard treasures and skills of national importance, the government has adopted a unique policy in which a small number of people who are skilled in the ancient creative traditions of that country (paper making, banraku puppets, pottery, traditional styles of acting, etc.) have been selected to receive the title 'Holders of important, intangible cultural properties'. They are, however, more commonly known as National Treasures and in return for a small annual stipend these people are entrusted with the responsibility of teaching and training apprentices as well as exhibiting their crafts to keep the ancient creative traditions of Japan alive.

In South Africa a similar policy could serve to forge powerful links with our traditional past and illuminate the future with the timeless spirit of days gone by.

However, in a country where the political situation is turbulent and fragile, the role of 'patron of the arts' would probably not be high on the government's list of priorities. But, this would be an ideal opportunity for museums. As sponsors of the great masters, they would ensure that the torch of our unique artistic and cultural heritage will live beyond the numbered days of those few practising craftsmen who still live in forgotten corners of our country.

At the National Museum of Botswana a project of this kind has been running with outstanding success for many years. From remote rural areas bordering the Kalahari Desert and Okavango Delta come some of Africa's most creative basket makers.

The museum, recognizing the exceptional talent of these people, organizes an annual national basket-making competition for them. Only baskets of the most traditional designs and exceptional craftsmanship are accepted for the exhibition and subsequent sale, at which museums and collectors from around the world are able to obtain the finest examples of this national handicraft.

177

This is not to say, however, that museums should focus all their attention on pristine unacculturated practices and reject all that has succumbed to modernization as not being genuine. An attitude such as this would tend to reinforce the notion of a disappearing people, or of a people unchanged by the world around them.

While black and other cultures have always occupied a small place in South African museums, the appalling reality is that they have invariably been portrayed as primitive societies in a timeless present – static, dark, mysterious and passive.

In a bid to appear sophisticated, museums in South Africa have tried to emulate their great European counterparts by building big exhibitions which then remain unchanged for twenty years or longer, giving an impression of undisturbed harmony. Yet the rate of change in exhibition subject-matter and issues is far greater than museums have ever had time to acknowledge.

Too inward-looking and oblivious or even hostile to the outside world around them, museums have failed to recognize that all around us traditional Africa is either rapidly vanishing or irrevocably changing.

Urban life, western-style economically rewarding occupations, and the lure of western mass-produced goods have either quickly replaced traditional cultural objects or provoked a response which has produced a unique mixture of the two – known in South Africa as transitional art.

Skilful borrowing and their inveterate frugality has led to the throwaway items of our society being incorporated into their traditional art forms. Bottle tops, beer can tabs, plastic bags, old toothbrushes, discards from medical clinics, broken zippers, buttons, striped telephone cable wire, plastic wrapping and metal from tin cans have all been incorporated into a striking display of objects.

In addition to this the market for traditional arts and crafts has also rapidly expanded, but in order to cater for a largely 'white' buyers' market the arts and crafts are changing. New materials, new techniques, new designs and new functions have been introduced, so that while the traditional techniques of basketry, beadwork and pottery, for instance, are not changing the shapes and designs are.

Far more square shopping baskets and colourful woven handbags are now made to cater for European tastes; the traditional colours and designs for beadwork are being replaced by fashion colours, styles and shiny disco beads; and traditional clothing is being updated and restyled in order to be able to cash in on the huge surge of interest in ethnicity, but in a suitably Europeanized way.

As you have perhaps realized, we are caught in a peculiar paradox in South Africa where on the one hand our traditional arts and crafts are in danger of dying out, but at the same time the surge of interest in 'things African' that is at present sweeping the world has by the unique response of our indigenous people not served to save them, but rather to hasten their extinction, through the evolution of the artistic forms themselves. All this has produced a uniqueness that is wholly South African, and there is a compelling need for museums to measure up to their responsibility of documenting these changes.

It would also seem to me illogical to try to separate the tangible from the intangible, and to assume that only 'objects' of cultural importance or interest should be preserved. The contribution of South Africa's black population cannot only be measured in terms of items suitable for museum display, but should also include all the foods, music, songs, dances, myths, legends, beliefs and customs that are so intimately associated with those objects. As keepers of the collective story, do museums not have a responsibility in defining national identity by providing the fullest picture possible, especially in South Africa where First World and Third World rub shoulders with inevitable exchanges affecting the traditions of both groups?

The potential of museums

At the Albany Museum in Grahamstown it has become one of my most pleasurable activities to tell traditional African stories to children at the beginning of every year. Brought up on a diet of 'Little Red Riding Hood', 'Cinderella' and 'Mother Goose', the majority of children have no idea of the rich treasury of stories about the people and animals of Africa that exist on our very doorstep.

Using items from the museum's collection to illustrate the stories, I have over the last six years been able to share a small part of the cultural heritage of our children with them in what I believe is a wholly enjoyable and extremely successful way.

In a rapidly changing world museums have the power to contribute to the richness of the collective human experience and to give the cultural diversity of a nation its fullest expression. They can achieve this through four key concepts:

1 Education in its broadest sense should be central to the museum's public service. By fostering a realistic sense of identity, heritage and contribution to the history of their country, museums can help a fragmented nation to regain a sense of self-worth and live in a state of truly multiracial harmony.
2 Museums must make a commitment to enlarge, enrich, understand and appreciate their collections so that they represent the full spectrum of the cultural diversity of our pluralistic society.
3 By broadening the base of their operations and programmes to include a wide spectrum of organizations and individuals, museums can foster partnerships and collaborative ventures which will make them more inclusive places that welcome diverse audiences and reflect an expanded public dimension.
4 Strong leadership and the commitment of funds are central to all these issues.

This is all very well but it leaves us with a serious question which may well have struck you right through this chapter. As stated earlier, a museum is a Eurocentric concept and as such is something which has no equivalent in traditional Africa.

179

Many comments and judgements have been made on the worth of museums, and it is generally agreed by First World nations that they are essential as a means of preserving the past, defining national identity, and giving purpose to and providing continuity in life.

Yet are any of these considered vital by a nation in the Third World? Considering that the majority of them have either been or still are struggling to throw off the shackles of a dominant political power, it would not be surprising if wanting to erase the past was top of their list of priorities.

With only the years ahead showing any prospect at all for a brighter existence, the past may well have little or no value at all.

And although this may only be conjecture, reality in South Africa adds even more complications and does not paint a brighter picture either.

Although museums in South Africa have always been open to all races and have always had free admission on at least one day of the week, black visitors have not been enthusiastic supporters and have tended to stay away.

This may well be a result of the appallingly inadequate representations of black culture in our museums, or a lack of understanding of what museums are about (many people hold the view that museums are full of dead bodies and are therefore frightening places). Similarly, imposing building styles and identity problems with other similar-looking institutions which until recently were not open to all races have also caused confusion. Furthermore, museums being a totally Eurocentric notion, it is not generally in the black tradition to visit them, and leisure time and weekends are reserved for traditional family activities.

To further complicate matters, the former Group Areas Act, by which the apartheid government forced people of colour to live far away from the metropolitan areas, has meant that visiting a museum is an expensive and time-consuming pastime for them.

How are we to reconcile these differences without falling straight on to the horns of the dilemma where on the one hand we in museums with our Eurocentric upbringing see it as our responsibility to act as conservators and protectors of an endangered and evolving culture in South Africa, and yet on the other hand run the risk of being accused of patronization and paternalism?

As pointed out by Professor Timothy Bergen of the University of South Carolina,

> [We] have sometimes been chagrined and shocked to find [our] well-intentioned plans utterly rejected by the very people whom they were intended to help. What [we] have often overlooked . . . is the fact that the well educated, middle class professional probably has a totally different set of perceptions [and hence values, attitudes and modes of behaviour] than his rural, lower class uneducated client.
>
> Merely because the professional sees merit in a particular proposal, in no way ensures that the client will view the proposal in the same way. Indeed

it would be nearly miraculous if he did. It is precisely because of this that the demand has grown for greater participation of clients in the planning of proposals intended for their benefit.

(Bergen 1993: 7–8)

Collaboration and action

It is my particular pleasure to share with you four excellent examples of collaboration between 'white' museums and 'black' people in South Africa, which form the basis of very special relationships between professional and client.

The first concerns what has become known as the Bulhoek Massacre:

> On the 24th May 1921 a force of some 800 members of the South African Police clashed with the Israelites, followers of a black religious prophet, Enoch Mgijima. The police were armed with rifles, machine guns and artillery. The Israelites were armed with Old Testament style weapons, swords and spears. At the end of the day 183 Israelites lay dead and nearly one hundred were wounded. One policeman was wounded and a police horse was killed. This incident became know as the Bulhoek Massacre.
>
> (Webb 1992: 1)

Following this a number of swords, scabbards, photographs and items of a religious nature associated with this day found their way into four nearby museums.

Time does not permit a detailed description of what happened on that fateful day; suffice it to say that the Israelites are part of a religious group known as African Independent Churches. Among their particular beliefs and rituals was one which prophesied that the end of the world was nigh and another which required all its members to come together for a week every April to celebrate Passover. Usually they erected temporary dwellings for the duration of their celebration.

However, in 1920, instead of doing this they began erecting permanent dwellings on the piece of commonage allotted to them. This was not in accordance with the local rules and regulations, and the authorities began to take steps to remove them. However, the Israelites took no notice, believing themselves to be God's chosen people.

By the end of 1920 between 1,200 and 1,400 Israelites were still firmly ensconced on the commonage, which led the government to decide that it had no option but to use force. In May 1921 the largest police force that had ever assembled in peacetime converged on the commonage. They opened fire and in the ensuing clash, 183 Israelites were killed and 100 wounded.

But what has all this to do with museums? In 1991 it was the seventieth anniversary of the Bulhoek Massacre, and the Israelites, who are as strong as ever today, approached the Historical Monuments Board and local museums to help them with their celebration. Among the projects embarked on were:

- an oral history project to get the Israelites' version of events;
- the researching and writing of a brief history of the affair;
- arranging a suitably worded plaque for the memorial wall round the graves of the Israelites killed on that fateful day;
- the updating and rearranging of the display relating to the Massacre in the Queenstown Museum;
- and, perhaps most interesting of all, a request by the Israelites to borrow a sword from the Kaffrarian Museum collection to be used in their anniversary celebrations. This was taken out of the museum, used in the ceremony and returned afterwards.

Although these may only seem like a small step, Bulhoek reflects a significant chapter in the nation's past and as such is one that is especially meaningful to formerly marginalized people. To those involved, the exercise has given them the confidence to embark on other projects and to build on this unique relationship that has begun to develop between them and their local community.

A similarly rewarding exercise took place in Natal between the KwaZulu Monuments Council, the museum and the Tribal Authorities on whose land the famous battlefield Isandlwana stands.

It was there that in 1879 the British Imperial army suffered one of its most humiliating defeats at the hands of an unconventional army. The shock waves that reverberated round the world after this defeat by the Zulu were considerable, and have put this great military disaster on a par with other similar disasters such as Colonel Custer's defeat at Little Big Horn.

For this reason the site has always been of great interest, but very largely to a narrowly defined group of Eurocentric military 'buffs' who have over the past 113 years held many commemorative events and erected many memorial stones to the fallen Imperial soldiers. In contrast to this, not one memorial exists to the Zulu fallen, yet this site recalls their nation at the zenith of its power. Until recently therefore the battlefield of Isandlwana had largely been a site of intense vandalism, grave robbing and general degradation on the part of the locals, who did not really have any idea of its importance.

About eight years ago, the Kwazulu National Monuments Council inherited this 'embarrassing mess' and, aware that they had a very saleable commodity in their hands in the guise of a historic site associated with the Anglo-Zulu War, decided to develop a master plan for heritage site development that would use as its guiding principle the direct benefit of the local communities on whose land the sites are located. Restoration of the historic integrity of Isandlwana involve the proclamation of a further 1,000 hectares as a heritage site, in addition to the already declared 2,8 hectares.

For the local Tribal Authorities this meant giving over agricultural land, the closure of a district road over the battlefield, and the demolition of a community school and a privately owned trading store. In return the Tribal authorities were offered an upgraded store in a new location, a new school capable of achieving high school status in the future, the building of a realigned all-weather access road to their community and the establishment of a trust fund to which 25 per cent of the battlesite gate fees would accrue.

Although the negotiation was long and laborious and took nearly eight years to conclude, the Isandlwana heritage site was formally opened in 1991. Besides the direct benefits to the local community as mentioned above, there have also been other spin-offs:

- local labour was employed for the restructuring of the site, allowing some to learn new skills and others to hone existing ones;
- five permanent new posts of general assistant were created;
- a programme to train local school-goers as accredited tour guides has begun;
- and probably, most satisfying of all, there has been renewed interest in the site by teachers on the local school circuits, who now make a visit to this historic battlefield an important part of their school curriculum.

In bringing this project to fruition, the developers tried to 'ensure that all interested and affected parties [were] consulted and provided with a forum for open negotiations'. In this way 'a new ethic of heritage conservation that has applicability and relevance to a broader spectrum of South Africans [has been sought]' (Van Schalkwyk 1992: 7).

My third example is the International Library of African Music (ILAM) which was founded by the late Hugh Tracey in 1954, and is devoted to the collection and study of music, musical instruments and the oral arts in Africa. In its brochure, Andrew Tracey, Hugh Tracey's son and now director of the library, points out that African music is an endangered heritage, because 'although music is the most widespread and universally practised of all the arts in Africa, it is also the most neglected'.

He goes on to offer a few thoughts which highlight the urgent need for collections of this kind:

- Ethnomusicology, a long-established discipline in all western countries, is still in its infancy in South Africa. There is no department of African music at any South African university, and few courses that deal with it.
- South Africa, probably alone among countries of its stature, still has no published collection of its indigenous folk music.
- The music taught in most black schools and black universities owes little to Africa, leaving most blacks knowing little about their own traditional music.
- There has recently been a worldwide resurgence of interest in South African indigenous popular music, yet the music recorded and broadcast on most South African radio and TV stations retains a heavy emphasis on overseas commercial music.
- Yet despite all this, traditional music still manages to continue in corners of the country, unrecognized, unsupported and largely unknown to all except its makers.

With its unique collection ILAM is truly a 'living' museum offering among other things:

- familiarization with and appreciation of the music of Africa, access to books, articles, records, tapes, films and a unique collection of authentic African instruments;
- instructions in the making and repairing of African musical instruments;
- performance on a variety of musical instruments from South Africa, Mozambique, Zimbabwe and other African countries;
- performances in Steel Band and other Afro-American music.

(International Library of African Music 1991)

Solomon Tshekisho Plaatje grew up in the Kimberley area of South Africa. Although he only had six years of formal education Sol Plaatje mastered eight languages and believed passionately in the power of the written word. He became a noted author and was the first black person to write a novel in English; he also translated at least four of Shakespeare's plays into Setswana.

When the ANC was founded in 1912 he became their first general secretary, and twice went abroad to petition against the 1913 Native Land Act, one of the most far-reaching pieces of legislation in South African history.

In 1921 he founded the Brotherhood Society which strove for co-operation and harmony among all races.

> Author, journalist, political spokesman and leader of his people, Sol Plaatje was one of the most gifted and versatile men of his generation who devoted his many talents to one overriding cause – the struggle of black people against injustice and dispossession.
>
> (MacGregor Museum 1991: 1)

Towards the end of his life, to show their appreciation for his kindness and devotion to his fellow men the black citizens of Kimberley bought him a house in which he lived until he died in 1932.

In 1991 the need to honour the achievements of this man was recognized and through generous sponsorship his home was bought and presented to the Mac-Gregor Museum in Kimberley. The two front rooms in the house have been restored and will be a museum dedicated to his life, while the rest of the house is being used as a 'living' monument to this far-sighted man. A 'bridge school' has been established here which will enable black children to cross the gap between their education system and that of their white counterparts. It involves a computer-based literacy programme designed to increase fluency in English and teach basic mathematical concepts. This has been such a success that within a few months the school had outgrown its premises and has had to flow into museum space as well. There are also plans for a library of African writers.

This museum is the first in South Africa to be dedicated to the memory of a black person, and as such is a triumph for all those involved in its realization.

These are by no means the only museums in South Africa that have actively sought to bond with their local communities, but it seems that we have finally reached a point where the wounds inflicted by a racist ideology are at last showing small signs of healing as we begin the slow process of transforming ourselves into a nation. We at museums should never forget that we are not above our community but are of it and the leadership of those mentioned above serves as an inspiration and shows that

> museums have the potential to nurture an enlightened humane citizenry that appreciates the value of knowing about its past, is resourcefully and sensitively engaged in the present, and is determined to shape a future in which many experiences and many points of view are given voice.
>
> (American Association of Museums 1992: 7)

Note

I would like to acknowledge with thanks the useful comments made by Mr Brian Wilmot, but most especially the wisdom and guidance of Dr Jay O'Keeffe who helped me to see the wood from the trees, and without whom none of this would have been possible.

References

American Association of Museums (1992) *Excellence and Equity, Education and the Public Dimension of Museums*, A report from the American Association of Museums, Washington, DC.

Bergen, T. J. (1993) 'The cultural determination of perception', *Education Journal* 101: 7–8.

International Library of African Music (1991) *Brochure*, Grahamstown, South Africa: Rhodes University.

Kahn, F. (1992) 'Heritage conservation: problems and proposals', *Conserva* 7(5): 9.

Levinsohn, R. (1984) *Art and Craft of Southern Africa: Treasures in Transition*, Johannesburg: Delta.

MacGregor Museum (1991) *Solomon Tshekisho Plaatje*, Draft press release, Kimberley, South Africa.

Stuckenberg, B. (1987) 'Stating the case: a synoptic view of the position of museums and the problems they face, in the changing and divided society of contemporary South Africa', *SAMAB* 17(7, 8): 297.

Van Schalkwyk, L. (1992) 'A new relevance for old monuments – the Isandlwana Model', paper delivered to the Southern African Museums Association Conference, Durban, unpublished.

Webb, D. A. (1992) 'Museums, monuments and the plan of God, a case study in community outreach', paper delivered to the Southern African Museums Association Conference, Durban, unpublished.

Part 3

Evaluating the communication process

17

Evaluating teaching and learning in museums

George E. Hein

Introduction

This chapter provides an overview of the methodology we have used for the past fifteen years to evaluate programmes and exhibits in museums. Our work has all been carried out within the framework of an educational theory that places major emphasis on the role of the learner. The first section of this chapter describes this constructivist educational theory to provide a background for our evaluation methodology. The second section outlines three examples of our evaluation work, emphasizing the methods we use and illustrating each with a single outcome from that work. The third section discusses the components of our evaluation approach which make them appropriate for the educational view to which we subscribe. Finally, our work is placed in a larger context of visitor research in museums.

Learning and teaching in museums

The last two decades have seen a tremendous growth in museum education: we now have major departments specifically devoted to this activity in most museums, the literature is expanding, students are graduating with degrees in museum education, and professional publications increasingly focus on aspects of museum education.[1]

Simultaneously, our ideas about learning theory, about what it means to learn, have undergone a sea change, not so much in that there are dramatic new ideas, but in that a coherent and interrelated set of ideas advocated by a steady stream of thoughtful commentators from Dewey and Piaget to Vigotsky (as well as a wave of current writers) now receives wide acceptance. These ideas cluster around the notion that the most important issues involved in understanding learning are derived from analysing the actions of the learner rather than in probing the nature of the subject to be learned. We now talk about *constructivism*, how the learner constructs meaning out of experience.[2]

Broadly conceived, museums have always had an educational function. The Harvard Museum of Comparative Zoology was built to refute Darwin (Gould

1981), the Louvre was opened to the public to demonstrate the glories of French imperialism, and other museums were designed to show off national aspirations, ranging from the demonstration of imperial wealth and prestige, to preservation of a disappearing culture. These examples are all of educational missions for museums which are primarily didactic in nature. The intention of the museum founders was to instil a specific message in the visiting public. A striking recent example of such a didactic function for a museum is provided by an article in the *New York Times* (1993), which includes the following paragraph:

> Today, Al-Serai Palace in Baghdad, once the seat of the Ottoman Turkish governor, now contains a museum devoted to the country's reconstruction effort. Models of every major industrial complex bombed by the allies show the damage inflicted and how it has been mended.

There can be no doubt of the didactic intention of this museum!

When an exhibit is built with a specific didactic function, it is also reasonable to ask whether that didactic function is achieved. We can ask: do visitors learn about the voyage of the *Mayflower* after they view an exhibit mounted on the dock where the *Mayflower* replica is berthed? Does the school group know some of the principles that underlie art deco design after it has participated in a programme based on an exhibition of American design in the early twentieth century? Do visitors know more about sexual reproduction in animals after a visit to the exhibition about sexual reproduction and gender roles? These are all didactic questions we were asked to address in the evaluations discussed below.

These questions, typical of the kind that evaluators are often asked to address, make sense within a model of learning and teaching that is based on the teacher's perspective, where the theory of education stipulates that the teacher decides what is to be learned and the task of education is to organize the material and present it in such a way that it is transmitted to the student.[3] The teacher (i.e. the museum) has chosen to teach something about the voyage of the *Mayflower*, about early twentieth-century design, about gender and reproduction, etc., and it is legitimate to ask whether what was taught by the teacher was learned by the student.

But constructivist theory requires that we ask a very different question. What we intend to teach is *not* the central concern in this theory; rather the focus is on what people learn, that is on what meaning they make out of whatever it is that we do and exhibit. In describing constructivism (Hein 1993a) we ask, what does the visitor (learner) make of our museum exhibit? What does she understand? What is the meaning for the visitor of the ship replica floating in Plymouth Harbor, of the pictures of skyscrapers and photographs of the modern factory, or the video of foetal development? Our intentions are not the beginning of our investigation, nor do they frame the questions we ask or structure the analysis of the answers visitors give; we have to start with the visitors and tell a story based on their experience. We can go so far as to say that our intentions are irrelevant![4]

The two approaches – seeing the museum as teacher and seeing the museum as a place to learn – are not only two aspects of the educational role of museums, but they are *not logically connected with each other*. That is, if we accept constructivist theory, we also have to accept the view that there is no *necessary* connection between learning and teaching. In fact, the conditions that favour learning are such that if we maximize them, we cannot predict with certainty what will be learned. I do not just mean how much will be learned, but in a very fundamental sense, we cannot predict what meaning learners will make of the experiences we provide for them. The more we construct a situation that allows and encourages learning, the more likely we are to construct something that is open, ambiguous and able to be manipulated in a variety of ways by the learner; thus, the less likely we are to be able to predict precisely what has been learned. Conversely, the more we structure a situation so that it will provide very specific teaching of content, principles or skills that we have predetermined, the less likely we are to fulfil the conditions under which learning can take place most fruitfully.[5]

This is the paradox of education, the dilemma that teachers have struggled with for centuries. Once we accept the idea of constructivism, the notion of the active role of the learner, then we realize that teaching and learning are not necessarily connected.[6] If I want to ensure that my student focuses on a specific task, attends only to it and achieves a precisely specified goal, then I am likely to shape an environment in which concentration on that task is assured, and use all my verbal and other skills to 'keep the student on task'. On the other hand, if I concentrate on the conditions of learning more broadly (for example, by patterning my education on what we know about how young children learn), then I am likely to provide a rich and varied environment, a number of ways to interact with the resources that are offered, and to subscribe to the attributes that developmental, constructivist theoreticians suggest to us.[7] But in doing so, and thus maximizing the opportunity to learn, I also increase the possibilities that the learner will focus on aspects of the situation that are not of interest to me. Precisely because the environment is rich, and multiple interactions are possible, I cannot limit the attention of the learner or ensure that the focus is on a specific concept/fact or skill.

The evaluation of teaching and learning in museums

We have struggled with the problem of documenting the results of teaching and of probing the consequences of environments for learning (*nota bene* the distinction!) for a number of years; the two issues are present in every evaluation study we carry out.

On the whole, our clients come to us because they know we use certain methods, methods that are variously called qualitative, naturalistic or interactive.[8] So we start out with a certain community of ideas in our work. This makes it likely (although not necessary) that they are interested in addressing the issue of learning as well as determining the specific consequences of their teaching.

But we still face the dilemma posed by any effort to determine both the outcome of teaching and the outcome of learning. The primary reason, but not the only one, why clients come to any evaluator, especially in the United States, is that their funding agency demands an evaluation. The next most common reason is that they want to know the results of their work.[9] And when we have the inevitable discussions about assessing the exhibition or the educational programme there is usually a strong interest in determining the outcome of teaching and a less strong, sometimes vague, interest in finding out what visitors 'make' of the exhibit, what meaning they gain from their experience. The challenge for us is that we have to, and want to, address both of these concerns, and need to develop a system that provides data relevant for both of them.

We have found that the primarily qualitative methods we employ, coupled with some simple quantitative measures (counting numbers of visitors, how long they stay in the gallery, etc.) can provide us with information that addresses both topics adequately, so that we feel we have learned something, and our clients appear to be satisfied since a significant fraction of them ask us to continue to work with them.

The key to organizing all this work is to be clear at the outset what questions we are addressing (both questions about the results of the direct teaching that takes place, and questions about what the visitors make of their experience), and then to follow the plan we have devised. We have found a matrix that links the issues of concern with our methods a particularly useful tool to guide our work.[10]

Examples of evaluation studies

What follows are three examples of evaluation designs we developed for three very different museum exhibits or programmes in history, art and science museums respectively. In each case the evaluation methodology is described to give some details of our approach, and then a single conclusion is presented which illustrates a way that visitors made meaning of the exhibition or programme independent of the didactic intention of the museum's staff.

Plimoth Plantation 'Mayflower' dockside exhibit

Some years ago, Plimoth Plantation, a first-person interpretation museum in Plymouth, Massachusetts, decided to place an explanatory exhibit on the dock in Plymouth Harbor where they had berthed a replica of the *Mayflower*. Visitors came on board the *Mayflower*, where they were greeted by costumed staff who provided first-person (seventeenth-century) interpretation of the ship, its crew and passengers. Staff at Plimoth Plantation wanted to improve the experience of visitors by providing a dockside exhibit that would serve as an introduction to the visit. We developed a matrix to guide our evaluation and agreed to carry out some evaluation activities to see whether the objectives of the exhibit were achieved.

Figure 17.1 shows the objectives we agreed to explore at the request of Plimoth Plantation education staff. These objectives included some that are directly intended to assess the results of teaching ('Visitors will know more facts about the *Mayflower* people') as well as others that are vague, but directed more towards assessing the results of the experience ('The exhibit will enhance the visitor experience'.) The four means we decided to use to assess these evaluation issues are illustrated in the matrix which combines means and methods, shown in Figure 17.2. We proceeded to gather data at three different times: before any exhibit was up on the dock and people just milled around until they were admitted on to the ship; few months later, when a temporary exhibit was mounted; and finally, a year later, when the permanent exhibit was mounted. It was clear after the evaluation that the exhibit had enhanced the visitor experience. Visitors knew more about the *Mayflower* and its voyage and could engage in more interesting discussions with the staff based on this increased knowledge. We were able to answer the didactic questions posed by the museum staff.

Plimouth Plantation, Mayflower Exhibit Evaluation Objectives

1. The exhibit should enhance and facilitate the interpretive process on the ship

   Because of the exhibit it should be easier for people to interact with the interpreters.

2. Visitors will:

   know more facts about the Mayflower people
   have a different attitude towards the historic period.

3. Visitors will have a greater sense of satisfaction from their experience

   Processing of visitors will be more efficient, they will feel that the visit has been more worthwhile, they will have learned during it.

4. The exhibit will help control visitor flow

   It will make flow more manageable, make the ship less crowded, improve the quality of interaction on the ship, help avoid problems when a bus tour arrives, and provide options while people wait.

Figure 17.1 Plimoth Plantation, *Mayflower* exhibit evaluation objectives

We also noted some other consequences of the visitors' interaction with the exhibit. I remember especially the older couples who stood before the map of England which showed from where the *Mayflower* passengers had departed. In carrying out our observations, we never heard visitors commenting that the Aldens had come from such and such a town or the Winthrops had come from

Mayflower Exhibit Evaluation	Evaluation means			
George E. Hein Program Evaluation and Research Group Lesley College Evaluation issues	Observation	Visitor interview	Visitor questionnaire	Staff interview
Enhance and facilitate interpretive process	✓	✓		✓
Increase knowledge and change attitude		✓	✓	✓
Increase visitor satisfaction		✓	✓	✓
Control visitor flow	✓			✓

Figure 17.2 *Mayflower* exhibit evaluation matrix

another. What many of them did do was to use the map to discuss where *their* own families originated.

Brooklyn Museum school group visits to 'The machine age in America'

The second example I want to discuss is an evaluation we did at the Brooklyn Museum (of Art) of a school visit programme. The Museum had mounted a major exhibit, 'The machine age in America, 1917–1941', and in conjunction with that installation, they had developed a school visit programme so that classes could get a guided tour of the exhibit followed by optional workshops where they did art work related to the exhibit.

The Museum staff had some objectives for the evaluation, in this case a rather ambitious and extensive evaluation agenda, which is illustrated in Figure 17.3.

Brooklyn Museum
School groups visits to
'The machine age in America'

Topics of interest for the evaluation

1. Content of learning: what do children learn from the group visits?

2. Do children learn about the nature of an art museum from this visit?
    Do they understand that this is an interdisciplinary experience?

3. What is the nature of the experience when they come?

4. What is the relation between the actual experience and the expectations of
    both students and teachers?

5. What in the environment teaches: the exhibit objects, the educational
    actitivies, the lecturing, the different settings?

6. What is the age appropriateness of the exhibit components and programs?

7. Are there connections between the school visit programs and the regular
    school curriculum? Should there be?

8. What are the logistics of the visit: process of signing in, movement through
    the galleries, interaction with the museum staff?

9. Should additional materials for teachers be developed? What should these
    contain? Should these be used for pre or post visit activities?

Figure 17.3 Brooklyn Museum school groups visits to 'The machine age in America':
topics of interest for the evaluation

We developed an equally elaborate set of sources of data, shown in Figure 17.4
and combined them into a matrix, illustrated in Figure 17.5. Again, the situation
is such that the issues we are investigating are broader than would be included if
we were only searching for evidence of the results of teaching specific topics. We
carried out the evaluation and answered most of the Museum staff's questions.
As in the previous example, some conclusions from the evaluation involved
visitor meaning-making that emerged from the data.

One example involves the wide difference between the culture of art museums
and the expectations of schools. Many school groups signed up for the
programme and happily participated in the guided visits. But there was a disson-
ance between the interests of the school groups and the interests of the curators
who had mounted the exhibit. The schools came essentially because the exhibit
had images (skyscrapers, bridges, paintings of workers and machinery, and
examples of objects, streamlined trains, art deco radios, etc.) that fitted into their
teaching of social studies in general and their mandated teaching about New

195

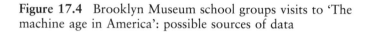

**Brooklyn Museum
School groups visits to
'The machine age in America'**

Possible sources of data

Children's work

Observations of visits

Teacher questionnaires

Professional staff and visitor questionnaires

Interviews with guards

Interviews with chaperones

Interviews with school children

Figure 17.4 Brooklyn Museum school groups visits to 'The machine age in America': possible sources of data

York City in particular in the fourth grade. But the exhibit curators had mounted the exhibit to make an aesthetic statement. The exhibition was not about social history, but about design. Their concern was not New York City in the 1920s and 1930s but the relationship between form and function.

We found out about this problem inadvertently. A hidden agenda for our evaluation was the desire by the Education Department to make a political case for themselves within the Museum. So we designed part of the evaluation to answer this need. Since the education group wanted their work better known within the Museum administration and staff (and this school programme was novel enough for various Museum staff to wander by to see what was going on), we enlisted the help of any such staff and asked them to fill in evaluation forms especially designed for this purpose.[11] We managed to get various administrative staff, and even one or two trustees of the Museum to observe an entire school group visit through this device. Among the people who observed the visits were curators, and they were not happy to find that their aesthetic exhibit was being used as background for a social studies lesson. Again, this instance illustrates a situation where the meaning attributed to the museum experience by the visitors is important and different from the intended meanings of the museum curators.

Boston Museum of Science: 'Two of every sort'

The third evaluation was a modest study of visitor responses to a temporary exhibition on gender and sexuality at the Boston Museum of Science. In this case our brief was not as specific: we were asked to get a general idea of how visitors viewed this exhibition, and again were concerned with what they learned from it. The Museum was particularly interested in visitors' responses to

Brooklyn Museum Evaluation Plan matrix 'The machine age in America' School Visits Program	Data Sources						
Evaluation topics	Observations of visits	Questionnaire: teachers	Quest: professional staff	Interviews: guards	Interviews: chaperones	Interviews: children	Children's work
Content	✓		✓		✓	✓	✓
Nature of Museum	✓	✓				✓	✓
Nature of experience	✓		✓	✓	✓		
Expectations		✓			✓	✓	
What teaches	✓	✓	✓	✓		✓	
Age appropriate	✓	✓					✓
Connection to school curriculum		✓				✓	
Logistics	✓	✓		✓	✓	✓	
Other materials		✓	✓				

Figure 17.5 Brooklyn Museum school visits programme matrix

the controversial nature of the exhibition, since its content included sexuality, reproduction and social issues related to these topics. The exhibition consisted primarily of wall text with some illustrations, a few traditional exhibit cases and a small number of video screens that showed 3–5 minute film loops on topics such as animal reproduction, foetal development or early infant response.

In this case, since our brief was less specific than in the previous examples, we did not develop a matrix. We combined some simple quantitative measures with a visitor questionnaire to obtain information about where visitors stopped and what they thought about the exhibit. Our information on visitor behaviour was obtained through a tracking study. We followed visitors through the exhibition and indicated where they stopped and what they did when they stopped.

It was no surprise to us that visitors overwhelmingly stopped at the video screens and seldom at panels with texts or photographs only, although the extent of the difference was quite dramatic. But most surprising was visitor response to our carefully worded question about the controversial nature of the exhibition. As good social scientists, we couched our question in a neutral, accepting format and asked : 'Some people think exhibits like "Two of every sort" should not be displayed in a museum of science, other people think it is a good idea to have such an exhibit here. What do you think, and why?' Visitors overwhelmingly responded not only that they had no objection to the exhibit in the Museum, but that they were even puzzled by our question. They gave us a surprised look as if to say, 'Why do you ask such a question? We all know that it is the job of museums to present this kind of material.' This answer even came from visitors who did not particularly agree with some of the messages in the exhibit. They indicated that although they might restrict their own children's access to the exhibit, they did not question the Museum's right to show it.

From other responses to open-ended questions, in which we asked them what they liked the most and the least, we found that the one controversial component of the exhibit was the display of an animal head, and other animal material which offended animal rights activists. This aspect of the exhibit, and its effect on one group of visitors, had not even entered the minds of the exhibit developers.

Discussion

The examples above can be used to generalize about the evaluation of both teaching and learning in museums. The way in which we carry out evaluations differs in significant aspects from the methodological style followed by more traditional evaluations based on behaviourist 'experimental' psychology. Some of these differences are the following.

1 The first difference comes in the way we state the issues. We do not insist on reducing the concerns of the museum staff to clearly stated behavioural objectives. On first glance, this seems obvious; the 'issues' we have listed in the matrix hardly fit the requirements for behavioural objectives (Mager 1975). But we also have to admit that the difference between our kinds of 'issues' and traditional objectives is not as large as the terminology might suggest. After all, no matter how naturalistic or qualitative we want to be, we are limited to observing behaviour. All we can directly discern about people is what they do and say; we cannot similarly note what they think or feel.

 But the difference between the two ways of describing what we are looking for is more than a matter of terminology, it is a matter of ideology. By framing the questions as we do, we leave ourselves open for the broader responses, for noting unexpected behaviours, and we do not shut out the possibility of documenting learning that is distinct from the teaching intended. By leaving our list of issues deliberately vague and general, we do not exclude the possibility of learning something about the visitors' experience that may be outside the framework of the museum staff's expectations.

2 Another distinction comes in the methods for data collection we use. Again, although we are limited to finding out about people's behaviour, we choose methods that are relatively open rather than constrained. If we have a questionnaire, it is likely to have (at least in part) open-ended questions. If we observe behaviour, as in our tracking forms, it is using a form that allows for the recording of unusual or unexpected activity. In every instance the emphasis is always on recording with the widest-angle lens possible, as distinct from providing a detailed specification of behaviour on the form/ questionnaire.

3 Characteristic of this type of evaluation is our use of multiple methods of data collection. The traditional forms of evaluation require that more time and energy be spent developing validated instruments which are relied upon to provide information, often based on the statistical differences between pre- and post-activity evaluation. We are more likely to follow the technique known as triangulation, where we validate our conclusions on the basis of the intersection of information from a number of sources. A particularly sharp insight can be gained when different methods provide similar information but different interpretations. Thus, when we asked curators and museum teachers about the exhibit at the Brooklyn Museum, they had different opinions, but these opinions differed on value and interpretation, not at the descriptive level.

4 Our matrix provides a convenient method of matching issues and means. It allows us to think through with the museum staff the possible sources of information and the way that the possible triangulation will take place. Setting up this matrix and, in general, the lengthy discussions we usually have with the staff before an evaluation are important components of our evaluation work.

5 But, although the methods we have developed permit us to address the questions associated with learning, with the meaning visitors make of the exhibits, they do not ensure that we will always obtain significant insight into what visitors are thinking. We use all the traditional probes of the field researcher who wishes to get at the meaning behind the behaviour – interview, observation, tracking, questioning, etc. – but all these qualitative methods work best in situations where the researcher spends considerable time with the people being studied. Participant observation and clinical interviewing are the typical methods of this style, with all the time commitments these imply. It would be wonderful to be able to spend in-depth time with visitors, but that usually is not possible for a variety of reasons. First, visitors themselves do not spend much time in the exhibit; second, the museum cannot afford such intensive shadowing of visitors; and third, the involvement of our staff would be so intrusive in relation to the limited nature of the museum experience that we would overwhelm the experience with the assessment of it. This is a major reason why our knowledge of museum visitors is so primitive in comparison, for example, with our knowledge of children in schools.[12]

6 Finally, I want to emphasize that our analysis usually consists of a combination of simple quantitative results (how many people stopped, who

recognized the picture, etc.) and a more complex qualitative analysis following the tradition of looking for emergent themes and cross-triangulation
among data sources. The extent to which each of these plays a role in the final
report depends on the nature of the data gathered, the time and resources
available and, sometimes, just plain luck. Some kinds of interviews turn out to
be more fruitful than others. Interviewing visitors is usually not a rich activity;
they are in a hurry, it's difficult to get them to say much, and their experience
has been too fragmented and brief (and recent) for them to be very articulate.
We have had better success with interviews of staff members, as we did at both
Plimoth Plantation and Brooklyn Museum, or even with volunteers.[13]

The relationship between visitor studies and learning/teaching in museums

On reflection, it seems to me that the methods we use are adequate to respond
to the questions from museum staff concerning their teaching objectives. They
are not adequate to explore fully all the meaning making that takes place (can
take place) in museums. This is not so much a limitation of the methods we use
as of the limitations which usually circumscribe evaluation studies. For any
reasonable question that is posed to us by the staff, for any objective they can
imagine obtaining as a result of the exhibit, we can make a good estimate of
whether and to what extent that has been achieved.

But on the whole, the means at our disposal when carrying out an evaluation
are usually inadequate to explore fully the learning possibilities of exhibitions,
the myriad ways in which visitors may make meaning out of the experiences. In
order to achieve the latter objective, we would need to broaden our evaluation
methods and carry out more open-ended studies, using the techniques of field-
based research. We need to provide 'thick descriptions' (Geertz 1983) of visitors'
experiences.

Some examples of the kinds of activities which might be particularly fruitful for
the understanding of visitors' making of meaning out of exhibits that have
appeared in the museum literature include:

1   careful analysis of visitors' conversations (Carlile 1985);
2   analysis of visitors' overheard conversations, using microphones (Lucas and
    McManus, 1986);
3   The detailed ethnographic studies of the kind first carried out in museums
    by Laetch's students (Laetch *et al.* 1980);
4   retrospective interviews about museum memories (Falk and Dierking 1992);
5   asking visitors to 'think out loud' as they view exhibits. Dufresne-Tassé and
    co-workers (Dufresne-Tassé and Lefèbvre 1994) have done such work,
    following the model of protocol analysis (Ericsson and Simon 1984)
    developed by cognitive psychologists;
6   the expansion of modalities for visitors to respond, as well as expansion of
    modalities for visitors to learn from;[14]

7 in-depth interviews (McDermott-Lewis 1990);
8 focus groups in which visitors discuss their museum experiences (Getty Center 1991).

Conclusion

Museums as teaching institutions (or more accurately exhibits and programmes with educational objectives which intend to teach their visitors/participants something) need to decide what they want to impart and how they plan to do it. This is hardly revolutionary. The problem in all this is the often implicit assumption that this task of deciding on educational goals requires a focus on the topic or subject. How shall we arrange the artists to get across our message? How shall we guide the visitor through the museum so he or she will understand what we want to impart? What label will be most understandable? (That is, from which label will the visitor best get the knowledge we wish to supply?)

I argue that most evaluation work in museums has been based on the premise that we need to modify our exhibits so as to maximize what visitors learn *of the content we want to teach*. This also assumes a close causal relationship between a particular way of installing an exhibit or devising a programme and the quantity and quality of learning for a majority of visitors. 'I tried this label and no one read it. I put up a different one and seven out of ten visitors stopped and could tell me what it said.' Therefore the second label accomplishes what I want.

But there is another whole world of learning that goes on in museums, the learning that is constructed by the visitor out of the experience and is not necessarily correlated closely with our teaching efforts. In order to understand the museum visitors and find out what they have learned, we need a broad approach to museum evaluation which includes a rich infusion of qualitative, naturalistic research into the museum field.

Notes

1 I have recently compiled a bibliography of literature on museum education (Hein 1993b). Without stretching beyond the field – into literature on learning theory that is relevant to museums, for example – I was able to describe almost seventy items, not counting journal articles, in the Unites States alone. This is particularly impressive, since there is almost no literature published by trade publishers; all of it is put out by professional organizations and university presses.

2 The discussion in this chapter represents an education perspective on a parallel issue discussed in this volume by E. Hooper-Greenhill (see Chapter 1) from a communications perspective and by I. Moroević (see Chapter 3) from a theoretical, semiotic analysis. Professor Dufresne-Tassé uses a a similar approach in her work described elsewhere in this volume (see Chapter 22).

3 In this chapter the language of teachers and students is used to emphasize that the discussion is based on writings about formal education. In the museum setting this language needs to be modified. In our context the 'teacher' is the museum, its exhibit designers and other staff, while the 'learner' is the visitor, regardless of his or her intention on entering

the museum. An issue, which I will not address in this chapter, is that the motivation of many visitors who come to museums is not to learn but to be entertained. Does this make teaching impossible? It certainly does not interfere with learning as defined by constructivist theory, since visitors will still make meaning out of their experience.

4 Proponents of so-called 'radical constructivism' (von Glaserfeld 1991) insist that there is no meaning besides the meaning attributed to something by the learner. That makes a teacher's intentions irrelevant.

5 That is not to say there is anything wrong or inappropriate in advocating didactic teaching. There are a myriad life conditions where the best approach is simply to 'teach' and not worry about the meaning making of the learner. Parents use this direct didactic approach in teaching children to take care in crossing the street (we do not wait to find out what meaning the child makes of the experience, or what cars signify to the child, we directly and forcefully instil in the child's mind the necessity of holding daddy's hand, and simply do not worry about the cognitive (or emotional) consequences of this action). Many other examples from school days, military 'indoctrination' (note we use a different word!) and other situations could be cited.

6 To put this in perspective we can contrast the view described here with a simple stimulus-response (S-R) theory. In S-R theory, it is argued that any stimulus produces a response and learning is simply the aggregation of responses to appropriate stimuli. Thus, given the correct stimuli, the organism *must* learn. A forceful argument against behaviourist theory is provided in the pioneering work of Feuerstein (1979) in diagnosing and educating children with severe biological limitations to their ability to learn. He emphasizes the active participation of mediators between stimulus and response in order for learning to take place.

7 One model for this type of learning in museums is found in the increasingly popular 'discovery' rooms. These are often rich learning environments without specific learning objectives, places where the learner can decide what to pursue.

8 The terminology for the kind of evaluation we carry out varies considerably among practitioners. Additional adjectives applied to it include holistic, illuminative, responsive, field-based, ethnographic and authentic. Opponents use other descriptive terms.

9 These two reasons are, of course, not mutually exclusive.

10 We have been using this approach for some time. See Engel and Hein (1981) and Hein (1982a, 1982b).

11 This is a generally useful technique in evaluations of popular or controversial activities, both to minimize the disruptive effect of visitors coming to observe and to maximize the sources of data.

12 There is a whole literature on life in classrooms, dating back to Jules Henry's (1963) pioneering application of anthropology to familiar settings. For example, see Armstrong (1980).

13 We once had great success in finding out about visitor behaviour by talking with the teenage boy scout volunteer guides at the National Museum of the Boy Scouts in Murray, Kentucky.

14 When we asked visitors about their knowledge of animal adaptation from viewing an enhanced diorama exhibit at the Museum of Science (Davidson, Heald and Hein 1991) they mentioned things they had learned from touching, from listening, from smelling and from conversation, not only items they could have learned from seeing or reading. In this exhibit we had people who told us they had not read the labels but could then recite them. The exhibit included recorded material that gave the label information. Visitors did not perceive that listening to the information counted as reading the labels (maybe it doesn't).

References

Armstrong, M. (1980) *Closely Observed Children, The Diary of a Primary Classroom*, London: Writers and Readers.

Carlile, R. W. (1985) 'What do visitors do in a science center?', *Curator* 28: 27–33.

Davidson, B., Heald, L. and Hein, G. E. (1991) 'Increased exhibit accessibility through multi-sensory interaction', *Curator* 34: 273–90.

Dufresne-Tassé, C. and Lefèbvre, A. (1994) 'Some data on the psychological functioning of the adult visitor at the museum and their implications for museum education', *International Review of Education*, in press.

Engel, B. S. and Hein, G. E. (1981) 'Qualitative evaluation of cultural institution/school education programs', in S. N. Lehman and K. Inge (eds) *Museum School Partnerships: Plans and Programs*, Washington, DC: Center for Museum Education.

Ericsson, K. A. and Simon, H. (1984) *Protocol Analysis: Verbal Reports as Data*, Cambridge, MA.: MIT Press.

Falk, J. and Dierking, L. (1992) *The Museum Experience*, Washington, DC: Whalesback Books.

Feuerstein, R. (1979) *The Dynamic Assessment of Retarded Performers*, Baltimore: University Park Press.

Geertz, C. (1983) *Local Knowledge: Further Essays on Intepretive Anthropology*, New York: Basic Books.

Getty Center for Education and the Arts (1991) *Insights, Museums, Visitors, Attitudes, Expectations, a Focus Group Experiment*, Los Angeles, CA: The J. Paul Getty Trust.

Gould, S. J. (1981) *The Mismeasure of Man*, New York: Norton.

Hein, G. E. (1982a) 'Evaluating museum education programs', *Art Galleries Association (U.K.), Bulletin*, September, 13–16.

—— (1982b) 'Evaluation of museum programs and exhibits', in T. H. Hansen, K.-E. Andersen and P. Vestergaard (eds) *Museum Education*, Copenhagen: Danish ICOM/CECA.

—— (1993a) 'The significance of constructivism for museum education', in *Museums and the Needs of People*, Jerusalem: ICOM.

—— (1993b) 'Museum education: a bibliographical essay', *Choice* 30: 1733–41.

Henry, J. (1963) *Culture Against Man*, New York: Random House.

Laetch, W. M., Diamond, J., Gottfried, J. L. and Rosenfeld, S. (1980) 'Naturalistic studies of children and family groups in science centers', *Science and Children*, March, 14–17.

Lucas, A. M. and McManus, P. (1986) 'Investigating learning in informal settings', *European Journal of Science Education*, 8: 343–53.

McDermott-Lewis, M. (1990) *The Denver Art Museum Interpretive Project*, Denver, CO.: The Denver Art Museum.

Mager, R. F. (1975) *Preparing Instructional Objectives*, 2nd edn, Belmont, CA.: Fearon.

New York Times (1993) 'Hussein rebuilds Iraq's economy undeterred by the U. N. sanctions', 24 January 1993.

von Glaserfeld, E. (1991) 'An exposition of constructivism: why some like it radical', in R. B. Davis, C. A. Maher and N. Noddings (eds) *Constructivist Views of the Teaching and Learning of Mathematics*, Washington, DC: National Council of Teachers of Mathematics.

18

Responsive evaluation in museum education
Ian Kelman

Introduction

Museums and galleries offer a wide variety of learning experiences. Their unique contribution is their emphasis on the development of sensory awareness based on work with real objects. C. G. Jung developed a theory that there are two psychological types with essentially different learning styles: sensing types and intuitive types. The sensing type relies to a greater extent on direct sensory experience. The intuitive type enjoys the complex abstract learning gained from probing the outward appearance of things. Children, being closer to the pre-linguistic stage of learning, have a strong preference for learning which has an active element, which engages their senses and stimulates their imagination.

While museum and gallery educators will continue to use methods which rely on reading and writing skills, they have the possibility to develop learning activities which are beyond the scope of most formal education. Over the past forty years a large body of research has developed in all areas of curriculum evaluation. Museum educators must decide which methods of evaluation are most appropriate to their work. This chapter looks at two models of evaluation: the objectives model and the responsive model. It shows how responsive evaluation can be used to gather information about the effectiveness of an education programme at the Laing Art Gallery, Newcastle upon Tyne, England.

Evaluation

Evaluation has traditionally not received much attention in museum and gallery education in Britain, partly because of the difficulty of defining the outcomes of a programme and partly because of the resources in time and money required to do the work properly. The present climate, particularly the moves to establishing performance indicators, is increasing pressure to evaluate many parts of the services undertaken by museums. As museum education comes to be seen as a core activity its work will inevitably be questioned. It is therefore important that those involved in this work begin to address the problem of seeking information about the effectiveness of programmes. Evaluation will take place in some form and it is far better that it is conducted by professionals who understand the nature of the enterprise. The purpose of evaluation is to inform current and future planning, known as formative evaluation, and to judge the effects of educational programmes, known as summative evaluation. Unlike research it is not concerned with developing theory or testing hypotheses. Evaluation aims to improve teaching and learning by close scrutiny of pupil behaviour. An important function of evaluation is to help define areas where new learning can be built on existing knowledge and skills. This is done by front end analysis. In the museum education context this can be achieved by liaison between schools, education advisers and museum education officers. It is important to discover what areas of the curriculum match the museum collection, what styles of learning and teaching are being used in the schools and what facilities are available to follow up work based on a gallery visit. Front end analysis should also ideally involve pilot testing of the programme before deciding on the final form of the learning experiences.

The objectives model

To pursue the rationale of evaluation a stage further it is important to consider the roles of formative and summative evaluation and to look at the methods used to carry out the process. It is at this point that we enter the debate about the relevance of using the objectives model against the so-called naturalistic or responsive model. The basis of the objectives model is summed up in the following way: 'Educational objectives are typically derived from curriculum theory which assumes that it is possible to predict, with a fair degree of accuracy, what the outcome of instruction will be' (Eisner 1985). In the 1940s and 1950s this approach to curriculum design held sway, particularly in America. The belief that learning could be broken down into discrete units led to the development, by Benjamin Bloom and his colleagues, of the Taxonomy of Educational Objectives (Bloom 1969). The first taxonomy, the Cognitive Domain, divided learning into a hierarchy starting with knowledge at the lowest level and continuing to evaluation at the highest. The Cognitive Domain was followed by two further taxonomies: the Affective Domain and the Psychomotor Domain. These have formed the basis for much curriculum development work. The use of objectives, making clear statements about what it is hoped to achieve, means that the work of educational establishments becomes more open to outside scrutiny. Critics of the objectives model point to the danger that it is not always possible to predict all the outcomes of a learning programme in behavioural terms and that instruction should not be limited to that which can be assessed by standardized tests. 'Objectives are future oriented and when the future becomes increasingly important we sacrifice the present in order to achieve it' (Eisner 1985). Behavioural objectives and standardized tests can have a place in museum education. There are clearly areas of learning which are amenable to the setting of predetermined goals. The problem is that this can induce a kind of tunnel vision where only the predetermined goals are seen as important and the evolution of other goals, along the way, is eliminated. An example of this is the simple type of museum worksheet which requires the acquisition of basic factual knowledge. In gathering the information and fulfilling the goals of the worksheet, the learner might miss many other opportunities for deeper insights into the objects. To avoid this, worksheets should include open-ended questions which encourage the learner to engage in more imaginative but less predictable learning from the exhibits. Used in appropriate ways the objectives model has a place in both formative and summative evaluation.

Responsive evaluation

Most educators in the arts will realize that programmes develop and evolve as they progress and outcomes which once seemed important are sometimes abandoned in favour of new ones. The approach, known as responsive evaluation, advocated by Robert Stake (Stake 1975) focuses attention on programme activities rather than programme intents. Evaluators seek responses from all the personnel involved in the programme and need to recognize that each has legitimate and differing concerns. They must put aside preconceived notions of success or failure and attend to what is actually happening. It is important that learning in the arts is seen as a highly individual activity that can take many divergent paths. Collection of data does not follow a standardized format. According to Robert L. Wolff: 'Naturalistic evaluation is a dynamic enquiry process demanding extensive interaction between evaluator and participants' (Wolff 1980). The work of Elliot Eisner in the realm of evaluation in the arts has added much to the debate. His evolving criticism of the application of the objectives model led him to develop the idea of evaluator as a critic and connoisseur of education. By adopting the approach of a connoisseur to the evaluation process it is hoped that many of the subtleties of learning can be revealed. Facial expression and body language may be just as important in the process as completed assignments. To achieve the level of discrimination needed, practice and experience in a wide variety of educational settings is required. The role of the critic is to reveal and communicate the findings of the data-gathering process. The skills of the ethnographic researcher need to be combined with those of the poet and the novelist in order to produce a complete picture of the learning process.

It can be argued that the naturalistic processes of evaluation are open to subjectivity and bias. This can be said of other types of evaluation and research. One way to compensate for bias is to have more than one person involved and to visit the site of the educational programme on a number of occasions. Moreover, most educational settings produce data which can be checked by other observers. The use of audio and videotape recorders can be helpful in providing material with which to compare the data collected by naturalistic methods. One of the major arguments in its favour is that it attempts to describe real learning situations. Predicting the outcomes of the learning process is only half the story. The naturalistic or responsive approach fills in the detail and attempts to reveal the process in a holistic way.

The choice of evaluation methods used in museum and gallery education must depend on the type of learning to be evaluated and the context of the programme. Some work may require the fulfilment of clear objectives, for example as part of an examination course. Evaluation data may be needed for the information of non-professionals where 'results' need to be seen. However, within the professional circles of museums and schools the responsive model would seem to provide the most useful data for those who seek to know how learning in an art gallery takes place.

Background to an evaluation project

To explore the practical problems of doing responsive evaluation I worked in co-operation with the Laing Art Gallery, Newcastle upon Tyne. The project sought to follow up groups of junior- and middle-school children who took part in an educational programme at the gallery. The programme was based on an exhibition of the work of Ralph Hedley entitled 'Ralph Hedley, Tyneside painter'. It ran from 8 November 1990 to 3 February 1991. The bulk of the exhibition consisted of 150 paintings and a number of sketch books and photographs showing many aspects of life in nineteenth-century Newcastle. The works were displayed in two rooms within which the paintings were grouped under themes such as 'The life of children', 'Working life', 'Unemployment' and 'Rural life'. Ralph Hedley lived all his life in the north-east and started work as a wood carver. He built a successful business and was able to develop his interest in painting. From humble beginnings he rose to become a pillar of Newcastle's artistic circle and a respected figure. From the early 1870s he was showing paintings regularly in local exhibitions. His paintings reveal a tendency towards Victorian sentimentality, but also a degree of sympathy for the plight of the poor. The paintings are fine examples of nineteenth-century genre work and in total make up a remarkable social document of the period. The narrative quality of the Hedley works, together with their realistic execution made the exhibition an ideal vehicle for education with local junior-school pupils.

Liaison between the gallery's education officer and the local authority advisers was instrumental in directing the marketing of the exhibition's educational content towards primary and middle schools. The schools were working on the National Curriculum core study unit entitled 'The Victorians' and this increased the potential audience for what the museum educational officer was planning. The schools were contacted through a letter circulated in the education authority post. Teachers were invited to come to a preview of the exhibition and were made aware that a teachers' pack was available. For schools wishing to participate two special activities were designed. They could choose either a session working with an artist who helped the children to make their own copies of the paintings in pastel or they could choose to work with two actors on role play situations. Both these activities were preceded by a period in the main part of the exhibition. Here the education officer was able to illuminate some of the important themes in the paintings and encouraged the pupils to discuss the works. The follow-up activities in the education area of the gallery were designed to involve all the children and to make them consider the paintings more closely. Their work with the artist concentrated on understanding the techniques which Hedley used to achieve the effects he wanted. There was discussion on the best ways to reproduce drapery and flesh tones and on the use of light and shade. The role play was intended to engage the pupils imaginatively with some of the paintings. For instance pupils were invited to improvise plays, to imagine what had led up to events depicted in the narrative paintings and to suggest what happened next. In the course of this work the children learned about social conditions, changes in the architecture of Newcastle, working life, costumes and many other aspects of the social history of the nineteenth century. The rich variety of learning experiences contained in the programme were not given formal objectives though some were articulated by the education officer at the Laing. Through discussion a number of issues were agreed which would form the focus of an evaluation project. Some issues related closely to the education programme for the Hedley exhibition and some were more general, looking at the service offered to schools at the gallery. The first issue was the effectiveness of the marketing of the programme and the level of communication between the gallery and the schools. The second issue focused on the organization of the school visits. The third issue to be evaluated was the quality of the learning which resulted from the sessions with the artist and the actors. The fourth issue was the extent to which both pupils and teachers valued the experience of visiting the gallery.

With the help of the gallery education officer a list of schools which had participated in the Hedley programme was drawn up. Letters were sent to the head teachers seeking permission to visit the schools and talk to the teachers and pupils who had taken part in the programme. A few days later ten schools were contacted by telephone and appointments made to visit.

Case-study methodology

The rationale for the evaluation was that the group of schools formed a case-study. The main method of gathering information was the semi-structured interview. Where groups of children could be seen, informal questioning in the classroom was also used. Other sources of data included pupils' work completed during and after the Hedley programme. As most evaluation of museum education is likely to be carried out by education officers rather than specially trained personnel the less formal methods favoured by ethnographic research seem more appropriate as a model. Such an approach requires a degree of understanding and mutual respect between those taking part in the evaluation. The methods used should endeavour to achieve an accurate picture of the results of the education programme and should try to uncover the successes and failures of the work without adopting a judgemental posture. The aim of the enterprise is to build a partnership between the museum and the schools where information can be exchanged for mutual benefit.

One of the important tools in the case-study approach is participant observation. While it was not possible to use this method during the course of the Laing study it is felt that some discussion of its merits is relevant. For the museum education officer, participant observation may be the only available method of gathering evaluation data. Observation has several advantages in the museum setting. It is superior to surveys when the data being collected are of a non-verbal nature. It enables data to be collected while learning is taking place, in a more natural environment, within the museum or the classroom. The main pitfall of this method is that if the evaluator is also the designer of the learning experience, then he or she will be biased in favour of seeing successful outcomes. Human nature being what it is, the problematical elements in the learning situation may be ignored. Here the use of a colleague armed with an observation schedule, which requires timed noting down of behaviour as it happens, can help to gain objectivity. The use of a video camera should also be considered. Where the objectives of the programme are not specified the case-study approach can be particularly useful. According to MacKernan (1991), 'Case study methodology may make the greatest contribution where project purposes or aims are unclear or ambiguous. The research may tend to clarify and tidy up misunderstandings.'

An important element of the case-study is its eclectic nature. The need not to rely on one method of data collection, such as participant observation, is essential for validity. An education officer who has a good rapport with local schools might consider the use of interviews with teachers and children as a way of gaining another perspective on the work they have done.

The semi-structured interview approach was adopted as a way of gathering a broad range of views on the work of the Laing and the value placed on museum education by the schools. Cohen and Manion (1984) characterize the research interview as: 'A two person conversation initiated by the interviewer for the purpose of obtaining relevant information'. To be effective in eliciting useful information the interviewer needs to gain the confidence of the person interviewed. There seems to be a middle course between being too much of an impartial researcher and the danger of 'going native' or becoming too identified with the person being interviewed. As an experienced teacher I found no difficulty in establishing a friendly, but business-like relationship with the head teachers and teachers who agreed to participate. It was possible to build up a degree of rapport through discussion of current educational issues such as the impact of the National Curriculum. I was asked some biographical questions by several of the teachers and this helped to establish the feeling that there was common ground. There are other factors which can affect the relationship between interviewer and person interviewed. These are outlined by Burgess.

> In addition to issues of gender and personal experience, a number of overt characteristics of the interviewer are involved in these situations – age, social status, race and ethnicity. Such characteristics create an immediate impression of the interviewer and will, in part, place limits on the roles that the interviewer may adopt.
>
> (Burgess 1984)

209

The skills of interviewing can only be learned as a result of practical experience, but certain guidelines can be followed. It is important to explain fully the purpose of the project at the start of the interview and to outline the kind of questions to be asked. This is designed to put people at ease. If a tape recorder is to be used then permission must be gained and if refused then the interviewer should be prepared to take notes. The person to be interviewed must be assured of complete confidentiality. In conducting a semi-structured interview it is necessary to have a list of areas of enquiry which are to be covered. In this case-study the following questions were used: (1) How had the teachers become involved with museum education? (2) What were the teachers' expectations and preparations for the gallery visit? (3) What were the teachers' views on how the gallery education programme had worked? (4) What were the outcomes of the programme at the Laing?

In talks with the children the following questions were used: (1) Do you remember your visit to the Laing Art Gallery? (2) What stands out for you from the visit? (3) What kind of work did you do? (4) What was special about your work at the Laing? (5) Has your visit helped you to do any good work at school? (6) Would you like to do some more work with the Laing? (7) Have you been back to the gallery since your first visit? (8) Did you talk to your parents about what you did? The questions were addressed in any order. It is important that the respondents do not feel they are being given a questionnaire. As important as the specific answers are the ways the respondents qualify and amplify their statements. The open-ended questions are important in the way they allow the respondent to enlarge on the themes to which they have been directed. The possibility of gaining a richer view of the events being evaluated and of understanding the motives and concerns of the respondents is the chief justification for adopting the semi-structured interview in responsive evaluation.

While most of the interviews for the Laing evaluation were with teachers, some of the school head teachers offered the opportunity to meet children who had visited the gallery. The talks with children generally took place in the presence of their teacher, but there were some opportunities to see children in small groups away from the main classroom. If such groups are made available it is important that they are representative of the class: 'it is natural that some teachers will want their schools to shine. Consequently you may find yourself with several very able pupils who are impressive but, nevertheless, unrepresentative of the class as a whole' (Moloney 1981).

Organizing evaluation data

The value of responsive evaluation is that it produces a mass of detailed information; the problem is that it is gathered in a rather disorderly way. As an aid to gathering and organizing the data the use of the Hein matrix (Hein 1982) is suggested (see Figure 18.1). The two axes of the matrix are the objectives of the programme and the sources of data. Where evidence of a successful outcome is seen the appropriate cell is filled in. In the survey of the ten schools which took

Data sources

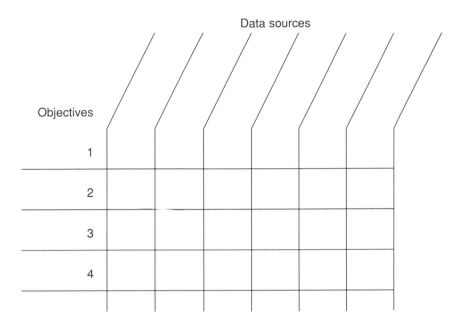

Objectives

1

2

3

4

Figure 18.1 The Hein matrix for organizing evaluation data (adapted from Hein 1982)

part in the Laing programme a separate set of matrices was used for each school. While this simple device might seem more closely related to the objectives model of evaluation, where intended outcomes are largely decided prior to the start of the programme, the matrix can have extra objectives added as the learning experience unfolds.

Conclusion

This chapter suggests ways in which museum educators might approach evaluation in a way which takes account of the unique qualities of learning from objects. Drawing on the work of educationalists and social science research it offers a way forward for museums to establish channels of feedback from one of their target audiences. The results of the Laing gallery evaluation revealed a high degree of success both in the quality of the learning experience and the strong partnership developed between the Laing Art Gallery and the schools of Newcastle.

References

Bloom, B. S. (ed.) (1969) *Taxonomy of Educational Objectives, Handbook 1: The Cognitive Domain*, London: Longman.
Burgess, R. G. (1984) *In the Field, an Introduction to Field Research*, London: George Allen & Unwin.

Cohen, L. and Manion, L. (1984) *Research Methods in Education*, Beckenham: Croom Helm.

Eisner, E. W. (1985) *The Art of Educational Evaluation*, London: Falmer Press.

Hein, G. (1982) 'Evaluation of museum programmes and exhibits', *Museum Education*, Danish ICOM/CECA, 21–6.

MacKernan, J. (1991) *Curriculum Action Research*, London: Kogan Page.

Moloney, K. (1981) *Guidelines for Education Fieldwork Research*, Leicester: Leicester Polytechnic.

Stake, R. (1975) *Evaluating the Arts in Education: a Responsive Approach*, Columbus, Ohio: Merrill.

Wolff, R. L. (1980) 'A naturalistic view of evaluation', *Museum News* 58 (6): 39–45.

19

The museum as medium in the aesthetic response of schoolchildren

Andrea Weltzl-Fairchild

Many visitors see museums as an invaluable educational resource. The variety of museums available offers many different possibilities to learn and to interact with the collections. In an art museum one expects that there will also be possibilities for the visitor not only to learn facts but also to have experiences which we call aesthetic. As pointed out, 'the aesthetic experience provides visceral, holistic, and greatly rewarding sensations that are absent from purely cognitive activities' (Csikszentmihalyi and Robinson 1990: 12). Yet not a great deal is known about people's aesthetic reactions in an art museum context. What do we mean by aesthetic response? What are the factors that influence aesthetic responses? Do we have to consider developmental issues when planning experiences for school-aged visitors?

There are two disciplines which inform the museum educator on theories on learning in a museum context: philosophy and psychology. Traditionally, philosophy, especially its sub-branch aesthetics, is concerned with the human response to beauty. It deals in a logical and systematic manner with the study of issues such as the nature of the art object and the reality of the aesthetic experience. However, this type of dialectic is not usually planned for in an art museum although it may happen for some of its visitors. The educational activities that take place therein, especially with schoolchildren, are not along the lines of a philosophical debate, but rather they are directed to imparting information and providing experiences which will capture the interest of the visitor.

The other discipline which has researched aesthetic response is psychology. Its preoccupation has mostly been with people's response to art objects in the context of a growing and developing mind. Psychological research has considered issues such as perception and the developmental sequence of aesthetic response. In fact, much of the literature on aesthetic response has come from this field, having a strong influence on educational practice and the notion of stages of growth.

The term aesthetic response can have many meanings depending on where one assumes the aesthetic quality lies. Is it in the quality of the experience or in the object? To avoid embarking on a debate which has already filled many books, we shall use this definition of an art educator, who states that aesthetics is 'the inquiry into the nature of *all aesthetic response, especially to those objects we call works of art*' (Lanier 1986: 7; my emphasis). In the context of this research, aesthetic response is the end-product of a process which starts with a perception of and experience with an art object and a verbal and non-verbal reaction to it. It is almost impossible to separate the parts of this sequence; we shall refer to the observable end of this sequence as aesthetic response.

Many psychologists such as Gardner and Gardner (1973), Machotka (1966) and Winner (1982) have studied perception, preference and judgement (among other aspects) in the general population to discover normative patterns in aesthetic response. A problem in applying their findings to a museum situation is that generally researchers only investigated single issues which interested them such as the relation of age to preference, or to criteria for judgement, or ideas about origins of the work in relation to age. This reductionist approach does not take into account the totality of the aesthetic experience or the possibility that there are other factors that will influence the experience besides age.

Although there are a few studies (Coffey 1968; Clayton 1974; Parsons *et al.* 1978; Housen 1983) which have focused on looking at aesthetic responses in their totality in order to generate a developmental schema which could be applied to the population as a whole, there are two problems with these studies. First, there is no true concordance between ages and the stages of aesthetic development that each suggests. Second, all of these started with a developmental theory to support and thus framed their questions to investigate issues as they pertain to age. Few researchers are concerned with the image used to elicit aesthetic response. Often the pictures used in research situations, generally semi-representational, have little to do with works of art. Yet works of art are exactly what are of interest to the museum educator, who is concerned with cultural artefacts.

Theories of aesthetic response

While there are few theories about aesthetic response in the literature, one researcher who has proposed a theory is Gardner (1973). His theory of participation in the arts depends on Freud's psychoanalytical theories and Piaget's cognitive developmental schema. For Gardner, looking at the arts is an ideal way to study both affective and cognitive developments. He conceptualized aesthetic development as a three-part system which he called Making, Perceiving and Feeling, all of which function better with increasing age. The three parts of the system also correspond to different modes of acting in the art field: the artist (Making), the critic (Perceiver) and the audience (Feeling).

According to Gardner, by the age of 7 or 8 years, the child has achieved the development needed to participate in most of art activities (making, perceiving and feeling in the arts). It is only in the role of critic that a person needs later phases of cognitive development: i.e. Piaget's Formal Operations. His research has investigated many aspects of cognitive development such as aesthetic judgement, preference and the effect of age on recognition of style in paintings (Gardner 1973: 37).

Another theory was found in the writings and practice of Horner (1988), an innovative art educator from Quebec. He starts with Winnicott's idea of the 'transitional object', such as a teddy bear or a blanket, which acts as the mother-substitute. This theory postulates that a person's stance to any cultural object is shaped by very early life experiences with the transitional object which eventually loses meaning but the predisposition to view the world by those early experiences is diffused over the whole cultural field.

> [T]his important area of *experience* in the potential space between the individual and the environment, that which initially joins and separates the baby and the mother when the mother's love, displayed or made manifest as human reliability, does in fact give the baby a sense of trust or of confidence in the environment factor.
>
> (Winnicott 1971: 103)

Horner also was influenced by theories from Reader Response Criticism which examines the role of the reader in the interpretation and understanding of the text. In Horner's view, an image or work of art is a text which engages the viewer in the same way as a written text. 'Meaning does not pre-exist in art works; nor does it pre-exist in a viewer' (Horner 1988: 7).

As a result of his work and reflection, he proposed a model of aesthetic response which has eight levels. This sequence of steps describes the aesthetic experience and can be divided into the internal and the external phases. The internal sequence is: Forgetting, Remembering, Reflecting, Revealing; these correspond to fusing the self with the art object, then remembering the experience, thinking about it and making it public. The external sequence is: Describing, Structuring, Interpreting and Retroactivating, which are a part of the public dialogue and deal with the art object.

These two theories were chosen for this study because each provided us with an explanation of what occurs in a situation when a visitor is said to be having an aesthetic experience. Gardner provided a developmental theory of aesthetic response while Horner conceptualized the sequence of the aesthetic experience under optimal conditions.

Keeping to the spirit of qualitative research, we aimed to understand the totality of the situation and the interplay of the factors that affected the aesthetic response of a group of schoolchildren. We identified three factors in the aesthetic situation (the subject, the pictures and the questions) which could be paralleled with a theory of educational interaction. Legendre (1983) proposed a model, SOMA, in which the *Subject* learns about the *Object* in a *Milieu* by the intervention of an *Agent*. The factors that influence the museum educational dynamics are: the subject's age and style, the pictures which are the object the subject is talking about, and the questions asked, which is the equivalent of the intervention of the agent. The museum milieu was not investigated as part of this study.

215

Description of the research

What follows below is a brief description of the subjects, the pictures and the questions asked to elicit aesthetic response and the results.

The subjects were chosen randomly from an elementary school: gender-equal numbers of schoolchildren of three different ages: 8, 10 and 12. Their interviews were videotaped and from the initial group, twelve interviews were transcribed and analysed in depth.

The pictures that were shown were chosen as examples of different visual representational systems. The reason for using such different styles of art reproductions is that we were interested in how the children would deal with such diversity. We had noted in the review of literature that the nature of the picture was rarely taken into consideration by researchers. Almost all had used realistic or semi-realistic works for their studies. However, an early study by Subès (1955) had noticed that very young children respond quite favourably to abstract art, which led us to follow up this indication. The images used were a highly realistic picture by Latour *La Diseuse de bonne fortune*, an abstract work by Jenkins, *Phenomenon Cat's Paw Reach*, and finally a semi-realistic work by Matisse, *L'Atelier rouge*.

The questions were derived from Horner's paradigm of aesthetic response, an instrument which we call 'phenomenological description'. The first four questions were open-ended and of a self-reflecting nature. (For example: Tell me where you went in this picture; where did you stay the longest?) Three additional questions were asked from other research to compare our results. (How did this picture come to be? Do you think adults would like this? Why?)

As all the subjects videotaped in turn as they spoke and moved in relation to the pictures, we were able to look at the non-verbal responses as well as the verbal commentary. The videos were transcribed and the non-verbal behaviour recorded next to the verbal comments.

The transcripts of the interviews were analysed and the different *topics* that each subject was talking about were identified (story, colours, memories, etc.). The topics were finally regrouped into three *domains*, which were: World of Art, Picture, and Self. Each of these corresponds to those larger categories which are a part of the aesthetic encounter: the world of art (theories, methods of work, museums . . .) or about the picture itself (forms, composition, story . . .) or about herself (feelings, memories . . .). We refer to this list as the inventory; this was the means whereby we answered our questions of research.

The results from the study

The factor of the subject: age and style of response

In this study, it was very difficult to come up with data that showed a definite developmental sequence given the numbers of subjects interviewed. There were a few topics that indicated developmental trends such as morality and concepts about the origin of the picture but most of others were elicited equally in all three age-groups. The factors of the effect of the picture and the different responding styles of the individual child were more significant than age.

Overall the older children responded more often than the younger ones in the domain of World of Art. They had a clearer idea of the work of the artist and art processes. They were concerned about art skills and standards and the notion that art should communicate. On the other hand, the youngest subjects were more liable to express personal and categoric preferences. They also related more stories about themselves and showed examples of synaesthesia (see below). They were more open to the experience of responding even if they had little hard knowledge about the art world.

There were more topics elicited in the middle age-group who showed both tendencies; they seemed to know more than the young subjects yet showed no inhibitions about letting themselves go and responding spontaneously. This demonstrates that much of what is considered as a higher stage in aesthetic response is based more on knowledge which has been learned. As a child becomes older, there is a shift from expressing personal feelings and interests to a more restrained, impersonal form of giving information.

This is not to suggest on the basis of this fairly small sample of children that there is no link between development and aesthetic response. Rather we are saying that the youngest subjects in this group were already in possession of many of the abilities to respond to art: to perceive, to feel and to respond. They support Gardner's thesis that this is achieved quite young and that from the age of 7 to 8 years onwards, there is an accumulation of facts and knowledge about art but not a reorganization in thinking about art. This also corresponds with Housen's developmental schema, where she noted that the factor of familiarity with art was more significant than the age of the subject (Gardner 1973; Housen 1983).

After analysis of the effects of the pictures, the questions and the ages of the subjects, we noted certain consistent modes of behaviour which were *independent of the age of the subjects*. These modes of behaviour were used by the subject as strategies or styles of response for all three pictures. In this study, the types or styles of responding we perceived were: the concrete, the empathetic and the conceptual styles. Given a larger sample, it might be possible to find other styles in another group of subjects.

Subjects from each of these styles had a characteristic approach to the art object which they used regardless of the picture. While the content of their talk was influenced by the picture and the questions asked, *the manner of speaking about that content was a matter of personal style, regardless of age*. The subjects with a concrete style were direct and idiosyncratic in their approach. They were not empathetic and found it difficult to project themselves into the work of art. They named objects and noted elements of the visual language without qualifying them.

The empathetic subjects, regardless of age, were just the opposite: they identified easily and related stories about their lives and the art work. They quickly linked their feeling and the stories in the picture. Sometimes, they went through the picture into their own world, which they described poetically. They easily saw metaphoric possibilities.

The intellectual subject, had a more 'advanced' notion of art than the others: he felt the pictures should communicate a message and he had greater knowledge of art concepts and a more developed sense of morality. However, he had little enjoyment of the picture as a sensual object and spent little time looking at it. He felt he did not have much to say personally about the pictures because he did not know the message. This child showed a very 'objective' approach, and he was reluctant to express any personal 'subjective' feelings, because of a lack of information.

Hand movements were made by all children, especially pointing to demonstrate and to explain verbal statements. Some subjects made many more hand movements than others but this did not seem linked to age. What was found to be different was the use of two hands, which was linked to response style. Those empathetic subjects who were in a state of fusion and very involved with their responses used two hand movements, stroking and touching the shapes as they spoke.

The non-verbal behaviours did not by themselves bring out data that could not be derived from the verbal. But they supported and elaborated the responses the subjects made. They also suggest a way to investigate aesthetic response with young children which should be investigated more thoroughly.

The factor of pictures

The pictures were also an important factor on the topics that the subjects talked about. The first picture, de Latour's *La Diseuse de bonne fortune*, was realistic and narrative. This picture elicited many explanations about the story and feelings that were noted. There were comments about morality across the three domains, the only picture to evoke this response.

Although it is almost photographically realistic, the people in the picture are dressed in eighteenth-century costume. This fact aroused many comments about the look of clothes, the hair and the face of the old gypsy. This was followed by suggestions that these should be changed in order to look 'right'. A normalizing set of standards is being applied which has much to do with a socializing process.

The abstract work, *Phenomenon Cat's Paw Reach*, by Jenkins, called forth as many types of response as the first picture but they were more often about the visual language: shapes, space and colour. This picture elicited rich personal narratives from the children about themselves, filled with imaginative details. Although many complained about messiness in this picture, it was one that brought forth the most imaginative and poetic responses from certain children.

In this picture, there were also examples of synaesthesia, an unusual kind of response. This is the production, from a sense impression of one kind, of an associated mental image of another kind. It is as if the lack of recognizable details allowed the children to imagine freely and to project themselves on to the picture, and respond in a variety of sensory modes. An explanation for this might be that the picture is an example of 'indeterminacy of text', a term borrowed from Reader Response theory, which states that if the text is open and amenable to different meanings, the viewer/reader will project meaning on to it, as Tompkins (1982) points out. In this instance, the text was the picture, which was 'open' because of its abstract form.

The other representational picture, Matisse's *L'Atelier rouge*, elicited almost as many stories about the self as the first picture but few comments about its most obvious feature, the overall red colour. The children were seduced by the subject-matter of both of these two pictures almost as if they were not aware of other formal or symbolic aspects. This picture represented a room; the responses dealt with the familiar, the tables, the chairs, and reorganizing these to conform to a habitual pattern. As pointed out in other research (Machotka 1966; Gardner and Gardner 1973), unless the aspect of content is removed, the primary concern of young children is focused on the subject-matter.

In summary, we noted that each of the three pictures called forth topics relating to their content. The narrative picture elicited stories; the abstract work elicited talk of visual elements, art making and personal narratives; and the picture of the room elicited comparisons between it and the child's lived reality. This corroborates Farrell's (1979) research where he found that the factor of the picture accounted for the differences of aesthetic responses between students of 9 to 16 years, rather than age as he had hypothesized.

The use of non-verbal measures also supported the importance of the picture in shaping the aesthetic experience. Upon analysing the 'Path', that is the tracing of where they looked while talking, we found that the Paths were fairly similar from child to child for the same picture; but Paths differed from picture to picture. When laid on to the picture, Paths were dependent on the composition of the picture. It did not matter greatly where the subject started, because the Path eventually touched upon the same areas in the pictures.

If aesthetic responses are a 'dialogue' between what is proposed by the artist in terms of form, line, colour, symbols and content, and the viewer who brings personal feelings, memories and acculturation, then responses to aesthetic objects will always be dependent upon the art objects as well as the viewer. It does not reside exclusively in one or the other.

The factor of the agent: the questions asked

Upon reflection, the first four questions of the instrument used by the agent were in effect a scenario that the researcher proposed to the subjects. There was a phenomenological sequence to them, whereby the subject was asked to contemplate, then enter, a picture and to empathize with the feelings, forms or events in the picture. This was followed by asking the child to remake the picture to his or her own image.

The second sequence, the last three questions, asked the subject to move out from the world of the picture and consider how the picture came to be, whether adults might like it, if the subject liked it or not, finishing with a judgement about the picture.

The questions had an important effect on the responses the subjects made. The questions from a phenomenological sequence, which were open-ended, elicited many more responses over a variety of topics than did some of the other questions. These tended to be clustered in the domains of Picture and Self; often these responses dealt with feelings that the subject saw in the picture and/ or within him or herself. We found this to be important as feelings are rarely investigated in research, even though most researchers define aesthetic response as having an affective component.

The last questions about the origin of the picture and about the work of the artist were focused on the domain World of Art. The answers were fewer because these questions dealt more with acquired knowledge of the art world. In fact, as demonstrated by Gardner *et al.* (1975) there is an influence of age on such information. Our youngest subject had little interest and insight into the origins of the picture. The answers to questions of personal preference were idiosyncratic, based on few criteria; the idea of adult preference, in almost all cases, was diametrically opposed to the child's preference. Few criteria were used to support judgement but these were different from the criteria for preference. Only one child said that the picture was good because he liked it.

In conclusion, the ideas and concepts raised by the questions were an important factor of aesthetic responses. They proposed issues for the subjects to consider and try to answer. Sometimes the children were surprised by the questions as if these were ideas that had never been considered. This has implications for the pedagogical situation, which will be discussed below.

Conclusion

To summarize, we set about answering our research questions by constructing an inventory of the verbal statements the schoolchildren made about three pictures. A list of non-verbal behaviours which could be analysed to enhance the verbal responses was also developed.

The eight questions asked were the instrument used to elicit aesthetic response; they constituted an intervention in aesthetic response which is equivalent to the role of the educator. We found that the sequence and the nature of the questions had an important effect on the statements that the children made. The sequence moved from taking stock of personal feeling about the picture to evaluating it. The subject was vested in the situation on several levels: affective as well as cognitive.

The questions were an important factor and because of their nature, allowed issues to arise which have rarely been discussed in other research: synaesthesia, for instance. As an educational tool, questions are part of a museum educator's repertoire which can be manipulated to produce different results. Our findings show that schoolchildren were very susceptible to the ideas embedded in the questions. These became teaching tools to expand the child's horizons and suggested areas about which to conceptualize and discuss.

The three pictures used in the study illustrated that while children normally attend to the subject-matter of a picture, if this factor is removed, they are able to respond to abstract work in equal measure. This is an important implication for the museum educator who should present a variety of pictures of different style, different representational systems, different content and different media to augment the repertoire of ideas and concepts in schoolchildren. Such variety will demonstrate the multitude of possibilities for expression in visual forms and give children a chance to explore this variety.

The importance of the picture was also demonstrated by a non-verbal indicator. The Paths, a non-verbal aspect of the subject's Journey indicating where the child looked, was dependent to a large extent on the composition of the picture. While there were variations between the different children's Paths, these depended either on which side the child stood on, or what strategies were used to look. But most of the Paths touched upon the main elements of the picture's composition. This is a very important finding as it underlines the role of the picture in shaping the aesthetic experience.

As to the factor of age, it was difficult to see much influence on the topics. There seem to be no restrictions on educational programmes for schoolchildren imposed by developmental considerations. All the subjects spoke of the domain Picture and Self about the same number of times. Mostly it was in the domain World of Art that there were differences to be noticed between the youngest and oldest children pointing out their knowledge about art. This supports Gardner's theory that by the age of 7–8 years most children have the necessary development to respond to works of art. Any later changes are the result of accumulation of knowledge and skills, not the result of a qualitative change in the mind.

If age did not play a very significant part in the aesthetic responses of these subjects, there were still differences between them that surfaced. We found that *responding styles* were more important than age as an influence on aesthetic response. Influenced by Housen-Grear's (1977) conception of aesthetic typologies and after analysing the videos, we were able to identify three different styles of response. These styles of response we labelled the concrete, the empathetic and the intellectual. We found evidence that this personal style could be seen in the verbal statements and some of the non-verbal behaviours. Other styles may well exist in other samples of the population.

Role of the museum educator

In the past, one of the concerns of educators has been to define the role of the art educator in the art-making process; this is true of aesthetics as well. As Feldman (1970) pointed out, if development is the motor that drives children's art-making there is no role for the teacher. In this study, we noted that age did not play an important part in the schoolchildren's responses.

What emerged was that the museum educator was very important in the interchange between art object and viewer. Not only as purveyor of facts and figures, the educator, by being aware of the different varieties of expression and of response, can suggest other positions to take in relation to the art work through the questions asked. By open-ended and varied questions, different issues can be examined in relation to the work.

The choice of art works in a museum to view and to respond to is another factor at the disposal of the educator. These art works are proof of a multiplicity of representational systems and modes of expression which allow many social and aesthetic concerns to be discussed. Museums by their richness and complexity have a major role to play in the visitor's aesthetic responses.

References

Clayton, J. R. (1974) 'An investigation into the possibility of development trends in aesthetics: a study of qualitative similarities and differences in the young', unpublished doctoral dissertation, University of Utah.

Coffey, A. (1968) 'A developmental study of aesthetic preference for realistic and non-objective paintings', unpublished doctoral dissertation, University of Massachusetts.

Csikszentmihalyi, M. and Robinson, R. (1990) *The Art of Seeing*, Malibu, Calif.: J. Paul Getty Museum and Center for Education in the Arts.

Farrell, E. (1979) 'Stages in aesthetic development: measuring aesthetic response', *Review of Research in Visual Arts Education* 11: 21–8.

Feldman, E. B. (1970) *Becoming Human through Art*, Englewood Cliffs, NJ: Prentice Hall.

Gardner, H. (1973) *The Arts and Human Development: A Psychological Study of the Artistic Process*, New York: Wiley.

Gardner, H. and Gardner, J. (1973) 'Developmental trends in sensitivity to form and subject matter in paintings', *Studies in Art Education* 14(2): 52–6.

Gardner, H., Winner, E. and Kircher, M. (1975) 'Children's conceptions of the arts', *Journal of Aesthetic Education* 9(3): 60–77.

Horner, S. (1988) '2B and not 2C; that is not the question', unpublished article.

Housen, A. (1983) 'The eye of the beholder: measuring aesthetic development', unpublished doctoral thesis, Harvard Graduate School of Education, Boston.

Housen-Greer, A. (1977) 'Levels of aesthetic development: a study of museum visitors', unpublished manuscript, Harvard Graduate School of Education, Boston.

Lanier, V. (1986) 'The fourth domain: building a new art curriculum', *Studies in Art Education* 28(1): 5–10.

Legendre, R. (1983) *L'Education totale*, Montreal: Les Editions Franco-Québec Inc.

Machotka, P. (1966) 'Aesthetic criteria in childhood justification of preference', *Childhood Development* 37: 877–85.

Parsons, M. (1986) 'The place of a cognitive approach to aesthetic response', *Journal of Aesthetic Education* 20: 107–11.

Parsons, M., Johnston, M. and Durham, R. (1978) 'Developmental stages in children's aesthetic response', *Journal of Aesthetic Education* 12: 83–104.

Subès, J. (1955) 'La sensibilité de l'enfant à l'art pictural', *Enfance* 8: 345–68.

Tompkins, J. (1982) *Reader Response Criticism*, Baltimore: Johns Hopkins University Press.

Winner, E. (1982) *Invented Worlds: the Psychology of the Arts*, Cambridge, Mass.: Harvard University Press.

Winnicott, D. (1971) *Playing and Reality*, London: Tavistock Publications.

20

Evaluation of school work in the Rutland Dinosaur Gallery

Kate Pontin

This chapter follows on from a research project developed for a Master's degree. As I am a museum education officer, the purpose of the research was to use a variety of evaluation techniques in the assessment of gallery use by schools, in particular in the learning of science. It was felt important to improve the quality of museum visits for the increasing numbers of school groups coming to the museum. This was part of a development plan to improve education services. The gallery chosen for the study was the Rutland Dinosaur at Leicester Museum and Art Gallery, which is popular with schools and has a selection of recently developed resources available for their use. The gallery was opened in 1985 and displays a dinosaur found in an Ironstone quarry in Great Casterton, Rutland, east Leicestershire, England. Displayed with it are a number of large sea reptiles found in north Leicestershire. These reptiles, plesiosaurs and ichthyosaurs were found in rocks of an age similar to those containing the dinosaur.

The gallery was designed by curatorial and design staff to appeal to the general public, particularly children. Information is brief and carefully written at an appropriate language level. All the panels are positioned at a low level and include graphics and items to touch. The curator's overall objectives were to answer the question 'what is a dinosaur?' and to display the local fossils, especially the dinosaur.

The Dinosaur Gallery has an average of 200 school visits a year totalling over 15,000 pupils, mostly from primary schools. It was an impossible task for the education officer to be present at all these group visits, so gallery support materials including an information pack and (more recently) handling material were developed. Evaluation was an important part of this resource development. The resources were written to support new National Curriculum topic areas. The government has introduced a detailed curriculum to be followed by all state schools, covering all subjects, each split into different areas of attainment at each key stage or age band. Although this initially narrowed the range of topics studied on museum visits it gave museums a great opportunity to target known areas of study. The advent of the National Curriculum and the inclusion of the use of primary source material has made museum visits more crucial. However, it is important to find out how effective the gallery visit is in achieving National Curriculum programmes. Did teachers find that the gallery and accompanying resources suited their needs? Did the pupils learn anything?

The evaluation programme therefore assessed whether teachers achieved their aims, what these were, and how much pupils gained from a museum visit, educationally and socially. The results were intended to help improve and develop gallery resources. The techniques of evaluation chosen made use of both naturalistic and scientific approaches, giving complementary information. The techniques included discussion and observation to discover visitor reactions and feelings, and a more formal and more quantitative approach in the survey. Thus, it was hoped to highlight successful areas and pinpoint any improvements using a variety of techniques – techniques which were set up to answer a set of predetermined questions (Table 20.1).

Table 20.1 Summary of approaches in evaluating schools' use of the Rutland Dinosaur Gallery

Objectives	Questions/information required	Method
To improve quality of children's experience; educational and social learning	What are children interested in? What makes them excited? What will help them learn more?	Observation of children Questionnaire, school study
To improve support for follow-up work	What are schools teaching? What is the gallery used for? What age group is using it most? What follow-up work do they do? How can this be developed?	Teachers' survey Observation, bookings Information, school studies Discussion
To provide activities for groups in the gallery	What are the teachers' and pupils' needs in the gallery? What do we offer to support this?	Surveys, observation, discussion, compare supported and non-supported schools
To provide teacher resources which give stimulus, educational support and science activities	What difference do support materials make? What are teachers' needs? What resources would support this?	Survey

Survey evaluation

Three surveys were developed: the teachers' opinion survey, the pupils' opinion survey (Figure 20.1) and the pupils' knowledge test questionnaire (Figure 20.2). Six teachers gave support to the project sending in survey returns, worksheets and comments. All of them used museum education resources including handling material, information packs and workshops.

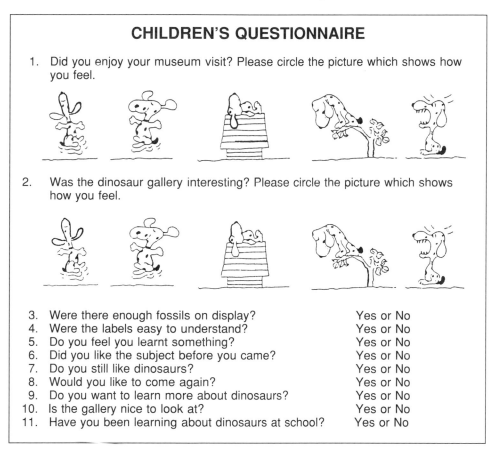

CHILDREN'S QUESTIONNAIRE

1. Did you enjoy your museum visit? Please circle the picture which shows how you feel.

2. Was the dinosaur gallery interesting? Please circle the picture which shows how you feel.

3. Were there enough fossils on display?   Yes or No
4. Were the labels easy to understand?   Yes or No
5. Do you feel you learnt something?   Yes or No
6. Did you like the subject before you came?   Yes or No
7. Do you still like dinosaurs?   Yes or No
8. Would you like to come again?   Yes or No
9. Do you want to learn more about dinosaurs?   Yes or No
10. Is the gallery nice to look at?   Yes or No
11. Have you been learning about dinosaurs at school?   Yes or No

Figure 20.1 Children's questionnaire. *Source*: Hopkins 1985

The pupils' survey was designed to find out how children themselves felt about the gallery visit. To aid the response the survey was designed in a pictorial way with smiling and frowning faces. The results from three groups reflected the opinions of primary pupils aged 6 to 9.5, 48 per cent boys. In general the responses were overwhelmingly positive. This may have been influenced by the style of survey using the 'Yes' and 'No' approach. However, the survey showed that most children were already interested in dinosaurs and got a great thrill from visiting the gallery. Their enthusiasm and enjoyment of the gallery encouraged them to want to learn more, in the gallery and back at school.

MUSEUMS EDUCATION
THE RUTLAND DINOSAUR AND FRIENDS

Please try to answer as many questions as possible.

The test is to find out how good the dinosaur gallery is at teaching children about dinosaurs; it is not meant to find out how brilliant you are!

1. What is the Rutland Dinosaur's scientific name?

2. Why do you think it was so large?

3. How do fossils form?

4. Why did the Rutland Dinosaur have a long neck?
    A   To reach leaves on the tops of trees
    B   To help it walk
    C   Some other reason

5. What is a dinosaur?
    A   A prehistoric animal
    B   A monster
    C   A prehistoric land reptile
    D   A sea reptile

6. What other animals did you see in the gallery that lived at the same time?

7. What was the climate like in Leicestershire when the dinosaurs were here?
    A   Cold and wet all year
    B   Warm and wet all year
    C   Like it is today
    D   Very hot

8. What sort of rock was the Rutland Dinosaur found in?
    A   Ironstone
    B   Chalk
    C   Limestone
    D   Shale

9. Why do you think dinosaurs became extinct?
    A   It got too hot
    B   It got too cold
    C   We do not know
    D   A meteorite hit the earth
    E   We do not really know

Figure 20.2 The Rutland Dinosaur and Friends questionnaire for children

Interestingly, the labels caused some problems, 32 per cent of pupils finding difficulty in reading them. This was probably partly because of some pupils' young age (the labels were designed for a reading age of 10). Solving this problem will be considered in any future resourcing.

The teachers themselves were also surveyed throughout the summer and autumn terms of 1991. The survey was sent out with an information pack on the gallery to every teacher booking a visit. The information gave background details on dinosaurs and on the gallery, including practicalities of visiting the museum and ideas for follow-up work. An activity was included to help teachers develop their own gallery session.

The survey was intended to find out how teachers prepared for a visit, in what context the visit was made and how they used the gallery. Most teachers replying had made a museum visit in the middle of the topic (68 per cent), a few at the end and the fewest, only two, at the beginning. This confirmed belief that most teachers feel a visit in the middle of the project allows for preparation and stimulates continuing interest.

Teachers' comments suggested that a school trip to the Leicester Museum and Art Gallery often involves visiting several galleries including the dinosaur gallery in one visit. This probably reflects restrictions on visits owing to lack of funds and curriculum pressures. Science Curriculum Studies work at school most frequently included dinosaurs, earth sciences and evolution, while local studies, geology and 'ourselves' were each mentioned by one teacher.

The most popular attainment areas within the Science Curriculum included Attainment Target 1, which considers scientific skills and method, especially the development of observation skills. Attainment Target 2 (as defined in the summer of 1992), the 'Variety of life', including fossilization, was mentioned by several teachers, while 'Life processes' and 'Genetics' (Attainment Target 4, 1992) were also mentioned. Areas from the earth sciences and environment attainment targets were each also mentioned by a teacher. Most groups were covering more than one science attainment target, although many teachers mentioned science study without specifying target areas. Other commonly mentioned curricula included English, maths and geography. Most teachers (60 per cent) took a cross-curricular approach covering more than one curriculum. With no mention of specific attainment targets from many teachers it seems that much of this work was general. Although it was disappointing not to see the gallery being used for a wider range of science work, teachers had obviously planned their visit to cover a range of curriculum areas.

The most important reasons teachers had for visiting are shown in Table 20.2. Of particular concern to them was the desire to stimulate and excite pupils through seeing real specimens. The scientific skill of observation was also seen as central to museum work.

The preferences show that teachers primarily organize school visits to stimulate, develop skills and observe original material (rather than teach factual information).

Table 20.2 Teachers' reasons for visiting the museum

Teachers' preferences	Percentage
To stimulate and excite	14
To see real specimens	12
To develop observational skills	7
To learn about dinosaurs	3
To learn about dinosaur extinction	2
To introduce the topic	2
To learn what a dinosaur is	1
To find out about Leicestershire in the past	1
To learn about dinosaur life style	1

On asking teachers about their evaluation of their visit they stated that they used class discussion to assess how effective the visit had been. Several used follow-up worksheets and one school used the visit to prepare for an assessment test.

Of the school groups, 50 per cent used worksheets in the gallery. Six groups (35 per cent) had adapted the worksheet enclosed in the pack. Although worksheets have many limitations they can provide more structure to a lesson than a general look round, giving a greater opportunity to learn and enjoy the experience. The non-participatory and unplanned work seen in other less well-prepared groups (see pp. 231–2) had a severely limited response from pupils.

Description of follow-up work was general; popular post-visit activities included art work, such as model making and drawing, and English work such as stories, poems and drama. In science, work included the study of time, early plants, shape, extinction, fossilization, skeletons and diet. Museum loans were used by two classes as part of their museum visit preparation, as were databases and technical lego.

Generally teachers liked the gallery, many adding additional comments to support this. Nearly all the teachers felt that there were enough specimens on display although there were requests for more handling materials. However, the labelling prompted comment again, half of the teachers finding the labels satisfactory but the other half finding that they were too difficult for their pupils. This was in spite of considerable effort having been put into the labels, with simple text, short sentences and large print. Young children had problems which, considering the reading age of the labels, were only to be expected. Teachers often read the labels and discussed their content with pupils. Other pupils with problems were those with English as a second language. Improvements will need to be considered including possibly foreign language translations of the basic panels but teachers will need to be informed of the age limitations of the labels.

Fifty per cent of teachers found the background information useful. Almost one-third of schools that replied had further support from the education officer in the form of an introductory talk with handling and discussion, intended to spark off enthusiasm. Ninety-four per cent of those teachers who had a workshop made comments that this had been an important addition to the school visit. Schools not using any extra museum services appear to have had more difficulty in using the display, particularly in using the labels.

A number of schools who had received museum education support returned results from the pupil questionnaire (Figure 20.2). It intended to test pupils' knowledge of dinosaurs, and in particular to test if the curator's exhibition objectives had been achieved. Many of the questions required looking at the display but some could be answered from information already gained from books. Initially it was hoped that teachers would be able to do a pre-test before their visit and a post-test following it. However this was very difficult to set up. Although statistical information would have shown the areas most pupils were interested in it required too much time from teachers and too much monitoring support from the education officer. Pre-test/post-test evaluation also required a control, using a non-museum visiting school, which was impossible in this case. The results were therefore assessed qualitatively rather than statistically.

Some interesting information did arise from the survey which offered an insight into pupils' perceptions in this subject area. The results will be used to help develop ways of supporting gallery use. They do not of course determine how successful the teacher was in achieving class objectives.

The results showed that the children were, on the whole, very knowledgeable about dinosaurs. They were keen to learn, although they often saw information as fact rather than as scientific theory. The high percentage of correct answers suggested that children's enthusiasm and interest helped them to learn. It also shows that those pupils whose visit had been planned, often with the use of museum resources, learnt more, both in the gallery and subsequently in class. Inaccurate answers to some questions suggested that pupils do not always look carefully at or read labels, and their own ideas often prevail even when the correct answer is available: for example, 'This is a baby dinosaur', referring to a model, and 'I knew this was a dinosaur', referring to a crocodile. It is clear that observational skills were not automatically present.

Qualitative analysis

Later qualitative analysis included a visit to a school following their museum visit, a project with a special school and gallery observation. The visit made to the school gave the opportunity to talk to the teacher and pupils about their visit and subsequent work. The teacher said that the visit to the gallery had been to stimulate interest in the project on 'the earth', to see real specimens and to develop maths and English skills. The teacher's comments in her survey return show that the pupils were studying evolution and had reached the reptile group. Their gallery work covered dinosaur extinction and also English Attainment Targets covering areas within listening, reading and writing. The teacher used a worksheet adapted from the one supplied in the pack and had prepared pupils before their visit. She planned follow-up work to continue looking at dinosaurs and to follow the story of evolution. She thought the specimens and labels appropriate and volunteered that it had been 'a very successful visit'. This was confirmed by the quality of the pupils' follow-up work and their responses to the questionnaire.

The children were completing project workbooks. These included largely teacher-led work with paragraphs of information and pictures. The work concentrated on facts, figures and names. There was little evidence of any child-led science work, other than a soil settling experiment. This was a little surprising as their other cross-curricular work was of a very high quality and largely child-initiated, including particularly good art and technology work.

Creative English work was also of a high standard. Other projects included model making and poems. The children were very proud of their work and enjoyed showing it to me. It seems that while many primary teachers provided a suitable background for pupils to produce high-quality work there is still a need for training in teaching science skills. Museums have an opportunity to support teachers in this area. Looking at the data from this particular pupils' survey returns, it shows that as well as producing good follow-up work the pupils enjoyed the gallery visit; in fact 66 per cent of pupils gave 'Yes' answers to all the questions (opinion survey, Figure 20.1). In the knowledge survey (Figure 20.2) the pupils produced results similar to the average. However, they described fossilization particularly well and gave correct answers to questions which required looking at labels and specimens.

Evaluating a museum visit in context

Another evaluation project was with a special school, one for children with special requirements because of either physical, mental or emotional impairment. In evaluating the museum experience it was important to consider the museum visit within the context of a learning programme, and so it was decided to develop a small project on dinosaurs with a group of pupils. A special needs class was chosen, partly to see what sorts of resources they might require, but also to consider other issues, such as social needs rather than subject needs. This class, in particular, was chosen because of the teacher's enthusiasm for the project and for his clear objectives. A visit to the museum was an opportunity to see new places outside the school, as well as to develop communication skills and appropriate behaviour for public places (considered important in all schools but not normally explicitly expressed).

The class consisted of five pupils aged from 12 to 14. They belonged to a special class in the school because of their lack of ability to fit in. This not only disrupted other pupils' work but also their own development. They had limited ability in writing and reading and had poor motor skills. More importantly though, they had emotional and behavioural problems.

The project was planned to last three mornings, over three weeks. The first session was one of preparation, the second a visit to the museum and the third a follow-up session. Pupils studied fossils and learned about dinosaurs on the first morning, following up the museum visit with discussion in the last session on how fossils formed, making fossil casts from plaster. The museum visit itself was structured with a variety of tasks, including drawing, maths and recognition of previously seen fossil types. Naturalistic evaluation techniques were used such as open interviewing and discussion. After three weeks their knowledge seemed upon initial inspection not to have improved very much but in fact for them it was significant, taking into account their restricted experience and ability. They gained an idea of life before humans and of the variety of different life forms. They learnt very quickly how to do plaster casts. More importantly, their confidence and communication skills were much improved.

Generally the project highlighted the need to prepare pupils for a visit, not only with background information but also on how to visit a museum. In preparing activities for the gallery session it was important to consider the ability of the pupils and their capability for learning abstract concepts. Gallery activities needed to focus on the development of practical and social skills, including those in communication as well as curriculum work. Important issues and information needed to be repeated throughout the activities to help pupils remember them. The progress of the children was continually assessed so that follow-up work could be adapted according to their achievement. Follow-up work was crucial in clarifying important information. Of most significance, though, was the need to remember how different the museum environment was from the classroom and how this affected pupil behaviour and learning potential.

Gallery observation

In the final qualitative project pupils were watched in the gallery while recording their conversations. These conversations fell into several categories. The first encompassed exclamations about the dinosaur, particularly its size and how much of it was real. The most frequent comments (approximately 20 per cent) included 'Wow', 'Is it real?', 'This one is my favourite' and 'What's this?'

The second category of conversation was organizational and included questions and comments on the work they were supposed to be doing – 'What are you doing?' 'What have we got to do?' – and discussions about stationery items. There were also one or two topic-based discussions which were a result of observation and questioning. Topics discussed included dinosaur skin, shape and skulls. However about 50 per cent of conversation was social chat among friends and was not directly relevant to the subject-matter. A substantial number of groups, particularly younger classes, had no worksheets or set tasks to do, and no museum support from the education officer. The pupils exhibited poor concentration and loud, over-energetic behaviour. Some group leaders attempted discussion on a variety of topics with, on the whole, little success. Although it is not possible to be sure how much was learnt it seemed minimal. All the excitement the pupils exhibited in the first few moments went to waste as they lost concentration and got bored with no tasks or programme to follow.

Most visits were short, approximately fifteen minutes, a little longer when they had worksheets. In the groups that did have tasks or worksheets much of the work was label-based. Many children copied labels with very little thought or observation of specimens. Others wanted to finish their worksheets as quickly as possible and consequently copied information quickly, often from each other.

Many children also thought they knew the answers before looking at anything – 'I knew it was going to be a brontosaurus', 'It's not real'. This appeared difficult to deal with, although some teachers developed a discussion around such comments, asking the group to check the statements. Discussion can be an effective way of teaching if pupils are used to such learning methods, otherwise they lose concentration quickly.

It seems that poorly prepared visits have low impact on pupils, the initial excitement not being used to develop ideas, skills or concepts. Sessions should have a planned programme to direct pupils to look at the specimens and to develop skills such as observation, and the assessment of information.

Conclusions

How far did the evaluations answer the questions set? These, as shown in Table 20.1, asked about pupil and teacher expectations of the gallery and how well these were met. Museums are not familiar environments for teachers or pupils, but skills can be developed to support curriculum and social learning and in particular observation through the study of specimens rather than labels. Pupils find the gallery exciting and visually stimulating and with preparation gain a great deal from a visit, which acts as a crucial stimulus to school work.

Evaluation largely confirmed professional feelings that the gallery was a successful educational experience, particularly when preparation took place and the museum's education resources were used. Most teachers required support materials, such as worksheets and handling specimens, in using the gallery to develop National Curriculum work. This covered a wide variety of curriculum areas including science, English and maths but focused on studying and observing real specimens. Many groups visiting used no museum education services, and had little or no structure to the lesson, with no participation from pupils. The excitement produced by the fossils was completely lost.

Quantitative results were particularly useful in establishing teachers' needs and gallery use, for example the popularity of the pack and handling material and the high proportion of teachers taking a cross-curricular approach. The fact that many teachers have found these resources useful shows the validity of spending more time improving them. Qualitative analysis was more useful in highlighting more specific points, as in the project with the special needs group. This revealed the importance of the museum as a place for social learning although it can also have a disruptive influence on subject learning.

The evaluation programme has shown how effective educational work is in museums and how essential dedicated education specialists are. To continue developing a high quality experience for all visitors, there needs to be more development of visitor support services, and in particular help in class preparation and teacher training. The study also shows the need for better links between display teams and education staff, particularly in considering communication of ideas and developing labels and also in providing a hands-on approach.

Future resource development will consider providing for more groups, in fact all groups, possibly through sending a pack to all booked parties and permanently storing in the gallery handling material with workcards. Casual use of the gallery will not be encouraged. It will also be crucial to continue supporting teachers in planning museum lessons. Training teachers to prepare pupils is essential to allow pupil-centred learning and thus gain the most from the museum experience. It is important that museum staff become more involved in teacher training.

The major limitation of the project was the non-completion of the pre-test, post-test questionnaire. As the pre-test was not completed there were no quantitative results to enable consideration of factual learning in the gallery. Future research will look at the learning of science skills in galleries.

References

Abbey, D. S. and Cameron, D. F. (1959) *The Museum Visitor: I – Survey Design*, Toronto: Royal Ontario Museum.

Adams, G. and Cole, H. (1990) *Survey of Museum and Gallery Usage by ILEA Schools: 1988–1989*, ILEA.

Alt, M. B. (1990) 'Four years of visitor surveys at British Museum (Natural History)', *Museums Journal* 80(1): 10–19.

Berry, N. and Mayer, S. (eds) (1989) *Museum Education History, Theory and Practice*, Reston, Va: The National Art Education Association.

Borun, M. and Flexer, B. K. (n.d.) 'The impact of a class visit to a science muscum – an experimental study', unpublished paper produced for UNESCO survey on museum education, The Franklin Institute Science Museum, USA.

Coleman, J. (1978) 'Sociological analysis and social policy', in T. Bottomore and R. Nisbet (eds) *A History of Sociological Analysis*, London: Heinemann.

Deutscher, I. and Ostrander, S. (1985) 'Sociology and evaluation research: some past and future links', *History of Sociology* 6(1).

Griggs, S. (1981) 'Formative evaluation of exhibits at the British Museum (Natural History)', *Curator* 24(3): 189–201.

Hein, G. F. (1979) 'Evaluation in open classrooms. Emergence of a qualitative methodology', in S. Meisels (cd.) *Special Education and Development*, Baltimore: University Park Press.

—— (1982) 'Evaluation of museum programs and exhibits' in T. H. Hansen, K. E. Anderson and P. Vestergaard (eds) *Museums and education*, Danish ICOM/CECA.

Henniger-Shuh, J. (1984) 'Talking with teachers about museums in Nova Scotia', *Museum*.

Hopkins, D. (1985) *A Teacher's Guide to Classroom Research*, Milton Keynes: Open University Press.

Kushner, S. (1989) 'Evaluation in the National Association of Arts Centres, arts centres in education', in *A for Arts: Evaluation, Education and Arts Centres*, The Arts Development Association Research in Education, Co. Durham and Centre for Applied Research in Education University of East Anglia, May.

Lawrence, G. (1991) 'Rats, street gangs and culture: evaluation in museums', in G. Kavanagh (ed.) *Museum Languages: Objects and Texts*, Leicester, London and New York: Leicester University Press.

McManus, P. (1985) 'Worksheet induced behaviour in the British Museum (Natural History)', *Journal of Biological Education* 19(3): 237.

Madden, J. C. (1988) 'Museums of natural history as educational resources', *Museums as a Learning Resource Seminar*, International Research and Exchanges Board United States/German Democratic Republic, Washington, DC.

Miles, R. S. and Alt, M. B. (1979) 'British Museum (Natural History): a new approach to the visiting public', *Museums Journal* 78: 158–62.

Otto, J. (1979) 'Learning about "Neat Stuff": one approach to Evaluation', *Museum News* 58(2): 38–45.

Rees, P. Thomas, D. and Brown, S. (1990) 'Education, evaluation and exhibitions: an outline of current thought and work on Merseyside', *Journal for Education in Museums* 11: 9.

Robinson, E. S. (1928) 'The behavior of the museum visitor', *Publications of the American Association of Museums Monograph, New Series* 5: 1–72.

Schetel, H. (1973) 'Exhibits: art form or educational medium', *Museum News*, September 32–41.

Screven, C. G. (1986) 'Exhibitions and information centres: some principles and approaches', *Curator* 29(2): 109–37.

Skramstad, H. K. (1988) 'The history museum as learning resource', *Museums as a Learning Resource Seminar*, International Research and Exchanges Board, United States/German Democratic Republic, Washington, DC.

Wolf, R. L. (1980) 'A naturalistic view of evaluation', *Museum News* 58(1): 39–45.

Wolf, R. L. (1978) and Tymitz, B. I. (1978) *A Preliminary Guide for Conducting Naturalistic Evaluation in Studying Museum Environments*, Washington, DC: Smithsonian Institution.

21

The evaluation of museum–school programmes: the case of historic sites

Michel Allard

Introduction

The increasing involvement of various orders of government in the funding of museums and similar institutions, as well as the growing number of visitors (Pronovost 1989), is encouraging, if not forcing, the heads of such institutions to commit themselves to a process and establish the necessary mechanisms for the evaluation of public programmes.

Nowadays most museum professionals agree on the need for programme evaluation. However, evidence suggests that some institutions do not evaluate their programmes in a rigorous and reliable manner. H. Shettel (1989), one of the pioneers of museum evaluation, suggests that lack of funds as well as passive staff resistance may explain this situation. Even though he identified approximately 325 museum evaluation studies, very few dealt with the evaluation of public programmes.

According to D. G. Hayward and J. W. Larkin (1983: 42), co-authors of a study designed to evaluate a programme developed and carried out at the Old Sturbridge Village historic site, 'Most museum studies so far have focused on indoor settings and elements such as exhibit rooms, display cases and signs. There remains, however, considerable need for understanding visitor experiences *in outdoor museum settings*' (my emphasis). Some ten years later, our own research confirms this diagnosis.

We systematically examined many bibliographical references and computer listings relating to programme evaluation in museums and at historic sites. We found no works, articles or reports specifically relating to the evaluation of educational programmes (also known as interpretation and communication programmes) developed by staff at historic sites for the general public or a specific category of visitors. All we found, here and there, were a few articles which, having described the developmental and operational steps of a programme, attempt to evaluate its impact on the public: in short, slim pickings indeed.

We also consulted a number of works on the presentation or organization of historic sites. Once again, little space is devoted to the evaluation of educational programmes. We can therefore assume that little importance is attached to their evaluation. For instance, a UNESCO work entitled *Un patrimoine pour tous: les principaux sites naturels, culturels et historiques* (1984) provides a very good description of the sites but makes no mention of the existence of educational programmes. Similarly, B. Mackintosh (1985), in a work on American national parks, says absolutely nothing about educational programmes. The National Trust for Historic Preservation (1983) merely proposes, for educational programmes, that sites should exchange information. In a major work on the interpretation of historic sites, W. T. Alderson and S. P. Low (1976) devote only a very short chapter to evaluation and limit themselves to a description of methodology. Lastly, Parcs Canada (1982), in a descriptive guide to national parks, merely lists for each park a few programmes for the general public.

Although historic sites are included in the International Commission on Museums' (ICOM) definition of the term 'museum', the appropriateness of this remains in question. Is it logical, given the fact that it is not accepted by persons working in the museum field? Take, for instance, the summer 1992 issue of the Hydro Québec's magazine *Forces*, which was devoted entirely to museums on the occasion of the ICOM's meeting held at Quebec. It gives no special place to historic sites despite the fact that there are quite a number of them in Quebec. Is this a deliberate exclusion or an oversight?

General remarks

Notwithstanding the above, we can make a few general observations about museum evaluation that may provide a better framework for the evaluation of historic sites.

1   The number of evaluations of museums and historic sites has increased steadily, especially since 1980 (Shettel 1989).
2   No holistic general evaluations of educational programmes have been carried out in museums, much less at historic sites.
3   A few fragmented studies deal with only one aspect of the question. They measure learning (Screven 1984); determine the influence of learning conditions (Falk 1976); describe visitor behaviour (Wolf and Tymitz 1979); and identify the socio-economic profile of visitors (Dartington 1984), etc. Historic sites are included in this typology. Some partial studies evaluate programmes *from one angle.*
4   A number of authors of magazine and periodical articles very often do no more than describe the educational programmes they have designed, developed or implemented. However, their evaluative comments go no further than to mention that participants have liked or loved their experience. Many articles on educational programmes at historic sites fall into this category.
5   Since 1986, many evaluations of museums of science and technology have been conducted. In this regard, they are in first place, followed by art museums and then history museums. Historic sites are at the very bottom of the list.

6 Most studies of museums and historic sites focus on visitors. Very few evaluate the quality of exhibits, the role of facilitators or the physical setting.

7 The overwhelming majority of studies, both of museums and historic sites, are descriptive in nature. They very often do no more than describe visitor behaviour without seeking to explain or establish links between such behaviour and the exhibits, the physical setting, and the role of facilitators. Most of the studies are thus descriptive in nature rather than explanatory or interpretative.

8 In evaluations of educational programmes in museums, authors are relying increasingly on the so-called 'naturalist' method. This method purports to evaluate the impact of a programme, not in terms of the visitor behaviour sought after or expected by the designers (behaviourist method), but in terms of the actual behaviour of visitors. Few studies of historic sites have used this approach.

Specific remarks

In our review of reports, articles and works on the evaluation of educational programmes at historic sites, we were not at all surprised to find no work devoted specifically to this topic. More important still, authors such as Loomis (1987) and Korn (1989), who have conducted a few general museum evaluations, make no distinction between museums and historic sites. Implicitly, they confuse them. Those who have dealt with evaluation in a general or collective work on historic sites include Alderson and Low (1976) and Munley (1989). They make no distinction between historic sites and museums.

Museums and historic sites are, of course, similar in many respects. But can one be confused with the other?

A historic site is inextricably bound to an event (e.g. a battle), a social phenomenon (e.g. a canal) or a well-known person (e.g. Jacques Cartier). Consequently, a site is not a matter of free choice, but is dictated by an event. A historic site must come to terms with the constraints imposed by its location, and this must be taken into account when evaluating its programmes. For instance, the Forges du Saint-Maurice, about 150 kilometres away Montreal or Quebec City, are not easily accessible to students of those cities. A large percentage of visitors at the Maison Cartier in Old Montreal are tourists. Visitors to Fort Lennox on Ile-aux-Noix arrive in small groups by boat. The canals in the Soulanges region are spread over several kilometres. And so on. Consequently, the location of a site will have an impact on any programme and thus on any evaluation.

More important still, the event necessarily determines the theme of any programme. In Châteauguay, the battle itself becomes the focus of any activity. The theme can, of course, be expanded somewhat by placing the Battle of Châteauguay in context and dealing with the society of the period. The theme can also be expanded diachronically by referring to other battles between the Americans and the Canadians. However, the fact remains that the necessary character of the theme restricts programme content and often the public to whom it is addressed. We cannot take it for granted that every segment of the public will be capable of understanding the Battle of Châteauguay. Thus, when we evaluate an educational programme at a historic site, we must take this factor into consideration.

In addition, the theme becomes a sort of central thread for any programme. In museums, it is not always easy to find the unifying element of an educational programme. For historic sites, the issue is not so acute. The interests and understanding of visitors must, of course, be taken into consideration, but we cannot change the nature of the theme to meet visitor needs, expectations and interests. The site thus imposes a quasi-obligatory theme for the programme.

Selected because it was the site of an important event, the residence of a person who became famous or because it reflects an activity or life-style of the past, a historic site gives a geographical space a significance beyond what it might normally have today. A historic site, like a manuscript or printed document, bears witness to a past that no longer exists. But, like any other witness of bygone events, the site has been subject to the erosion of time and cannot achieve the impossible dream of bringing the past to life in a fully authentic manner. A much more realistic goal is to try to evoke a few events of the past as precisely and faithfully as possible.

The events are already situated in their original space. However, the natural environment has sometimes been subjected to change over the years or centuries, and some work is needed to restore, at least in part, the aspect it had at the time of the event that gives it its importance and meaning. With the exception of a few archaeological sites, this task is made somewhat easier in North America because the sites refer to events that date back less than five centuries.

In most instances, however, reorganization of the natural landscape is not enough to bring alive the context in which the past events occurred. What is also needed is restoration of the buildings and other elements present at the site when the historical events to which reference is made occurred. If they are not restored, then fairly faithful reconstitution is satisfactory. The site will then partially or totally reflect the physical landscape and organization that obtained when the events it commemorates took place.

But restoration or reconstitution of the site, no matter how perfect, is still very static. More is required to bring it to life: maps, brochures, books, guides, facilitators, audiovisual presentations, information activities and interactive terminals. But all these types of animation remain, in the final analysis, piecemeal. Ideally, à la Orson Welles, the events themselves should be relived. The public should become direct witnesses or, better still, actors in the events themselves. In other words, the events should be simulated. But how do we relive the Battle of Châteauguay? Can we simulate the life-style of the nineteenth century? Since we cannot fully reconstitute events, we must try to present them as faithfully as possible: guides and facilitators wearing the clothes of the period; re-creation of activities such as bakeries and tailor shops; and group activities such as the parade ground exercises of a military company. Sometimes theatre can be used to reconstitute an event. In ideal circumstances, the visitors themselves become actors. In this way, the natural landscape comes alive through human activity and the historic site becomes, to varying degrees, a living museum.

However, no one is deceived by such re-creations, restorations and reconstitutions. They may pique curiosity, stimulate interest and better define content, but they cannot make us relive the past in every respect. They can evoke a situation but not recreate it. The objective assigned to historic sites – to reconstitute the past as faithfully as possible – raises a number of issues about efforts to evaluate their impact on the public.

1   No one can deny that reconstitutions and restorations focus the visitor's attention, but to what degree we do not know. In addition, we do not know if reconstitutions and restorations help visitors understand the event or confuse them even more.
2   Any reconstitution or restoration leaves much to the imagination. Visitors must be given an understanding of an event or aspect of society through the site itself, its objects, buildings and sometimes theatrical presentations. But how can they do so without calling on their imagination? Any evaluation must therefore identify, if not measure, the impact on the imagination as well as on the cognitive and affective faculties of visitors to the site.
3   But if imagination, or at least a certain degree of abstraction, is required to understand or relive events of the past, does the site itself provide the necessary focus? In this regard, evaluations of programmes at historic sites should not be limited simply to their impact on visitors; they should analyse the relationships established between the subject (the visitor), the object (the site) and the agent (the facilitator or guide). The issue, then, is more complicated than for a museum. If we cannot isolate the environmental variable in museums and analyse it in terms of how it relates to the other variables mentioned above, at a historic site the object and the environment become one.

At a historic site, the object and the environment become two almost inextricably interwoven variables. Based on today's research, we are unable to determine the influence of either of these variables. We therefore see how difficult it is to evaluate the impact on visitors, if not of a site, at least of the educational programmes put in place.

A historic site has its own characteristics and requires a specific type of evaluation. While historic sites can borrow forms and techniques of evaluation from museums or other educational institutions, it should nevertheless adapt them to its own needs or, at best, find its own approaches. Historic sites should not, because of their nature, be confused with museums.

Epistemology and the current state of knowledge dictate that great care should be taken when developing and implementing models and techniques to enable historic sites to be more satisfactorily evaluated.

239

Types of evaluation

We can make a distinction between two major types of evaluation. The first, of a disciplinary nature, focuses on the exhibit(s). The second, focusing on the public, seeks to measure or describe the impact of the exhibit(s) on visitors. Let us now examine how these two types of evaluation are carried out for historic sites.

Disciplinary evaluation

In the case of a historic site, it is essential and fundamental to evaluate the site itself. This approach draws heavily on the historical method. The first step is to conduct an external critique of the 'document'. We must establish if the event commemorated really did take place and, if so, if it occurred at the location designated as a historic site. Museum evaluation is not in the slightest concerned with this feature. Therein lies a fundamental difference between a museum and a historic site.

The second step of the evaluation involves an internal critique of the site, particularly with respect to the reconstitution of buildings and its internal and external physical arrangement.

The third and last step is to analyse the historical interpretations conveyed by the site as a whole and in information found on plaques, in brochures and in other materials.

Our research has uncovered few studies of this type (Alderson 1975). We believe, however, that such studies should necessarily precede any study of impact on the public.

Evaluation of impact

A second type of evaluation examines the impact of interpretation, communication or educational programmes established for the public. In this type of evaluation, we distinguish between several major categories of studies.

A first category describes the socio-economic characteristics of visitors to historic sites. The purpose here is to gain a better understanding of the public. Data on age, sex, profession and income are some of the variables most often collected. Some studies compare the characteristics of visitors to historic sites against those of the general public. We have found several studies of this type. But we are well aware that most sites undertake this type of study. According to Loomis (1987), unpublished studies conducted locally may be much more numerous than those that are published.

A second category of studies analyses the impact of programmes on visitors in terms of the goals and objectives of the designers (Dartington 1984). These quasi-experimental studies measure, through pre- and post-tests, the knowledge acquired by the public during their visit to the site. Most of these studies limit themselves to cognitive development and ignore changes of an affective nature, particularly attitudes. These studies usually examine only factual knowledge about the events in question; information of a conceptual nature or that relating to the development of intellectual skills is usually ignored or set aside. Several studies of historic sites fall into this category (Knopf 1981; Mullins 1979).

A third category of studies are of the naturalist type and purport to identify the actual impact of programmes on visitors. Based on observations and non-directed interviews with visitors and sometimes museum staff, they describe visitor behaviour and try to identify needs, interests and perceptions (Harrison 1980). Although this type of evaluation is becoming more frequent in museums of science and art, virtually none is conducted at historic sites.

Lastly, a fourth category of studies includes those that focus on the description of educational programmes designed for the general public or for a specific clientele. Their authors describe the programme activities, explain in detail how they are presented and conclude with a summary evaluation based on their own observations and impressions, or do not evaluate them at all. For historic sites, we have found several studies of this type (Grant 1987).

Most articles on the evaluation of educational programmes offer very poor foundations on which to build a coherent, effective, relevant and general policy. However, our study has not been a waste of time. It should be placed in an overall perspective and be considered as the first step in what P. M. Wortman and R. W. Marans (1987) call, in the case of existing programmes, 'pre-evaluation research'. According to these authors, if we wish to ensure the effectiveness and validity of an evaluation, we must, in addition to a feasibility study, conduct research whose purpose is to determine the actual objectives of the evaluation and validate the investigative tools and techniques. Once the pre-evaluation research has been successfully concluded, the real evaluation may begin.

Future outlook

In line with Wortman and Marans (1987), we propose the following plan of action:

- In light of the studies already completed in museums, particularly historical studies (importance of the object) and those relating to 'external' education (importance of the setting), a pre-evaluation research project to develop a model specific to historic sites could be undertaken. Unlike the studies we have listed and examined, such research would not be restricted to a single facet of a historic site. It would study each aspect, not only in itself, but also in terms of its relations with other objects (Allard and Boucher 1991). It would analyse the adequacy or inadequacy of the educational programme in terms of the object (site theme), the public (children, teenagers, adults, seniors; family, school and other groups) the agents (conservationists, facilitators, guides) and the setting (natural, developed, restored, reconstituted). The result would be a non-fragmented but holistic (i.e. general and complete) evaluation model that could be applied to all historic sites.

241

- The pre-evaluation research could be conducted at many historic sites across the world. Thus the validity and the fidelity of the model would be confirmed.
- The pre-evaluation research could use the following steps: analysis, by an evaluator or evaluation team, of the material produced for educational or any other purposes by staff of the historic sites involved; analysis of this documentation by external experts such as historians, history teaching consultants, etc.; in addition, interviews could be held with authors of documentation and/or staff of the sites where it is used; the sites could be the subject of a general analysis involving, in addition to the measures already set out, the exploratory study of a group of visitors; the theoretical and practical studies conducted at the sites could be combined with information collected during the bibliographical study and be used as a basis for developing an evaluation model for historic sites.
- Introduction of the model.

This plan, in addition to responding to the demands of a 'scientific' methodology, could be conducted in stages. It would be relatively inexpensive and could be revised at each step in the process.

References

Adams, C. and Miller, S. (1982) 'Museums and the use of evidence in history teaching', *Teaching History* 34, October, 3–6.

Alderson, W. T. (1975). 'Les objectifs de la préservation des sites historiques', *Museum* 27(3): 101–4.

Alderson, W. T. and Low, S. P. (1976) *Interpretation of Historic Sites*, Nashville: American Association for State and Local History.

Allard, M. and Boucher, S. (1991) *Le Musée et l'école*, Montreal: Hurtubise H.M.H.

American Association for State and Local History (ed.) (1991) *Fall Catalog*, Nashville.

American Association of Museums (ed.) (1982) *An Annotated Bibliography for the Development and Operation of Historic Sites*, Washington, DC.

Andel, M. A. (1990) 'Digging for the secrets of time: artifacts old foundations and more', *Social Studies and the Young Learner* 3(1): 9–11.

Anderson, J. (1984), *Time Machines. The World of Living History*, Nashville: The American Association for State and Local History.

Armstrong, S. (1983) 'Living history at Sainte-Marie among the Hurons', *History and Social Science Teacher* 18(4): 241–3.

Barclay, D. (1983) *Interpretation of the Environment. A Bibliography*, London: The Carnegie United Kingdom Trust.

Borden, R. (1983) 'Planning and evaluating interpretative programs', in B. Dysart, *Interpretation Seminar Proceedings*, Irondale, Ont.: Council of Outdoors Educators of Ontario.

Borhegyi, S. F. and Hanson, I. A. (1967) 'Chronological bibliography of museum visitor surveys', in E. Larabee (ed.) *Museum and Education*, Washington, DC.

Center for Museum Education (ed.) (1978) *Programs for Historic Sites and Houses, Sourcebook no. 3*, Washington, DC: George Washington University.

Cizek, E. D. and Sensat, L. L. (1989) 'Sun Oak', *Art Education* 42(2): 27–8.

Cyr, S. (1992) 'Les parcs canadiens. Simplement naturel', in Association québécoise des professeurs de sciences (ed.) 'Les sciences, quand les musées s'en mêlent', *Spectre* 21(5).

Dartington Amenity Research Trust and Psychology Department of the University of Surrey (1984) *Interpretation in Visitors' Centres*, Gloucester: Countryside Commission.

Dauphin, S. and Archambault, J. (1987) *Bibliographie subjective sur les musées et la communication efficace avec les visiteurs*, Montreal: UQAM, Service de l'audio-visuel.

242

Everhart, W. C. (1972) *The National Park Service*, New York, Washington and London: Praeger Publishers.

Falk, John H. (1976) 'Outdoor education: A technique for assessing student behaviors', *School Science and Mathematics* 75: 226–31.

Gottesdiener, H. (1987) *Évaluer l'exposition, définitions, méthodes et bibliographie sélective commentée d'études d'évaluation*, Paris: La documentation française.

Grant, D. (1987) *The Topic is Sandy Hook: A Program for Gifted and Talented Students at Sandy Hook*, Lincraft, NJ: Brookdale Community College.

Harrison, N. K. (1980) 'Development and implementation of educational programs in selected history museums and suggested practices for future programming', doctoral thesis, The University of Oklahoma, Oklahoma, USA.

Hayward, D. G. and Larkin, J. W. (1983) 'Evaluating visitor experiences and exhibit effectiveness at Old Sturbridge Village', *Museum Studies Journal* 1(2): 42–51.

Heath, A. M. (1979) 'Programmes d'excursion à travers les musées, sites et monuments en tant que "sources de savoir"', *Museum*, 31(3): 210–18.

Howard, D. F., Hunnecutt, H. H. and Draver, D. D. (1980) 'Writing local history: a new look at Old Portsmouth', *Childhood Education* 56(5): 264–7.

ICOM (1986) *Bibliographie muséologique de base 1986*, Paris: ICOM, Centre de documentation, Unesco.

International Laboratory for Visitor Studies (1988) *ILVS Bibliography and abstracts*, second edition, Exhibit Communication Research, Milwaukee: University of Wisconsin, Department of Psychology.

Kavett, H. (1984) 'Architectural awareness: an important aspect of historical study', *Social Studies*, 75(1).

Knopf, R. C. (1981) 'Cognitive map formation as a tool for facilitating information transfer in interpretive programming', *Journal of Leisure Research* 13(3): 232–42.

Koedel, R C. (1980) 'Teaching local history in the community college', Paper presented at the annual conference of the Eastern Community College Social Science Association, Baltimore.

Korn, R. (1989) 'Introduction to evaluation: theory and methodology', in N. Berry and S. Meyer, *Museum Education: History, Theory and Practice*, Reston, VA: The National Art Education Association.

Loomis, J. (1987) Bibliography, in J. Loomis *Museum Visitor Evaluation: New Tool for Management*, Nashville, Ten.: American Association for State and Local History.

McCutcheon, K. (1979) 'The historic site and the class visit: a cooperative approach', *Ontario Museum Association Quarterly*, summer.

Mackintosh, B. (1985) *The National Parks: Shaping the System*, Washington, DC: National Park Service (Department of Interior).

Mason, J. L. (1980) 'Annotated bibliography of field trip research', *School Science and Mathematics* 80(2): 155–66.

Mullins, G. W. (1979) *Participation and Nonparticipation in Interpretation: a Study of People, Places and Activities*, doctoral thesis, Texas A & M University.

Munley, M. E. (1989) 'Intention and accomplishments of museum evaluation research', in J. Blatti (ed.) *Past Meets Present. Essays about Historic Interpretation and Public Audiences*, Washington DC: Smithsonian Institution Press.

National Trust for Historic Preservation (ed.) (1983) *With Heritage so Rich*, Washington, DC: Preservation Press.

National Trust for Historic Preservation, Literacy of the University of Maryland, College Park (1988) *Index to Historic Preservation Periodicals*, Boston: C. K. Hall.

Parcs Canada (ed.) (1982) *Historique. Guide des parcs historiques nationaux du Canada*, Ottawa.

Patrick, J. J. (1989) 'Heritage education in the school curriculum', Paper presented for the National Trust for Historic Presentation and the Waterfront Foundation, Washington, DC.

'Pleins feux sur les musées', (1992) *Forces* 98, summer.

Pronovost, G. (1989) *Les Comportements des Québécois en matière d'activités culturelles de loisir*, Québec: Les publications du Québec, Gouvernement du Québec.

Samson, D. and Schiele, B. (1989) *L'évaluation muséale, publics et expositions, Bibliographie raisonnée*, Paris: Expo-Médias.

Schlereth, T. J. (1978) 'Historic houses as learning laboratories. Seven teaching strategies', *History News* 33(4).

Screven, C. G. (1984) 'Educational evaluation and research in museums and public exhibits: a bibliography', *Curator* 27(2): 147–65.

Shettel, H. (1989) 'Evaluation in museums: a short history of a short history', in D. Uzzell (ed.) *Heritage Interpretation. Vol. 2: The Visitor Experience*, London and New York: Belhaven Press.

Swan, M., Stark, W., Hemmerman, D. and Lewis, C. (1983) *Research in Outdoor Education: Summaries of Doctoral Studies, vol. 3*, Reston, VA: The Council on Outdoor Education.

UNESCO (ed.) (1984) *Un patrimoine pour tous: les principaux sites naturels, culturels et historiques dans le monde*, Paris.

Wolf, R. L. and Tymitz, B. L. (1979) *The Pause that Refreshes: A Study of the Discovery Corners in the National Museum of History and Technology, Smithsonian Institution*, Washington, DC: Smithsonian Institution.

Wolf, R. L., Andis, M. F., Tisdal, C. E. and Tymitz, B. L. (1979) *New Perspectives on Evaluating Museum Environments: An Annotated Bibliography*, Washington, DC: Smithsonian Institution.

Wortman, P. M. and Marans, R. W. (1987) 'Reviving preevaluative research. An illustration from the arts', *Evaluation Review* 11(2): 197–215.

22

Andragogy (adult education) in the museum: a critical analysis and new formulation[1]

Colette Dufresne-Tassé

Andragogy[2] is another name for adult education first advocated by certain European authors and then adopted and popularized in North America (Knowles 1981a). This term is now in common use throughout the world.

There exists little documentation on adult education in the museum. In a survey of the literature conducted in 1986, I found scarcely more than a mere three dozen documents (Dufresne-Tassé 1986) and their number does not seem to have increased significantly since then. This scarcity does not matter very much since eight of these documents present the essentials of andragogy in the museum and were written for the American Association of Museums by four eminent practitioners of andragogy: L. Allen (1981a, 1981b), R. Hiemstra (1981a, 1981b), M. Knowles (1981a, 1981b) and A. Knox (1981a, 1981b). Since I have noted no disagreement between these four authors and since they represent very well what others have written about adult education in the museum (see for example: Bunning 1974 and Carr 1985), I shall base my own text on the synthesis of their writings.

I shall first present the major points of this synthesis and indicate their difficulties; I shall then consider two series of data which I shall adopt as what I consider to be the basis of a more satisfactory museum-centred andragogy.

The recommendations given by adult educators to museum staffs are abundant but often divergent, and thus of little interest here. I shall therefore focus only on andragogy's underlying principles. These principles, of which there are four, should, according to these adult educators, orient museum activities.

1 The principal function of the museum is to foster learning.
2 The goal of the knowledge and skills that are acquired there is to satisfy needs or to solve problems specific to a particular phase of adult life.
3 The accomplishment of this learning requires the museum institution to equip itself with an extremely wide range of activities, capable of treating all adult problems, including domestic or health problems. Hiemstra (1981b: 128) gives this idea concrete form by proposing that the museum should become a Community Resource Centre.
4 The activities offered by the museum must not be primarily inspired by its collections, but rather by the needs of the population it serves.

Criticism

Each of the above principles poses an important problem. First of all, while learning is the predominant concern of museums such as science centres like the Exploratorium in San Francisco, it is hard to imagine it becoming the major preoccupation of all types of museums. Indeed, as shown by the latest texts published by the National Art Education Association (see for example Berry and Mayer 1989) or the most recent *Cahiers* of the Centre Georges Pompidou (especially that of 1989, published under the direction of Yves Michaud), it is normal that a fine arts or contemporary art museum would attribute greater importance to communication with the work and its appropriation, or to aesthetic pleasure, rather than to formal learning.

Next, it is obvious that adults do not go to museums to find solutions to their problems. The abundant national and institutional statistics accumulated over the last twenty years emphasize on the contrary that they go for amusement, to spend a pleasant time in company with family or friends or even to be seen. Thus, the notion of problems as conceived by the adult educators does not fit the museum situation. Moreover, the importance they give it is responsible, in my view, for their homeostatic and puritanical conception of learning that ignores the gratuity, playfulness and wonder so important for the visitor (Dufresne-Tassé, Lapointe and Lefebvre, forthcoming).

Although advocated by certain museologists (see for example Gurian 1991), the transformation of the museum into a community resource centre poses as many problems as the adult educators' other recommendations. Indeed, this change would cause the museum to neglect activities for which it possesses important and even unique resources in western society and to venture into areas where other institutions have already demonstrated their pertinence and effectiveness, thus running the risk of not doing what it can do and of doing badly what it does.

Lastly, although endorsed by certain museologists such as Alt and Shaw (1984), the fact of limiting the museum's action to satisfying the needs of the population proves embarrassing. First, the idea of service to the community is probably suited to regional museums but, in my opinion, loses its pertinence in the case of other types of museums, especially museums of international standing such as the Louvre, the Pergamon, the Metropolitan or the British Museum. Second, for a museum to neglect the potential for action represented by a collection and the expertise of a staff in order to place itself solely at the public's service prevents it from fully playing its role. In actual fact, society expects the museum, while serving the population, to be a force that dynamizes individuals and the community, which it can only do by using its own resources to the full.

While the application of the principles of andragogy has given rise to spectacular successes in the academic context and in popular education – for example, in literacy training and health education – it must unfortunately be concluded that the application of these principles to the museum environment leads to aberrations. Is this because, in academic or popular education, adults study to satisfy a need or to solve a problem, while in the museum setting they act for pleasure? I cannot say. However, this conclusion leads me to seek the basis of adult education in the museum elsewhere than in these principles.

Examination of data

I shall now examine two types of information: first, what is known in the United States as visitor studies (Bitgood *et al.* 1988), and second, a series of investigations carried out at the Université de Montréal concerning the psychological functioning of the adult in a museum gallery.

Studies of visitor behaviour and socio-cultural characteristics

There are now abundant data concerning the adult visitor. After analysis, I have classified it into six categories (Dufresne-Tassé 1991c). This classification has shown that the data focus either on visitors' behaviour or on their socio-cultural or psychological characteristics, but have almost nothing to say about their psychological functioning or their experience in contact with the objects they observe. This will be apparent from an examination of the various categories, grouped together here to facilitate description.

1 Studies on the way in which the public perceives the museum and its services: see in particular the research of Griggs and Hays-Jackson (1983), Merriman (1989), National Museums of Canada (1979) or Rieu (1988). These studies are multi-functional. The aspect which interests us here is their contribution to the forecasting of the behaviour of each category of the public associated with an institution.
2 Clientele studies such as those of Abbey and Cameron (1960, 1961), Brière *et al.* (1990–1), Ganzeboom and Haanstra (1989), Griggs and Alt (1982), Mason (1974) or O'Hare (1975), or more theoretical studies like that of Merrimam (1989). Usually conducted by a museum or by a state, these are analyses which identify who comes to the museum and who does not, as well as the reasons why a person decides to visit a museum. This type of survey reveals the visitor's expectations and, by extrapolation, possible reactions.
3 Specifically sociological studies (see, as a Canadian example, the study Duhaime *et al.* 1989) of which Bourdieu and Darbel (1969) is the classic example. These describe the socio-cultural factors that influence attendance at any kind of museum and the behaviour of the visitor inside it.
4 Studies on visitor behaviour in a museum form three categories. The first contains research on the attracting and retaining power of exhibits inspired by Melton's observation methods (1933, 1936, 1972). These surveys reveal the objects in front of which the visitor stops and for how long (see in particular Abrahamson *et al.* 1983; Kearns 1940). In the light of these data, the researcher can trace the visitor's path within an exhibition gallery. The second includes surveys on precise but limited actions by the visitor, such as use of the signage (Griggs and Alt 1982). Lastly, the third includes observations that attempt to characterize the visitor's general behaviour, sometimes comparing it with the behaviour of certain animals, ants, fish, etc.

(see Véron and Levasseur 1983). These surveys lead to a classification of visitors and the prediction of behaviours corresponding to each type.

5   Evaluation studies, especially summative evaluation. These studies concern either the exhibition as a whole or some aspects of it, and, of course, depend on the questions that a museum asks itself. Although these studies are interested in visitor reactions, they are of little relevance here for the visitor reactions are studied in terms of a particular context and not in a general visitor functioning comprehension perspective.

6   Learning studies. These studies appear in two forms: experimental research and descriptive research. The experimental surveys consider learning once completed, in other words as a product that depends on various factors: characteristics of the exhibits (for example, Screven 1975; Sneider *et al.* 1979); the visitor's personal characteristics (for example, Falk *et al.* 1985; Greenglass 1986) or behaviour (for example, Barnard *et al.* 1980; Kimche 1978). Most of the time, the descriptive studies (for example, Falk *et al.* 1986; Miles and Alt 1979) also focus on the acquisitions made by the visitor. Had they treated learning as a process or an approach, these studies might have contained information on the visitor's functioning. But this is not the case: they view learning as the culmination of an activity about which they are silent. Why is this the case? Because, as Screven (cited by Kimche 1978: 272) claims in a purely behaviourist spirit: 'Learning cannot be directly observed. It must be inferred usually from observed changes in what a visitor can do before and after exposure to an exhibition.'

Obviously, the studies of the six categories described may reveal visitors' social, cultural and psychological characteristics and state of mind, or perhaps their movements, gestures, and reactions or the product of their activity; in short, their behaviour, a series of factors likely to explain it and certain products stemming from it.

These studies could have given rise to a whole series of inferences concerning psychological functioning and the elaboration of a model of this functioning. To the best of my knowledge, nothing like this has been done. On the other hand, by means of theoretical studies, an attempt has been made to describe the phenomenon of learning (Hooper-Greenhill 1988) and, from a pedagogical point of view, to determine an approach that facilitates this task.

Indeed, the only information available until quite recently on the subject came from individual insight arrived at under unknown conditions. The very functioning of the visitor thus remains to all practical purposes an unmapped territory. This conclusion, explicit here, is implicit in several recent syntheses of the accumulated knowledge about the visitor (see in particular that of D. Worts, forthcoming).

Study of the visitor's psychological functioning

A preliminary study completed in 1985 made me think that it is possible to penetrate into the universe of how visitors function. It is possible to learn how they enter into contact with an object, giving it meaning and internalizing this meaning; it is possible to know how their emotions, imagination and reasoning skills contribute to this process.

Since there was scarcely any accurate information on the subject, I thought it was worth while setting up a whole research programme to study it. This is now under way. I shall present the underlying concept of visitor functioning, the approach that characterizes it and its inherent investigation potential.

A dynamic concept

Functioning, as I understand it, is not a global entity to be drawn from a set of data; it is not the residue of a series of manipulations, a figure or a quality attributed to an individual. Recorded as the visit proceeds, it is what an individual does to give form to an experience (Dufresne-Tassé, forthcoming).

Two approaches to the visitor's functioning

I designed the investigation in such a way as to align the visitor's functioning as seen by the researcher and as seen by him or herself. The aim of the design is to compare these two viewpoints, not to correct that of the researcher, but to identify the difference between the two and to explore the universe of meanings that it constitutes.

Apart from the visitors' own perception of their functioning, I collect, by means of a pre-visit questionnaire or a post-visit interview, the explanation that they give of this functioning as well as of the psychological benefits they believe they have derived from their tour around the exhibition gallery.

I obtain the researcher's perception by analysing what the visitor says in front of the objects being looked at. Since the instructions given to the visitor upon arrival at the museum are very important, I quote them in full.

> The aim of the study is not to verify anything, not even what you can remember. It is to know your experience. Because, at present, we know almost nothing about it. Everything you can tell me is valuable. I would like you to lend me your eyes, your sensitivity, your intelligence, your imagination. I have been working here too long – I can no longer see things with a fresh look. I would like you to tell me as you go along what you see, what you think, what you feel, what you imagine; in short, everything that happens to you.

A researcher accompanies the visitor at a comfortable distance and tapes his or her remarks. When the visit is over, the researcher invites the visitor to talk about his or her functioning to describe it and attempt to explain it.

All the material collected is verbal. It then has to be transcribed to be examined. The material that is taken from the pre-visit instrument or from the interview is studied by the simple process of content analysis. However, the remarks made during the visit itself must be processed by means of a special instrument that took considerable time to elaborate.

Four angles of analysis

The instrument developed permits four aspects of the visitor's functioning to be monitored simultaneously:

1   The mental *operations* performed by the visitor to process the experience. They are thirteen in number: manifesting; noting; identifying; situating; evoking; comparing-distinguishing; grasping; explaining-clarifying-justifying; transforming-modifying-suggesting; solving; anticipating; verifying; judging.
      These thirteen operations suffice to process any kind of attempt on a visitor's part to give form to the experience;

2   The particular *orientation* if the visitor's psychic activity at the moment the operation is performed. This orientation may be: cognitive (possibility of distinguishing its imaginary orientation) or affective;

3   The *direction of attention* during the operation. The most pertinent breakdown of the fields of attention differentiates: the object observed; the creator of this object; other objects; the museum context in which the object is exhibited (distinguishing the labels and panels); other contexts, other situations; the visitor; other people;

4   The particular *form* the operation may take or, if preferred, any additional information to that obtained from the three previous analytical approaches. Contrary to what happens in these three sectors, the list of characteristics established remains open. At the present time, it includes six elements: question; hypothesis; action; learning; hesitation; exclamation.

Some characteristics

The analytical design that I have just described is based on a dynamic view of the visitor's psychological functioning. Moreover, it obeys a general conception of this functioning. Indeed, each of its first three aspects views the visitor's entire activity from a certain angle. In short, it is not simply a tool utilized in a particular study. It is a real instrument that can be used by any researcher or professional. Each of the concepts it contains has received a definition and the extent of this definition has been fixed by a set of rules. This instrument has been tried out in three types of museums (fine arts, history and natural history) and reworked until a stability within and an agreement between analysts of over 85 per cent have been obtained. A series of codes has been developed, so that the data it provides can be computerized, with the support of an appropriate programme.

Some data and their meaning

By means of this instrument applied to what the visitor says in the exhibition gallery and the analysis of the discourse on these sayings during a post-visit interview, my research team explored the visitor's questions, hypotheses and learning, wider phenomena such as his or her contextualization or appropriation of the objects observed, the role played by metacognition in these processes and the benefits that derive from a visit to the museum. In addition, these data were examined to detect possible differences introduced by age, sex, length of schooling and the museum attendance habits of the persons who participated in this research.

I shall not dwell on the results of these studies for they either have been published or will be soon (see the asterisked entries in the References). I shall merely point out that while some studies confirm the traditional ideas concerning adults' functioning in the museum, most contradict them. Here are some examples:

1 As we guessed, for an adult, the most obvious benefit of a visit to the museum is not learning, but a cognitive and intense affective functioning because this determines a series of pleasures not afforded by learning. The benefit may be:

   • Aesthetic pleasure, resulting from the observation of beautiful or important objects;
   • pleasure of recognizing and identifying oneself with what is beautiful, valuable, rare;
   • pleasure of using one's intellectual skills to imagine, remember, acquire knowledge, extend it, reflect, modify one's ideas;
   • pleasure of easily overcoming a major difficulty;
   • pleasure of coming into contact with something new, internalizing it or having new ideas.

   A close look at these pleasures reveals that they form opposite pairs. Pleasure of contemplation and action. Pleasure of manipulating the outside world and pleasure of turning in on oneself. Pleasure of what is revealed when the attention is fully focused and pleasure of overcoming the difficulty. Pleasure of the sensation, the emotion and the pleasure of intellectual activity. Pleasure of novelty and pleasantness of habits. In my view, these data illustrate quite strikingly the complexity of the visitor's functioning and suggest that a museum approach based solely or even mainly on a single element such as learning is inadequate.

2 The results of a study on visitor questioning challenge the belief long held by educators that a question demonstrates an intense intellectual activity and the more encouragement people are given to ask questions, the better. I have observed that the search for a reply is not an easy task in the museum because visitors are obliged to proceed by discovery. Thus, they must simultaneously and without help find an effective method and a pertinent way to find a reply. Moreover, they must ensure that their conclusions are exact. If they therefore pursue their questioning, it is an exacting process and anxiety awaits them; if they give up, the result is frustration.

   In reality, the manipulation of visitors' questioning is a delicate matter and a wise museum educator curbs the temptation to force its emergence or intensity, in so far as he or she has not provided in his exhibits satisfactory replies or simple ways of replying in the exhibits.

3 In the same vein, I have observed that, faced with objects displayed as in a jeweller's store – each piece separate and briefly identified – visitors are not passive, as is often stated. They devote more psychological activity to building

on what they observe and verifying what they elaborate than in simply noting what they are looking at. Moreover, this tendency applies equally to the visitor with little education as to the visitor with a university background.

In short, these observations suggest that, usually, adult visitors are active as soon as they become interested in an object. They elaborate the latter's meaning and experience pleasure in doing so provided that their functioning is easy and intense.

Perspectives

The interest of the above results is probably not negligible. But, in my view, the approach that enabled them to be obtained is even more important. Indeed, it provides the researcher with means of recording visitors' real procedure, the way they go about entering into contact with the object, to give it a meaning and to internalize it. It gives access to the main points of this approach, its development and its variations according to the visitor's socio-cultural characteristics, and according to the types of objects, exhibition presentation and museum institution.

In my view, far from duplicating or competing with the knowledge provided by the different categories of visitor studies described above, the data collected concerning the visitor's psychological functioning complete this knowledge and at the same time enhance its meaning. Indeed, visitors' expectations, state of mind and, more indirectly, socio-cultural characteristics all become factors that explain their functioning while their gestures, reactions to the objects presented or their learning are all consequences of this functioning. All these elements thus form a whole that I call the *visitor functioning dynamics*.

New formulation

Before attempting to review museum andragogy, two levels of analyses must be distinguished: the first, the micro level, corresponding to the detailed description of a type of educational relationship; the second, the macro level, including the goals attributed by society to the educational action and the achievement of these goals through a group of institutions.

Tension and optimal functioning of the visitor

I shall use what we have seen concerning the visitor's psychological functioning to reformulate the micro level of museum andragogy, but I shall first have to structure the subject by formulating the following principle. The actualization of the educational function in the gallery must take into simultaneous account the obligations inherent in this function (see Parker-Parélius and Parélius 1978), the specific nature of the museum institution and the conditions that the latter creates for the visitor. The statement of this principle leads me to formulate a four-part proposition.

1 The museum facilitates by various means the visitors' spontaneous functioning, their attempts to enter into contact with the exhibit, to acquire knowledge concerning the exhibit, to situate this knowledge within their perception of the world, to internalize the lot; to use their imagination and affect suitably in this process and to derive from it all the benefit and pleasure they are capable of.

2 The museum offers the visitor the knowledge and criticisms accumulated by its specialists or by university experts on the objects it exhibits.

3 The museum, over time, enables the visitor to enhance his or her skills of acceding to specialized knowledge, to be moved, to appreciate objects, and to derive more profit and delight from them.

4 The museum modulates its three previous interventions so as to adapt them to the characteristics of the publics that visit it.

More precisely, at the micro level, the articulation of the museum's educational function depends on the interaction of the educator or, if preferred, of the exhibit in the broad sense of the term, with the visitor's functioning. This is the way in which this interaction is articulated. We have seen that, usually, visitors are active as soon as they become interested in an object; they elaborate its significance and experience pleasure in doing so provided their functioning is intense. Since we can know this functioning we can determine what aspect of it requires support and what aspect comprises an unexploited potential. It is thus possible to offer visitors what they need for their activity to encompass all the profits they desire, and to introduce, wherever they can absorb them, elements that they have not anticipated and that correspond with the museum's knowledge and expertise. This introduction creates a tension in the visitors and this tension peaks when their skills are used to the full. Until there is evidence to the contrary, I consider that this full use is achieved when the abilities of observation, elaboration of significance are themselves achieved, and when those of being moved, deriving pleasure are fully exploited and entertain an optimal interrelationship. The exhibit–visitor interaction can then be formalized as follows. An *optimal exhibit* entertains in the visitor an *optimal tension* which, in turn, underlies an *optimal functioning*.

The same type of interaction that prevails during a visit may be reproduced in the museum's long-term relations with the visitor in order, this time, to facilitate the development of cognitive and affective skills, as well as a competence to derive pleasure from the relation to the object.

In this view of educational activity in the gallery, two actors, the educator and the visitor, interact through different roles and in different ways to achieve a common goal: the optimal functioning of one of the two. This optimal functioning is therefore always a creation and, in this production, the actors are always interdependent.[3]

The autonomy of thought and critical sense of the citizen

The data that have enabled me to construct the various modalities of educational intervention, in other words the micro level of education, are of little use in determining its macro level, and more particularly its ultimate goals. However, these goals are of the greatest importance for the adult educator. While the teacher or the professor operates within organizations for which the state determines the goals, the adult educator usually acts either within structures such as hospitals, whose primary mission is not education, or perhaps outside any state structure, for instance in disadvantaged citizens' groups. Adult educators must therefore almost always clarify the immediate and long-term goals of their intervention for these goals are not set by a political authority.

Here, as above, data must be found on which museum andragogy can be based. As my work on these data has only just begun, I shall merely, after a summary contextual description, formulate a proposition whose intuitive character is obvious.

Two characteristics of the museum institution seem to me to have a great influence on the orientation of its educational function: the highly polysemic significance of the objects that society entrusts to it and its intervention in the citizens' leisure space.

Taking into account these two characteristics and the mission of other institutions such as the school, I propose that, as well as supporting general adult development, the major role of the museum should be to elicit, maintain or enhance the adult's autonomy of thought, critical sense and creative spirit, as it fulfils its task of presenting objects and the knowledge that accompanies them. Thus, andragogy in the museum, based on the visitor's optimal functioning, would aim to make the visitor increasingly capable of addressing not only the museum objects, but also the situations of daily life in a personal and productive way.

I believe that the legitimacy of this concept of andragogy, which focuses simultaneously on its micro and macro aspects, stems in great part from its coherence with the structure of western society today.

Notes

1 This research was funded by the government of Canada (Social Sciences and Humanities Research Council of Canada), by the government of the Province of Quebec (Fonds pour la formation de chercheurs et l'aide à la recherche) and by the Université de Montréal.
2 Originally written in French, this text has been translated by N. Côté.
3 That schema could be regarded as an attempt to detail an aspect of constructivist museum education as described by Hein (1991) and see Chapter 17 in this volume.

References

Abbey, D. S. and Cameron, D. F. (1960) *The Museum Visitor 2: Survey Results. Reports from the Information Services*, Toronto, ON: Royal Ontario Museum.
—— (1961) *The Museum Visitor 3: Supplementary Studies. Reports from the Information Services*, Toronto, ON: Royal Ontario Museum.
Abrahamson, D., Gennaro, E. and Heller, P. (1983) 'Animal exhibits: a naturalistic study', *Museum Education Roundtable, Roundtable Reports* 8: 6–9.

Allen, L. A. (1981a) 'Basic concepts and assumptions about adult learners', in Z. W. Collins (ed.) *Museum, Adults and the Humanities*, Washington, DC: American Association of Museums.

—— (1981b) 'Community involvement', in Z. W. Collins (ed.) *Museum, Adults and the Humanities*, Washington, DC: American Association of Museums.

Alt, M. B. and Shaw, K. M. (1984) 'Characteristics of ideal museum exhibits', *British Journal of Psychology* 75: 25–36.

Barnard, W. A., Loomis, R. J. and Cross, H. A. (1980) 'Assessment of visual recall and recognition learning in a museum environment', *Bulletin of the Psychonomic Society* 16: 311–13.

Berry, N. and Mayer, S. (1989) *Museum Education History, Theory and Practice*, Reston, VA: The National Art Education Association.

Bitgood, S., Roper, J. T. and Benefield, A. (1988) *Visitor Studies – 1988. Theory, Research and Practice*, Jackson, AL: The Center for Social Design.

Bourdieu, P. and Darbel, A. (1969) *L'amour de l'art: les musées européens et leur public*. Paris: Les Éditions de Minuit.

Bunning, R. L. (1974) 'A perspective on the museum's role in the community adult education', *Curator* 17: 56–63

Brière, M. A., Légaré, B. and Lirette, Y. (1990–1) *Rapport d'enquête: Le public du CCA*, Montreal, QU: Centre Canadien d'Architecture.

Carr, D. (1985) 'Self-directed learning in cultural institutions', in S. Brookfield (ed.) *Self-Directed Learning: From Theory to Practice; New Directions for Continuing Education no. 25*, San Francisco, CA: Jossey-Bass.

Chamberland, E. (1988) 'La création de contexte dans une situation d'apprentissage spontané', in J. L. McLellan and W. H. Taylor (eds) *Les Actes du VIIe congrès annuel, Canadian Association for the Study of Adult Education*, Calgary, AL: Faculty of Continuing Education, The University of Calgary.

—— (1989) 'Contexte et contextualisation, deux notions fondamentales pour la compréhension de l'apprentissage adulte', in R. Bédard (ed.) *Les Actes du 8e congrès annuel de l'Association canadienne pour l'étude de l'éducation des adultes*, Cornwall, ON: University of Ottawa.

—— (1990a) 'La démarche de contextualisation chez le visiteur de musée', doctoral thesis presented to the Faculté des études supérieures de l'Université de Montreal.

—— (1990b) 'Les caractéristiques de la contextualisation chez les adultes dans une situation d'apprentissage libre', in B. Stolze-Clough (ed.) *Les Actes du 9e congrès annuel de l'Association canadienne pour l'étude de l'éducation des adultes*, Victoria, CB: University of Victoria.

—— (1991a) 'La démarche de contextualisation du visiteur adulte', *Musées* 13: 72–8.

—— (1991b) 'Les thèmes de la contextualisation chez les visiteurs de musée', *Canadian Journal of Education* 16: 292–313.

Chamberland, E. and Dufresne-Tassé, C. (forthcoming) 'Les caractéristiques de la contextualisation chez des adultes visitant un musée', *The Canadian Journal for the Study of Adult Education*.

Danis, C. and Dufresne-Tassé, C. (1988) 'Problèmes et éléments de solution liés à la définition de l'objet d'étude en recherche qualitative; trois illustrations', in J. L. McLellan and W. H. Taylor (eds) *Les Actes du VIIe congrès annuel, Canadian Association for the Study of Adult Education*, Calgary, AL: Faculty of Continuing Education, The University of Calgary.

Dufresne-Tassé, C. (1986) 'Examen critique des recommandations de quatre éducateurs d'adultes éminents aux gens de musée', *Musées: Actes du colloque Musée et éducation: modèles didactiques d'utilisation des musees*, Montreal, QU: Société des musées québécois.

—— (1988a) 'Connaissance du fonctionnement intellectuel et affectif de l'adulte comme base de l'intervention éducative dans les musées', in J. L. McLellan and W. H. Taylor (eds) *Les actes du VIIe congrès annuel, Canadian Association for the Study of Adult Education*, Calgary, AL: Faculty of Continuing Education, The University of Calgary.

—— (1988b) 'L'approfondissement de certains processus comme celui que vit le visiteur de musée échappe-t-il à la recherche qualitative?', *Revue canadienne de l'éducation* 15: 100–11.

—— (1989) 'Variation du fonctionnement intellectuel et affectif du visiteur de musée adulte en fonction de son âge', *XXIIe Journées d'Etudes de l'Association de Psychologie Scientifique de Langue Française*, Geneva.

—— (1990a) 'Extension des connaissances et développement muséal', in G. Racette and L. Forest (eds) *Pluralité des enseignements en sciences humaines à l'université*, Montreal: Editions Noir sur Blanc.

—— (1990b) 'L'éducation au Louvre en 1789', in P. Ansart (ed.) *1789 Enseigné et imaginé; regards croisés France-Québec*, Montreal: Editions Noir sur Blanc.

—— (1991a) 'Approches didactiques et âge des visiteurs', *Musées* 13: 58–61.

—— (1991b) 'Introduction: L'éducation muséale, son rôle, sa spécificité, sa place parmi les autres fonctions du musée', *Canadian Journal of Education* 16: 251–8.

—— (1991c) 'Effets pervers d'une utilisation intensive des résultats de la recherche sur le visiteur dans une optique behavioriste', communication given to the Congrès de l'Association Canadienne Française pour l'Avancement des Sciences, Montreal, QU.

—— (forthcoming) 'Six études sur le fonctionnement psychologique de l'adulte au musée', Université de Montréal et Société des musées québécois.

Dufresne-Tassé, C. and Dao, K. C. (1991) 'Quelques données sur le questionnement du visiteur de musée', in M. H. R. Baskett (ed.) *Proceedings of the 10th Annual Conference of the Canadian Association for the Study of Adult Education*, Kingston, ON: Queen's University.

Dufresne-Tassé, C. and Lefèbvre, A. (1986) 'Exploration de trois questions sur la recherche qualitative à partir d'un projet de pédagogie muséale', *Revue canadienne de l'éducation* 11: 407–24.

Dufresne-Tassé, C. and Martineau, G. (1990) 'L'apprentissage et le fonctionnement rationnel de l'adulte au musée', in B. Stolze-Clough (ed.) *Les Actes du 9e congrès annuel de l'Association canadienne pour l'étude de l'éducation des adultes*, Victoria, CB: University of Victoria.

Dufresne-Tassé, C., Dao, K. C. and Lapointe, T. (forthcoming) 'Epistemological aspects of the adult questions in the museum', *McGill Journal of Education*.

Dufresne-Tassé, C., Lapointe, T. and Lefèbvre, H. (forthcoming) 'Etude exploratoire des bénéfices d'une visite au musée', *The Canadian Journal for the Study of Adult Education*.

Dufresne-Tassé, C., Lapointe, T., Morelli, C. and Chamberland, E. (1991) 'L'apprentissage de l'adulte au musée et l'instrument pour l'étudier', *Canadian Journal of Education* 16: 281–92.

Duhaime, C., Annamma, J. and Christopher, A. (1989) *A Picture Speaks a Thousand Words: The Conception of Contemporary Art*, Montreal, QU: Groupe de recherche en gestion des arts de l'Ecole des Hautes Etudes Commerciales.

Falk, J. H., Koran, J. J. and Dierking, L. D. (1986) 'The things of science: assessing the learning potential of science museums', *Science Education* 70: 503–8.

Falk, J. H., Koran, J. J., Dierking, L. D. and Dreblow, L. (1985) 'Predicting visitor behavior', *Curator* 28: 249–57.

Ganzeboom, H. and Haanstra, F. (1989) *Museum and Public, The Public and the Approach to the Public in Dutch Museums*, Rijswijk: Ministry of Welfare, Health and Culture.

Greenglass, D. I. (1986) 'Learning from objects in a museum', *Curator* 29: 53–66.

Griggs, S. A. and Alt, M. B. (1982) 'Visitors to the British Museum (Natural History) in 1980 and 1981', *Museums Journal* 82: 149–55.

Griggs, S. A. and Hays-Jackson, K. (1983) 'Visitors' perceptions of cultural institutions', *Museums Journal* 83: 145–51.

Gurian, H. (1991) 'The opportunity for social service', Keynote paper presented to the Annual Conference of ICOM CECA, Jerusalem.

Hein, G. E. (1991) *The Significance of Constructivism for Museum Education*, Keynote paper presented to the Annual Conference of ICOM CECA, Jerusalem.

Hiemstra, R. (1981a) 'The state of the art', in Z. W. Collins (ed.) *Museums, Adults and the Humanities*, Washington, DC: American Association of Museums.

256

—— (1981b) 'The implications of lifelong learning', in Z. W. Collins (ed.) *Museums, Adults and the Humanities*, Washington, DC: American Association of Museums.

Hooper-Greenhill, E. (1988) 'The "art of memory" and learning in the museum', *The International Journal of Museum Management and Curatorship* 7: 129–39.

Hrimech, M. (1991) 'Problèmes d'identification de l'apprentissage de l'adulte au musée: éléments de solution', in M. H. R. Baskett (ed.) *Proceedings of the 10th Annual Conference of the Canadian Association for the Study of Adult Education*, Kingston, ON: Queen's University.

Isaacs, C. (1977) 'The visitor and the museum visit', in L. Draper (ed.) *The Visitor and the Museum*, Washington, DC: The American Association of Museums.

Kearns, W. E. (1940) 'Studies of visitor behavior at the Peabody Museum of Natural History, Yale University', *Museum News* 17: 5–8.

Kimche, L. (1978) 'Science centers: a potential for learning', *Science* 199: 270–3.

Knowles, M. S. (1981a) 'Andragogy', in Z. W. Collins (ed.) *Museums, Adults and the Humanities*, Washington, DC: American Association of Museums.

—— (1981b) 'The future of lifelong learning', in Z. W. Collins (ed.) *Museums, Adults and the Humanities*, Washington, DC: American Association of Museums.

Knox, A. B. (1981a) 'Motivation to learn and proficiency', in Z. W. Collins (ed.) *Museum, Adults and the Humanities*, Washington, DC: American Association of Museums.

—— (1981b) 'Basic components of adult programming', in Z. W. Collins (ed.) *Museum, Adults and the Humanities*, Washington, DC: American Association of Museums.

Lapointe, T. (1991a) 'L'adulte au musée et ses souvenirs', in M. H. R. Baskett (ed.) *Proceedings of the 10th Annual Conference of the Canadian Association for the Study of Adult Education*, Kingston, ON: Queen's University.

—— (1991b) 'Le fonctionnement mnémonique de l'adulte au musée', in G. R. Roy (ed.) *Contenu et impact de la recherche universitaire actuelle en sciences de l'éducation*, Sherbrooke, QU: Université de Sherbrooke.

Larocque, D. (1988) 'Le questionnement spontané de l'adulte dans une situation d'apprentissage informel, la visite de musée', in J. L. McLellan and W. H. Taylor (eds) *Les Actes du VIIe congrès annuel, Canadian Association for the Study of Adult Education*, Calgary, AL: Faculty of Continuing Education, The University of Calgary.

Lefèbvre, A. (1986a) 'Des difficultés de la pédagogie muséale', in G. Racette (ed.) *Musées: Actes du colloque: Musée et éducation: modèles didactiques d'utilisation des musées*, Montreal: Société des musées québécois.

—— (1986b) 'Prolégomènes à une didactique muséale en histoire', in G. Racette (ed.) *Musées: Actes du colloque: Musées et éducation: modèles didactiques d'utilisation des musées*, Montreal: Société des musées québécois.

—— (1988) 'Les enseignants et les musées', in J. L. McLellan and W. H. Taylor (eds) *Les Actes du VIIe congrès annuel, Canadian Association for the Study of Adult Education*, Calgary, AL: Faculty of Continuing Education, The University of Calgary, 1988.

—— (1989) 'L'enseignant et la chose muséale', in R. Bédard (ed.) *Les Actes du 8e congrès annuel de l'Association canadienne pour l'étude de l'éducation des adultes*, Cornwall, ON: University of Ottawa.

—— (1990) 'Des enseignants approchent la chose muséale', in G. Racette and L. Forest (eds) *Pluralité des enseignements en sciences humaines à l'université*, Montreal, QU: Editions Noir sur Blanc.

—— (1991a) 'Des groupes d'enseignants font l'expérience de quelques types de visites de lieux muséaux', *Musées* 13: 124–30.

—— (1991b) 'Une visite guidée par les pairs dans le Vieux Montréal', *Canadian Journal of Education* 16: 313–31 .

Lefèbvre, A. and Dufresne-Tassé, C. (1991a) 'Fondements d'une pédagogie muséale auprès des adultes', in R. Roy (ed.) *Contenu et impact de la recherche universitaire actuelle en science de l'éducation*, Sherbrooke, QU: Universite de Sherbrooke.

—— (1991b) 'L'apprentissage de l'adulte en milieu muséal', in M. H. R. Baskett (ed.) *Proceedings of the 10th Annual Conference of the Canadian Association for the Study of Adult Education*, Kingston, ON: Queen's University.

Lefèbvre, B. and Lefèbvre, H. (1991) 'Le visiteur, le guide et l'éducation', *Canadian Journal of Education* 16: 331–8.

Lefèbvre, H. (1988) 'Réflexion au sujet des bénéfices du visiteur de musée', in J. L. McLellan and W. H. Taylor (eds) *Les Actes du VIIe congrès annuel, Canadian Association for the Study of Adult Education*, Calgary, AL: Faculty of Continuing Education, The University of Calgary.

—— (1989) 'De la relation besoin-bénéfice dans le contexte de l'éducation muséale', in R. Bédard (ed.) *Les Actes du 8e congrès annuel de l'Association canadienne pour l'étude de l'éducation des adultes*, Cornwall, ON: University of Ottawa.

—— (1990) 'La personne âgée: un défi pour l'université', in G. Racette and L. Forest (eds) *Pluralité des enseignements en sciences humaines à l'université*, Montreal, QU: Editions Noir sur Blanc.

Lefèbvre, H. and Lefèbvre, B. (1991) 'Le visiteur de musée: motivations et bénéfices', *Musées* 13: 88–91.

Marcousé, R. (1969) 'Animation et information', in H. L. Zetterberg (ed.) *Rôle des musées dans l'éducation des adultes*, London: Hugh Evelyn for the Conseil International des Musées.

Martin, W. W., Falk, J. H. and Balling, J. D. (1981) 'Environmental effects on learning: the outdoor field-trip', *Science Education* 65: 301–9.

Mason, T. (1974) 'The visitors to Manchester Museum: a questionnaire survey', *Museums Journal* 73: 153–7.

Melton, A. W. (1933) 'Some characteristics of museum visitors', *Psychological Bulletin* 30: 720–1.

—— (1936) 'Distribution of attention in galleries in a museum of science and industry', *Museum News* 14: 6–8.

—— (1972) 'Visitor behavior in museums: some early research in environmental design', *Human Factors* 14: 393–403.

Merrimam, N. (1989) 'Museum visiting as a cultural phenomenon', in P. Vergo (ed.) *The New Museology*, London: Reaktion Books.

Michaud, Y. (1989) 'L'art contemporain et le musée', *Les Cahiers du Musée d'art moderne*, Paris: Centre Georges Pompidou.

Miles, R. S. and Alt, M. B. (1979) 'British Museum (Natural History): A new approach to the visiting public', *Museums Journal* 78: 158–62.

Morelli, C. (1988) 'Composantes de l'interaction entre le visiteur et l'objet de musée', in J. L. McLellan and W. H. Taylor (eds) *Les Actes du VIIe congrès annuel, Canadian Association for the Study of Adult Education*, Calgary, AL: Faculty of Continuing Education, The University of Calgary.

—— (1989) 'La résistance à l'objet muséal comme contexte du refus d'apprendre de l'adulte', in R. Bédard (ed.) *Les Actes du 8e congrès annuel de l'Association canadienne pour l'étude de l'éducation des adultes*, Cornwall, ON: University of Ottawa.

—— (1990) 'Caractéristiques des modes de pensée du visiteur adulte au musée', in B. Stolze-Clough (ed.) *Les Actes du 9e congrès de l'Association canadienne pour l'étude de l'éducation des adultes*, Victoria, CB: Université de Victoria.

—— (1991) 'Composantes de l'expérience psychologique du visiteur adulte dans un musée de sciences naturelles,' mémoire de maîtrise présentée à la Faculté des études supérieures de l'Université de Montréal.

National Museums of Canada (1979) *A Report on Visitor Surveys Conducted at the Canadian Railway Museum*, St-Constant, QU: The Canadian Railway Museum.

O'Hare, M. (1975) 'Why do people go to museums? The effect of prices and hours on museum utilization', *Museum* 27: 134–46.

Parker-Parélius, A. and Parélius, R. J. (1978) *The Sociology of Education*, Englewood Cliffs, NJ: Prentice Hall.

Rieu A.-M. (1988) *Les Visiteurs et leurs musées. Le cas des musées de Mulhouse.* Paris: La Documentation Française.

Sauvé, M. (1990) 'L'appropriation des objets de musée, une activité importante chez le visiteur adulte', in B. Stolze-Clough (ed.) *Les Actes du 9e congrès annuel de l'Association canadienne pour l'étude de l'éducation des adultes*, Victoria, CB: Université de Victoria.

——— (1991) 'La visite de musée comme expérience intégratrice chez l'adulte', in G. R. Roy (ed.) *Contenu et impact de la recherche universitaire actuelle en sciences de l'éducation*, Sherbrooke, QU: Université de Sherbrooke.

Screven, C. G. (1975) 'The effectiveness of guidance devices on visitor learning', *Curator* 18: 219–43.

Sneider, C. I., Eason, L. P. and Friedman, A. J. (1979) 'Summative evaluation of a participatory science exhibit', *Science Education* 63: 25–36.

Touchette, C. (1989) 'A comparative study of andragogy (adult education) as a field of academic study in the world', in A. N. Charters and B. Cassara (eds) *Papers on Comparative Adult Education*, Syracuse, NY: The Coalition of Adult Education Organization, Syracuse University and University of the District of Columbia.

Véron, E. and Levasseur, M. (1983) *Ethnographie de l'exposition: l'espace, le corps, le sens*, Paris: B.P.I./Centre Pompidou.

Wetlzl-Fairchild, A. (1991a) 'Describing aesthetic experience: creating a model', *Canadian Journal of Education* 16: 267–81.

——— (1991b) 'Phenomenological description: an instrument to elicit aesthetic response', *Musées* 13: 141–7.

Worts, D. (forthcoming) 'In search of meaning: "reflexive practice" and museums', *AAM Source Book*.

23

Communicating and learning in Gallery 33: evidence from a visitor study

Jane Peirson Jones

Introduction

In his essay on 'Culture and representation' in the volume *Exhibiting Cultures: The Poetics and Politics of Museum Display* Ivan Karp proposes that:

> Cross-cultural exhibitions present such stark contrasts between what we know and what we need to know that the challenge of reorganising our knowledge becomes an aspect of the exhibition experience. This challenge may be experienced in its strongest form in cross-cultural exhibitions, but it should be raised by any exhibition. Almost by definition, audiences do not bring to exhibitions the full range of cultural resources necessary for comprehending them; otherwise there would be no point in exhibiting. Audiences are left with two choices: either they define their experience of the exhibition to fit with their existing categories of knowledge, or they reorganise their categories to fit better with their experience. Ideally, it is the shock of non-recognition that enables the audience to choose the latter alternative. The challenge to exhibition makers is to provide within exhibitions the contexts and resources that enable audiences to choose to reorganise their knowledge.
>
> (Karp 1991: 22)

Gallery 33 is a cross-cultural anthropology exhibition in Birmingham Museum and Art Gallery which aims to communicate to visitors in the manner which Karp has described. The primary theme in the exhibition is cultural relativism and a secondary sub-theme is cultural representation in museums. These themes are conveyed in a variety of 'contexts and resources' both within the exhibition and in its locale.

This chapter examines the nature of the communication and learning which is taking place in Gallery 33, based on a synthesis of the results from a recent summative evaluation study.[1] The discussion will focus on the effectiveness of five different styles of exhibit or communication vehicles in use in Gallery 33. Ham defines a 'communication vehicle' as the communication mode in which themes are developed and which are strategically selected to enhance audience interest (Ham 1983: 22). The five key vehicles to be discussed are: (i) cross-cultural groups of artefacts in cased displays, (ii) the diorama of the Collectors' House; (iii) the exhibition script; (iv) low-tech hands-on features; and (v) the interactive videos. The communication goals will be outlined for each vehicle and their relative effectiveness will be discussed.

An Evaluation Plan developed by Dr McManus and the author identified a nine-point battery of information-gathering projects designed to investigate the major features of the gallery. The aim was: (i) to provide a demographic description of the audience;[2] (ii) to describe the volume and pattern of visitor use; (iii) to assess the intellectual and emotional responses of visitors; and (iv) to provide an in-depth study of the effectiveness of the interactive video exhibits (Peirson Jones 1993: 5).

Dr McManus carried out four principal studies. They were: (a) an Exit Questionnaire on a sample of 100 randomly selected visitors; (b) a Tracking Study in which a hidden observer plotted the tracks and timed the stops of a random sample of fifty visitors; (c) a Memories Study based on 136 discrete memories submitted by twenty-eight individuals – visitors who left their address on the Comments Stand and who were contacted on average seven months after their visit and invited to write in about their memories; (d) a Questionnaire Survey of Visitors' Reactions to the *Collectors* interactive video. A random sample of 109 visitors who stayed for more than five seconds after the introductory sequence had finished were timed, observed and interviewed at the *Collectors* interactive video.

Three further studies were undertaken: (e) Comments Analysis by the author on almost 1,000 written comments left on the Comments Stand during the first six months after opening; (f) an interactive video 'hit count' analysis by Philip Watson; and (g) a report on the pilot study of school use of the interactive video *Collectors in the South Pacific* by Susan Werner. The results of the seven studies have been published in full (Peirson Jones 1993).

Summative evaluation of this depth and complexity is rare. As the projects complement and cross-reference one another it is possible to build up a dynamic picture of the way in which Gallery 33 functions. Each study stands alone but taken together a picture emerges of who visits Gallery 33, what they do and think while they are there and what they remember afterwards.

Aims of Gallery 33

The purpose of the Gallery 33 project, commenced in 1986, was to redisplay Birmingham Museum's ethnographical collection of art and material culture from North America, Africa and Oceania in an innovative way. The exhibition is about human societies, their customs, social relationships and traditions. The aim as outlined in the Initial Design Brief was to create a didactic exhibition which is interesting, challenging and fun to visit and which encourages visitors to question the assumptions they make about their own and other people's culture. In doing this the exhibition aims to encourage visitors to gain a greater understanding of and respect for both their own and other people's culture (Peirson Jones 1987: 2).

Items from the ethnographical collection had not been on public display for over twenty years. The challenge was therefore to redisplay the collection for an audience who had little experience locally of this type of museum material and to do it in a way which was pertinent to Birmingham as it is today rather than as it was when the museum collections were first assembled and interpreted for public benefit. I have discussed the issues this challenge raised and the eventual outcomes elsewhere (Peirson Jones 1992: 221).

The exhibition title serves as its mission statement. It is 'Gallery 33: a meeting ground of cultures; an exhibition about beliefs, values, customs and art from around the world'. The principal theme or concept explored is cultural relativism. In each exhibit the cross-cultural presentation offers an opportunity to compare and contrast the way different cultures have resolved similar problems of social organization. The communication goal is to assist visitors in thinking about their own cultural identity in relation to others via the constructions of 'self' and 'other' which are offered for consideration.

The aim was to engage visitors' attention sufficiently so that they pause for thought once, perhaps only momentarily, to consider their own cultural identity. Sufficient arousal might be provoked by only one thing in the exhibition: an arte-fact, an image or a piece of technology. This condition of limited intellectual engagement need happen only once in the course of a visit to the exhibition for the communication goal to be reached (Peirson Jones 1989: 13).

The secondary theme in Gallery 33 is the issue of cultural representation in museums. By this I mean the political acts of collecting, preserving and interpret-ing cultural heritage. Cultural representation is an issue in all exhibitions and it would have been impossible to have redisplayed the Birmingham collection for a present-day audience without making explicit reference to this issue. At the heart of this lies the key question of who has authority to control the process of cultural representation at each stage of the museum process. The word 'authority' in this context carries three shades of meaning: the possession and exercise of power, the notion of expertise and the notion of authorship.

The issue of authority was addressed by taking approaches in project manage-ment and exhibit development which were a departure from current practice in Britain at the time. The project was managed in such a way that the curatorial authoring voice was broadened by the involvement of specialist advisers. The production of the exhibition was personalized by the acknowledgement of all the team members. Authorship was explicitly discussed in the orientation video and its limitations defined. The *Collectors* interactive video was developed as a multivocal exhibit to address subjects such as the return of cultural property where a single monovocal storyline would have been inadequate.

The broadening of the authoring voice has necessitated not only the involvement of other specialists, but also the inclusion of visitors' views and interventions. To facilitate this, visitors are invited to enter into a dialogue about cultural representation at several places in the exhibition, notably in the orientation video and in the Collectors' House diorama. The communication goal is not to present a received opinion or to affect attitudes but merely to draw attention to the essentially open-ended issues which underlie museum processes. To do this it was necessary to reveal something about these processes and to call for comment. In several places visitors are also invited to take part in the processes under review by carrying out some cultural representation for themselves, for example in the *Collectors* interactive video and the Totem Pole.

Cross-cultural groups of artefacts

There are just over 300 artefacts from about 100 distinct cultural groups in the exhibition. Two-thirds of the artefacts are in six cased exhibits accompanied by colour photographs and label text. These cross-cultural presentations explore topics such as 'Body decoration', 'Signs and symbols' and 'Masks'. A seventh case, called 'Societies', explores the nature of human society. Artefacts and images from all over the world are mixed with those from Britain in sometimes unexpected arrangements.

Normally, traditional displays separate and classify museum 'things'. Gallery 33 attempts to challenge these classifications and mix the familiar with the unfamiliar, the past with the present, and the 'minority' with the 'majority'. In doing so it forges unfamiliar classifications and juxtapositions which are intended to attract visitors' attention and challenge their sense of order, their sense of other and thus their sense of themselves (Peirson Jones 1992: 228). As Baxandall says 'The juxtaposition of objects from different cultural systems signals to the viewer not only the variety of such systems but the cultural rela-tivity of his own concepts and values' (Baxandall 1991: 40). Karp expresses a similar idea in a slightly different way: 'When cultural "others" are implicated, exhibitions tell us who we are and, perhaps most significant, who we are not' (Karp 1991: 15).

Given that the idea of challenging visitors about their cultural identity is a key goal, does it in fact happen? Table 23.1 summarizes evidence from the visitor studies to support the view that visitors do think about their cultural identity in Gallery 33.

In the Exit Questionnaire 64 per cent of visitors said that the exhibition had made them ponder about the factors in their cultural heritage which are simi-lar to or different from factors in other cultures. McManus states that:

> This is a satisfactory finding as it indicates that the exhibition presents material in such a way that visitors to it are enabled in their efforts to think about culture in an abstract way. This is a considerable achievement when the casual, social, low-key character of a museum visit is considered.
>
> (McManus 1993a: 28)

Table 23.1 Evidence for visitor consideration of cultural identity in Gallery 33

• Reflected on cultural similarities and differences	64%
• More conscious of own cultural heritage	40%

Source: McManus 1993a: Tables 2.14, 2.13

In a further question, 40 per cent of visitors reported having been made more aware of their own cultural heritage by the exhibition. McManus suggests that this is a harder question than the previous one. In her view,

> the result gives a strong indication of the power of the exhibition to raise questions about a person's cultural identity. The exhibition helps visitors to undertake the hard work of considering various cultural elements in order to consider their own cultural heritage in an analytical manner. Not all casual visitors to museums can be expected to engage with the exhibition at this level.
>
> (McManus 1993a: 11)

She goes on to suggest that the 60 per cent who said they were not made more conscious of their cultural heritage by the experience of visiting the exhibition is likely to include some people who believed that they already had a strong awareness of their cultural heritage and others who will be prompted by the exhibition to consider these issues in later real-life situations (McManus 1993a: 27).

In the Comments study a cluster of visitors' comments within the Requests category asks for further treatment of named cultures. Over a period of time it has become clear that these requests do not single out one, or even a few, specific cultures, but rather an increasingly diverse list of cultures have been mentioned. At first, perhaps predictably, subjects requested included 'Africa', 'Ireland' and 'Jewish culture'. However, over time, the range has extended to include, for example, 'Sweden', 'Eastern Europe' and 'Australia'.

At one level these comments can be read as an expression of dissatisfaction with the superficial treatment which a cross-cultural presentation inevitably achieves. However, there is also a more subtle interpretation for this group of comments. It is possible that they represent an expression of cultural self-assertion which arises out of the experience of being challenged by the cultural relativism of the exhibition. Visitors, having been confronted by so much cultural 'other' in Gallery 33, respond by requesting enhancement or special treatment for the group (cultural, ethnic or national) to which they feel greatest affinity (Peirson Jones 1993: 149).

The collectors diorama

The remaining third of artefacts on display are in the Collectors' House diorama. This is a centrally placed exhibit which features three collectors. They are Ida Wench, who was a missionary in the Solomon Islands, Percy Amaury Talbot, an officer in the colonial service in Nigeria, and Arthur Wilkins, a private collector in Australia. Models of the three are located on the verandah of a house inside which can be seen a display of artefacts from their collections. The aim was to develop an emotive display which examined museum processes from collecting to display. It was also designed to support the nearby interactive video and to rehearse the issues raised there.

The Tracking Study showed that the diorama is a middle-ranking exhibit in terms of frequency of stops made (ranking sixteenth) but that its text panel with the all-important explanatory text ranks twenty-seventh (McManus 1993b: 3, Table 3.3). The diorama ranks twenty-fourth in terms of viewing time and as it is a large exhibit which has the potential to be browsed over this finding indicates that the exhibit is less attractive and engrossing than it might be (McManus 1993b: 46, Table 3.15). This is also reflected in the finding from the Exit Questionnaire that only 25 per cent of visitors had any knowledge of how exhibits got to Birmingham (McManus 1993a: 24, Table 2.10). However, the Collectors' House is well-remembered, ranking third of the 'objects and things' remembered. Further examination reveals that it is remembered as both a missionary hut and a house (McManus 1993c: 64).

The Collectors' House is in fact a composite diorama. The exterior is based on photographs of the missionary's house in the Solomon Islands and the interior is based on photographs of Arthur Wilkins's display in his house in Sydney. McManus's findings indicate that the complex nature of this diorama is not being communicated fully. Changes to the content and location of the labelling may improve communication at this stage. However, it is likely that the diorama would have been more effective if it had simply focused on one collector rather than three.

The exhibition script and written information

From the outset the aim was that the exhibition script should be brief and simple. It was also the intention to provide information at multiple levels of complexity for visitors to select at their preferred level. The view was taken that visitors would read the script if it was relevant and meaningful. The graphics system was designed by Morag Bremner[3] to be attractive and lively in order to offer further motivation to the visitor.

The higher orders of text in the labelling hierarchy (for example the mission statement plus photomontage and case panel headers) aim to set a strong conceptual context in which visitors can examine the artefacts and images before them. These texts are concerned with ideas. The lower order texts such as artefact labels and information sheets are concerned with data on specific artefacts or subjects at increasing levels of detail.

The key feature of the case panels is the use of header captions phrased as questions to which the middle-order texts offer answers. The questions are there as an invitation to visitors to interact intellectually with the exhibits. Visitors can make their own sense of the groups of photographs and artefacts assembled before them. This was done in full recognition of visitors as active interpreters who make their own interpretations based on their own cultural baggage of beliefs, values and prior museum experiences (Falk and Dierking 1992).

The use of questions in this way has the immediate effect of changing the relationship between the exhibition 'author' and visitors. Questions serve to empower visitors and sensitize them to the relative 'authority' of the text. Questions also cue visitor behaviour. Visitors are expected to be active participants rather than passive receivers in Gallery 33.

Visitors' reactions to the interrogative approach were examined in the Exit Survey. Visitors were invited to choose statements which reflected their feelings about being asked questions. Table 23.2 indicates their response. More than half the visitors reported that they enjoyed having questions raised in the exhibition. The same number of visitors but not necessarily the same people indicated that they had enjoyed having questions raised and had actively engaged intellectually with the questions posed. Others would have liked the approach to have been taken even further. Detailed examination of the responses of those who said they preferred stories revealed that only 12 per cent of the entire sample actively disliked the questioning approach. The conclusion is that the majority of visitors approve of the communication approach and engaged happily with the exhibition on its own terms (McManus 1993a: 11).

Table 23.2 Opinions about questions in exhibitions

Rank	Opinion	%
1	I enjoy having questions raised	52.0
2	The questions made me think	52.0
3	I prefer stories in exhibitions	26.0
4	I didn't notice any questions	14.0
5	The questions didn't go far enough	11.0
6	It's confusing to be asked questions	5.0

Note: More than one response was possible.
Source: McManus 1993a: Table 2.9

The three information stands were developed to carry an additional, more detailed level of information than that contained in the exhibition script and object labels. One stand provides back-up for the 'Welcome' photomontage. It contains data about the population and the languages spoken in Birmingham. Another stand contains additional information about the collectors featured in the diorama. A third stand contains articles about cultural representation in museums.[4] The 'pages' on the A3-sized lecterns were designed to be bright and informal as an incentive to visitors to investigate them. However, the Tracking Study shows that the information stands attract very little attention. McManus suggests that their status in the gallery should be reviewed. Either they should be removed if they are not really necessary as carriers of information or they should be radically redesigned so that the visitors notice and use them (McManus 1993a: 12).

This is a disappointing finding because they were developed in an attempt to furnish visitors with additional detailed information on important issues. I still feel sure the principle is worth while and I would like to see them maintained but with better signage and with the contents presented in more attractive and accessible forms yet to be identified. The *Collectors* interactive video survey shows that some visitors wanted more information. This is in fact available but they failed to find it. Here is an opportunity to make significant changes in the hopes of improving communication and of meeting a stated need.

Interactive videos

The interactive video exhibit *Collectors in the South Pacific* was developed to support the Collectors' House diorama as a means of communicating issues about cultural representation.[5] The aim was to offer a well-documented rich archival source which was capable of supporting alternative opinions on open-ended issues and which could be accessed by visitors at a level of detail appropriate to them (Peirson Jones 1990). The *Collectors* interactive video was the subject of a detailed questionnaire survey to find out how visitors use it, what they think about it and what they learn from it.

The observation and timing of visitors sampled indicates that those who use the interactive video commit time to it. McManus found that there is considerable evidence from duration of visit that visitors find the programme content to be engrossing.

> It is extremely successful in holding the attention of the visitors who use it – it could be said to show good 'holding power'. Published research has shown that it is the usual case that immediately after the initial engagement of a sample of visitors with an exhibit there is a marked dropping away of engagement. This is not the case with 'Collectors' as the attention spans shown by visitors to it build up over 2½ minutes before gradually trailing away. The longest visit recorded was 18 minutes and 9 seconds in duration.
>
> (McManus 1993d: 79)

The Tracking Study showed that *Collectors* attracted the most repeat visits (McManus 1993b: 45, Table 3.4). The interactive video appears to intrigue visitors sufficiently for them to want to return to it. However, it may also be the case that visitors move away from this exhibit when someone else wants to use it and return later to reuse it in solitude.

The Tracking Study revealed that the interactive video is frequently used as a completely separate exhibit from the diorama of the Collectors' House. Only one-third of the visitors looked at the object display in connection with their visit. Clearly the link between the two exhibits is not explicit enough (McManus 1993d: 82, Table 5.4). Additional signage on both exhibits may correct this now. However, perhaps each exhibit should have been designed to stand alone, or very explicit reference to the diorama should have been made in the interactive video.

Table 23.3 summaries visitors' reaction to the *Collectors* interactive video. Most people sampled enjoyed using the programme and found the instructions easy to follow. When invited to comment on what they made of it 65 per cent of visitors responded positively.

Table 23.3 Summary of visitors' reactions to the *Collectors* interactive video

• Easy to use	90%
• Enjoyed using it	91%
• Positive response	76%
• Right amount of information	64%

Source: McManus 1993d: Tables 5.7, 5.6, 5.8, 5.9

While the majority of visitors were satisfied with the level of information provided by the programme, around one-third of visitors thought that they had not been given enough information. McManus suggests that there are three points to consider. First, visitors may find the exhibit so interesting that their engagement in the topic goes beyond the scope of the exhibit. Second, many visitors had not made links to the Collectors' House and could well have had a more satisfying experience had they done so. Third, a small number of visitors may be missing out on sections of the programme because they do not under-stand its instructions or menu layouts (McManus 1993d: 88).

Almost one-third of the sample reported that the *Collectors* programme made them think of matters related to the collection of artefacts which had never occurred to them previously. A significant one-third of the sample reported that the programme had influenced their views on whether objects such as those on display in Gallery 33 should be kept in museums. Similarly one-third of the sample reported that the programme had influenced their views on the repatriation of artefacts of cultural significance to their countries of origin.

Table 23.4 summarizes these findings which, taken together, suggest that two of the conditions for quality learning as defined by Richard T. White are being met. Quality learning takes place when old and existing beliefs are permanently discarded in favour of new propositions which are found to be relevant and intelligible. A permanent commitment to new knowledge requires comparison of it with the older beliefs so that dissatisfaction with the old and fruitfulness of the new can be realized. Shallow learning, by contrast, implies the acquisition of knowledge from another authority without deep commitment or deep consideration (White 1992: 157). Those visitors who admit to having new questions raised in their minds are expressing dissatisfaction with old

Table 23.4 Evidence of quality learning

• Raised new questions	32%
• Influenced view on returns	29%
• Influenced view on museums	25%

Source: McManus 1993d: Tables 5.10, 5.20, 5.21

knowledge. The visitors who said the interactive video had influenced their views are acknowledging that new propositions presented to them are relevant and fruitful.

There is a second interactive video called *Archives* which is an image bank of artefacts featured in the exhibition.[6] The overall visitor response to both the interactive videos is very positive. In the Exit Questionnaire 11 per cent of the sample selected the interactive videos as their favourite exhibits. This ranked as the third most popular choice (McManus 1993a: 15, Table 2.7). The Tracking Study shows that on average visitors spent the longest amount of time at *Collectors*, with *Archives* ranking third of all exhibits. Both exhibits hold visitors attention significantly longer than other exhibits and thus appear to be fulfilling their function (McManus 1993b: 47, Table 3.5). The Comments Analysis shows that of the 'things' referred to, the interactive videos rank second (Peirson Jones 1993: 148, Table 8.2). The Memories Study shows that the interactive videos are the most memorable objects in the exhibition, mentioned in 24 per cent of memories (McManus 1993c: 63, Table 4.4).

Table 23.5 summaries the overall positive response to the interactive videos. They are very attractive exhibits. They have strong holding power and they arc influential in stimulating quality learning. They also appear to be very memorable exhibits. It is clear that the experience the visitor has of the interactive video exhibits will be very influential in the final opinion arrived at in respect of a visit to Gallery 33.

Table 23.5 Overall response to interactive videos

• Favourite exhibit	3rd rank
• Viewing time for *Collectors*	1st rank
• Viewing time for *Archives*	3rd rank
• Memories (things)	1st rank
• Comments (things)	2nd rank

Source: McManus 1993a: Table 2.7; McManus 1993b: Table 3.5; McManus 1993c: Table 4.4; Peirson Jones 1993: Table 8.2

Hands-on exhibits

The intention behind the hands-on exhibit was to try to adapt some of the techniques used in hands-on science centres to the development of cultural history exhibits. The goal was threefold: first, to invite active participation by visitors; second, to enable intellectual engagement with the concept or theme being presented; and third, to provide an enjoyable experience as an aid to learning.

In addition to the interactive videos there are several low-tech hands-on features in Gallery 33. The hands-on features are fully integrated into the exhibition and each one was designed to complement a cased exhibit. Each hands-on exhibit offers an opportunity to explore in an experiential way the concept being addressed in the adjacent artefact display. For example the 'Signs' lightbox is situated next to the 'Signs and symbols' display. It offers an opportunity to use unfamiliar sign systems including the Egyptian alphabet, Pacific coast totems and European heraldic emblems. The 'Trying-on masks' feature offers an experience of the transformation process which masking invokes by the use of hand-held replica masks. It is situated next to cased displays of masks and includes replicas of masks on display. There are other participatory features such as the Totem Pole, to which visitors can attach personal symbols or mementoes, and the Comments Stand. These last two items have a very considerable potential as participatory exhibits which I feel has not been fully exploited as yet. They require considerable maintenance, flexible and inventive manipulation and experimentation. They could form key means of creating change in the exhibition.

Table 23.6 summarizes findings about the replica mask exhibit which suggest it is the most popular exhibit in Gallery 33. In the Exit Questionnaire almost one-third of the sample nominated it as their favourite exhibit. Together with the adjacent display of museum masks the two exhibits collected 40 per cent of the choices of favourite exhibit. The Tracking Study revealed that 'Trying on masks' is the most frequently visited exhibit in the gallery. Half the sample visited it. This display ranks joint second for repeat visits and fifth in terms of viewing time. In the Comment Analysis masks are the most commented upon 'things'. Masks are the second most memorable 'things' in the Gallery with 20 per cent of the sample memories mentioning them.

Table 23.6 Trying on masks

• Favourite exhibit	1st rank
• Frequency	1st rank
• Viewing time	5th rank
• Memories (things)	2nd rank
• Comments	4th rank

Source: McManus 1993a: Table 2.7; McManus 1993b: Table 3.3, 3.5; McManus 1993c: Table 4.4; Peirson Jones 1993: Table 8.2

The hands-on features have proved very popular and they have withstood heavy use. The briefest observation of the 'Trying-on masks' exhibit also shows how effective it is. Some 9 per cent of all memories are about 'doing something' and 'activities' also form the subject-matter for many written comments. The hands-on features form a significant part of the Gallery 33 experience.

Conclusions

There is abundant evidence from memories and comments, and from the replies to specific questions in the surveys, to show that many visitors to Gallery 33 are actively engaging with the concept of cultural identity which is the main theme of the exhibition at many different levels. McManus found that 97 per cent of the sample in the Exit Questionnaire had perceived the underlying theme of the exhibition. Some of the associated comments indicate a genuine and reflective engagement with the theme (McManus 1993c: 68; McManus 1993a: 26–8). Cultural identity is a very personal and emotive issue for everyone because it involves the consideration of gender, sexuality, religion, nationality and economic group as well as race and ethnicity. There is evidence to suggest that, in Gallery 33, as Karp (1991) predicted, it is 'the shock of non-recognition' which provokes an emotive response which is sometimes expressed in terms of cultural self-assertion (Peirson Jones 1993: 149).

Visitors coming to Gallery 33 as part of a schools or event programme take part in a highly mediated experience in which an exploration of cultural identity becomes a key focus. There is some evidence from work with schoolchildren and my own work with adults that members of so-called 'majority' groups have trouble articulating cultural identity because they cannot necessarily single out factors of specific identity from what appears to them as the cultural norm. On the other hand perceptions of difference, and by extension cultural identity, tend to be more pronounced among members of so-called 'minority' groups (Werner 1993: 138).

The secondary theme about cultural representation in museums is less success-fully communicated. The Visitor Study indicates that three of the exhibits specifically designed to convey this theme are among the least well used in the gallery. The diorama of the Collectors' House is less effective than it could be. One information stand contains further information about the Collectors and another containing provocative articles on cultural representation are two of the least frequently visited exhibits. This leads to the conclusion that some visitors cannot find the opportunities available to engage on this theme.

It has to be said, however, that cultural representation is not an issue of popular concern. Rather it is an intellectual construct which is primarily, I suspect, a professional preoccupation. The museum-visiting public have little idea of what goes on in museums. (This is borne out by the fact that only 2 per cent of visitors sampled in the Exit Questionnaire claimed a previously-formed idea of how artefacts in Gallery 33 might have come to Birmingham (McManus 1993a: 25).) Visitors also have a low expectation of their opinions being canvassed on procedural issues. Until recently museums did not reveal what went on behind closed doors and the aura of expertise and objectivity so maintained is difficult to dispel. As visitors become empowered to judge museum activities in an informed way more sophisticated critical responses may be anticipated.

The invitation to engage with the exhibition at several different levels is eagerly and successfully taken up by visitors. The conclusion is that visitors do indeed come to Gallery 33 as active interpreters. Both their physical and intellectual involvement form memorable parts of their experience.

The way in which the Totem Pole is decorated and the comments pages are regularly filled demonstrates that visitors are happy to take part in making representations of themselves. The majority of visitors sampled acknowledged some intellectual engagement with the exhibition via the interrogatory script. Expressions of enjoyment of the activities available form a significant group of written comments and memories. Evidence from several visitor studies show that the 'Trying-on masks' exhibit and the interactive videos provide popular and memorable hands-on experiences.

David Carr, in a paper on adult learning in museums, suggests that 'learning requires a moment when people redefine themselves and their roles . . . they become individuals in the process of transforming their experiences' (Carr 1990: 11). He goes on to say that the best way to assist the process of transformation is to encourage the development and articulation of questions and to create opportunities for the learner to find answers which lead to the construction of personal meaning: in essence the same process as that described by Karp as the challenge to exhibition makers to provide within exhibitions the contexts and resources that enable audiences to choose to reorganize their knowledge.

The various visitor studies carried out in Gallery 33 provide evidence which suggests that some visitors are indeed in a process of transforming their experiences. Affirmations, contained in questionnaire responses, that particular exhibits have raised new questions, increased awareness, caused reflection and influenced views suggest that visitors are in the process of constructing personal meanings.

Carr adds that 'the moment of definition for the adult learner in the museum is the moment of asking an epistemic question – that is a question that has to do with the production of knowledge and the regulation of interactions between the learner and the environment' (Carr 1990: 11). In this respect two categories of memories about Gallery 33 become significant. McManus categorized 15 per cent of all the memories as those which recalled accounts of feelings experienced at the time of the visit which are concerned with intellectual and affective responses to Gallery 33. A further category, containing 10 per cent of all memories, consists of executive summary memories generated by feeling, thus reflecting critical assessments of the exhibition communication (McManus 1993c: 68).

It is possible to conclude that 'mature' or 'quality' learning is taking place in Gallery 33. The learning process, defined by Carr and White respectively, is similar in essence to the process described by Karp quoted at the opening of this chapter. The evidence presented here suggest that Gallery 33 does provide 'contexts and resources that enable audiences to choose to reorganise their knowledge' (Karp 1991: 22).

In management terms the opening of an exhibition is often seen as the end of a project. In fact it is the beginning of the most important stage in an exhibition's cycle when the real work of interaction between audience, exhibition and exhibition makers takes place. The evaluation programme has provided a window through which to observe this interaction. I hope that this chapter demonstrates that a two-way learning process is taking place. Visitors and exhibition makers are both learning from the interactions which are taking place in the 'context and resources' provided in Gallery 33.

Notes

1 The study was carried out by Dr Paulette McManus and funded by grants from the Gulbenkian Foundation and the West Midlands Area Museums Council. The results are published in full as J. Peirson Jones (ed.) (1993) *Gallery 33: A Visitor Study*, Birmingham: Birmingham Museum and Art Gallery. Copies are available from the Department of Archaeology and Ethnography, Birmingham Museum and Art Gallery, Chamberlain Square, Birmingham B3 3DH; Tel. 021-235 4201, Fax 021-236 6227. The author wishes to acknowledge Dr Paulette McManus, Dr Bill Brookes and Dr Eilean Hooper-Greenhill for their comments on this paper.

2 Demographic characteristics of random samples of visitors were available for the Exit Questionnaire and the 'Collectors' Questionnaire (see Table 23.7). The results are consistent in all important respects. They are also broadly consistent with findings in an unpublished survey of visitors to Birmingham Museum and Art Gallery carried out in 1990. Full details are given in the published study (Peirson Jones 1993).

Table 23.7 Visitor profile summarized

• White/European	86%
• Black and ethnic minority	14%
• West Midlands residents	31%
• Birmingham residents	48%
• Male to female	13:10
• Adult groups	41%
• Family groups	22%

Source: McManus 1993a: Tables 2.2, 2.3, 2.4, 2.5

On this evidence Gallery 33 does not attract an audience specific to itself. In most respects the Gallery 33 audience reflects the type of visitors coming through the main entrance. This is to be expected as 82 per cent of the audience reaches Gallery 33 by chance. A further 8 per cent of the sample heard about Gallery 33 from family and friends and 8 per cent from promotional material. McManus comments that

> as the exhibition is located in an area of the museum remote from the main entrance it would benefit from improved publicity near the reception areas. Improved orientation signage throughout the museum would also help in directing visitors to galleries of interest to them.

> (McManus 1993a: 12)

She further suggests that 'These findings also imply that the exhibition has received a low level of sustained and effective publicity outside the environment of the museum' (McManus 1993a: 18).

It is unrealistic to expect one exhibition alone in a large multidisciplinary museum building to effect major change in the visitor profile, especially since the museum's overall promotional strategy has remained unchanged. Considerable effort went into developing a strong image so that the gallery could be individually promoted and targeted at potential audiences but that opportunity has not been exploited. It is also a misunderstanding to see Gallery 33 as specifically 'for' black and ethnic minority visitors. Gallery 33 was designed to speak to existing audiences as well as potential audiences.

In order to build a regular audience to Gallery 33 there needs to be consistent programming linked to effective promotion over a considerable period of time. Regrettably Gallery 33 has not received that level of support to date. However, gains have been achieved by personal networking and the potential has been demonstrated in some of the Saturday events. First-time visitors have been attracted to Gallery 33 as performers or as friends and relatives of performers: for example the Chinese New Year Festival in 1991 brought in members of the Vietnamese community for the first time.

3 Gallery 33 was designed by Bremner and Orr Design Consultants Ltd, 53 Long Street, Tetbury, Gloucestershire GL8 8AA.

4 The articles on display are: Hakiwai, A. (1990) 'Once again the light of day? Museums and Maori culture in New Zealand', *Museum* 165, vol. XLII, 1: 35–3; Lavine, S. D. (1989) 'Museums and multiculturalism: who is in control?', *Museum News* March/April: 39–42; Phillips, R. B. (1988) 'Indian art: Where do you put it?', *MUSE* Autumn: 64–6.

5 The *Collectors* interactive video was based on a concept by the author and Professor Nick Stanley, University of Central England in Birmingham. It was produced and directed by New Media, 12 Oval Road, Camden Town, London NW1 7DH.

6 Both the *Archives* and *Collectors* interactive video programmes have been subjected to a hit count analysis which has examined the menu choices made by visitors. Full details can be found in Watson, P. (1993) 'Video hit count analysis' in J. Peirson Jones (ed.) *Gallery 33: A Visitor Study*, Birmingham: Birmingham Museum and Art Gallery.

References

Baxandall, M. (1991) 'Exhibiting intentions: some preconditions of the visual display of culturally purposeful objects', in Ivan Karp and Steven D. Levine (eds) *Exhibiting Cultures: The Poetics and Politics of Museum Display*, Washington, DC: Smithsonian Institution Press.

Carr, D. (1990) 'The adult learner in the museum', in Janet Solinger (ed.) *Museums and Universities: New Paths to Continuing Education*, American Council on Education, New York: Macmillan.

Falk, J. H. and Dierking, L. D. (1992) *The Museum Experience*, Washington, DC: Whalesback Books.

Ham, S. H. (1983) 'Cognitive psychology and interpretation: synthesis and application', *Journal of Interpretation* 8(1): 11–25.

Karp, I. (1991) 'Culture and representation', in Ivan Karp and Steven D. Levine (eds) *Exhibiting Cultures: The Poetics and Politics of Museum Display*, Washington, DC: Smithsonian Institution Press.

McManus, P. (1993a) 'Gallery 33: Exit Questionnaire' in Jane Peirson Jones (ed.) *Gallery 33: A Visitor Study*, Birmingham: Birmingham Museums and Art Gallery.

—— (1993b) 'A tracking study investigation into visitor use of Gallery 33', in Jane Peirson Jones (ed.) *Gallery 33: A Visitor Study*, Birmingham: Birmingham Museum and Art Gallery.

—— (1993c) 'A study of visitors' memories of Gallery 33', in Jane Peirson Jones (ed.) *Gallery 33: A Visitor Study*, Birmingham: Birmingham Museum and Art Gallery.

—— (1993d) 'A survey of visitors' reactions to the interactive video programme "Collectors in the South Pacific"', in Jane Peirson Jones (ed.) *Gallery 33: A Visitor Study*, Birmingham: Birmingham Museum and Art Gallery.

Peirson Jones, J. (1987) 'Initial design brief', unpublished paper, Birmingham Museum and Art Gallery.

—— (1989) 'Cultural identity, colonial legacy and the community: the Gallery 33 project', unpublished paper presented at the Salzburg Seminar.

—— (1990) 'Interactive video and the Gallery 33 project', *Museum Development*, June, 10–16.

—— (1992) 'The colonial legacy and the community: The Gallery 33 project' in Ivan Karp, Christine Mullen Kreamer and Steven D. Lavine (eds) *Museums and Communities: The Politics of Public Culture*, Washington, DC: Smithsonian Institution Press.

—— (1993) *Gallery 33: A Visitor Study*, Birmingham: Birmingham Museum and Art Gallery.

Werner, S. (1993) 'Report on pilot study of schools' use of the interactive video "Collectors in the South Pacific"', in Jane Peirson Jones (ed.) *Gallery 33: A Visitor Study*, Birmingham: Birmingham Museum and Art Gallery.

White, R. T. (1992) 'Implications of recent research on learning for curriculum and assessment', *Journal of Curriculum Studies* 24(2): 153–64.

24

Family groups in museums: an Indian experience

B. Venugopal

Introduction

A museum is a public place where people of all ages and types meet and interact. The museum public is heterogeneous and varies with the museum concerned. Of all museum visitors, families constitute an important category (Alt 1980; Conway 1974; Falk *et al.* 1985; Lakota 1975; Venugopal 1986). Families cut across age and special interest groups and are represented in every socio-economic group. Museum visiting is for many people a social activity (Ambrose and Paine 1993). Families provide many facilities to their members. These are the basic nutritional, shelter and protection functions, the sexual regulation and access functions, the reproduction and nurturing functions, appropriate education functions regarding economic production and consumption, the property transmission function and the social status and placement functions (Kelly 1983).

Despite the fact that families constitute a major portion of museum visitors, specific museum-based research on family visitor behaviour in museums is generally scarce (Falk and Balling 1982; Lakota 1975; Screven 1974). In Indian museums, where visitor study is in its infancy, it is all the more difficult.

With the emergence of nationalism in the Third World, museums have become powerful tools for a radical socio-economic transformation (Ghose 1992). In order to realize this social role, the first task for the museums of the Third World is to get more baseline data about its visitors.

The museum scene in India is at a crossroads. The recent changes in the media scenario due to liberalization of the economy and an unprecedented exposure to the international market-place are going to affect Indian museums. In this critical stage of competition with other leisure/entertainment centres for the attention of visitors, it is important for Indian museums to increase their visitor services. The first step in this direction is the collection of details about its visitors.

Other than simple statistics on attendance numbers, not many data on visitors are collected in Indian museums. The National Museum of Natural History (NMNH), New Delhi, is perhaps the only museum in India to incorporate evaluation of visitors as a regular feature of its programmes. Various researchers have been collecting data about its visitors. In a cross-cultural investigation of the novel field-trip phenomenon, Falk's (1983) study at the NMNH reinforced the importance of understanding the effects of the setting upon learning. Singh (1987) was interested in the NMNH as an environment for informal learning. The studies of Naqvi and Venugopal (1987) and Naqvi *et al.* (1991) centred on the effectiveness of various types of exhibits.

I have been interested (Venugopal 1986, 1991) in the efficacy of various educational activities of the museum. Recently I have been concentrating on family visitors to the NMNH. In this chapter an attempt has been made to study some aspects of the demography of the family group visitors of the National Museum of Natural History (NMNH), New Delhi, India.

Methodology

For the purpose of this study a family group was defined as a group that consisted of one or both parents or any other adult accompanied by one or more children, not necessarily their own.

Data were collected on the size and structure of the family groups. The relationship between family size and the frequency of visits was also looked into. Members of the families were divided into five class structures based on age: children, teenagers, youth, adult and the old. Babies were excluded.

The families were observed as they entered the mezzanine of the First Gallery of the NMNH. The museum's visit opening hours were divided into two equal sessions, 10.00–13.30 and 13.30–17.00 . Observations were carried out for one session per day for twelve days of the month of May 1986 covering every hour of the day (10.00–17.00 hours) and every day of the week (Tuesday to Sunday; museums are closed on Monday) at least once. In total, data for forty-two hours representing 25 per cent of the total museum opening hours of the month for May 1986 were taken into account. A total of 626 people who visited the museum as members of 146 families were observed.

Results

A summary of the arrival of families at the NMNH by the time of day and day of the week is given in Table 24.1. Sunday accounted for the maximum number of families and Thursday the least. The pattern in relation to the timing of family museum visiting shows a bi-modal distribution, one before noon and the other after noon. The frequency shows a gradual increase from the first hour of the museum opening, reaching a maximum during the next two hours; it decreases considerably during the lunch session, but then rises up and reaches a second peak; it then slowly decreases reaching the lowest during the last hour of the museum opening.

Table 24.1 Time of arrival of family groups in the National Museum of Natural History, New Delhi, in May 1986

Time of arrival	Tuesday	Wednesday	Thursday	Friday	Saturday	Sunday	Total
10–11	6	2	0	7	3	8	26
11–12	4	2	4	13	3	5	31
12–13	5	3	1	9	2	11	31
13–14	3	1	2	2	2	3	13
14–15	4	4	3	1	2	4	18
15–16	3	2	1	1	4	5	16
16–17	2	1	1	1	3	2	10
Total	27	15	12	34	19	38	145

The size of the families ranged from two to eleven (Table 24.2). The most frequent size was three (26 per cent). The smallest-sized family visited the museum twenty-four times, whereas the largest-sized one was observed only once.

Children and adults formed the majority of visitors by age-group (Table 24.3). Teenagers constituted 7 per cent of the sample whereas the youth and the old formed 6 and 4 per cent respectively.

Discussion

When the late Shri Rajiv Gandhi, then Prime Minister of India, introduced the five-day week for government offices in 1986, Saturday became a holiday for most other office-goers as well. The idea was to tone up the administration and to give more leisure to the general public. So museum visits on Saturdays and Sundays were expected to increase. The results of the study showed that Sunday was the most popular day for museum visits. But Saturday occupied only fourth position. Since the occupational backgrounds of the families had not been attended to during this study the causal factors for the low turn-out on Saturdays could not be understood.

It was also found that families visited the museum more often during the forenoon hours, and the least during the lunch hour and the final hour.

About twice as many families visited the museum during the forenoon as during the afternoon session. Thirteen families visited the museum during the lunch hour. When the rate of visitors was taken into consideration, the maximum number of families visited the museum from 11.00 to 12.00 hours and the minimum during the last hour, 16.00–17.00 hours.

Table 24.2 Size of family group visiting the National Museum of Natural History, New Delhi, in May 1986

Size	Tuesday	Wednesday	Thursday	Friday	Saturday	Sunday	Total	%
2	5	2	4	4	4	5	24	17
3	7	4	4	3	3	18	39	26
4	7	2	0	17	4	4	34	24
5	1	0	2	3	3	3	12	8
6	5	2	1	4	2	3	17	12
7	0	2	0	1	0	2	5	3
8	0	0	1	1	0	1	3	2
9	2	1	0	1	2	2	8	6
10	0	1	0	0	1	0	2	1
11	0	1	0	0	0	0	1	1
Total	27	15	12	34	19	38	145	100

Table 24.3 Breakdown by age of the family groups visiting the National Museum of Natural History, New Delhi, in May 1986

Age-group	Tuesday	Wednesday	Thursday	Friday	Saturday	Sunday	Total	%
Children	48	37	19	68	37	54	263	42
Teenager	9	4	1	11	4	15	44	7
Youth	6	3	2	12	7	7	37	6
Adult	45	34	20	51	37	71	258	41
Old	4	2	3	6	3	6	24	4
Total	112	80	45	148	88	153	626	100

The number of visits by size of family showed a general trend. Although the smallest-sized family was not the most frequent, it could otherwise be generally said that the families frequenting the NMNH most were the small-sized ones. This is to say that the number of visits is inversely proportional to family size.

When the different age-groups were compared, it became clear that most of the families were composed of children and adults only. It may be that in India the old find it physically exhausting to go out of their houses to leisure places including museums, or they are influenced more by home leisure opportunities like video and television. The teenagers and the youth are assumed to prefer to go out in peer groups.

Summary

This paper summarizes the findings of an evaluation study conducted in the National Museum of Natural History, New Delhi, India, during May 1986 on 626 visitors in 145 family groups.

Indian families generally prefer to visit the museum during holidays and weekends. They visit the museum more often during the morning than the afternoon. The number of visits by families is in inverse proportion to their size. The majority of family members visiting are children and adults.

References

Alt, M. B. (1980) 'Four years of visitor surveys at the British Museum (Natural History). 1976–1979', *Museums Journal* 80(1): 10–19.

Ambrose, T. and Paine, C. (1993) *Museum Basics*, London: Routledge and ICOM.

Conway, W. G. (1974) *Zoo Education: Recent Interpretations, Proceedings of the first conference of New York State Zoological Parks and Aquariums*, New York: Zoological Parks and Aquariums.

Falk, J. H. (1983) 'A cross-cultural investigation of the novel field-trip phenomenon: National Museum of Natural History, New Delhi', *Curator* 26(4): 315–25.

Falk, J. H. and Balling, J. D. (1982) 'The field-trip milieu: learning and behaviour as a function of contextual events', *Journal of Educational Research* 76(1): 22–8.

Falk, J. H., Koran, J. J., Dierking, L. D. and Dreblow, L. (1985) 'Predicting visitor behaviour', *Curator* 28 (4): 249–57.

Ghose, S. (1992) 'People's participation in science museums', in P. Boylan (ed.) *Museums 2000*, London: Museums Association.

Kelly, J. R. (1983) *Leisure Identities and Interactions*, London: George Allen & Unwin.

Lakota, R. A. (1975) *An Experimental Analysis of Behavioural Performance*, Washington, DC: Office of Museums Programmes, Smithsonian Institution.

Naqvi, A. and Venugopal, B. (1987) 'An evaluation study of the First Floor Gallery of the National Museum of Natural History, New Delhi', *Journal of Indian Museums* 43: 126–37.

Naqvi, A., Venugopal, B., Falk, J. H. and Dierking, L. D. (1991) 'Analysis of the behaviour of family visitors in natural history museums: the New Delhi National Museum of Natural History', *Curator* 34(1): 51–7.

Screven, C. G. (1974) *The Measurement and Facilitation of Learning in the Museum Environment: An Experimental Analysis* (Publication in Museum Behaviour), Washington, DC: Office of Museums Programmes, Smithsonian Institution.

Singh, D. P. (1987) 'An investigation of natural history museums in India as a medium of non-formal education', unpublished Ph.D. thesis, Jamia Millia Islamia.

Venugopal, B. (1986) 'Families visiting the National Museum of Natural History', *Journal of Indian Museums* 42: 39–48.

—— (1991) 'Family groups in museums: with special reference to the National Museum of Natural History, New Delhi', unpublished M.Sc. dissertation, University of Leicester.

Venugopal, B. and Menon, U. (1993) 'Natural history museums and conservation education', in M. Balakrishnan (ed.) *Environmental Problems and Prospects in India*, New Delhi: Oxford and IBH.

25

Here to help: evaluation and effectiveness

Sandra Bicknell

'Here to help' sounds a little trite – though that is far from my intent. I genuinely believe evaluations can help – help, that is, with the effective communication between a museum (or, rather, its staff) and the museum's audience.

One of my more awkward moments as an evaluator was when I was observing visitors to an exhibition, using a scale map to mark how individuals were using the space. I was tracking a woman and her two children when she suddenly looked round and latched on to me and my name badge. There was nothing I could do to avoid her, so I put my clip-board and map behind my back and waited for her question. 'Is there a particular way round this [exhibition]?' she asked. I replied that I was not sure and it was up to her. She seemed to accept this answer and went back to the children. This was all somewhat ironic considering that one of the recommendations to come from this evaluation was that a map of the exhibition together with clearly discernible sections could have been useful to the visitors. As we said:

> The implementation of these ideas will help communicate the messages of an exhibition more effectively to visitors, because it gives them a conceptual framework within which to receive the information. It would also give people the ability to dip into the aspects of the exhibition that most interests them without having to search for them.
>
> (Bicknell *et al.* 1991: 36)

My intent

The UK is experiencing a small boom of interest in museum-based evaluation work. Like many other booms it is associated with unconditional enthusiasm, ignorance, cowboys (and cowgirls) and some hostility. I hope that the examples I am going to share with you will move us towards a common understanding of what sort of findings can come from evaluation work and which methods can be used. In this chapter I first explain evaluation in a museum context and how it fits into a general communication strategy, and then I use the findings from four case-studies to illustrate both process and consequence. Finally I synthesize the general and the specific to confirm the title 'here to help'.

I should come clean about my motivations. I have spent some five years learning, on the job, how to do evaluation work, I push for recognition of the worth of this work and I believe it is essential. The explanations are quite straight forward:

- I believe I am accountable to the Science Museum's actual and potential visitors;
- I believe the visitors' views are no less important than those of professional staff;
- I believe museums are a medium of mass communication and true communication is a dynamic process;
- I believe visitors have a right of access to museum collections both in a physical and in an intellectual sense.

All the work I do in the Science Museum is underwritten by these personal tenets.

What is evaluation?

Every day, in almost all areas of our lives, we evaluate – make judgements of worth. My favourite example is the daily torture of buying a newspaper. Life was simpler a few years ago when only the *Guardian* tempted me. Now life is complicated by the trauma of choosing between the *Guardian* and the *Independent*. I have to read the content summaries of both and weigh up which paper is offering more – which is worth more to me. I make an evaluation.

Within the context of a museum, evaluations are statements of worth from the visitors which are mediated via the evaluator and via the method, or methods, used to gather this information. But evaluation reports do not just deal with whether an exhibition, or whatever, was worth the visitors' time, money or attention: they are also instruments of change.

The holistic: audience research

It would be unwise to write about museum-based evaluation without setting out the broader picture and mentioning audience research. Minda Borun (1992: 269) has made a clear distinction between audience research and evaluation:

- Research asks: what is the nature of the museum experience? What is its impact on the visitor?
- Evaluation asks: is this exhibit or programme doing what its developers intended it to do?

Audience research, or the investigation of actual and potential audiences, can help identify characteristics unique to a particular audience, or segment of the audience, that can have an effect on visiting.

A proportion of the population visit museums but the actual size of that proportion in the UK seems unclear (Merriman 1991: 47–8). One researcher in

North America has suggested that only 20–25 per cent of a population visit museums (Kelly 1992: 27); another researcher's data suggested that just over a half of the community she surveyed go to museums (Hood 1983: 54). Data from the western world suggest that the average is around 50 per cent. However, as Hood points out, only some of the visitors (14 per cent) will understand 'the code'. Inaccessibility through ineffectual presentations means limited appeal, limited audiences and ultimately limited public support. Understanding your actual and potential audience can help with effective targeting, planning and timing, and an efficient use of resources. As Hood has noted:

> Gathering quality information for long-term decision making is worth effort, time and money ... by incorporating the findings ... [into] planning and programming [and providing] ... a heightened awareness by the staff of the diversity of visitors' expectations, leisure values and needs ... the study results prompted staff to think beyond only internal concerns.
>
> (Hood 1983: 57)

The atomistic: evaluations

The nomenclature of museum evaluation can be most confusing. As one practitioner has written: 'I suspect ... there is considerable confusion at the present time as to the best way to do evaluation and how to define different parts of the process' (Loomis 1992: 272). There are descriptions of method, of approach, of intent, of data and of the time-frame of the work.

A *plea for pluralism*

There is a superbly non-conformist view of method and approach in Mary Daly's *Webster's First Intergalactic Wickedary of the English Language*:

> Methodolatry (n): common form of academic idolatry: glorification of the god Method; boxing knowledge into prefabricated fields, thereby hiding threads of connectedness, hindering New Discoveries, preventing the raising of New Questions, erasing ideas that do not fit into Respectable Categories of Questions and Answers.
>
> (Daly 1987)

I have a feeling that there is a lot of this about. There have been a number of attempts to categorize evaluation methodology. This 'boxing' of methods is, in my view, isolationist. It suggests either/or scenarios. One is either a supporter of the naturalistic approach, or one is a supporter of the scientific approach; the study is either goal-oriented or goal-free; I am labelled a behaviourist if I watch what visitors are doing, or a follower of the school of cognitive psychology if I try to find out what visitors have learnt (not, I should add, that I do this sort of testing); I use the tools of either the anthropologist, or the ethnographer, or the sociologist, or the psychologist, or the media critic; you either do quantitative work, or you do qualitative work; you do it either before the event or after; you either observe or you ask.

I, however, do not make such 'either/or' choices. I am an unashamed pluralist who uses multiple methodologies as part of an evaluation scenario which has the clear intention of providing answers to the questions my colleagues want answered. I use multiple methods to give greater rigour, reliability and depth to the work I do. Each element is designed both to test and to complement the findings of other elements. The different methods add layers of information but also provide a means of identifying inconsistencies and weaknesses.

Communication models

I work from a communication model in which a message travels from sender to receiver, via the medium of communication, with a feedback loop (Figure 25.1). There are three messages: first, the message dispatched by the member of staff; second, the message transmitted by the medium; and third, the message interpreted by the individual visitor. In any communication the meaning of the original message can be altered by the medium, and the message that is received is determined to some extent by the visitors and their own unique circumstances (their previous experience, their knowledge, the reaction to their environment, how they are feeling, and so on). The role of an evaluation is, in essence, to see how the message dispatched compares to the one received. The evaluation provides feedback. However, this smacks of only a goal-oriented evaluation – a standard form of evaluation which assesses the success of the aims of the project, and one of these aims should be the accurate transmission of the project's messages.

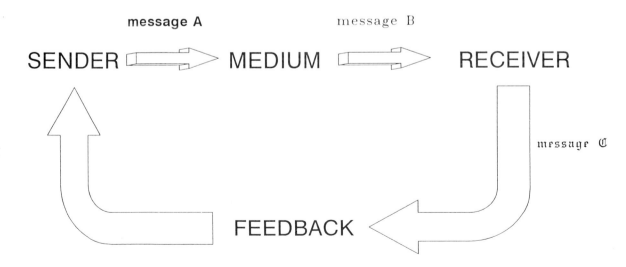

Figure 25.1 Communication model for goal-oriented evaluations

284

An alternative approach is that of goal-free evaluation where either the aims of the project are ignored, or there are no aims. These evaluations are more open-ended and explore possible consequences rather than the predetermined expectations of the project. Let me suggest another model, one that may be better related to goal-free work (Figure 25.2). Here we have the museum sending a number of defined, conscious messages (and perhaps a few unconscious ones). There is distortion associated with the medium and there are the received messages. Visitors may receive the key messages, albeit slightly modified according to their own experiences, but they may pick up something entirely different. A goal-free evaluation might investigate all of these potential messages.

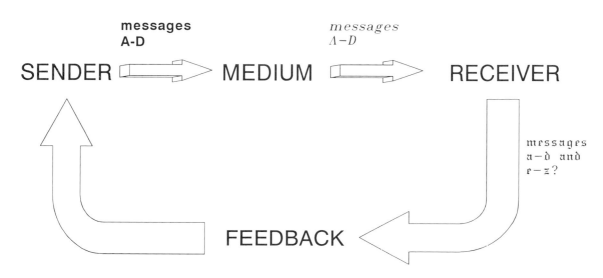

Figure 25.2   Communication model for goal-free evaluations

The above models are implicitly summative – looking at the end-result of a project such as a temporary exhibition. However, they could be used for front-end and formative work where we are looking to see what messages might be received, rather than what actually has been received.

Case-studies

Some specific case-studies might serve to illustrate various types of evaluation, and how they can help with effective communication.

Science Information Service – formative

One evaluation for a project called PUBSTIC formatively tested names for an information service which aimed to answer visitors' queries about science and technology. Museum staff had been asked to suggest titles, and seven were tested.

An appropriate title is one of the most important elements of any service to the public, be it an exhibition or an information service. The title needs to provide a key to understanding the purpose and function of the service to prevent unfulfilled expectations, disappointment or confusion on the part of the visitor. Visitors were asked about proposed titles for this information service: did the title interest them, and why? What would they expect from a service with such a title? Comments from fifteen visitors were recorded for each title. The responses gave a feel for the general visitor response to the title. Examples of the conclusions drawn from the visitors' responses included:

Quest
Half of the visitors interviewed to could not say what sort of service *Quest* would provide. The majority of those who did respond suggested services that were unrelated to the aims of the PUBSTIC project.

Ask Here
It would appear this might be considered as a title for a general enquiry desk, but the specific nature of the PUBSTIC project was not identifiable from the title.

Spark
Although this title caught the imagination of the visitors questioned, it neither suggested a science/technology information service nor a general information service to them.

Science and Technology Information Service
This title was seen by the majority of the sample as uninteresting, but this did not prevent visitors from grasping the purpose of the service.

So the most appropriate title was Science and Technology Information Service. It conveyed to the visitors what the service intended to provide, i.e. something more than general information. Although it was not seen as particularly 'interesting', I argued that it was more important that visitors should know what the service was about than it was to have a catchy, but misleading, title. The title was eventually shortened to 'Science Information Service'.

Health Matters – front-end, audience data

Evaluations and audience research can help with many elements of planning a gallery. For example, an answer to key questions such as how many visitors might be expected, at what sort of rate per hour they might arrive, and how long they might stay can help with the design of an exhibition. The following example shows how past evaluations and audience work can help with the development of new projects.

The old aeronautics gallery in the Science Museum attracted some 40 per cent of all visitors (Heady 1984: 81). Various evaluations conducted within the Science Museum have indicated the appeal of the personal and have indicated people's interest in things medical. A brief assessment of visitors' expectations of a gallery with the title Health Matters suggested great interest. This led me to propose that some 60 per cent of visits to the Science Museum would include a tour of this gallery. Translating this into visit numbers for the life of the gallery produced a figure which greatly encouraged the sponsors: some six million visits over a ten-year life.

To assess how many visitors might be expected in an hour meant looking at flow rates into the museum and the range of visitation during the year. Analysing data from the admissions tills suggests that peak influx times are between 11.00 and 12.00 and between 14.00 and 15.00. There will be a build-up during the day and a time-lag as visitors move round the building, suggesting that peak times for visits to the gallery would be 11.00–13.00 and 14.00–16.00 hours. Looking at the daily visitor figures, the Science Museum had an average in 1992 of 3,000 visits a day. However, averages, when dealing with museum visiting, can be unhelpful.

What this means for the Health Matters gallery is that on average days the gallery might expect to attract 180 visitors an hour at quiet times (i.e. one family per minute) and 270 people an hour at the busier times of the day (i.e. a family and a couple every minute). With 6,000 visits – a busy day – the figures rise to 360 and 540 an hour (or, if you prefer, two to three families a minute).

And how long will they stay? This is a difficult question, but because of work in other galleries I can answer it at least in part. Averages are not necessarily helpful and average stays in a gallery are particularly unhelpful. For example, I have tracked a sample of visitors in a temporary exhibition, grouped the data into blocks of times (Figure 25.3), and calculated an average length of stay, in this case 4 minutes 46 seconds. This gets me nowhere with my problem of predicting how long visitors will spend in the Health Matters gallery, because this is not a good fit to a normal distribution and associated standard deviation is high. If, however, I plot these data in another way (Figure 25.4) a more useful picture emerges. The graph shows how long people stayed in this gallery. It shows that everyone stayed at least 5 seconds and one person stayed 22 minutes. It also shows how long it took for half the sample to have left the gallery, i.e. just over 3 minutes. This type of curve also shows that in another 3 minutes half the remaining people will also have left the gallery, and so on. The curve, sometimes called a 'survival curve', is like a radioactive decay curve, and the time it takes for half the sample to leave (or decay!) is the half-life.

This model is so useful because it shows what actually happens: most visitors stay for a short period, some for a long time, and there is a spread between these extremes. Five half-lives is a long stay – in the case of this gallery that means over 15 minutes. The model also allows us to work out how many people will stay that long. If this gallery had 2,000 visitors on one day then 1,000 people could be expected to stay more than 3 minutes, 500 to stay more than 6 minutes, 250 to stay over 9 minutes, and so on.

The model has been confirmed by the results from six other exhibitions: the half-life changes but the pattern is the same. For example, work done in the Land Transport gallery (Figure 25.5) shows the same pattern but with a half-life of 10 minutes – in this case the dedicated visitors will be staying over 50 minutes.

% of visitors

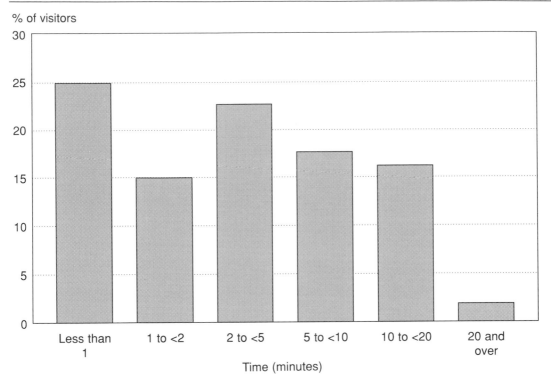

Figure 25.3 Bar chart of time spent by visitors in 'Making the difference: Babbage and the birth of computing', a temporary exhibition in the Science Museum

Returning to the Health Matters gallery, I compared the half-lives for the galleries looked at previously and, bearing in mind the subject-matter, size and routes, I suggested a half-life of 5 minutes. This means that on an average day, with 60 per cent of the museum's visitors going to Health Matters, some 900 visitors can be expected to stay less than 5 minutes and 900 to stay longer.

One reason for this sort of number crunching was that the engineering consultants wanted to do some calculations about heatloads in the gallery, and one of the main sources of heat in a gallery is its visitors. If you can predict how many visitors will come to the gallery, and how long they will stay, you can then calculate the total number of person-hours that will be invested in the gallery with every hour of opening. In this case this works out at something like 45 person-hours per hour (i.e. 300 visitors an hour with a visit half-life of 5 minutes is equivalent to 45 people being there for the whole hour).

Science Box – summative

Science Box is a series of small temporary exhibitions which address issues of contemporary science, technology and medicine for an audience of non-specialists. The exhibitions are intended to explore current issues in an authoritative but entertaining way. The first Science Box was on DNA fingerprinting and opened to the public in March 1991. The second exhibition, 'Living with lasers', opened about three months later.

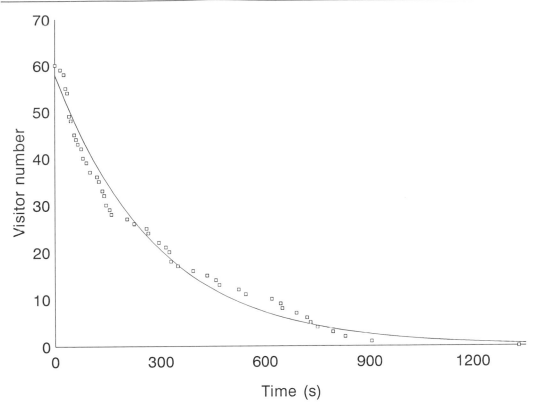

Figure 25.4 'Survival curve' for time spent by visitors in 'Making the difference: Babbage and the birth of computing'

There are some general points that can be made about visitors' use of both these exhibitions. One way to assess this use is to track visitors. This is done as discreetly as possible and various levels of interaction between the visitor and the exhibition are recorded on a scale plan of the exhibition. The data can then be transformed into 'contours of attention'. For example, the results from the DNA fingerprinting exhibition can be plotted and the resulting contours show very clearly which aspects of the exhibition visitors found most and least attractive (they can also show what holds visitors' attention). The same was done with the lasers exhibition. Both of these plots showed 'dead' space – areas where visitors did not seem to invest their time and attention. The suggested reasons for this finding were practical: the areas were hidden behind other parts of the structure, they were areas with more text; in general, they were less accessible both physically and intellectually.

The issue of popularity – which parts of the exhibition attracted the most attention and why – was developed further in a questionnaire. Visitors were asked what they liked most and least from the various elements of the exhibitions. In general the popular aspects were the unusual, familiar, and personal features and those with some form of interaction. The findings from each Science Box evaluation are used to develop subsequent exhibitions.

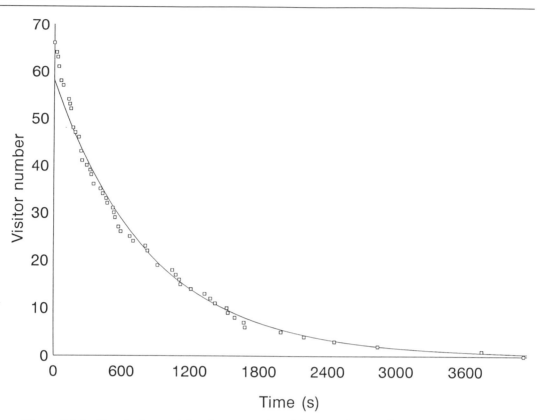

Figure 25.5 'Survival curve' for time spent by visitors in the Land Transport gallery, Science Museum

The 'kitchen sink' evaluation: drama in the Science Museum

This last example shows what can be done if you have the resources to do it. The Science Museum's use of drama to interpret topics in the history of science, technology and medicine began in 1987 with a single experimental role. In 1992 there was a daily programme from a repertoire of about twenty roles performed by a company of actors. The study of drama in the Science Museum was commissioned for three main reasons. First, I wanted to assess the here and now, to assess whether the present drama provision is meeting its goals, and, certainly no less importantly, to see how visitors are reacting to the presentations. So, the intent is both goal-oriented and goal-free. Second, the evaluation was designed to identify potential improvement to what is already offered. My colleagues and I wanted to know the strengths and weaknesses of the presentations as a medium of communication. If there were weaknesses I wanted suggestions and recommendations for appropriate changes. Third, the study has provided data to help develop new projects for drama in the Science Museum – data to guide our thinking and to enable informed decisions.

The present goals are an amalgamation of the views of a number of interested groups (or stakeholders): actors, managers, interpreters and curators. In general these views fall into a range of categories: from issues to do with generating warmth to communicating information and complexity. The overriding concern is to give the museum a human face. Preliminary interviewing identified several key concerns: interpreters were concerned about how to maximize communication and comprehension; curators wondered whether the visitor/actor interactions were consistent, i.e. whether the information given stayed the same and the script was uncorrupted; drama managers were concerned whether drama was considered a serious communication tool and whether it would continue to be used in the museum; actors wondered how they could develop their skills; and visitors were concerned about whether it was embarrassing or enlightening.

These points illustrate some of the complexities of this study. The consultants contracted to do the evaluation describe their method as 'everything but the kitchen sink': they used observation sessions, group discussions, accompanied visits, and questionnaires (with open and closed questions), and they let teachers loose with small hand held tape recorders. The consultants looked at six of the presentations, a workshop and some 'street theatre'. We have quantitative and qualitative work: the early qualitative work was used to develop the quantitative (the questionnaires). The evaluation can be viewed as summative, and formative and front-end.

I am reluctant to summarize the richness of this study into a paragraph but the overview is that the drama received a ringing endorsement by visitors, participant and non-participant alike. Children seem to be the socially acceptable means of access for adults into the drama, and the children are also seen as the main beneficiaries. Children enjoy the drama and make a beeline for the actors, whereas adults are inhibited. It appears that adults are socially wrong-footed by drama, and they are on the defensive. This was despite the fact that visitors are not cajoled into engaging with the actors – they can walk by. The general recommendation (from both actors and visitors) is that the museum should prepare people for the actors, and give them a sense of the rules of the game. As with other evaluations conducted within the Science Museum, staff address the findings, decide if action is to be taken, and if so determine the form of that action.

Conclusions

Let me finish with two views of museum visiting. The first is by Fay Weldon:

> in Darcy's Utopia it will be very bad form to hark back. . . . A museum will be the only place for the artefacts of the past ages, and let them be as gloomy and dismal as can be. In Darcy's Utopia it will be accepted that museums are very boring places indeed. If you want to subdue the children you only have to take them on a visit to a museum, and they will behave at once, for fear of being taken there again.
>
> (Weldon 1990: 197)

I prefer a more optimistic image, one from Posy Simmons in her book *Lulu and the Flying Babies* (1988). Lulu wants to go out and play, and she wants to go out now. Unfortunately she has to wait for her baby brother, Willy, to be loaded up into the baby back-pack, and dressed for the cold weather. Finally they leave but when they get to the park it has started to snow and is too cold for Willy, so Dad says they will have to go to the museum. Lulu doesn't want to go to the museum, she wants to play in the snow. Lulu is cross and creates a big fuss, especially when they get to the museum. Rather than suffer more, Dad leaves Lulu sitting on a bench sulking – 'horruble Daddy', says Lulu.

As she sits there feeling sorry for herself she wipes her nose on her sleeve. 'That's filthy!' says a voice; it belongs to a cherub from the painting behind Lulu. Lulu, a little surprised, is adopted by yet another cherub and they take her off to play in the snow – the snow in a picture! They also growl at a tiger, pat a king, and paddle in the sea; but then they get lost in a wood. Like all good children who get lost in museums they go and find a warder, a security guard, to help them find their parents. Lulu is not cross any more and she enthusiastically tells her Dad that she 'went with flying babies. . . . We rolled in the snow! We splashed in the sea . . . we growled at a tiger . . . we . . .'. 'Fancy that!' says Lulu's Dad as she dances her way back home through the park.

The challenge is how to realize these images: how can we make the objects in museums come to life? I believe evaluation work can help – more effective communication means greater accessibility which offers a more rewarding visit. In crude terms, this can mean a greater likelihood of return visits or word of mouth encouragement for friends to visit. We cannot be complacent about such issues. Museum openings were the boom of the 1970s and early 1980s; I fear museum closures will be the boom of the 1990s. I believe it is vital to document how visitors view a museum and its communications: are they worth while to the visitor? Whether you like it or not, the reality in the UK in the early 1990s is that of the Citizen's Charter: are customers receiving a service they find acceptable? Public expenditure is justified in terms of the user and not the provider.

Evaluations and audience research can help museums to be even more effective communicators, but there is a wider role: that of supporting the continuing existence of museums. That is why I am here to help.

References

Bicknell, S. E. (1988) 'Excellent at everything', unpublished audience research, Science Museum.

Bicknell, S. E. and Bunney A. (1992) 'Making the difference: Babbage and the birth of computing', unpublished summative evaluation, Science Museum.

Bicknell, S. E. and Bywaters, J. (1992) 'Presenting contemporary science to the public: the visitor and the museum', unpublished paper, ECSITE conference, Barcelona.

Bicknell, S. E. and Mann, P. M. (1993) 'A picture of visitors for exhibition developers', in D. Thompson, A. Benefield, S. Bitgood, H. Shettel and R. Williams (eds) *Visitor Studies: Theory, Research, and Practice, Vol. 5*, Jacksonville: The Center for Social Design.

Bicknell, S. E., Bunney, A., Uttley, C. and Weisz, N. (1991) 'Michael Faraday and the modern world', unpublished summative evaluation, Science Museum.

Bicknell S., Farmelo, G. P. and Leonard, S. J. (1993) 'Evaluation of an exhibition on laser applications', *Physics Education* 28(4): 209–14.

Borun, M. (1992) 'Part 1: Where do we go from here?', in A. Benefield, S. Bitgood and H. Shettel (eds) *Visitor Studies: Theory, Research, and Practice, Vol. 4*, Jacksonville: The Center for Social Design.

Daly, M. (1987) *Webster's First New Intergalactic Wickedary of the English Language*, London: The Women's Press.

Farmelo, G. (1992) 'Drama on the galleries', in J. Durant (ed.) *Museums and the Public Understanding of Science*, London: Science Museum.

Fiske, J. (1990) *Introduction to Communication Studies*, London and New York: Routledge.

Heady, P. (1984) *Visiting Museums: a Report of a Survey of Visitors to the Victoria and Albert, Science and National Railway Museums for the Office of Arts and Libraries*, London: Her Majesty's Stationery Office.

Hood, M. G. (1983) 'Staying away: why people choose not to visit museums', *Museum News* 61(4): 50–7.

—— (1992a) 'Audience research helps museums to make informed decisions', in A. Benefield, S. Bitgood and H. Shettel (eds) *Visitor Studies: Theory, Research, and Practice, Vol. 4*, Jacksonville: The Center for Social Design.

—— (1992b) 'Significant issues in museum audience research', *ILVS Review: a Journal of Visitor Behavior* 2(2): 281–6.

Hooper-Greenhill, E. (1991) 'A new communication model for museums', in G. Kavanagh (ed.) *Museum Languages: Objects and Text*, Leicester, London and New York: Leicester University Press.

Kelly, R. (1992) 'Museums as status symbols III: a speculative examination of motives amongst those who love being in museums, those who go to "have been" and those who refuse to go', in A. Benefield, S. Bitgood and H. Shettel (eds) *Visitor Studies: Theory, Research, and Practice, Vol. 4*, Jacksonville: The Center for Social Design.

Korn, R. (1989) 'Introduction to evaluation: theory and methodology', in N. Berry and S. Mayer (eds) *Museum Education: History, Theory, and Practice*, Reston, Va: The National Art Education Association.

Lawrence, G. (1991) 'Rats, street gangs and culture', in G. Kavanagh (ed.) *Museum Languages: Objects and Text*, Leicester, London and New York: Leicester University Press.

Loomis, R. (1992) 'Part 2: Where do we go from here?', in A. Benefield, S. Bitgood and H. Shettel (eds) *Visitor Studies: Theory, Research, and Practice, Vol. 4*, Jacksonville: The Center for Social Design.

Merriman, N. (1991) *Beyond the Glass Case*, Leicester, London and New York: Leicester University Press.

Miles, R. (forthcoming) 'The evaluation of interpretive provision', in R. Harrison (ed.) *Manual of Heritage Management*, London: Butterworth.

Schlereth, T. (1992) 'Object knowledge: every museum visitor an interpreter', in *Patterns in Practice: Selections from the Journal of Museum Education*, Washington, DC: Museum Education Roundtable.

Screven, C. G. (1990) 'Uses of evaluation before, during, and after exhibit design', *ILVS Review: a Journal of Visitor Behavior* 1(2): 36–66.

Shearman, A. and Wood, R. (1992) *Front-end Evaluation of an Exhibition about Innovation in Australian Industry*, Powerhouse Museum Research Series No.1, Haymarket, NSW: Powerhouse Museum.

Simmons, P. (1988) *Lulu and the Flying Babies*, London: Jonathan Cape Ltd.

Weldon, F. (1991) *Darcy's Utopia*, London: Flamingo.

Index